Thomas Francis Wildes

Record of the One Hundred and Sixteenth Regiment

Ohio Infantry Volunteers in the War of the Rebellion

Thomas Francis Wildes

Record of the One Hundred and Sixteenth Regiment
Ohio Infantry Volunteers in the War of the Rebellion

ISBN/EAN: 9783337116521

Printed in Europe, USA, Canada, Australia, Japan

Cover: Foto ©ninafisch / pixelio.de

More available books at **www.hansebooks.com**

RECORD

OF THE

ONE HUNDRED AND SIXTEENTH REGIMENT

OHIO INFANTRY VOLUNTEERS

IN THE

WAR OF THE REBELLION

By THOS. F. WILDES,

Late Lieutenant Colonel of the Regiment, and Brevet Brigadier General
U. S. Volunteers.

"*The world is cold to him who pleads;
The world bows low to knightly deeds.*"

SANDUSKY, O.
I. F. MACK & BRO., PRINTERS.
1884.

To the Relatives and Friends

OF ITS HEROIC DEAD,

AND TO THE

SURVIVING OFFICERS AND ENLISTED MEN

OF THE

ONE HUNDRED AND SIXTEENTH REGIMENT,

THIS RECORD

IS HUMBLY DEDICATED.

The Author.

NOTE.

General Wildes had, as he thought, the manuscript of this work ready for the publishers, and, in fact, had partially arranged for its publication, but delayed it to make some necessary corrections, which he was engaged in doing, when he was so suddenly called from his labors. Some of the changes, he anticipated making, had been so far advanced, as to enable those, into whose hands the result of his labors was entrusted, to carry out his plans, while some additions which he proposed making had to be abandoned. Every page of the original manuscript bears witness to the care taken by the author to avoid mistakes, while the voluminous correspondence pertaining to this work shows how earnestly and faithfully he labored in its preparation. The writer knows whereof he speaks when he says the men of the 116th had no truer friend than the author of this work. Many times subsequent to his leaving the regiment, did he express himself in no measured terms as to the bravery, efficiency and soldierly bearing of the regiment, and said it was an honor for any man to be able to say, "I belonged to the 116th."

AUTHOR'S PREFACE.

In entering upon the work of writing the History of the One Hundred and Sixteenth Regiment, I am forced to confess that I have considerable faith in what Oliver Wendell Holmes once said: "I would not give a fig for a man, every one of whose geese is not better than any other man's swans." I always felt some such partiality as this sentiment expresses, for the regiment, and while I shall strive to make its history appear as it really is, it is quite possible that my own feelings may color some parts of it too highly. Shortly after the appearance of the history of the 34th Massachusetts regiment, General Lincoln, who wrote it, was asked "if there was any other regiment besides the 34th Massachusetts in the service." Perhaps the same criticism may be made of the history of the 116th, but, if so, it shall be regarded as a compliment, for everything stated in these pages will be verified by reports, records and data, concerning the accuracy of which there can be no question. I have depended upon my recollection, or impressions, for very little, but have relied upon official records and diaries, letters and memoranda written at the time by myself and others. Through the kindness of the Adjutant General of the War Department, the Adjutant General of Ohio, and Ex-President Hon. R. B. Hayes, I have been furnished with copies of the reports of all the battles in which the regiment was engaged. From the same and other sources, I have received many other valuable records, such as official lists of casualties, burial places of those dying in rebel prisons and elsewhere, promotions of officers, the names of enlisted men awarded "Medals of Honor," and promoted for special good conduct. I am greatly indebted for valuable assistance and information to Colonel Washburn; Majors Morris, Hull and Karr; Captains Mann, Henthorn, Chaney, Welch, Frame, Knowles and Mosely; Lieutenants Cline, Walker, Heald, Sibley, Knight and Myers; Sergeants King, Hoyt, Drake and Bartley; Corporals Campbell and Thompson, and to a great number of private soldiers, notably to Charles L. Eberle, of C, for a valuable diary covering nearly the whole term of three years; Leroy D. Brown, of H, for a paper prepared by him on "Sheridan in the Shenandoah Valley"; Edward H. Bradley, of G, for a correct list of G, the rolls of which were very imperfect; John W. Reusser, of E, and Jacob L. Gregg, of H. As will be seen, I have quoted freely from official reports and records, giving some of the most important in full, and made free use of diaries, memoranda and letters. Fortunately all my own letters written during the war were preserved by my wife. A very serious obstacle in the way of accuracy was met in the imperfect condition in which I found the rolls in the Adjutant General's office at Columbus. This involved a great deal of correspondence, and finally a resort to the Adjutant General of the War Department. There may yet remain some errors and omissions in the record of enlisted men, but I trust not many.

THE AUTHOR.

INTRODUCTORY.

In letters to the undersigned, received many months ago, General Wildes thus writes: "I am now engaged in writing the history of my own regiment, the 116th Ohio, of our own gallant first brigade, and intend making it sufficiently cosmopolitan to include a general history of our own campaign and a particular history of the first brigade, our own military family. If I could send you enough proof matter, or give you a general enough idea of it in any other way, I would ask you to write an introduction. The 116th Ohio and the 34th Massachusetts served together in the same brigade in many of the decisive battles of the war, and were side by side during the whole of the last year. I can see a fitness in you of Massachusetts doing this for us of Ohio. You must see at once how much pleasure it would give our whole regiment to see the book introduced by one of their old comrades of the gallant 34th Massachusetts." What was thus lightly undertaken then, was rendered a duty when information was afterwards received that the warm friend and gallant officer had been removed from earth's labors, his task but partially completed. "It is an awful big job," continues the General, "to do the work in a way that will not class it with the hundreds of useless, utterly silly, *bombastes furioso* books issued and called histories of regiments. But with all the battle reports in the Valley in 1864 and around Richmond, added to Pond's and Humphrey's works, I think I ought to get some things right. You see I will have many advantages over you."

In entering upon his work, General Wildes aimed to make it a *history in fact;* one wherein should be given the minute incidents of interest to each man, as well as the more general matter in which the regiment as a whole was concerned. He knew, if in no other way, by correspondence with those who with more or less success had been engaged in similar works, how almost entirely he must rely upon himself; how little aid he would receive from even those of his old associates from whom he might expect assistance. It is fortunate that his work has been delayed to this day, because thereby he has had access to sources of information denied to others who preceded him. In another respect he has been fortunate that almost to the last he was with his command, actively engaged in its organization, going with it into its first rendezvous, being its first commissioned field officer (having been appointed its Lieutenant Colonel in August, 1862) being for a long time from various causes, its actual commander, and remaining with it until February, 1865, when he received promotion to the full Colonelcy of the 186th, a new regiment of Ohio infantry. So that he had that full knowledge of the military life of his regiment which intimate association only could give. He is said to have had no previous military training. Indeed, the condition of himself, his brother officers and his men can only be appreciated by his own amusing description of it when marching orders were first received.

"With little preliminary drill, not even once having been in line as a regiment, the men armed with old Belgian rifles, rusty and in demoralized condition generally, without an adjutant, and only one field officer; scarcely an officer having a sword or even a shoulder strap, and none with an uniform, no one knowing how to form a battalion, how to move it after it was formed, what orders to give or how to give them," they suddenly "were directed to hasten to Parkersburg." Loyal men that they were, they rose to the emergency like good soldiers, and "concluded to let Captain Teters go ahead and the rest follow as best they could." Within an hour they were on their way. Here going into camp, "the whole regiment was busy as a hive in learning the art of war." In one branch, at least, they were apt scholars, as is proved by the fact that upon a march which soon followed they could burn "wet rails" and have for breakfast "roast pig and turkey," and "on reaching Buckhannon were followed by a train of twenty-seven loaded wagons and a cloud of citizens loaded with complaints against us for pressing horses, etc., into service," drawing from General Milroy the remark that from what he knew of them "they could take care of themselves." Of all the scoutings and skirmishes; the hurried marches up, and sometimes the more hurried marches down, the Valley of the Shenandoah; of the battle of Piedmont, where "every color bearer and every man of the color guard was wounded"; of that before Lynchburg, where its "colors were the only ones of the whole army that waved over the enemy's works"; of that at Opequan, where "Early was sent whirling thro' Winchester"; of that at Fisher's Hill, where the 116th "received the fire of a battery when only 100 yards from it, and captured it in the very smoke of its discharge"; of Cedar Creek, (where now by the death of Colonel Wells, Colonel Wildes succeeded to the command of the brigade) "where the army that had swept in triumph at dawn, was a mass of fugitives at night." General Wildes is enabled from his active participation to give full and vivid descriptions. His words burn with the pride he feels in the splendid record his men had made. Having no fear of the "rules and regulations," he expresses with great plainness of language the contempt in which he, in common with others, held "General Sigel and the crowd of foreign adventurers" who surrounded that officer during his short command; for whom, as he writes, "not an officer or a man retained a spark of respect or confidence." And with equal directness and justice he comments upon the "blundering and blind pursuit of Early by Wright from Washington and Hunter from Harper's Ferry, over which the evil genius of Halleck hovered, making it the worst handled and most fruitless campaign of the war." The movement to the James in response to General Grant's call for the "best division in the Army of West Virginia," to which the 116th belonged, and the life at the winter cantonment there is passed over rapidly. Here Colonel Wildes received his well-earned promotion and left his old command. He shows, however, his love for his old boys in the glowing language, in which he describes their after service; their gallant charge on Fort Gregg, and hand-to-hand struggle for its possession; their long and rapid marches to head off Lee in his retreat, spoken of in General Gibbon's order

from "behind Richmond" as being "superior to anything
of the kind heretofore witnessed," and leading Crook, the
loved leader of their Valley campaign, to exclaim that
"there was little use for his cavalry while this division was
present"; their triumphal entry into Richmond, and inglorious ease in quiet encampment there, followed soon after
by their muster out of service, and welcome home. Here
ends the narrative of the service of the regiment. Some
chapters follow containing a sketch of prison life, notice of
deceased officers, the death roll and roster, the whole
closed by an eulogy of the General from the pen of an old
friend. Too much cannot be said in praise of the manner
in which the work is done. Sub-divided into chapters, each
is occupied by descriptions of particular campaign or battle,
and what is of especial value is the list of killed, and
wounded (in which is given the name and nature of the
wound) and of the missing. One word of a personal nature before conclusion. In letters, hurriedly written at the
time, after only a short observation of the troops brigaded
with the 34th Massachusetts, I thus wrote: "Except the
34th Massachusetts, these troops are neither drilled nor disciplined, this, however, from no fault of their own. The
rank and file of the commands were captured at Milroy's
defeat last summer. They were paroled soon after, and
have been scattered in small squads along the B. & O. Railroad as picket guard. The officers, however, were retained
as prisoners, and many are in fact still in rebel hands. It
looks as if we were to suffer from the connection." Almost
twenty years later, extracts from these letters, without re-
vision, were taken to make the history of that body, and a

copy sent to General Wildes. He, perhaps slightly disturbed by the apparent depreciation of his own command, now writes. "The fact is, the 34th then regarded itself as badly mismated with us. True enough, they had performed garrison and patrol duty in Washington from their enlistment up to '63. It had a well trained brass band and was in every way prepared for serenades, parades and reviews, while we poor fellows, with constant marching, scouting and picketing, to say nothing of now and then a little fighting, would make a sad display in either of these three ornamental positions. But before we separated in Richmond, the 34th felt as much pride in the history the first brigade had made for itself as was felt by any regiment in it. It was not then ashamed of the connection formed fourteen months before, nor was there an officer or man in it who felt he had suffered by the connection." To all of which by General Wildes, the present writer cheerfully assents, and without at all qualifying the statements then made, rejoices in the present opportunity of stating that the 116th Ohio, if not then thought to bear comparison with the 34th Massachusetts in "drill and discipline," and if, as General Wildes writes, "it could claim to have no ornaments," did on actual trial, prove to have what was of far greater value, men of willing hands and fearless hearts, and gallant souls, who in all the essential qualities of a true soldier were the peers of the noblest in the service.

WM. S. LINCOLN,
Late Colonel 34th Massachusetts Infantry, and
Brevet Brigadier General U. S. Volunteers.

THOMAS F. WILDES.

The writer of the following regimental history, was born at Racine, Canada West, on the first day of June, 1834. He died at his home in Akron, Ohio, Wednesday, March 28, 1883, and was therefore unable to see his work—to him purely a labor of love—in print. His modesty respecting his own services as a Union soldier is so marked in what he has here written, as in itself to call for a brief sketch of his career. The general worth of the man also so emphasizes this demand that the volume would be incomplete without some account of its deceased author. As the tribute, therefore, of a "comrade" who knew General Wildes as a man, soldier, lawyer, I offer this, imperfect as it must be, in the limited space at my disposal—to be published as a preface to the book which he has left—a gift of his heart and brain to the members of the regiment yet surviving, and record, so far as it can be made, of the honored dead who went with it to the field, no more to return.

General Wildes was of pure Irish blood. His grandfather was an ardent revolutionist, who suffered loss of property and home for his love of liberty. The General's parents came to Portage County, Ohio, in 1839. He at once sought the advantages of liberal education, and after great effort spent two years at Wittenberg College, Springfield, Ohio. He was also two years—1859-60—superintendent of the graded schools in Wooster. Hence, while he did not complete a collegiate course, he reached a position in scholarship which was highly respectable in itself, and was of great aid to him in the further work of his life. During his struggle for educational training, he became acquainted with Miss Eliza M. Robinson, a refined and intellectual lady, to whom he was married in 1860, and who survives to mourn in his death a loss irreparable.

General Wildes' public life began with his purchase of that always able and influential paper, the Athens, Ohio, Messenger, in 1861. He at once assumed editorial charge, and showed himself eminently able and fit for the position. Hardly was he established in this new field when the outbreak of treason against the Union of slavery against freedom occurred. An ardent Republican, he became of necessity an equally ardent advocate of liberty and Union. And it was not long until his hot Irish blood drove him from the pen to the sword in defending American freedom, and the Union, which is its safeguard, against the treason and slavery he so thoroughly understood and hated. Hence August, 1862, found him in military service, active and energetic, as was his wont. There I first saw him. He was made Lieutenant Colonel of the 116th Ohio Infantry.

"With this command he served in Virginia at Moore-
"field, Romney, in the Shenandoah Valley under Sigel, par-
"ticipating in the battles of Piedmont, Snicker's Gap, Ber-
"ryville, Opequan, Fisher's Hill and Cedar Creek. During
"all this time Colonel Wildes was with his regiment in
"every march, skirmish and battle in which it was en-
"gaged. At the battle of Piedmont, by concussion from
"a shell, and at Winchester he was seriously hurt by being
"thrown from a horse. During a portion of the Shenan-
"doah campaign, including the battle of Cedar Creek, and
"other minor engagements, he commanded the First Bri-
"gade, First Division of the Army of West Virginia. He
"retained this command until February, 1865, when he was
"promoted to Colonel of the 186th Ohio. With this regi-

"ment he went to Nashville, and afterward to Cleveland,
"Tennessee, where he received his commission as Brevet
"Brigadier General for gallant conduct at Cedar Creek,
"Virginia, October 19, 1864, to date from March 11, 1865.
"He was appointed to the command of a brigade at Chat-
"tanooga, which he retained until his muster out in Sep-
"tember, 1865." *Ohio in the War. V. I. 951.*

As a soldier, General Wildes was able, brave, energetic, active, always ready and willing for duty. His patriotism never cooled. War meant to him the finding and hurting of the enemy. He believed thoroughly in crushing treason by force, and at all times was ready to act upon that conviction. No one entered the great conflict through which he passed, more fully devoted to the cause which called those who loved the Union and human liberty to the field of battle, than himself. His tongue, pen, sword, the man in all his powers, was for the time wholly given to that cause.

In 1866 General Wildes graduated at the Cincinnati Law School. He at once entered upon the practice of law at Athens, Ohio, with Judge Brown, an old and distinguished member of the bar of that city. From there he removed to Akron, where he had made a high position for himself as a man and as a lawyer at the time of his death. With his powers of application and the abilities which he always manifested, that he would have made his mark among able men, had another decade of life been granted him, none doubt, I think, who knew the man. Cut off in the prime of his strength, we can only sorrow as we think of his loss to friends and to the community in which he was making the way to distinction. In temper he was warm and impulsive, a fast friend, and open, active opponent. The man he did not like was quite sure to find it out. Plain, sometimes severe, in speech, it was impossible that his energetic life should not at times create personal opposition and resentments. And so, in fact, in some instances it did. Yet when the heat cooled and the real disposition of the man was felt, I think in most cases ill-feeling was removed, and often warm friendship took its place. General Wildes was possessed of a vigorous intellect, which he could make felt with tongue and pen. To me it seemed natural for him to express himself in written discourse. But in the one way or the other, he was clear, forcible, convincing, often able. His work was always with a definite purpose, which came clearly out, and for which he seemed to care more than for mere graces of style. Terse force was his characteristic as a speaker and writer. He had something to say, and he said it in a way that "plain people" never failed to understand. The living members of "the old 116th," as he used proudly to call our regiment, will join me, I know, in expression of common sorrow at the loss of our old commander, so suddenly and unexpectedly cut down by death.

"A flash of the lightning, a break of the wave,
Man passeth from life to his rest in the grave."

Hiram L. Sibley,
Lieut. Co. B, 116th O.V.I.

CONTENTS.

CHAPTER I.

Preliminaries — Esprit de Corps of The Regiment — Recruiting — Military Committees — Patriotism of The People of The District — Remembrance of The Dead — John Frame and Elmer Armstrong — Hon. John R. Morris and Others — Woman's Work for The Soldiers. . 1

CHAPTER II.

The Organization — To the Rescue of Parkersburg, Then of Gallipolis — Mustered into The U. S. Service — Into West Virginia — Our First Fight — We Defeat General Jones and 4,000 Cavalry at Moorefield — General Milroy's Congratulations. 13

CHAPTER III.

The March to Romney — The Winter at Romney — A Forage Train Under Captain Brown Captured — Paroles — A Bad State of Feeling — Patriotic Action of The Regiment — March to Winchester. 40

CHAPTER IV.

At Winchester — A New Brigade Commander — Scouts and Marches — Death of Dr. Gilkey — Battle of

Winchester, June 12th, 13th and 14th, and Bunker Hill, June 13th — The Retreat and Battle in The Night — Escape of Milroy's Army from Lee Over in Pennsylvania and Maryland — List of Killed, Wounded and Prisoners — Back to Martinsburg — A Word in Defense of General Milroy. . 50

CHAPTER V.

The Fall and Winter at Martinsburg — Along The B. & O. R. R. — Preparing for the Campaign of 1864 — Regiment Ordered to Harper's Ferry — Brigaded Anew — General Sigel takes Command — Up The Valley — A Sham Battle — Battle of New Market — Retreat. . 72

CHAPTER VI.

Hunter Relieves Sigel — His Order on Assuming Command — Short of Rations for the First Time — Battle of Piedmont — Bravery of The Regiment — List of Casualties — One or Two Amusing Incidents, and Some not so Amusing, Connected with The Battle — On to Staunton. . 89

CHAPTER VII.

Destruction of Property at Staunton — On The Move, Still Going South — Return to Staunton to Meet a Supply Train — Hard Marching to Overtake The Army — To Lexington — Destruction of Rebel Property and of Washington College — And on we go — Regular Army Engineering Superseded by Western Ideas — Lynchburg — Battle of Lynchburg —

A Gallant Charge—Reports—Retreat to Gauley
Bridge—At Parkersburg—At Martinsburg again. 101

CHAPTER VIII.

Early in The Valley—His Advance into Maryland and
upon Washington—March to Harper's Ferry—
To Hillsboro—Snicker's Gap—Battle of Snicker's
Ferry—Wounding of Colonel Washburn—Hard
Fight of The Regiment on The Right—Brave
Conduct of Officers and Men—List of Casualties. 126

CHAPTER IX.

To Winchester—Battle of Kerntown—List of Casu-
alties—Retreat—Report of General Crook—At
Harper's Ferry Again—A Hot, Hard March—At
Monocacy Junction—Back to Bolivar Heights—
Arrival of General Sheridan, 6th and 19th Corps,
and Torbert's Cavalry—Dawn of A New Era in
The Valley. 140

CHAPTER X.

Sheridan in Command—For The First Time We Are
Part of An Army Equal in Numbers to The Opposing Enemy—March to Cedar Creek—Skirmish
on Three Top—March Back again—Battle of
Halltown, August 26th—List of Casualties—Battle of Berryville, September 3d—List of Casualties. 150

CHAPTER XI.

An Ambulance Train Captured and Re-captured—
Action Taken by The Officers on Learning of The

Death of Captain Keyes — Another Accident in the Regiment — Sheridan's Opportunity — Getting Ready for A Fight — Battle of Opequan, September 19th — Another Gallant Charge — List of Casualties — A Major's Report of Our Charge. . 165

CHAPTER XII.

Still Going Forward — Enemy at Fisher's Hill — Battle of Fisher's Hill — Another Charge — List of Casualties — Extracts from Reports of Colonel Wells, Generals Sheridan and Crook — Also General Early — Tardy Justice Done to Captain Varley of Company E — March to Harrisonburg — Death of Lieutenant Meigs — Buildings Ordered Burned — Order Revoked as to Dayton. . . . 180

CHAPTER XIII.

March Back to Cedar Creek — Destruction in The Valley — Election Day at Cedar Creek — Battle of Stickney Farm — Death of Colonel Wells — List of Casualties — Colonel Wildes in Command of the Brigade — A Reconnoisance — Battle of Cedar Creek, October 19th — Defeat of The Morning — Sheridan's Arrival — We "Go for Them" — A Glorious Victory — List of Casualties — Reports of Colonel Wildes and General Crook — A Rest — Promotions — At Opequan Crossing — Thanksgiving Turkeys Ordered to The Army of The James. . 193

CHAPTER XIV.

Good-bye Shenandoah Valley — On the Cars to Washington — Ride on the Water — Arrival at Deep

Bottom — Promotions — Drilling and Inspections — High Standing of the Regiment in the 24th Corps — Rebel Rams and Gunboats Create An Excitement — More Promotions. . 225

CHAPTER XV.

Off for Petersburg — Continuous Hard Marching — Hatcher's Run — Skirmishing — List of Casualties — A Narrow Escape for Captain Mann and Forty Men — Fort Gregg Carried by Assault — Some Incidents Connected with The Charge — Report of Lieutenant Colonel Potter — Casualties of The Regiment — After Lee — Farmville and Rice's Station — List of Casualties — A Good Day's March — Lee's Retreat Cut Off — Appomattox — The White Flags — Surrender — General Gibbon's Order. . 235

CHAPTER XVI.

March to Lynchburg — Back to Richmond — Triumphal Entry of The Rebel Capital — Preparing to go Home — Mustered Out — Transfers to the 62d Ohio Regiment — Off for Home — Home. . 260

CHAPTER XVII.

Prison Life — The Cruelty of Rebels to Prisoners — Barbarities of Prison Keepers — The Experiences of Several of our Officers and Men — The Death Roll. . 272

CHAPTER XVIII.

Sketches of Deceased Officers — Captain F. H. Arckenoe — Captain E. Keyes — Lieutenant Robert Wilson — Lieutenant Levi Lupton — Surgeon Thomas J. Shannon — Captain Alexander Cochran — Captain Edward Fuller — Captain William Myers — Surgeon Walter R. Gilkey — Hospital Steward James T. Moran — Lieutenant M. A. Ellis — Major John Hull. . . 305

ROSTER OF THE REGIMENT
  Field and Staff, . . 322
  Company A, . 323
  Company B, 327
  Company C, 331
  Company D, 336
  Company E, 340
  Company F, 344
  Company G, 349
  Company H, 353
  Company I, 358
  Company K, . 362

CHAPTER I.

PRELIMINARIES—ESPRIT DE CORPS OF THE REGIMENT—RECRUITING—MILITARY COMMITTEES—PATRIOTISM OF THE PEOPLE OF THE DISTRICT—REMEMBRANCE OF THE DEAD—JOHN FRAME AND ELMER ARMSTRONG—HON. JAMES R. MORRIS AND OTHERS—WOMAN'S WORK FOR THE SOLDIERS.

The One Hundred and Sixteenth Ohio Regiment made a history during the war of the rebellion worthy of preservation, and I have long felt that some one ought to undertake the task of writing it out for publication. I appreciate that the history of the regiment ought to be fair and impartial to be of any value to any one, and so start out with the purpose to make it as nearly so as possible. If ever such a history is to be written, it ought to be possible to write it now—eighteen years after its return from the war.

From the outset of its services, the 116th had faith in itself. Its officers and men had faith in each other, and the people of the group of counties from which it was recruited had faith in it, and have always felt a pride in its career. But unless the permanency of history be soon given to its services, there will be little left beside tradition, camp stories, and the fireside recollections of its few survivors. At first it would seem an easy task to write its history, but when it is considered that a regiment in active service forms an integral part of an army, and perhaps of many armies, and that to give a comprehensive history of a regiment is necessary to give much of the history of the armies with which it served, a different estimate of the task will soon be formed. When the war-worn regiments of the Union Army returned from the field in 1865, there was a feeling among the soldiers and their friends that it would be a pleasing luxury to forget the long story of their perils and sufferings. The blessed benediction of peace shut out forever the anxieties of war, and in a contest in which whole armies had done so nobly, the achievements of particular regiments did not seem, either to the soldiers or to their friends, to demand special mention or record.

But as the years went by, the vast importance of the results attained by the war began to grow more and more apparent. Then there arose a new interest in the minor actors in the struggle. Time had healed the wounds which the close of hostilities had left bleeding, and the lengthening vista of years had exalted the sufferings of the people and their army to the dignity of a holy sacrifice. Each recurring May had seen the church yards and cemeteries of the whole country visited by the people, who, with reverence and regard, scattered the sweet flowers of spring upon the graves of their soldiers, and consecrated their graves anew with prayer, eulogy, and sacred and patriotic song. Everywhere the people sang—

> "From the lily of love that uncloses
>   In the glow of a festival kiss,
> On the wind that is heavy with roses
>   And shrill with the bugles of bliss,
> Let it float o'er the mystical ocean
>   That breaks on the kingdom of night—
> Our oath of eternal devotion
>   To the heroes who died for the right!

> "Ah, grander in doom-stricken glory
>   Than the greatest that linger behind,
> They shall live in perpetual story,
>   Who saved the last hope of mankind!
> For their cause was the cause of the races
>   That languished in slavery's night;
> And the death that was pale on their faces
>   Has filled the whole world with its light!

> "To the clouds and the mountains we breathe it,
>   To the freedom of planet and star;
> Let the tempests of ocean enwreath it,
>   Let the winds of the night bear it far—
> Our oath, that, till manhood shall perish,
>   And honor and virtue are sped,
> We are true to the cause that they cherish,
>   And eternally true to the dead!"

So during these years, there has arisen a new interest in the more minute details of the great conflict. The history of the great leaders is familiar to us all, but only in the details of a regimental history can we see and learn the record of the *private soldier*, to whom, after all, is due the glory of the victory.

It is true that the history of the regiment in the concrete belongs to the State and the Nation, and nothing that can now be said or done can add to, or take from, the record it has made. But while this is true, the *individual* history of its officers and men is the *home* history of each fireside that contributed to its ranks; and it is due to the memory of its noble dead, to the mothers, fathers, wives and friends of both living and dead, that, while opportunity lasts, the story of the regiment be written and its lessons of heroism, patriotism and devotion to country be preserved.

It shall not be claimed for the 116th that either its officers or its enlisted men possessed greater courage or patriotism than inspired other regiments of Ohio soldiers. All we shall claim is that it marched and fought when and where duty called; that from Moorefield, where it first met the enemy in battle, to Appomattox, where the white flags of the rebellion were thrown to the breeze before its skirmishers, it never wavered or faltered in its duty or failed to perform the part assigned it in the work of destroying treason to the flag, and planting the imperilled nation anew upon the firm rock of peace.

The sacrifices made, the sufferings endured, the weary marches, the lonely night vigils, the days and nights of hunger and fatigue, wounds, sickness, death in battle and in hospital, and that worse than death—long lingering in Southern prison pens—the thrill of the bayonet charge, the steady tread of brave men advancing to the battle shock, the gloom of disaster and defeat and the loud peans of victory, these constitute the material out of which the history of a regiment is made. To portray these properly we must follow the trail of the men in the ranks. Some of this we approach with pleasure and pride, much of it with hesitation and pain. To how many is "the 116th" the synonym of woe. How many hearts are made to bleed at the sad recollections its mention revives? And yet to these bleeding hearts may it not be a solace and a balm to feel and know that their heroic dead are not forgotten by their surviving comrades; that it is in their honor we write; that had we no dead there would be no honor, no glory, no fame, no history worth recording, and that with us, as with them, reverence for our dead

"Is never old and never new,
Because it is eternal."

The history of the 116th would not be properly begun without referring to the noble men who exerted themselves in recruiting it, who gave their time, their money, their voices and their influence to filling its ranks. To the military committees of the different counties very great credit is due, and that they may be known to all the friends of the regiment they are given below:

ATHENS COUNTY—M. M. Greene, Hon. J. W. Bayard, H. T. Brown, S. W. Pickering, Hon. L. L. Smith, Capt. J. M. Dana, E. H. Moore, W. R. Golden, T. F. Wildes.

MONROE COUNTY—Hon. Wm. F. Hunter, Hon. J. A. Davenport, John Kerr, Stephen S. Ford, J. M Kirkbridge, Nathan Hollister.

NOBLE COUNTY—J. Belford, E. G. Dudley, John M. Rounds, B. F. Spriggs, Wm. H. Frazer, John W. Tipton, Dr. M. Martin.

MEIGS COUNTY—Hiram G. Daniels, David R. Jacobs, J. V. Smith, Ed Tiffany, N. Stanbery, Geo. Eiselstein, G. W. Cooper.

WASHINGTON COUNTY—Col. W. R. Putnam, Geo. W. Barker, S. F. Cooke, Mark Greene, John Newton.

All of these men took a very active part in raising the regiment, but many others helped. In Athens County Elmer Armstrong, Joseph Herrold, Elza Armstrong, N. O. Warren, John Frame, W. F. Pilcher, A. D. Jaynes, the Glaziers, the Postons, William Golden, Hon. W. Reed

Golden and many others, took an active part. Conspicuous in the work was Elmer Armstrong. He organized the "amen corner" at the meetings, to which he especially invited all the "Bible Democracy."

The 92d was full on August 15th. The call of the Governor for two full regiments from the district was issued July 9th. The 92d was raised in two weeks after the work of recruiting was begun. As soon as the 92d was full, every one kept at work to raise the 116th. In Monroe County, prominent in the work of recruiting was Hon. James R. Morris, Democratic member of Congress. There never was in Ohio such a deep-seated, universal feeling of patriotism, as was witnessed during the months of July and August, 1862. The women took as deep interest in the work of recruiting the 92d and 116th as did the men. They attended the meetings. Many "basket" meetings were held at which the women furnished excellent meals, and no troops passed on the railroads without being well fed. The enthusiasm was unbounded everywhere all over the district. But great as was the enthusiasm in the other parts of the district, it was excelled in Monroe. That county had seven companies to raise under the quota. Such men as Hon. James R. Morris, Hon. Wm. Okey, Jacob Mitchell, S. L. Mooney, J. B. Noll and William Read, in connection with the military committee which we have named, took the work in hand. After all arrangements were perfected for the work of recruiting, these gentlemen, with many others, took the county by storm, and in less than three weeks the quota of Monroe County was full, two companies going into the 92d and five into the 116th; and the people of Monroe County have ever since availed themselves of every opportunity to do honor to the 116th regiment.

Very few regiments from Ohio exceeded the 116th in personnel. It was composed of the very best men of the counties from which it was recruited. They had not gone out in the first hot flush excited by the firing on of Fort Sumter and the opening of hostilities, but the necessities of the Government, now so pressing and so apparent, appealed to their judgment as well as to their patriotism, and with equal alacrity and determination with those who had gone before, they stepped into the ranks and went forth to fight the battles of their country against the gigantic conspiracy which threatened its existence. There was now real danger, which was not clear until now, of the dissolution of the union between the States, of the arresting of the progress, the paralyzing of the energies of the whole country, and the destruction of the peace of the Nation forever. The whole people felt the imminence of the danger which now threatened their liberties in the destruction of not only the form, but of the very framework, of their republican institutions. The conspirators had been in deadly earnest from the outset, while we had not been more than half in earnest. Till now Nation and people had been half tampering, half pleading with treason, but now both had determined henceforth to battle against it in earnest,

> " And taking counsel but of common sense,
> To strike at cause as well as consequence."

The stake in the contest was now seen to be human rights and civil liberty. No man who loved his country, on whose soil and under whose flag had grown the perfect embodiment of liberty, could turn a deaf ear to this appeal. Beneath the beneficent influences of the government established under our constitution, humanity had asserted its dignity and its truth; intelligence had become the birthright of all; peace had reigned supreme; and over boundless states, territories, hills, valleys, plains, rivers and lakes, the jubilant bells of a happy people rang out their never ending praises of the perfect freedom they enjoyed. All this was put in jeopardy by a ruthless and treasonable faction now advanced so far in its purpose that naught but its utter annihilation would save the country. The alternative thus presented to the people was soon chosen. To hesitate now was to perish. The American pro-slavery rebellion never had any foundation in truth, no defense in law, no justification in equity or good conscience. Even had the ends proposed and promised been attained it could not justify itself before a single nation in christendom. With "slavery as the cornerstone" it would have been a blotch upon the face of the earth and a disgrace to the nineteenth century. But the war into which this causeless rebellion plunged the country could not end in its success without resulting in the downfall of the civil liberties of the people of the whole country. In its triumph slavery, with all its attendant curses, would have been the rule and freedom the exception all over the country, and the proud name of *American*, so far from being an honor above title of nobility or stars of an emperor's decoration, would be the object of the scorn and derision of the civilized world. It was to this peril the country was approaching when the President called for twice 300,000 men in the summer of 1862, and it was to thwart this that a half million of our people were inspired to step into the ranks of the Union Army. War had no charms or allurements for them, else they had seized the sword at the first alarum of war. They were rather of those who suffer much before resenting insult, but who, when aroused, are the more formidable antagonists.

The war had now assumed the character of a revolt of the union-loving, freedom-loving people of the republic against the insolence of treason and slavery. This now was not only *felt*, but it was *seen*. It was either an inglorious peace and disgraceful submission, or a complete crushing out of the military power of the rebellion. The whole people, with very rare ignoble exceptions, had determined upon the latter conclusion of the contest. And so, without thought or respect of party, in every county of our military district, as well as all over the State, there was a unanimity in the work of recruiting for the new regiments never before seen.

Two men in Athens County, both Democrats in politics, were so conspicuous in the work that we feel it due to them to make special mention of their services. We refer to John Frame, of Coolville, and Elmer Armstrong, of Hibbardsville. They were men of considerable wealth and prominence, and peculiarly enthusiastic in their method of doing everything they took hold of. Throwing their whole strength and power into the canvass for recruits, there was soon aroused all over Athens County the highest state of excitement and enthusiasm. They traveled, talked and worked day and night, until their county's quota was full; and when our regiment was organized they were both strenuously urged to take charge of the sutler's department, where we knew they would be of great service to the men. Mr. Frame felt himself too old and infirm to attempt it, but Mr. Armstrong accepted the appointment, which he soon shared with A. J. Frame, a son of John Frame. Another son, A. B. Frame, was a lieutenant in company "I." Of the military committees we have named, it would be invidious to speak of one in more flattering terms than of another. They each and all did all that men could do, not only before, but after the regiment went to the field, continuing their kind offices and interest in its welfare until the expiration of its term of service.

It will not, I hope, be considered foreign to the the purpose of this volume to mention that great popular work which made care for the soldiers and their families the business of life for our tenderest and best at home while the war lasted. Of much of it no man may speak. Like charity it recoils from publicity. It would be intruding to attempt to measure the love of the mothers, sisters and wives at home for the soldiers in the field. But who could attempt it? Who can chronicle the prayers and the labors to shield them from death and disaster? Who can find words to describe the womanly fervor which counted loss, suffering, self-denial and even life as nothing so that God might give victory to the Union arms in the battle for liberty and the right? But to the soldiers in the field the tangible results of the great work for their relief carried on by the women at home were so many, so varied, so valuable, so life-saving, that no regimental history would be complete without their mention and their grateful acknowledgment. In fact, it would be cruel thoughtlessness and deep ingratitude for any regiment to overlook woman's work during the war. No soldier could turn in any direction without meeting with something that bespoke her thought, her care, her love and her constant effort to lighten the burdens, and soften the hardships of his lot.

Immediately after the organization of the "Cincinnati Branch of the Sanitary Commission" in November, 1861, branch "Soldiers' Aid Societies" were organized in all the counties. Early in May a "Soldiers' Aid Society" had been organized in Athens with Mrs. E. M. Wildes as president. About the same time similar societies were organized in Pomeroy, Marietta, Coolville and surrounding towns. These societies connected themselves with the Sanitary Commission at Cincinnati as soon as it was established, thus gathering into one receptacle the fruits of all their joint labors. "Camp Jewett" being established at Athens early in 1861 brought to the very doors of the kind hearted women of Athens the care of many sick soldiers. The entire county was soon after organized for relief work through the efforts of the society at Athens, and it so remained through the war. It would be impossible to recount the work done there, much less throughout the other counties of the military district. Hundreds of sick, and hungry, and wounded soldiers were cared for through the instrumentality of these aid societies. Every battle was the signal for sending forward large stores for the relief of the wounded. After very many of the more serious engagements, urgent calls for relief came from the battle fields and these were responded to with the greatest promptness and generosity. After the battle of Shiloh, a strong appeal for help came. Several large boxes of hospital and camp supplies were sent off on the 7th of April, the last day of the battle, in charge of a committee, Messrs. Twombly, F. L. Ballard and the writer. Day and night the women of all the societies in the county worked, and on the 9th, the 10th and the 11th, other supplies were sent to the Sanitary Commission at Cincinnati. Among the old files of the "Athens Messenger" we find, among many others, the following letter of acknowledgment:

CINCINNATI, April, 14th, 1862.

Mrs. E. M. Wildes, Pres. Soldier's Aid Society, Athens, Ohio:

DEAR MADAM: On behalf of our Commission, I acknowledge the receipt of your present, as well as of former contributions. Please accept our thanks for the same. The demands now made upon us are very great and pressing, and we welcome aid from every quarter. Very Respectfully,

CHAS. E. CIST, Cor. Sec'y *pro tem.*

Not a person connected with all these aid societies received a farthing for her untiring, constant work. Every dollar and every dollar's worth went to the soldiers in some needed form. In short, it was Christian integrity and scrupulous fidelity in charge of the people's contributions for their men in the ranks. The good thus done can never be written, and perhaps never ought to be written, for it was the work of the heart. In every hospital, in every camp, on every march, on every battle field, the soldier was met by the agents of the Sanitary Commission with the fruits of these hard worked women's toil and care. How much suffering was alleviated, how much prevented, how much comfort afforded, how many sick beds made easy, how many wounds healed, how many precious lives saved through the instrumentality of woman's work in these societies, can never be told on earth. Like the gentle dew their kind charity fell and like it disappeared, leaving a memory only that shall blossom into blessings in the immortality of their beneficent results.

But this was not all of woman's good works to the soldiers in the field. Our regiment was a great portion of its time engaged in active campaigning. After we were free from our "base of supplies" and often, too, our "communications were cut off," no one who has not seen it can imagine the joy of "meeting a mail" and reading a "letter from home" from a mother, a father, a wife, a sister, or a sweetheart after such a time, and no one would, if he could, describe the sore disappointment of some boy when he found after waiting expectantly until the last letter was handed out by the chaplain that there was none for him.

The women—old, middle-aged and young—earned many a "God bless you" for the encouraging letters they wrote to the soldiers. Many a letter from a mother, wife and sister, written to cheer and comfort a son, husband or brother, bore the marks of scalding tears, and required a braver heart to write than it did to face the storm of battle. The agonizing sufferings in the homes out of which the light had gone, and the long, dark days and nights of waiting and watching for its return, could only be endured by the patient heart and strong hope of woman. It would have killed more men than it did women. The aid societies and every act done and word written by the women were a power of good for loyalty. While the union sentiment of a town was sure to crystallize around its "Aid Society," the hearts of the soldiers in the field were cheered and strengthened by the knowledge of the agencies employed at home for their comfort.

When the future historian writes the true history of the War of the Rebellion, woman will be given a first place in the great work of crushing treason and restoring peace and union. No better expression has ever been given to the noble work, the silent pain and courageous suffering of woman, in that great struggle for civil liberty, than that found in the following beautiful poem by T. Buchanan Read, entitled

"THE BRAVE AT HOME."

"The maid who binds her warrior's sash
    With smile that well her pain dissembles,
The while, beneath her drooping lash,
    One starry tear-drop hangs and trembles,
Though Heaven alone regards the tear,
    And Fame shall never know her story,
Her heart has shed a drop as dear
    As ever dewed the field of glory.

"The wife who girds her husband's sword,
    'Mid little ones who weep and wonder,
And bravely speaks the cheering word—
    What though her heart be rent asunder?
Doomed, nightly in her dreams, to hear
    The bolts of war around him rattle,
Hath shed as sacred blood as e'er
    Was poured upon the plain of battle.

"The mother who conceals her grief,
    While to her breast her son she presses,
Then breathes a few brave words and brief,
    Kissing the patriot brow she blesses;
With no one but her secret God
    To know the pain that weighs upon her,
Sheds holy blood as e'er the sod
    Received on Freedom's field of honor."

CHAPTER II.

THE ORGANIZATION—TO THE RESCUE OF PARKERSBURG, THEN OF GALLIPOLIS—MUSTERED INTO THE U. S. SERVICE—INTO WEST VIRGINIA—OUR FIRST FIGHT—WE DEFEAT GENERAL JONES AND 4,000 CAVALRY AT MOOREFIELD—GEN. MILROY'S CONGRATULATIONS.

The One Hundred and Sixteenth Ohio rendezvoused at Camp Putnam, Marietta, on the 25th of August, 1862. Several of its companies had for some days been guarding the Marietta and Cincinnati Railroad, then supposed to be in danger of destruction by rebel raids from the Virginia side of the Ohio river. Some of the road's bridges had been burned and others set on fire.

But three or four officers of the 116th had ever seen any military service. The military committees of the several counties, in which the companies composing the regiment had been raised, met at Marietta on the 17th of August and selected the following field and staff officers for recommendation to the Governor: James Washburne, of Monroe County, Colonel; Thos. F. Wildes, of Athens County, Lieutenant Colonel; W. Thomas Morris, of Monroe County, Major; W. Reed Golden, of Athens County, Adjutant; Artemus W. Williams, of Meigs County, Quartermaster. Subsequently Frederick L. Ballard, of Athens County, was selected Adjutant, *vice* Golden, whom the Governor declined to receive because he was lame. These officers were all commissioned by Governor Tod. At a later date the officers held a meeting and elected Rev. E. W. Brady Chaplain and Elmer Armstrong Sutler. Dr.

Walter R. Gilkey was assigned to the regiment as surgeon. Dr. J. Q. A. Hudson, first assistant surgeon and Dr. James Johnson second assistant surgeon. Milton A. Ellis was appointed Sergeant Major, William J. Lee Quartermaster Sergeant, and Ezra L. Walker Commissary Sergeant. Colonel Washburne had been a captain in the 25th Ohio, from which he came with an excellent record for bravery and efficiency. The date of rank of these officers was: Washburne, August 22; Wildes, August 18; Morris, August 19; Ballard, September 8; Williams, September 3.

Companies A, C, D, E and F were raised in Monroe County, Companies B and G in Meigs County, Companies I and K in Athens County, and Company H in Noble County. Some drilling was done at Camp Putnam by squad and company, but the regiment was never in line there. Lieutenant Colonel Wildes joined the regiment on the 25th of August. On the 1st of September the regiment was ordered to Parkersburg to watch the movements of Jenkins, who was supposed to be threatening that place. At this time neither officers nor men had been mustered in. All were without uniforms, accoutrements, blankets, cooking untensils and camp equipage except that belonging to Camp Putnam. The men were armed with an old Belgian rifle, intended more for show than use, and they did not even make a good show, being rusty and out of order, and in a demoralized condition generally. The men had been in camp and doing duty of various kinds for several days without a change of clothing. There was yet no Adjutant with the regiment and only one field officer; scarcely an officer had a sword or even a shoulder strap, and none had uniforms; there was not a horse in the regiment; not an officer with the regiment knew how to form a battalion, how to move it after it was formed, what commands to give or how to give them. Such was the situation of affairs when Col. Putnam hurried into camp late in the afternoon of September 1st, with orders from Gov. Tod, directing the 116th to hasten to Parkersburg. Imagine the surprise and indignation of officers and men on the reception of this order under the circumstances! Had any one in camp known anything of war or its regulations there would without doubt have been loud murmurings, if not a mutiny then and there, but there was nothing of the kind. On the contrary, the order was obeyed with as much alacrity, as the regiment ever afterwards obeyed an order, and within an hour we were on the march to Parkersburg. There was no pageant in that march from Camp Putnam to the depot that evening. No banners waved over those men, no music cheered them, no bugle stirred their souls with its flaring blast. As we have said, there was not even a uniform among them. The farmer, the professor, the student, the smith and the miner were in that line. The farmer marched in the garments he brought from the furrow, the professor and student in those they had worn in the school-room, the smith and the miner were attired as they had been in the shop and the mine. Here were the sturdy yeomanry of Southeastern Ohio marching to the scenes of war. From the hills and quiet fields of Monroe, were five hundred of her hardy sons of toil; from Meigs two hundred, at the head of one a farmer, and at the head of the other a professor, and behind him marched his whole academy; from little Athens, two hundred, at the head of one a jolly business man, and behind him the very flower of the village of his residence, at the head of the other "a good carpenter but not much of a soldier," as he often used to say of himself, and following him were the stoutest and hardiest of the miners of the Hocking Valley; from Noble, one hundred, headed by an intrepid and dauntless wounded soldier, followed by the pick of her chivalric youth, and by the irrepressible "Private Dalzell." And these thousand true men, loved well at home, and made of sterling staff, were on their way to war, to actual war. And their untaught, uncouth and unprepared condition made the spectacle of their march to the front as the sun was going down the sky that evening more interesting and more impressive, than if they had been clothed in all the panoply of war. It was long after dark when we were ferried over the Ohio to the trembling city of Parkersburg. Of course it rained! What soldier ever knew it not to rain when he was least prepared for it? And so now it fairly poured as though the Heavens were baptizing us with their waters, preparatory to the baptism of fire which we were for years to receive in that State of Virginia, to whose shores we were being slowly ferried across the beautiful Ohio, which ran neutral between its loyal and disloyal banks.

Without tents or blankets and without quarters, we took possession of the Baltimore and Ohio Railroad depot, and after satisfying ourselves that Jenkins was not likely to burn the town before morning, we spread out a great quantity of sacked grain, with which the depot was stored, and lying down, slept soundly until morning. The town and the roads leading into it were picketed by some of the officers of the regiment most of the night. Before daylight next morning we were up and ready to move to a camping place selected a mile or more out of town. Here we found rations enough prepared for four regiments. A company in command of Captain J. H. Dickey stationed there, knowing our condition and expecting more in the same plight, had been cooking nearly all night, and now we partook of an excellent breakfast. As we were preparing to leave the depot that morning the old freight agent arrived, and seeing the use we had made of his freight during the night, was the maddest man for a few minutes any of us ever saw. He actually knocked down a couple of men who had the impudence to laugh at his rage, and to avoid further demonstrations of that sort the men tied him to a post, where he securely remained whilst the regiment was making its escape to camp.

About the streets were a good many old soldiers, some on furlough and more who were stragglers from the recent engagements in that part of Virginia. We felt uncomfortable in their presence and when we began to prepare to move out to camp we realized more than ever our untaught condition. How to form we did not know, so we concluded to let Captain Teters go ahead and the rest to follow him as best they could. How we got out to camp none of us ever knew, but when we got there and found breakfast ready, we knew just what to do. Here was something, after all, that we had done before. That day Colonel Mulligan's "Irish Brigade" and other troops arrived and we did our first guard and picket duty. The loyal Governor Boreman was in Parkersburg at that time, and an order was issued, that no citizen could pass in or out, until recognized as a Union man by him. It gave the Governor plenty of work to do for a couple of days. Colonel Mulligan's men camped beside us, and seeing our destitute condition, generously loaned us their cooking utensils, and gave our men a great many useful lessons in army life. Our men never forgot this kindness, and whenever they afterwards caught sight of the green flags of those gallant and whole-souled Irishmen, they gave them "three cheers and a tiger."

One of the first things we did was, to tear down a whisky shanty and empty the filthy contents of several barrels, kegs and bottles into the gutters. We found the keepers of the place to be old acquaintances from Athens, who had been treated the same way there by some soldiers from Camp Jewett and compelled to leave the town. They would sell whisky to soldiers wherever they were, orders or no orders, and none but extreme measures were appreciated by them, so we broke up their business.

On the 4th, Colonel Washburn and Major Morris arrived in camp. Sometime before our appearance in Parkersburg, General Cox left the Kanawha Valley with all the available troops to join the Army of the Potomac, in which he performed gallant services, as will be remembered, in the battles of South Mountain and Antietam. He had left Colonel Lightburn in command, whose force was soon driven to the Ohio River. On the 2d, Colonel Rathbone surrendered the 11th West Virginia regiment to Jenkins, at a point a few miles from Parkersburg. He and his officers were paroled and came into Parkersburg on the 3rd. About the same time General Morgan began his retreat from Cumberland Gap to the Ohio River at Gallipolis, which he reached about the 4th. On the 6th of September, we were ordered, with about the same haste as from Marietta, to Gallipolis. As we passed through Athens early in the morning of the 7th M. M. Greene, who happened to be at the depot, said if we would wait fifteen minutes the citizens would give us our breakfasts. We waited and they did not disappoint us. Before the time was up the road leading to the depot was thronged with men, women and children bringing coffee, bread, meat, pies, cakes, etc. Many were at their breakfasts and brought all they had on their tables. The entire regiment was fed bountifully. Some of the companies from the other counties were surprised at this swift way of doing things. We landed at Oak Hill that evening, and, after supper, marched to Centerville, where we went into camp about 10 P. M. Arrived at Gallipolis early next day and went into camp in the Fair Grounds. Some of General Morgan's troops on arriving here looked about as hard as we did after the Lynchburg raid. All the Union forces in West Virginia and Eastern Kentucky were now lying along or near the Ohio River and the line of the Baltimore and Ohio Railroad, most of them on the Ohio side. The "Home Guard" and militia in all the counties bordering on the Ohio were called out and ordered to Gallipolis, and when we arrived there the country about the city was full of soldiers. A very large force of militia was here, among them a company of 130 men from Athens County in command of Captain A. D. Jaynes. Two other companies from Athens were also there, one under Captain F. H. Hackman, the other under Captain Silas Pruden. Adjutant Ballard went to Cincinnati from here on business for the regiment, and Lieutenant H. L. Karr acted as Adjutant in his absence. On the 12th Colonel Washburn was sent up the Kanawha, with the three companies of the 92d O. V. I. and some other troops, to reinforce Colonel Lightburn, who was fighting above Charleston and falling back toward the Ohio before a vastly superior force of rebels. He was gone three days, Lightburn's forces, in the meantime, having reached the Ohio at Point Pleasant, where he fortified. General Morgan soon organized the miscellaneous companies and regiments into a formidable army. In a few days after our arrival General Cox arrived and assumed command. Our first camp was some distance above Gallipolis, where we entered upon the work of drilling in real earnest. Upon the arrival of General Cox we were moved three miles below Gallipolis. From our first camp we could occasionally see the rebels on the opposite side, seemingly content with having driven the "Yanks" off the "sacred soil." Colonel Lightburn's forces arrived at Point Pleasant from Charleston on the 20th. On the 16th and 17th of September, the regiment, excepting companies K and F, which were not quite full, owing to some desertions and some rejections which reduced them below the minimum, was mustered into the United States service, and we received clothing, camp and garrison equipage, and better arms. Over forty of Captain Hull's men refused to be mustered and left camp as deserters. This conduct was very disgraceful and left company K with less than the minimum, so that it could not be mustered. One of his lieutenants, Miers, also refused to be mustered. General George B. Wright paid us a visit shortly after our arrival at Gallipolis, and made a speech to the regiment, in which he complimented us very highly on our willingness and promptness in obeying orders in moving from point to point to defend the border before we were mustered in, or properly equipped.

The officers and men rapidly improved in the manual of arms and in squad and company drill. We had now a fine looking regiment. Most of the men were very large, healthy, strong fellows, giving promise of great endurance and a capability of making their regiment and themselves a record in whatever field of service they might be called to act. Officers' school was also established, and the whole regiment was soon as busy as a hive in learning the art of war. Some battalion drill was also indulged in, but it was not performed with much skill and generally ended in disgust all round.

Among the troops we met at Gallipolis was the 40th Ohio. Very strict orders were in force, at one time, in regard to passing any one in or out. One day, as Captain Teters was on duty on the river road east of Gallipolis, Colonel Taylor of that regiment rode up to the guard and attempted to pass out. He had on a "linen duster" and no sign of his rank was visible. Captain Teters ordered him to halt. This he declined to do, until the Captain caught his horse by the bridle and stopped him. He made a motion to draw a revolver from his holster, when the Captain drew his from a holster on his sword belt, and getting the "drop" on him ordered the Colonel to "dismount and surrender." The Colonel obeyed promptly. Colonel Taylor then told who he was and again demanded to be passed through the lines. Teters' mettle was up by this time, and he held the Colonel a prisoner, refusing to recognize his rank or his right to pass his guard without authority from General Cox's headquarters. High words ensued, and the Captain was about ordering his prisoner under guard to the Provost Marshal, when General Cox, with some members of his staff, happened to ride up. Explanations followed and the Colonel rode off a wiser if not a better officer. General Cox personally thanked Captain Teters for his care in enforcing orders and reproved Colonel Taylor for his conduct.

While we lay here was probably the darkest and gloomiest period of the war. A despondent feeling overspread the whole North. Union men were discouraged and the disloyal element was correspondingly jubilant. President Lincoln had on the 22d of September issued his proclamation "that on the first day of January, 1863, all persons held as slaves within any State, or designated part of any State, the people whereof shall then be in rebellion against the United States, shall be then, thenceforward and forever free." Partisan feeling ran high, even in the army. Many officers resigned, declaring they would no longer serve in an "abolition war." The newspapers, according to their partisan bias, applauded or denounced the proclamation. The large enlistments during the months of July, August and September, had drained the country of many of the warmest supporters of the Government at home, and at the October elections, many of the Northern States, including Ohio, seemed to manifest their disapproval of the proclamation and the conduct of the war by voting for the Democratic party, which refused its sanction to any scheme of emancipation. In the army, and especially in the Army of the Potomac, the predominant feeling was suspected to be adverse to the proclamation. If the October elections could be taken as an expression, the majority of the Northern people were also adverse to it. Many efforts were made to turn the tide of discontent and re-establish the confidence of the country. The meeting of the "Governors of the Loyal States" at Altoona, Pa., was a notable effort in this direction. Among other things done by this meeting was the adoption of an address to President Lincoln and the country, in which, among other things, they said: "We hail with heartfelt gratitude and encouraged hopes the proclamation issued on the 22d instant, declaring emancipated from their bondage all persons held to service or labor as slaves in the rebel States where rebellion shall last until the first day of January ensuing." With a view to suppressing the disloyal tendencies of many and to restrain their interfering with and discouraging enlistments, President Lincoln issued another proclamation on the 24th of September. We quote from it as follows:

"WHEREAS, It has become necessary to call into service not only volunteers, but also portions of the militia of the States by draft in order to suppress the insurrection existing in the United States, and disloyal persons are not adequately restrained by the ordinary processes of the law from hindering this measure, and from giving aid and comfort in various ways to the insurrection,

Now, THEREFORE, be it ordered:

First, That during the existing insurrection, and as a necessary measure for suppressing the same, all rebels and insurgents, their aiders and abettors, within the United States, and all persons discouraging volunteer enlistments, resisting militia drafts, or guilty of any disloyal practices, affording aid and comfort to the rebels against the authority of the United States, shall be subject to martial law and liable to trial and punishment by court martial or military commissioners."

The address of the Governors and the latter proclamation by the President had the effect to restore, in a great measure, the confidence of the loyal people, and to suppress open demonstrations of hostility to the Government on the part of those opposing enlistments, the draft, the suppression of the rebellion by force of arms, and the emancipation of the slaves of the South. But while this was true as to open opposition, there were organized immediately afterwards secret political societies all over the North, prominent among which was the one known in history as the "Order of the Knights of the Golden Circle," all of which were notoriously disloyal in character and design. These two proclamations of the President sharply defined the future policy of the Government, and as sharply developed the antagonisms and prejudices of the people in relation to the vexed question of slavery. The anti-slavery element of the country regarded the emancipation proclamation as a blow at the root of the rebellion, and believed that it would lend new vigor to the efforts to suppress it and new life and hopes to the hearts of the people. To this element had been added by this time a vastly more numerous one composed of patriotic people, regardless of party in all parts of the country, who had come to believe that slavery was an element of strength to the rebellion and who favored its destruction as a means of destroying and suppressing the rebellion. To this latter class belonged Governor Tod, of Ohio, Governor Pierpont, of Virginia, Governor Bradford, of Maryland, Governor Morton, of Indiana, what was known as the "Douglass Democracy," and, in short, the great body of the loyal people of the country. Among them now there was but little division of opinion on the importance of slavery to the rebellion, and hence their hearty endorsement of the emancipation proclamation. And so it followed that they also endorsed the proclamation which aimed at those who discouraged enlistments and resisted the draft as a necessary war measure. But with the opponents to the proclamation, with the lukewarm supporters of the Union, and with the avowed opponents of the war, the two measures were denounced as "arbitrary interferences of the

Government with the personal rights of a citizen," and the feeling aroused by their discussion was bitter and vindictive beyond anything ever before, or since, witnessed in this country. The feeling ran so high, and discussion became so bitter and hostile in the Army of the Potomac, that General McClellan on the 7th of October issued an order forbidding discussion of the proclamation. Other army commanders found it necessary to follow his example in this respect. Our own regiment was not free from this feeling, and it did not entirely abate until after the action taken at Romney in January following. Enlistments were almost entirely checked, as Colonel Washburn found, who, taking companies K and F back to Camp Putnam, tried to fill them up. Such, then, was the state of public affairs, when the 116th entered the service in the fall of 1862.

On the 16th of October the regiment left Gallipolis for Parkersburg. On the march we passed through Meigs and Athens Counties, the homes of many of our men. The first night we stopped at Cheshire, in Gallia County. The next day we passed through Pomeroy and that night camped at Chester. The next day we took dinner at Tupper's Plains, the home of Captain Keyes and most of his company, and that night we camped at Coolville, the home of Captain Fuller and most of his company. We met with grand receptions at all these places, the people turning out *en masse* to greet us, having everything prepared in most lavish abundance for our comfort on our arrival at each place of stopping. We arrived at Belpre, opposite Parkersburg, on the 19th, from which point Colonel Washburn went to Camp Putnam with companies K and F. He did not succeed in filling them until the 28th of October, when they were mustered into the service. It required more hard work to secure about a dozen men each for those two companies, than it did to recruit all the rest of the regiment. On the 22d, the balance of the 116th crossed the river to Parkersburg and took the cars to Clarksburg, arriving there the following morning. That night ride to Clarksburg was a terribly disagreeable one. It was very cold, and there being no fire or means of making fire in the old rickety cattle cars in which we were being moved, the men were in imminent danger of freezing. Finally, as the men expressed it, a "council of war" was held, and this plan adopted to warm the cars: The lining of the cars was torn off, whittled or broken up, the doors closed and fires built on the board seats. When in danger of burning through a seat it would be moved to another spot, and so on during the night, with regular guards detailed to keep up the fire and watch it. Of course the smoke had to be disposed of. This was done by standing it as long as they could, when the doors would be opened on both sides of the cars to allow the smoke to blow out. Looking forward from the rear car the train appeared almost entirely enveloped in smoke. But when we arrived in Clarksburg the next morning, the charred seats, the absent lining of the cars, and the blackened hands and faces of the men showed pretty plainly, how they had spent the night in fighting the cold. At Parkersburg, we were put into a brigade commanded by Colonel Latham, and Lieutenant Sibley was detached from the regiment and assigned as an aide on his staff. At Clarksburg, we met the 36th, 23d and some other regiments just returned from making for themselves a glorious record on the South Mountain and Antietam battle fields. We met many acquaintances among them, and were deeply interested in their stirring accounts of those battles, and especially of the desperate stand made by General Cox's Kanawha Division, the left of the army during the first day's fight at South Mountain. Now that we were soldiers, we found ourselves taking a sort of family interest in the deeds of other soldiers never so strongly felt by us before. Here we also met General Milroy, who had just been assigned to command the "Cheat Mountain Division," of which we were to form a part. General Crook, who had won his star in the battles named, was also there. At Clarksburg, we received further equipments in the way of teams and Sibley tents. On the 26th we started on the march for Buckhannon, reaching there on the 27th. The roads could hardly have been worse, if made to order, and added to this, it rained hard from almost the moment of starting from Clarksburg. That night it continued to rain even harder than during the day. "Sibley stoves" had not yet been issued and the boys complained terribly because they had nothing to burn but "wet rails." Sibley tents did not draw very well, and the fires built in them soon filled them with dense volumes of smoke. For raw soldiers, that was a very uncomfortable night, but dismal as it was, some of the men went out "foraging" and next morning several had breakfast of roast pig and turkey. On reaching Buckhannon that day, the regiment was followed by a train of twenty-seven loaded wagons, and a cloud of citizens loaded with complaints against us for "pressing" their horses, etc., into the service. General Milroy was hard pressed for an apology for us, but finally getting all the citizens' horses and wagons together, he dismissed them for their homes, each with his own vehicle and enough good army rations to keep them in good cheer on their journey. From what he knew of the 116th on the train from Parkersburg, and this, too, he said he thought the 116th Ohio would take care of itself. We thought so, too.

On the 30th, the 123d Ohio joined us with the same teams again, they having even a larger train than we had. By this time, Milroy's stock of patience began to give out, and he issued an order forbidding the army to molest the property of citizens, unless we had satisfactory evidence of their disloyalty, which "evidence" was not hard to get, when we wanted anything. There never was much trouble in getting this kind of "evidence," whenever we found ourselves in want of transportation, and we were always in want of it, for every soldier, now, had three times as much stuff as he ought to have in active field service. Colonel Washburn joined us on the 31st with companies K and F, and now we had a full regiment, completely equipped, rather *too* completely, in fact, and ready, as we thought, for any service assigned us. We were now brigaded with the 122d and 123d Ohio regiments, with Colonel Washburn as Brigade Commander. Colonel Washburn made Adjutant Ballard his Assistant Adjutant General, and Quartermaster Williams his A. A. Q. M. Quartermaster Sergeant W. J. Lee accompanied the Quartermaster. Lieutenant Hiram L. Sibley, of company B, was detailed as Acting Adjutant. What became of our other brigade no one seems to know and but few remember ever having even seen our first brigade commander. At any rate Lieutenant Sibley came back to us at Buckhannon, just in time to assume the duties of his new position of Adjutant of his regiment. Lieutenant Alexander Cochran, of company I, was detailed as Acting Quartermaster of the regiment, and Corporal George K. Campbell, of B, was appointed Acting Quartermaster Sergeant. We kept up our drilling with great diligence, and were every day improving in the tactics, while the discipline was strict, and as the men sometimes thought, severe. Lieutenant Robert Wilson, of company A, an officer who gave bright promise of being one of the best in the regiment, was here stricken down with fever, was sent home, and soon afterward died. His was our first death. We found General Milroy a very kind and courteous officer, full of energy and loyalty. No slave was ever turned back from *his* lines, for he ardently supported the policy of the Administration, embodied in the emancipation proclamation.

The enemy was quite active in guerilla warfare in all

West Virginia, and we had plenty of scouting and picketing to do, all of which was teaching our men the value of discipline and strict obedience to orders in and out of camp. But, notwithstanding, there would sometimes occur grave misconduct and violation of orders. One night it was discovered that quite a number of men were out of camp and away in the country foraging on their own account. Strong guards were placed at different points about the camp, and a detail sent out after the foragers. They were met some distance out, returning to camp loaded down with honey and fresh meat of different kinds, and marched to headquarters. It was afterwards learned that another party had been out earlier the same night which had gotten safely back to camp with their plunder. Search was at once made and most of the plunder, and the men who had it, discovered. Colonel Washburn was just about assuming command of the brigade, having received his orders, but discovering this, he stopped awhile to discipline these unruly fellows. The boys never forgot the short, sharp lecture he delivered to them, and going out of camp after plunder during the night was put a stop to for some time afterwards. Nobody was punished and all agreed to be good boys in the future, and they kept their word.

November 9th, we broke camp and started for Beverly. That night we camped at the middle fork of the Tygart Valley River. Just as we stacked arms, a team ran away. The wagon was upset and a general smashup made of everything. The soldiers made a rush for the wreck with the double purpose of catching the runaway team and helping the unfortunate mule driver. The wagon proved to be loaded with medical stores, among which was a large quantity of bottled wine, whisky and brandy, and observing the contents of the dilapidated wagon, the soldiers very soon captured "the bottles with corks out," as they afterward said, when called to account, but it was more than suspected that they also captured all the bottles whose "corks" could be *pulled* out. It was, however, always claimed by the men of the 116th that the 123d appropriated the bottles whose corks could be pulled out, and that they, acting simply on the maxim "waste not, want not," took only the bottles with corks out. It was too intricate a question to settle off hand in the conflicting state of the proof, and was dropped as one of those things "no fellow can find out." Major Morris, to whom an investigation of the matter was referred, was found next morning with several bottles with "corks out," which he said "had been offered in evidence." We reached Beverly next day, passing over the battle ground of Rich Mountain, and through some of the most beautiful mountain scenery in Virginia. While lying here, we were the recipients of many kindnesses from Mrs. Arnold, the only surviving sister of Stonewall Jackson. She was a thoroughly loyal woman, and kept the stars and stripes constantly flying over her house. She was, besides, kind-hearted and attentive, beyond the power of pen to tell to the Union soldiers, many and many an one owing his life to her care. Colonel Washburn went from here to Clarksburg and thence to Columbus for a better class of arms. On the night of the 10th, for the first time, our men "slept on their arms," our post being threatened with an attack. Our stay at Beverly was an enjoyable season, if we may believe the statements contained in a letter before us, dated November 12th, 1862: "It would do you good to look in upon us to-night. We ate our supper—a good one—just before dark, after which the Major, Doctor Johnson, Lieutenant Cochran, Lieutenant Sibley and a few others came in and seated themselves around as charming a fire as you ever saw in civilization. Then we ate apples and drank cider! What do you think of that? Let me explain. The apples and cider were 'foraged' to-day. Then we smoked and chatted, and finally the Major led off in a song. What a splendid bass voice he has! Our fire is built in a chimney—all that remains of a house that once stood here. Our tent is put up close to the chimney, the fire-place opening into the tent. Orderly Morrison says he will put a mantle-piece up to-morrow, and decorate it with plaster of Paris angels, birds, dogs, squirrels, etc. But the mail has arrived, and though it is raining quite hard, the men are running about through the camp following the 'postmaster.' Commissary Sergeant Walker has just come dancing in, exclaiming 'a letter from my wife.' Here comes the Orderly now with headquarters mail, and a letter is announced for 'the Colonel,' another for 'the Major,' and so on until nearly all of us are supplied. Then one after another went to his own quarters to read his letters from home, and we are alone with Waterman and the Orderly again. Nothing does a poor, forlorn soldier so much good as a cheerful letter from home. A great many of our officers and men left their homes very unceremoniously, and their families were left to do and care for themselves almost without notice or warning, and now, that winter is coming on, I can see that a great many of them are in great trouble about the comfort of their families. A letter, assuring them that all is right and comfortable at home, removes many a dark cloud and heavy trouble. I can see its effect at once in their countenances and cheerful discharge of duty."

We lay at Beverly until the 15th, when we took an early start for Webster, marching twenty miles the first day, and twenty-two the next. On this march, we passed over the battle ground of Phillippi. At Webster, our wagon train was left to go overland to New Creek in care of our wagon master, Hiram L. Baker, while we, next day, took the cars on the Baltimore and Ohio Railroad. A few days after our arrival at New Creek, the men of the regiment presented a field glass to Colonel Washburn, Quartermaster Sergeant Lee making the presentation speech.

The Colonel responded briefly, thanking the men for their kindness, and remarking in closing that he hoped soon to have the opportunity of leading the Third Brigade to battle against the enemy. Up to this time the regiment had enjoyed excellent health, but now the measles broke out among us and in a short time fully one-fourth of the regiment was prostrated with the disease. We met our old friends of "The Irish Brigade" here, and acting on the principle that "friends are of no use unless you use them," we induced Colonel Mulligan to detail a number of his best drilled Sergeants to drill our men, and his Adjutant to drill our officers. The result was most satisfactory. On the 28th of November, company H, in command of Captain Teters, was sent to St. George, in Tucker County, with instructions to thoroughly scout that vicinity, and clear it of a band of bushwhackers and thieves infesting it. He did the work thoroughly and returned to the regiment on the 11th of December. But the measles in their worst form had been among his men also, and he was obliged to leave fourteen men in hospital at St. George. We were, also, pretty thoroughly vaccinated at New Creek.

On the 12th of December, we broke camp and marched to Burlington, leaving 124 men in hospital at New Creek, who were afterwards sent to the general hospital at Cumberland, Maryland. We lay at Burlington until the 17th, when we started for Petersburg, which we reached on the evening of the 18th, going into camp in a plowed field, on the bank of the south branch of the Potomac. The country was now full of rebel cavalry and guerrillas, and the large trains we had with us had to be heavily guarded at all points to prevent their capture. Fourteen teams were allowed to a regiment, but in addition to these sometimes nearly as many more were "pressed into the service" to carry the heavy knapsacks of the men, and the great quantities of baggage belonging to the officers. On the march to Petersburg, Lieutenant Colonel Hunter, of the 123d, becoming separated from his command, was captured by a single rebel who met him with his gun drawn up. The Colonel was, however, recaptured in a few moments afterwards, together with his captor. Captain Brown and Lieutenant Cochran went out one day, while we lay at Petersburg, beyond the picket lines foraging and were fired upon by rebel cavalry. It was with the greatest effort they escaped to camp. The boldness and strength of the rebels in our vicinity caused the greatest vigilance in camp and in guarding forage trains. On the 21st of December Captain Teters and Lieutenant Karr were sent out with 100 men on a scout, and returned next day with nineteen prisoners. We had captured quite a number of prisoners, up to this time, and on the 23d, Lieutenant Mallory was sent to escort them to Wheeling. On the 28th, the 116th, a section of battery D, 1st West Virginia Light Artillery, Lieutenant Daniels commanding, and a company of cavalry left Petersburg, reaching Moorefield in the afternoon of the same day. There we relieved other troops which were ready to move out on our arrival, accompanied by General Milroy. Colonel Washburn remained at Petersburg with the 123d Ohio, a section of the same battery under command of Lieutenant Chalfant and a company or two of cavalry. As the troops bound for Romney were yet in sight of our camp, the rebel Captain McNeil made a descent on their train and cut loose and ran off the horses and mules of thirteen wagons. General Milroy himself was only a short distance in advance of the point where the train was attacked. The rebels, encouraged by the success of their raids and increasing numbers, were constantly threatening our positions at Petersburg and Moorefield. Union people and "contrabands" had conveyed us information that the rebel forces were concentrating under General Jones to capture these two posts. Petersburg was thirteen miles from Moorefield, and the nearest point on the other side of us was Romney, thirty-five miles away. Our position was, therefore, very critical, if attacked by a large force. General Milroy, who had established his headquarters at Winchester, had nearly 10,000 men, mostly new regiments, in his command, but they were scattered in small bodies over a wide extent of territory, except at Winchester, where the main portion was concentrated, and these very generally not in supporting distance of each other.

As soon as we were fairly settled in camp at Moorefield, we began scouting the country, entrenching, making ourselves acquainted with the roads, and watching the movements of the enemy, especially in the direction of Strasburg, where we soon learned quite a large force lay under General Jones. Inquiring by telegraph of General Milroy what rebel force was at Strasburg, he replied as follows:

"Dec. 30, 1862.

"*Lt. Col. T. F. Wildes, Moorefield, Va.:*

"I will take care of the rebels at Strasburg soon. If you are attacked, fight till the 123d can come to your relief. You can whip any force that comes against you.

"R. H. MILROY, Maj. Gen."

This was encouraging, at least. Moorefield and vicinity was most thoroughly rebel. Only five Union families lived in the place. The women were exceedingly insolent to our soldiers. A great many of the finest houses in the place were vacant, whole families having gone further south to follow the fortunes of the Confederacy. A very fine hotel, with its furniture, carpets and fixtures in place, was transformed into a hospital. General Milroy ordered that we subsist off those who would not take the oath of allegiance to the United States, and to arrest and confine all who refused to take the oath. Upon notifying him of the capture of a notorious rebel bushwhacker living in Moorefield, he telegraphed:

"Good! Stick him in jail and keep him there till you catch a horde of them that are about there, and then send them, with descriptions of their crimes, to Major Darr, at Wheeling, Va."

The women becoming daily more and more insolent, we determined to administer a little discipline to them. Accordingly, as one of them tucked her clothes close about her as she was passing one of our officers on the sidewalk, one day, he politely took her by the arm, and escorted her to the Provost Marshal's office, where she was requested to take the oath, which she very reluctantly did. She then departed "with her feathers all adroop like a rained-on-fowl." As she left the office, however, she walked far out into the street to avoid walking under the stars and stripes floating from the Provost Marshal's window. She was at once arrested again and sent to Wheeling. As usual, we found the negroes all loyal, trustworthy and vigilant to obtain news of importance to us. In a letter written December 31, 1862, we said: "If we are attacked, it will be within three days, and we are almost sure to be." This shows what was expected.

On the morning of the 3d of January, 1863, before it was yet quite light, our pickets were fired upon on the Petersburg road, and one officer, Lieutenant Okey, and seventeen men taken prisoners. We were prepared for our visitors. The vigilance maintained and the state of preparation kept up since our arrival at Moorefield found us in position for defence. The regiment numbered about 650 men. General Jones, who attacked us, had about 4,000 cavalry and a battery of artillery. We occupied an excellent position on rising ground east of the village which was skirted on three sides by woods, or thick underbrush, which formed a good cover for our men and their movements. The enemy first sent a large body of dismounted men under cover of his artillery, across the open fields from the direction of the Lost River road, down which he had come. Here he was met by companies B, G and F, and driven back with some loss. In a short time, another attempt to advance upon us was made from the same direction. By this time, one of our cannon had been planted in an open space in the woods, a little in the rear of the infantry. Allowing them to come within a few rods of the foot of the hill, the infantry and our one gun opened upon them a well directed fire, and put them to flight a second time. In a few minutes after this, a large force advanced from the direction of the Winchester road, where they were met by companies E, C and K, under command of Major Morris. They were again repulsed. About the same time a large body of mounted men advanced on the Petersburg road into the village. Captain Teters, with company H, treated them to some fine, vigorous street firing, and drove them out again on the run. In the meantime, their battery had kept up a rapid exchange of compliments with our two guns, which were manned by a brave and competent officer. About 10 A. M., the rebels drew off, and their battery ceased firing. Shortly after this, quite a large body of cavalry with one gun was seen forming on the opposite side of Moorefield. One of our guns was placed in position to meet this threatened attack, and company I sent down to reinforce H. About noon the enemy fired a shell from the gun on the opposite side of Moorefield. While the smoke was yet curling about it, a shot from our gun dismounted it. This was a most lucky and remarkable shot, and the sergeant who fired it was at once promoted to a lieutenancy in the 5th West Virginia regiment, in which we met him at the rebel works in front of Lynchburg in June, 1864. Company A was now sent down from the hill to confront a force gathering on the Romney road, on our right, and I and C brought in as a reserve. Our section of battery now selected a well protected spot, and began shelling in earnest the rebel battery near the Petersburg road, soon disabling another gun. The artillery duel was not of long duration, before the rebel battery ceased and withdrew. Matters remained very quiet now until about 3 P. M. Whenever the enemy showed any large number, we would shell them and drive them to shelter, and so we watched their movements closely, every moment expecting a charge from some direction, for they were all around us. About this time everything indicated preparations for a final dash upon us, from all sides, with overwhelming numbers. Their artillery opened fire afresh, and lines of skirmishers advanced carefully towards us. But just as we were expecting their lines, now in plain sight, to charge us, artillery was heard out on the road toward Petersburg, and the rebel lines at once fell back from all sides. "What had happened?" "Is Washburn coming?" every one inquired. Field glasses failed to detect any force in that direction, but the smoke of guns out there could be seen from our hill. Now we saw shells exploding in the vicinity of the rebel battery which we knew we did not throw. We placed our colors on a commanding point in full view of the point from which the firing came on the Petersburg road, for we all concluded these guns were, with reinforcements, coming to our relief. Our own guns were opened afresh on the rebel battery, which was now giving its attention to these new comers, and between us it was silenced and withdrawn. A courier was now started to try to get through the rebel lines, and ascertain who our friends were, and convey to them a dispatch, containing suggestions of a combined movement for the capture of that portion of the enemy on the opposite side of Moorefield. Several attempts to get through failed. The enemy was in strong force between. Finally the dispatch was given to Hiram L. Baker, and we attempted to clear a way for him with our artillery. He was successful, and at the same time a courier came through to us who announced that Colonel Washburn was there with his force from Petersburg. We then moved a portion of our regiment out to intercept the rebels on the other side of Moorefield, but without attempting to rejoin General Jones on the Lost River road, they retreated over the mountains and escaped, taking with them Elmer Armstrong, our sutler, whom they had captured at the house of Major Harness, where he had gone with the view of concealing some of his money and goods. Major Harness was an old acquaintance of Mr. Armstrong, they having had dealings in cattle before the war. After taking him away several miles, they released him and the next day he returned to us at Moorefield in a terribly dilapidated condition. Being a "Bible Democrat" did not shield Mr. Armstrong from misusage and insult at the hands of his captors. He was listened to with great interest by the men in his relation of the sad experience he had in riding a raw-boned, bare-backed horse for several miles on the run, and then being released to find his way back through the mountains on foot. The 123d Ohio and the rest of the Petersburg troops joined us at Moorefield before night, the rebels retreating over the Lost River road. They were without tents, blankets or cooking utensils, and the 116th boys were only too happy to supply them with everything necessary to their comfort during the night, for we felt that they had without doubt saved us either a severe and bloody fight, or capture, and perhaps both. Our loss was three men wounded by fragments of shell, and twenty prisoners. Corporal Wm. Scott, of company I, was wounded in the shoulder by a fragment of shell, being the first man in the regiment wounded in battle. Two others were slightly wounded, whose names we cannot ascertain. The prisoners were Lieutenant Henry Okey, company D; Sergeant Benjamin Sheffield, company K; Rawley Ausburg, company K; Byron Battin, company K; Wm. H. Brown, company K; Abraham Butterworth, company K; Joseph Cullison, company K; David Gross, company K; Asa Ladd, company K; Isaiah Matheny, company K; William Robinett, company K; George Sigler, company K; Daniel F. Weddle, company K; John Wilkinson, company K; Corporal Harrison Cochran, company E; Corporal Andrew W. Henthorn, company E; Adam H. Ollam, company E; John J. Walter, company E; Robert J. Hathaway, company E; Samuel Luthey, company E. Lieutenant Henry Okey, who was captured that morning, had tendered his resignation some time before, and it was accepted only the day before his capture. The order for his discharge had not, however, yet reached the regiment. As soon as it did reach it, the information was duly sent to the rebel authorities, and he was soon after released. Lieutenant Okey was too old a man for the service, and its hardships soon broke down his health. But he was a patriotic, good man, and his heart was in the cause. He would gladly have remained with us had his health permitted.

The next day Colonel Mulligan arrived with his "Irish Brigade" and O'Rourke's battery, and the day after his arrival our whole force moved up the Lost River road several miles. We found abundant evidence of the haste with which the enemy retreated on the 3d. Ascertaining that they had moved as far south as Staunton, we returned to Moorefield the same evening. There was no use in infantry trying to catch up with cavalry. General Milroy, Colonel Mulligan and Colonel Washburn commended the 116th very highly for the defense it made of Moorefield against the vastly superior numbers of the enemy, which we afterward learned numbered over 4,000 cavalry and six pieces of artillery. Mr. Armstrong said that when he told them our strength, they called him a "d——d old Yankee liar," and claimed that we had at least three regiments of infantry and a battery of artillery. It was fortunate for us that they thought so, for had their whole force attacked us at once, we could not hope to have successfully resisted them. Though this was the first time the 116th was under fire, it behaved splendidly. Up to this time there had been a good deal of grumbling at the strict discipline maintained and the constant drilling kept up. All now hastened to acknowledge the benefit of this, and from that time on the men of the 116th were never heard to complain of drill or discipline. The day following the battle, General Milroy sent us the following message:

WINCHESTER, VA., Jan. 4, 1863.

"*Lt. Col. T. F. Wildes, Moorefield, Va.:*

"Accept my congratulations and thanks, yourself and your gallant command, for the courage and skill with which you defended your post against such overwhelming numbers of the enemy. I thought I was not mistaken when I told you, Dec. 30th, 'you can whip any force that comes against you.' I bespeak for you and your noble regiment a glorious record.

"R. H. MILROY, Maj. Gen'l Commanding"

No compliment paid us during the war was more highly appreciated and none more deserving.

CHAPTER III.

THE MARCH TO ROMNEY—THE WINTER AT ROMNEY—A FORAGE TRAIN UNDER CAPTAIN BROWN CAPTURED—PAROLES—A BAD STATE OF FEELING—PATRIOTIC ACTION OF THE REGIMENT—THE MARCH TO WINCHESTER.

On the 20th of January we left Moorefield for Romney. Sergeant Charles P. Allison and Carmi Allison, of company K, and Sergeant Robert G. Wells and D. J. Haning, of company G, remained behind for some purpose, as we moved out of Moorefield, and were captured by the enemy, who occupied it as soon as our rear guard left, and while it was yet in sight of the town. These men were all paroled. On our march we were accompanied by a great many colored people fleeing from slavery. The threatened proclamation, liberating the slaves, had been issued, on the first of January, by President Lincoln, and though West Virginia had been excepted from its provisions, the colored people did not know it. They only knew that an emancipation proclamation had been issued by the President, and, hence they flocked into Moorefield in large numbers during the night before we moved, colored people inside our lines having sent the news of our intended movement next morning to a great distance outside. It snowed hard the first day, it was very cold, and the roads were about as bad as they could well be. Toward the middle of the afternoon, two colored women were given a ride by the hospital steward. Somehow the incident, which was thought nothing of, got home in the shape that "Colonel Washburn and

Lieutenant Colonel Wildes had turned sick men out of their ambulances and put niggers in to ride." The story lost nothing by repetition and traveling, and soon assumed very ugly proportions. Finally the officers of the regiment united, in a card to the press, explaining the silly story, which squelched it. We here reproduce the card of the officers:

Editor Messenger, Athens:

Our object in addressing you, is to publish an extract from a letter from one of our friends in Athens, and set the matter it contains in its true light before your readers. The extract is as follows:

"Letters written home, either by the line officers or privates, all have their effect on public opinion. We have had some experimental facts in the case, and some of them I must take the liberty of asking you to give me the truth of, as the stories sent home by one or two writers, and circulated by their friends, demand immediate attention if not true; if *true*, I would like to know it, as your humble servant and your friends here have pronounced them *lies*. I have been told by Reed Golden that his *brother John* had written to his father, that while your Regiment was on a march, some three or four contraband negroes were found coming into your lines and asked protection; whereupon Colonel Washburn ordered some sick boys that were riding in an ambulance to *get out*, and *put the contrabands in to ride*, and that a private had written home to his father that the contraband negroes were wenches, and that Lieut. Col. Wildes ordered the sick boys out and let the negroes ride."

The undersigned, officers of the 116th Reg't O. V. I., are acquainted with the circumstances that gave rise to the story above mentioned, and we do hereby pronounce it an *unmitigated lie*, and we brand *any man* as an *unprincipled liar* who would be so lost to every sense of manliness as to construe what *did* occur, to make it appear as represented by "Reed Golden" and said "private."

The facts in the case are simply these: When our Regiment left Moorefield two female contrabands, desiring, it seems, to leave their good masters, came within our lines and started *on foot*, in company with a few other contrabands, in the wake of our Regiment. The hospital steward, who was driving an ambulance full of sick soldiers, overtook them and kindly asked them to ride on the driver's seat, where sick soldiers cannot very well ride, and could not, *especially that day*, as it was storming. Neither Col. Washburn nor Lieut. Col. Wildes *knew* that said contrabands were riding, and *we* say, under the circumstances, "*what if they did?*" The two females brought through on that march are now doing good service in the hospital of the regiment—one being an excellent cook, the other a laundress.

JOHN HULL, Capt. Co. K.
LEVI LUPTON, 2d. Lieut. Co. C.
W. S. MARTIN, Lieut. Co. F.
JAS. P. MANN, 1st. Lieut. Co. C.
E. W. BRADY, Chaplain 116th.
C. W. RIDGEWAY, Capt. Co. A.
H. L. SIBLEY, 2d. Lieut. Co. B.
WM. MYERS, Capt. Co. D.
JOHN VARLEY, Capt. Co. E.

H. L. KARR, 1st. Lieut. Com'g Co. G.
MATHEW BROWN, Capt. Co. F.
W. R. GILKEY, Surgeon 116th.
T. MALLORY, 1st. Lieut. Co. B.
EDWIN KEYES, Capt. Co. H.
A. B. FRAME, Lieut. Com'g Co. I.
R. F. CHANEY, 2d. Lieut. Co. D.
F. H. ARCKENOE, Capt. Co. C.

Of this matter Jesse VanLaw, the editor of the "Athens Messenger," said:

> "We need not say that we never believed this report, as the enemies of Col. Wildes, as well as his friends, will agree that no man in Athens County has excelled him in kindness and care for the sick and hungry soldiers that came to this place, while he resided in it. The idea that he would turn out the sick of his own command to allow any body to ride is absurd to any one not gone stark mad with 'nigger phobia'."

In justice to Captain Golden, we should state here, that he positively denied writing anything of the kind to any body, and even if he had not denied it, we would never have believed that he did. Looking back to this from the midst of our changed condition, what was then thought of sufficient importance for all the officers of a regiment to stop to explain, looks now very ridiculous and absurd. Yet such was then the bitter prejudice against the colored people, that their action seemed not only advisable, but really necessary, in order to relieve the public mind from the impression gained that the 116th had officers who would throw their sick men out of ambulances to make room for "niggers." Such were the absurdities some people were ready to believe, whenever the "nigger" was involved in the story.

When we camped at the end of the first day's march, there was a foot of snow on the ground, and the "top rails" in our vicinity were rapidly consumed. We reached Romney the next day, the 11th of January. We lay here two months and were constantly engaged in drilling, foraging and picketing. On the 18th day of January, a four days' mail was captured by a party of twenty-five guerrillas, between Romney and the railroad. It was the result of a most disgraceful piece of carelessness on the part of a cavalry escort. A few days after this, a soldier of company I came to headquarters, and wanted to be authorized to act as a scout, and thus be able to convey news of the proximity of rebel bands in time to avoid such attacks and surprises as the one just mentioned. After some conversation, he was asked if he thought he could deceive the rebels as to his identity in case of his capture. After a moment's reflection he replied: "I guess I can. I have deceived everyone I have ever had anything to do with so far in life." He was given the authority to scout, and some days afterward was found at a house close by the picket line, where he had been all this time "sparking" a girl. His authority to scout was revoked, but his ability to "deceive" remained unquestioned ever afterwards.

A most disgraceful affair took place here on the 16th of February. Captain Brown, of company F, with his company and some cavalry, all under his command, when about seven miles from Romney on their return from a foraging expedition, with a loaded train, allowed his men to straggle and wander about the country, thus leaving the train unprotected. He and his Lieutenant, Martin, were riding quite a distance in front of the train, giving it no attention whatever. In this situation the rebel McNeil, with about forty mounted men, dashed in between Captain Brown and his train, and captured it and his men in detail, without any resistance. The men were all paroled, the horses and mules cut loose from the wagons and their loads burned. Captain Brown ran off at full speed to camp, never making even the slightest attempt to join his men, or avert this disaster. McNeil took about sixty prisoners, fifty horses and eight mules, and beat a hasty retreat, and though followed, as soon as the news reached the camp, by a large body of cavalry, he made good his escape with all his capture, except the prisoners, whom he paroled. He sent word to Captain Brown by the paroled prisoners to send him out his shoulder straps. The affair aroused the greatest indignation, and Captain Brown and Lieutenant Martin were placed in arrest. Charges were preferred against them, and they were tried by a court martial and acquitted with a public reprimand! It is proper, in justice to Lieutenant

Martin and the members of company F, to say, that they thoroughly redeemed themselves in their subsequent conduct, and that the responsibility of the whole affair wholly rested upon Captain Brown. No braver officer belonged to the 116th than Lieutenant Martin afterwards proved himself; and no company of men did any more gallant service than company F performed throughout its term of service. Of Captain Brown, more will appear hereafter. Lieutenant Sibley was Judge Advocate of the court martial here. At Romney Captains Ridgeway, Fuller and Golden, Lieutenants McElfresh and Sears, and Assistant Surgeon James Johnson resigned, all on account of failing health.

Quite a despondent and unpatriotic feeling extensively prevailed among the men at this post during this winter, and large numbers procured themselves to be captured by guerrillas and paroled. On being paroled they would, on their own responsibility, go home, or on returning to camp, refuse to do duty. Suspicion led to an investigation, which developed the fact, that rebel citizens in the vicinity kept on hand paroles, signed by guerrilla chiefs, and that the men, aware of this, were in the habit of going out and getting them, sometimes paying for them in coffee, sugar, etc. There seemed to be an understanding established between our soldiers and the rebels. Paroles became as common, at one time, as sutler's checks, and the uncomfortable feeling that this state of affairs created among officers can hardly be imagined. It was determined to put a stop to it at all hazards, for it was simply another way of deserting. Accordingly, orders were sent home to cause the arrest and return of all soldiers, in whose possession were found paroles and *no furloughs*, and all in camp were armed and returned to duty. Paroles soon became a badge of cowardice, and when once thus branded by the better class of soldiers, the business suddenly came to an end. This was a shrewd scheme on the part of the rebels to deplete our army. Had they sent their prisoners to Libby and Belle Isle, the terrors of prison life would have been in their minds, but so far from this being the case, the paroled prisoners had the picture of a pleasant, indefinite visit to their home and friends held before their eyes, and in the home-sick condition of many, this was a temptation too strong to resist. When Captain Brown's train guard was attacked, McNeil cried out to the men, before either side fired a gun, "I don't want to hurt you, throw down your arms and I'll parole every devil of you and you can go home." This was the policy pursued by the rebels all through that part of West Virginia during the winter of 1862 and '63, and it did us far more harm than to have sent their prisoners off to the rebel prisons of the South would have done. We have said that probably while we lay at Gallipolis in the fall of 1862 was the darkest and gloomiest period of the war. Perhaps the time we lay at Romney ought to be excepted. During this period the disloyal element of the North exercised its most baneful influence, and its greatest sway over the minds of the soldiers, and no one had any doubt that the policy of paroling our soldiers originated with and was suggested to the rebels by Northern rebel sympathizers. Letters advising soldiers to desert often came to camp. In these letters, rebel victories were magnified, and Union victories disparaged, and we were hearing on all sides that we could never quell the rebellion. Seeing the poisonous effect of such letters and newspapers upon the minds of the men, General Milroy suppressed a few papers, notably the "Wheeling Register," and it was threatened to suppress the mails altogether, if such letters and papers continued coming to our camps. A general meeting of officers and men was finally held in February, at which a stirring address appealing to the patriotism of the Northern people was adopted, together with a series of resolutions deprecating, in strong terms, the course pursued by disloyal men in the North, urging the loyal people everywhere to take new heart, to stand up fearlessly for the cause of the Union, and to do all in their power to encourage the army in the field. This address and these resolutions were published throughout the counties in Ohio in which the regiment was raised, and the effect was soon made visible in the advanced *morale* and temper of the men. We here copy the resolutions.

At a meeting of the officers of the 116th Regiment O. V. I., held on the evening of the 10th inst., at Romney, West Virginia, the following officers were appointed a committee to draft resolutions expressive of the sentiments of the officers and men of said Regiment, viz: Lieut. Col. Thos. F. Wildes, Captain John Varley, Captain Wm. Myers and Lieutenant Hamilton L. Karr.

The committee reported on the evening of the 12th inst., the following preamble and resolutions, which were adopted by every officer on duty with the Regiment. On the following day they were read to the Regiment while on battallion drill, when not one man dissented, but all adopted them with a deafening AYE!

WHEREAS, We, the officers and men of the 116th Regiment Ohio Volunteer Infantry, firmly believing in the justice and holiness of the cause in which we are engaged, and solemnly avowing our purpose anew of fighting its battles till the last rebel in arms is laid low at the foot of our glorious banner of Light and Liberty, do, therefore—

Resolve, That nothing but "*unconditional surrender*" will answer the demands of the true soldier and patriot.

Resolved, That we are still actuated by the same motives that induced us to first lift our arms against rebellion; that we are mindful, and believe, that service rendered to our country is service rendered to our God, whose boon our country is to a people determined to be FREE, and, with these convictions to inspire us, we will war against treason till its last vestige is swept to its native hell, with a devotion unfelt and unknown by any but the true soldier.

Resolved, That we will hail with feelings of delight the dawning of PEACE; but we can think of no peace worth having short of crushing out the rebellion, and the complete restoration of the authority of the Government over every foot of her soil, East, West, North and South.

Resolved, That we, as a loyal soldiery, acknowledge the Administration the medium through which the destruction of the rebellion is to be made effectual; and that we owe it to all we hold sacred in our blood bought, free institutions, to give it such support as will enable us to hand down to generations to come, intact, this glorious Union of ours.

Resolved, That any party, or set of men who, by factious opposition to the Administration, the Government, or the prosecution of the war, injure our noble cause, will meet with *overwhelming and popular indignation from the soldiery both now and* HEREAFTER.

Resolved, That we hear with regret, though with *hearts full of condemnation and repudiation, the murmurings*, and insane, disloyal conduct of the "copperheads"—so called by the soldiers—in our loyal and gallant State.

Resolved, That we regard the efforts of these "copperheads" in Ohio to demoralize the army by writing treasonable letters to the soldiers in the field, urging them to desert their flag, misrepresenting the Administration and the objects of the war, much of which is done to cover up their own cowardice and justify their treason, as unworthy American citizens, and as more heinous and execrable than the efforts of armed rebels who meet us in deadly conflict on the battle-field.

Resolved, That we regard any attempt to injure or depreciate the value of the currency of the Government—in which the soldier is paid—as a direct blow at the soldier and his family, and a stab at the very vitals of the Government itself, conduct of which no one friendly to the perpetuation of our free institutions and the restoration of the union of the States would be guilty.

Resolved, That we regard the prospects of a speedy termination of the war resulting in the utter discomfiture and the consequent overthrow of the rebellion, as bright and encouraging—all the boasts of rebels and the sneers and jeers of "copperheads" to the contrary notwithstanding.

WM. MYERS, President.

H. L. KARR, Secretary.

ROMNEY, WEST VIRGINIA, Feb. 12, 1863.

The January proclamation of emancipation had added much to this bad state of feeling in the army and among the people. For a time, party spirit was so excited, that it was feared that the North itself might become the scene of civil strife. But now the army everywhere began to express itself upon the state of affairs. In the same month the Army of the Cumberland had a monster meeting at Murfreesboro, at which an address was adopted, containing a powerful appeal to the patriotic people of the land "to stay, support, and uphold the hands of the soldiers," and denouncing in unmeasured terms those who were clamoring for "peace on any terms." While the storm of passion was at its height, threatening the safety of the country, there came a sudden lull, calming popular agitation and allaying factional discord. The Government, just before tottering under the tumult of contending parties, now suddenly resumed its firmness, sustained by the steady support of the people. This surprising change, as surprising to one side as the other, and as mysterious as the varying phenomena of nature, was accompanied by circumstances which astounded the whole country. Popular leaders who but a few days before had denounced the "radical" policy of the Government as fatal to the cause of the Union, and counselled opposition, now praised the one and deprecated the other. Many attempts were made to solve the mystery of this sudden and remarkable change. Some attributed it to the stand taken by the army against opposition to the Government; some to the scorn with which the enemy had treated rebel sympathizers in the North; some to a discreet fear of an Executive, endowed with almost absolute power, and now thoroughly determined to exercise every mite of his power, to the work of crushing out the rebellion; while the real explanation of this sudden political conversion was doubtless attributable to the patriotic notion of checking the rising anarchy by a sacrifice of personal opinion to the general welfare. But whatever caused the mysterious change, the fact of the change itself remained, to be seen and felt on every hand. Patriotic letters and counsels took the place of the late seditious and treasonable ones, and soon not a vestige of the unpatriotic feeling we have mentioned was any where to be found. It was as dead as the same men helped to make the rebellion within the next two years. And from that time forward the people and the army were one harmonious whole, and both labored in perfect accord and unison to accomplish the overthrow of the rebellion and the restoration of the Union. With the disappearance of this state of feeling, the slumbering fires of patriotism were kindled anew, and every one went about the discharge of his duty in the good work before him with a renewed zeal and a firmer determination than ever.

February 17th Private Amos S. Byers, of company C, was instantly killed by the accidental discharge of a musket. It created a great sensation in the regiment, and caused greater care of arms ever afterwards. Byers was a good man and an excellent soldier, and his sad death was greatly mourned. The headquarters of the regiment were in a large brick house while we lay at Romney, and having plenty of fuel and rations and good sleeping apartments, we passed the time very comfortably. No happier military family could be found anywhere than ours. Major Morris, Adjutant Sibley, Quartermaster Cochran, Sergeant Major

Ellis, Commissary Sergeant Walker and Acting Quartermaster Sergeant Campbell, Clerk Waterman and Orderly Webster formed a happy party. Several of them were good singers. One or two good fiddlers were generally about. Sibley, for drollery and comic speaking and story telling, excelled, and when all other duties were performed, the *ennui* of camp life was kept very far away from those quarters by genuine fun and amusement. From one of the numerous letters written from Romney, we make the following extract as showing the enjoyments of headquarters: "In the Adjutant's office just now is heard the sweet sounds of the violin, and the Major's strong bass voice with the Sergeant Major's fine tenor, while, overhead, in the Quartermaster's room, is heard the fun and frolic of Lee, Walker and Campbell, and the useless protests of the matter-of-fact old Quartermaster. I would like to take this whole headquarters crew home with me and show them to you. You would think us wild barbarians no doubt, and it is more than likely we have all forgotten the ways of civilized life, but we are all apt scholars, and with good teachers would soon learn them again." But the foundation of the future good record of the regiment was also laid at Romney in study, drill, officers' and non-commissioned schools, and in the preservation of excellent discipline. On the 15th of March we moved from Romney for Winchester, reaching there on the 17th.

CHAPTER IV.

AT WINCHESTER— A NEW BRIGADE COMMANDER—SCOUTS AND MARCHES— DEATH OF DR. GILKEY— BATTLE OF WINCHESTER, JUNE 12TH, 13TH AND 14TH, AND BUNKER HILL, JUNE 13TH— THE RETREAT AND BATTLE IN THE NIGHT— ESCAPE OF MILROY'S ARMY FROM LEE— OVER IN PENNSYLVANIA AND MARYLAND— LIST OF KILLED, WOUNDED AND PRISONERS— BACK TO MARTINSBURG— A WORD IN DEFENSE OF GENERAL MILROY.

We were now brigaded anew and placed under command of Brigadier General W. S. Elliott. The brigade consisted of the 110th, 116th, 122d and 123d Ohio infantry regiments, the 12th and 13th Pennsylvania cavalry, and Battery L, 5th U. S. artillery, a very strong brigade, but a curious mixture of arms. This returned Colonel Washburn, Adjutant Ballard, Quartermaster Williams and Quartermaster Sergeant Lee to their regiment, and Lieutenant Sibley, and Lieutenant Cochran, and Corporal Campbell to their companies. It would be hard to find words to express how well these three men— Sibley, Cochran and Campbell— discharged the duties assigned them at Buchanan. Each man was exactly the right man in the right place, and they now returned to their respective companies with the good will of everybody and with the assurance that they had faithfully and efficiently done their work. On the 1st of April the enlisted men of the regiment purchased a fine sword for Lieutenant Colonel Wildes, which, on account of an injury he had received, was not formally presented to him until the last of May. It bore the engraved inscription, "Presented to Lt. Col. Thomas Francis Wildes, by the enlisted men of the 116th O. V. I., as a testimonial of their appreciation of his courage, zeal and kindness. April 1st, 1863." A very graceful and feeling presentation speech was made by Private W. H. Bassett, of company C, which was responded to in brief remarks by Lieutenant Colonel Wildes, in which he thanked the men most heartily for their splendid gift.

During the time we lay in Winchester, there was a great deal of serious sickness and many deaths among both citizens and soldiers, typhoid fever being the prevailing disease. Dr. W. R. Gilkey, our surgeon, died of fever on the 4th of June. Dr. J. Q. A. Hudson, our first assistant surgeon, was detached from us, and assigned to the charge of the hospital for insane soldiers at Louisville, Ky., almost immediately after the organization of the regiment, and seeing no prospect of being returned to us he had resigned on the 23d of March. As before stated, Dr. Johnson resigned at Romney on the 19th of February, and for a long time, during which a great deal of sickness prevailed, Dr. Gilkey was alone and he was overworked. He really fell a sacrifice to his extraordinary devotion to duty. Dr. Thomas J. Shannon was appointed to the vacancy occasioned by the death of Dr. Gilkey, and Drs. Smith and Brown to the vacancies created by the resignations of Hudson and Johnson.

From the time of its arrival in Winchester, the regiment was almost constantly engaged in foraging, scouting, or skirmishing with the enemy. Several very long and hard marches were made on scouts. One of these, on the 22d of April, was to Strasburg, twenty miles distant, where our cavalry only had a tilt with the enemy. We returned, next day, with thirty prisoners. But long scouts up the valley were a weekly occurrence, but as nothing more than heavy marches resulted from them it would be tedious to give them in detail. On the 25th of April, we again started out with our entire brigade of infantry, cavalry and artillery, accompanied by a pontoon train. The next day we reached Wardensville, where we went into camp, passing through Capon Springs, a beautiful watering place, on the way. On the morrow, we marched to Lost River, and finding the bridges all gone, we returned to our camp ground of the night before. We were now in the midst of some of the most enchanting scenery in Virginia. During the day Lost River was bridged with pontoons, and next morning we crossed and resumed our march to within nine miles of Moorefield. We then turned about, and marched back to Wardensville, where we again camped over night. During the night four of our pickets were shot by bushwhackers. The next morning early, we were on the road toward Strasburg, where we came up with the enemy, and had a sharp engagement. The 13th Pennsylvania cavalry was led into an ambush here and lost a few men, but the enemy was repulsed with considerable loss, retreating up the valley. The Union loss was six killed and several wounded, all from the cavalry. On the next day, the 29th, we returned to Winchester, having marched about 100 miles. On the 5th of May we started out with a week's rations and forty rounds of ammunition. Went as far as New Market, and meeting with nothing more formidable than a few bushwhackers, returned to Winchester on the 9th. Soon after this we were engaged several days in macadamizing the road to Martinsburg, which was put in good shape for several miles out of Winchester. Several promotions took place at Winchester on account of the resignations at Romney. The following is the list:

> First Lieutenant T. Mallory, to Captain, *vice* Ridgeway, resigned.
> First Lieutenant H. L. Karr, to Captain, *vice* Golden, resigned.
> First Lieutenant Alex Cochran, to Captain, *vice* Fuller, resigned.
> Second Lieutenant H. L. Sibley, to First Lieutenant.
> Second Lieutenant W. M. Kerr, to First Lieutenant.
> Second Lieutenant Richard Chaney, to First Lieutenant.
> Second Lieutenant Wilson F. Martin, to First Lieutenant.
> Second Lieutenant J. C. H. Cobb, to First Lieutenant.
> Second Lieutenant A. B. Frame, to First Lieutenant.
> Second Lieutenant John F. Welch, to First Lieutenant.
> First Sergeant John Manning, to Second Lieutenant.
> First Sergeant Samuel D. Knight, to Second Lieutenant.
> First Sergeant Ransom Griffin, to Second Lieutenant.
> First Sergeant Richmond O. Knowles, to Second Lieutenant.
> First Sergeant Gottleib Schenkey, to Second Lieutenant.
> First Sergeant Wm. B. Henry, to Second Lieutenant.
> Sergeant Major Milton A. Ellis, to Second Lieutenant.
> Sergeant James M. Dalzell, Company H, was appointed Sergeant Major.

On the 3d of April the regiment was armed with new Springfield rifles, and now we felt, for the first time, that we had a serviceable and respectable arm. On the 4th there was a grand review of the army by Gen. Milroy. On the 4th of June Private Jacob Butts, of company G, died in hospital. He was a fine man and one of the strongest physically in the regiment. His was the first death in the company. On the 5th companies A and I, with two companies of the 87th Pennsylvania, were sent, under command of Major Morris, to Bunker Hill. On the 6th company G, under Captain Karr, was sent out about nine miles on the Romney road, to break up, and, if possible, capture a band of rebel horse thieves infesting that section. The company captured two notorious thieves, besides a rebel militia captain. He told Captain Karr that the Union forces had been after him eighteen times, and he had always eluded them until now. Captain Karr replied, "Yes, but this is the first time company G of the 116th Ohio has been after you."

For two or three days prior to the 12th of June, the whole army was on the *qui vive*. We were in line of battle ready for orders, or on the move from one point to another, day and night. On the afternoon of the 12th the 116th and 123d Ohio, 12th West Virginia, a regiment of cavalry and a battery were ordered out on the road leading to Kernstown. Soon after passing our picket lines, we met the enemy's skirmishers, which we drove back beyond Kernstown. In this movement the 116th was on the right. We met a strong line a short distance beyond Kernstown. The 116th was quickly thrown around to a position from which it enfiladed the line, and pushing our advantage, pressed them under a hot fire, until they broke, when we charged and drove them from the field in a rout. We captured a large number of prisoners, meeting ourselves with only slight loss in wounded. It was soon seen, however, from a point of high ground which we reached in the pursuit, that we had met but a small portion of the force actually in our front. The roads for miles up the valley indicated the approach and near presence of a large force. Information to this effect being sent back to Milroy at Winchester, he came out and reconnoitered. We remained in line of battle until after dark, when we fell back to Winchester. We now expected hot work on the morrow. While we wondered at our remaining there in the presence of so large a force, it was only ours to obey such orders as were given us, ask no questions and cast no reflections. So all that night we lay on our arms behind the entrenchments. History shows that the main body of Lee's army then lay within a few miles of us, and that the movement he was then carrying out was commenced on the 3d of June. Lee says in his report of the Gettysburg campaign: "On the night that Ewell appeared at Winchester, the Federal troops, in front of A. P. Hill at Fredericksburg, recrossed the Rappahannock, and the next day disappeared behind the hills of Stafford. General Ewell left Culpepper Court House on the 10th. Crossing the Shenandoah near Front Royal, he detached General Rhodes's division to Berryville, with instructions, after dislodging the forces there, to cut off communications between Winchester and the Potomac. General Rhodes attacked the force stationed at Berryville on the 13th, drove it into Winchester, and on the 14th entered Martinsburg."

Fighting began early on the morning of the 13th all along the line in front of Winchester, and continued during the day until after dark. The 116th was engaged constantly. Towards evening, it was driven with other troops from the outer entrenchments to the second line. In the afternoon of the 13th, the two companies at Bunker Hill were attacked by a portion of Rhodes' division. The little command under its intrepid leader, Major Morris, made a gallant stand and held its ground against vastly superior numbers, until nearly half its number was killed, wounded or captured. Among the severely wounded and left on the field was Captain Alex Cochran, of company I, and among the prisoners were Lieutenant R. O. Knowles of the same company, and Lieutenant Manning of company A. The remainder sought to reach an old brick church, and the enemy made an effort to cut them off from it, but they fought their way into it bravely, and using loop-holes which they had previously made for their rifles, soon drove the enemy beyond their reach. Here they remained until about 2 o'clock the next morning, when, finding a gap in the enemy's lines surrounding them, they made their escape, and by a long and tiresome march reached Winchester about 7 A. M. of the 14th. The troops driven out of Berryville reached Winchester also the morning of the 14th. They were followed and attacked at the crossing of Opequan Creek. This force was in command of Col. McReynolds, of the 1st New York cavalry.

General Doubleday, in his account of the battles of Chancellorsville and Gettysburg, in "The Campaigns of the Civil War," says: "Soon after the affair at Opequan, Major Morris, with 200 men, was attacked at Bunker Hill, an outlying post of Winchester. He occupied a fortified church, but moved out to meet the enemy, under the impression it was only a small raiding party. When he found 2,000 men in line of battle, he retreated, fighting, to the church again. There, as the doors were barricaded, and the walls loop-holed, the rebels could make no impression, and were obliged to fall back to a respectful distance. In the night the Major managed to steal away, and soon rejoined the main body at Winchester." Among those conspicuous for bravery and coolness at the battle of Bunker Hill, was Lieutenant A. B. Frame, of company I, upon whom the command of the company devolved, after the wounding of the gallant Captain Cochran. He was highly praised by Major Morris, and ever afterwards retained the confidence and esteem of his men. Under a most galling fire, he covered the retreat to the church, keeping his men in hand as well and as coolly as on a parade ground, and was among the very last to enter the church. More than half of his company were made prisoners, by being cut off from the church, and from reaching him from the skirmish line. Mere boy, though he was, he that day showed himself possessed of great courage, and superior soldierly qualities.

On the morning of the 14th the battle began in earnest, bright and early. The 116th fought at different points in the entrenchments, re-enforcing, and being re-enforced, wherever and whenever the battle was most desperate, and our lines were most hotly pressed. It was wonderful, even to ourselves, how we held that overwhelming army at bay. Just before night, however, the rebels, in overwhelming numbers, attacked us on all sides, and drove Milroy's little army from its entrenchments into the forts, and the works in their vicinity, on Applepie Ridge. In the last charge made, Captain Frederick H. Arckenoe, as brave, noble and gallant an officer as the regiment ever had, was killed. For some time prior to the rebels' advance on Winchester, Captain Arckenoe's company, "C," had been detached from the regiment to support a battery, occupying a line of works about one mile northwest of Winchester, on Flint Ridge. On the morning of the 14th, the 110th Ohio, Col. Keiffer, was added to the force at this point. At the time of the general advance of the enemy, on the afternoon of the 14th, this position was assailed by a large division of rebels, and twenty-four pieces of artillery. Captain Arckenoe fought his men with remarkable coolness and bravery, and fell, shot through the head, as he was firing his pistol in the very faces of the rebels, as they swarmed over the works in his front. Besides the Captain, Sergeant Oswald Heck was killed, and a number of men wounded, which we will mention hereafter. Lieutenant Lupton and about one-third of the company were captured. With the balance, Lieutenant Mann reported to Colonel Horn, of the 6th Maryland regiment, in one of the large forts, where he was assigned to duty on the left, and with which regiment he remained during the day. The 116th thus had three companies substantially used up—A and I at Bunker Hill, and C at this spot, with a loss of one officer killed, one wounded, and four captured. The rebels now opened a terrific fire of artillery upon us, and charge after charge was made by their infantry, which they renewed again and again, until long after dark. Often times they charged in heavy masses right up to the ditch surrounding the forts, only to be hurled back again and again in a shower of balls, and grape, and cannister. But they were unable to gain a footing at any point, and about 10 o'clock at night, withdrew beyond our reach. During the whole of this deadly struggle, General

Milroy stood in a lookout, high up on the flag-staff in the center of the main fort, coolly directing every movement, and encouraging his troops. About 10 o'clock the firing ceased, and arrangements began for our escape during the night. The prisoners we had taken during the day, and everything else, confirmed to prove that we were in the presence of Lee's Potomac Army. As a result of a council of war, after spiking all the cannon, we moved out of the forts quietly, about 2 o'clock in the morning of the 15th. The enemy lay very close to us on our front and flanks, but, for some reason, did not close the gap in our rear, which they might have done as well as not. But we knew they were in strong force, four miles below us, on the road to Martinsburg, and that to escape we must cut our way through them. At the point expected, we met the enemy drawn up in line of battle, where the road to Harper's Ferry turns off from the Winchester and Martinsburg turnpike, thus covering both roads. The 116th occupied a position on the left of the line, and some distance left of the turnpike. We were in line of battle, and as soon as the rebel line was discovered in the darkness, we made a determined charge, and broke through, at the same time capturing several prisoners. On the extreme right, several regiments, including the 110th and 122d Ohio, did the same thing. The whole of our second line, under orders of General Milroy, now moved quickly to the right, without attacking the enemy, and with the 110th, 122d, and other regiments, made their way to Harper's Ferry. The 123d Ohio and 18th Connecticut were in the centre, and met the enemy in strong force, and though they made two or three desperate charges, were unable to cut their way through, and were obliged to surrender, portions of each regiment, however, escaping in the darkness. On the left, beside the 116th, were the 12th West Virginia regiment of infantry, a battalion of the 1st New York cavalry, and a portion of the

12th Pennsylvania cavalry, under Major Adams. From our present position, the enemy was in strong force between us and Harper's Ferry, and also between us and Martinsburg. Company C went through to Harper's Ferry with the 6th Maryland, with which it had operated the latter part of the day before. General Milroy, on being informed of our position, ordered us to move off to the left, and try to reach the Baltimore & Ohio Railroad at some point west of Martinsburg, at Hancock, if possible. We then quickly moved to the left, westward, through a piece of woods, skirmishing with an unseen foe as we went, until we reached an open field beyond, where we halted and reformed. We found we had the two regiments named, besides fragments of several others, a battalion of the gallant 1st New York cavalry, and about half of the 12th Pennsylvania cavalry. A course of retreat was soon settled upon. The infantry moved out in advance, the cavalry covering the rear. Colonel Washburn was in command of the infantry, and Major Adams of the cavalry. Knowing precisely the direction to take, and the point to make, we were enabled in the confusion following the engagement, aided by the mist of early dawn, to get well on our way before we were discovered by the rebels. When they did discover us, they followed with a considerable force, determined to cut us off from a gap in the mountains, which we were aiming, with all speed, to reach. The detachment of the 1st New York cavalry did splendid service now in protecting the rear of our column, and preventing the enemy's cavalry from obstructing our march. The 12th Pennsylvania cavalry went forward to possess and hold the gap that we were endeavoring to reach. They performed their work well. By dint of hard marching, and considerable maneuvering and skirmishing, we reached the gap, and entering the narrow mountain pass, we were safe against further successful pursuit by almost any amount of force.

That our route may be recognized by others, it may be stated, that we took the route on this march pursued by Collis' zouaves, in Banks' retreat of the year before, crossing the mountains at the same place, and marching thence through Bath and Berkley Springs, to Sir John's Run. Reaching the Springs, we rested a few hours, the men, meanwhile, taking occasion to bathe and wash up. As we were about starting again, we learned that a force of rebel cavalry was trying to get possession of certain mountain roads ahead of us a short distance, in order to cut us off from the ford of the Potomac at Sir John's Run. Hastily throwing a few companies forward, to command these roads, we moved out quickly, and crossed the ford without molestation, but we were scarcely across before the enemy appeared on the opposite bank of the river. We halted at Hancock, and placed a strong guard at the ford. From here we sent our regimental horses and mules to Cumberland, in charge of Captain Powell's company of cavalry. We rested at Hancock until 10 P. M., marched all night, and the next day, in the afternoon, reached Orleans Station, on the Baltimore & Ohio Railroad, where we procured rations, and met a part of General Conche's division, collected from guarding the railroad. Here, learning that the enemy was in Cumberland in large force, we received orders from General Milroy, at Harper's Ferry, to proceed to Bloody Run, Pennsylvania, at which point he would meet us, for co-operation with the Army of the Potomac. We reached Bloody Run on the 19th. Milroy was as good as his word and met us on the next day after our arrival. It was a sad meeting. The "Old Grey Eagle" looked gloomy and broken-hearted, but we drew up in line to receive him, and, as he approached, presented arms, and cheered him loud and long. Stacking arms, officers and men gathered about to shake his hand, and learn the fate of the rest of his little army. Many a heart was saddened at the news that our old associates of the 123d Ohio were prisoners. We must not pass from Bloody Run without mentioning the fact, that, upon hearing of our coming, the people of that place prepared a glorious feast for us. Long tables were placed in the middle of the principal street, which were loaded with warm and cold meats, potatoes, bread, pickles, splendid hot coffee, and great bowls and pails of milk. We were nearly starved, and no meal we ever ate was so heartily relished. The good people of Bloody Run will be remembered as long as there is a member of the 116th living. Finding we were in no condition for immediate service, General Milroy left us to await further orders. Remaining here until the 30th, we then moved to Bedford, where we remained until the 3d of July. On that day, we moved back to Bloody Run. Next day, starting at 4 A. M., we marched six miles, and stopped for breakfast. During the day we passed through the small village of Mount Zion, and camped that night six miles from McConnellsburg. It rained hard from 6 A. M. till 3 P. M. July 5th we passed through McConnellsburg to Loudon, which we reached about 2 P. M. Just after dark we received orders to move by a forced march to Mercersburg, to guard trains captured by our cavalry. We reached Mercersburg about 1 o'clock next morning. Here we met Col. McReynolds, through whose disobedience of orders, on the morning we left Winchester, a portion of our force was captured, and by whose conduct the successful escape of our whole command was thwarted. We were far from glad to see him, and every one expressed hopes that he would not be allowed to remain in command of the troops. Our hopes were gratified, for he was ordered from there in arrest, and his gallant regiment remained in command of Major Adams, and the rest of the troops breathed freer when they learned they were relieved from any further risk from his treachery. Early in the morning, we started back with the captured trains, and about 1,000 prisoners, to Loudon. Other portions of our cavalry had now joined us, and we watched closely for opportunities to strike Lee's trains, which were passing in front of his defeated army from Gettysburg. Opportunities soon came, when our cavalry, supported by our infantry, struck his trains and captured, in the aggregate, over 400 wagons, a large number of which were loaded with wounded. The wagons, horses, and mules were run off to a safe distance from the rebel line of retreat, while the wounded prisoners were distributed in Loudon and adjoining farm houses. We hung upon the flank of Lee's retreating column, until they passed through Hagerstown, making frequent dashes upon his trains, capturing large numbers of stragglers and foraging parties, thus protecting the country from being plundered by his half-famished hordes. From a letter written from Loudon, under date of July 6th, I take the following: "We are doing good work here, harassing the rebels on their flank, cutting up their trains, and picking up their stragglers. There probably never was so complete a rout as Lee's army sustained. A train six miles long passed by on the Cumberland pike yesterday. It was terribly cut up by our cavalry and Pleasanton's. It will probably all be captured, or destroyed. Providence is favoring us with such copious rains. The Potomac has risen several feet. A large pontoon bridge of the enemy was swept away yesterday, near Williamsport. This was the point aimed at by the rebel train mentioned. The demoralization of Lee's army is something awful to witness, and if General Mead would press it hard, fully half of it would certainly be destroyed, or captured. Why he does not press forward is a mystery to us, who can see its hopeless condition here, as it passes by." On the 13th we marched to Greencastle, and the next day started for Hagerstown, where we met the Army of the Potomac in pursuit of Lee, now too late to accomplish what it might so easily have accomplished a week before. And here, after a month of fighting, skirmishing and hard marching, (much of the marching being night and day and forced), we stacked arms, and partaking of the first square meal we had eaten since we left Bloody Run, laid down to rest and sleep. I can never forget the appearance of those sleepers. They looked more like dead than asleep. They were utterly exhausted. For the four days prior to reaching Hagerstown, we had scarcely rested an hour at a time, had hardly closed our eyes in sleep, night or day, and had had nothing to eat, save what we could pick up as we passed rapidly along the roads, or through the fields and woods.

The next day we moved to Sharpsburg, passing over the battle field of Antietam, and then, on the 4th of August, moved to Martinsburg, by the way of Harper's Ferry. On the way, we passed the house in which John Brown prepared for his raid on Harper's Ferry. From the 13th of June our regiment had lost 203 men in killed, wounded and prisoners. The following is a list of our killed, wounded and prisoners:

KILLED AT BUNKER HILL.

COMPANY A—Simpson Smith, John Welch and John A. Bowman —3.

WOUNDED AT BUNKER HILL.

COMPANY A—Abel Hall, Henry Harman, Daniel P. Hubbard, James Lafevere, James W. Oliver, Jacob Ring, Jacob Zimmerly, Hiram Shafer, Solomon Shafer, Cyrus Spriggs, Samuel Tidd, Edward J. Tillett, Aaron Weekly, George C. Williamson, Samuel Steel, and Corporal Newton Meek.—16.

COMPANY I—Captain Alexander Cochran, Caleb L. Baker, George W. Burch—3.

PRISONERS.

COMPANY A—Lieutenant John S. Manning, Sergeant Mann Smith, Sergeant James H. Worder, Sergeant Daniel C. Hurd, Corporal Benjamin F. Dye, Corporal Jesse Keyser, Corporal William Brock, Corporal Newton Meek, Privates, John D. Brown, Albert Gates, Joseph R. Brock, John C. Bean, William Bonam, Jesse Coulter, Abraham Coulter, William Danford, William S. Dyer, Frederick Edge, Samuel Gates, Jefferson

Gratton, Abel Hall, Henry Harman, Daniel P. Hubbard, Joseph Paith, Jacob Ring, Cyrus Spriggs, Samuel Todd, Edward J. Tillett, Samuel Zimmerly, James Lafevere, Samuel H. McHugh, George C. Williamson, Benjamin Ring.—33.

COMPANY I Captain Alexander Cochran, Sergeant George Bean, Privates, William Scott, John O. Athey, Jacob E. Athey, John C. Bailey, Caleb I. Baker, Elias Baker, Bradly P. Barrows, Jesse Burton, George W. Burch, James A. Campbell, Samuel H. Cramblett, John A. Dennis, Samuel P. Fleak, (escaped June 16th), Ephraim W. Frost, James H. Gilchrist, Samuel McCulloch, William McMillan, Leonard S. Mickle, Joseph Morrison, John J. Norris, Sheldon Parker, Hopson L. Sherman, George W. Tasker.—25.

KILLED AT WINCHESTER.

Captain Frederick H. Arekenoe, Co. C; Sergeant Oswald Beck, Co. C; Samuel Luthey, Co. E; Theodore Mathias, Co. E.—4.

WOUNDED.

John H. Lang, Co. C, in arm; Charles D. Watson, Co. C, right shoulder.

PRISONERS, JUNE 15TH.

Chaplain E. W. Brady, Q. M. Sergeant William J. Lee, Elmer Armstrong, Sutler, Mrs. Colonel Washburn.—5.

COMPANY B Lieutenant Hiram L. Sibley, Sergeant Edward P. Tiffany, Privates Henry Jennings, Leonard J. Cooley, Benjamin McLane, John Campbell, Daniel Rose, Aurelius P. Wiley.—8.

COMPANY C Lieutenant Levi Lupton, Corporal Oliver A. Hardesty, Privates Wilson A. Mann, David A. Mann, John Mahoney, Miller Booth, Jacob Butt, Eli Evans, Robert E. Chambers, George W. Gannon, William Montgomery, Reinhard Straub, Jacob Walton, John Latchaw, George W. Matchet, George W. Sampson, John Egger, William Bush, Clarkson W. Adams, William W. Wheaton, Citizen H. Henderson, Samuel Dobbins, Emon H. Beardmore, James A. Preshaw, Henry Fleishman, Lewis Stenber, Charles L. Eberle, Alexander Robbins. 28.

COMPANY D Corporal William A. Ferrell, Privates Isaac Price, Jackson Cox, Leander A. Eddy, Henry Mowder, Thomas Rawley, Sampson Patterson, Robert Armstrong, Hugh Thompson, James Simmons. 10.

COMPANY E Corporal John J. Walter, Privates Robert S. Hutchison, John Smith, John Morrow, Benjamin J. Ridgeway, Jacob Fisher, Jacob S. Hurd, Jacob Walter.—8.

COMPANY F Privates William H. Bell, Junius Early, Charles Latch, James Marsh, Christian Rhuer.—5.

COMPANY G — Lieutenant J. C. S. Cobb, Privates Ira Wood, James Davis, William. M. Davies, Jacob Fisher, George W. Hysell, Eben Hysell, Samuel L. Smith, Isaac C. Swett, William J. Chase.—11.

COMPANY H Privates Daniel Bock, Joseph Geralds, Mathew Grandon, E. J. Mathews, Lafayette Moore, Michael J. Moore, Hugh Shater, Joseph Dudley, James Smith, Stephen C. McCoy, Jacob Wannhas, Samuel B. Mathews.—12.

COMPANY I Lieutenant Richmond O. Knowles, Sergeant John B. Humphrey, Corporal Wisley Mickle, Corporal Joseph P. Parrish, Privates George Bates, Asher Buckley, Alvah D. Carlton, Luther B. Clayton, James W. Glazier, Morris Humphrey, William S. Parrott, Rufus B. Stanley, Enoch Taylor, Charles W. Waterman.—14.

COMPANY K - Corporal Carmi Allison, Drummer Boy Lucius Hull, Privates John Koons, Reason Risley, Hiram Pitcock, William Butter, Abraham Butterworth, John Hartley, S. Fenton, George McDonald, Harley Gilbert, Craven Ayers, Emory Newton, William Robinett, Asa Ladd, Corporal Jesse Allen. 16.

Making a total loss of 7 killed, 21 wounded, 175 prisoners— 203.

Lieutenant Sibley was recorder of a military commission at Winchester, of which Colonel Keifer was president, when the attack was made upon the place. He was at the time quite unwell. The morning of the attack he got out of bed the first time for a week, and went to the room of the commission to be excused by Colonel Keifer. While they were talking, the rebel artillery opened. Keifer buckled on his sword, saying: "I think there won't be any further use of this commission," and left to command his regiment. Sibley was alternately in camp and hospital, until the night we moved out, when he rode Surgeon Smith's horse, and was finally captured in Colonel Ely's surrender in the morning attack. Many of the prisoners at Winchester were sick in hospital, but it is impossible to distinguish, from any records or papers in my possession, who were captured in hospital, or who in action. Company C, after reaching Harper's Ferry, was assigned to the 110th Ohio, and served with it until August 1st. On the evacuation of Harper's Ferry, the stores were sent down the canal to Washington, the troops marching as an escort, company C accompanying the 110th on the march. Arriving at Washington, the news of Lee's defeat at Gettysburg was received, and it accompanied the 110th back to follow the retreating rebels. Reaching Frederick City, Maryland, it, with the 110th, was assigned to the 2d Brigade, 3d Division, 3d Army Corps, and marched in pursuit of Lee through Williamsport, London, Upperville and Manassass Gap, where they skirmished with the enemy. Arriving at Warrenton, Virginia, the company was ordered to rejoin its regiment, which it did at Sharpsburg, on the 4th of August, having marched, in the meantime, about 250 miles, besides traveling by rail several hundred miles more. A captain's commission awaited Lieutenant Mann. Lieutenant Lupton was promoted to First Lieutenant, and Orderly Sergeant William T. Biddenharn to Second Lieutenant, and were assigned to duty with their old company.

Now a few words in general about the campaign, ending with our arrival at this point. General Milroy had 6,900 men when attacked at Winchester, on the 12th of June, by Ewell's corps, in the advance of Lee's army. He was severely censured for the "loss of his army," as the critics of those times put it. He was placed in arrest, and, after waiting a time, and no charges being preferred, he asked and obtained a court of inquiry. There never was any division of opinion among Milroy's army, but that he did the best that bravery and skill could do, under the circumstances. From it he received never a word of censure. But the public, and some others, demanded a sacrifice for the confessed blunder of leaving General Milroy's little army in Winchester until it was surrounded by Lee. General Halleck was then the commander-in-chief of the army of the United States. General Hooker, who was then in command of the Army of the Potomac, until the 28th of June, testified before the Military Court of Inquiry, "that as early as the 28th of May, he communicated information to General Halleck of the enemy's movements towards the Shenandoah Valley, and that he suggested sending General Stahl's cavalry there." But the evidence showed, that not even an intimation of this was sent to General Milroy. General Halleck communicated the information to General Schenk, but the latter never sent it to Milroy. Hooker also testified "*that he believed the holding of Lee's army in check, during the 12th, 13th and 14th of June, saved Harrisburg, and perhaps other important cities of the Union, from destruction."* The testimony before the Court fully exonerated General Milroy, and, in this, Judge Advocate General Holt fully concurred. President Lincoln subscribed his approval to the endorsement of Judge Advocate Holt. In his approval the President said: "Some question can be made, whether some of General Halleck's dispatches to General Schenck should not have been construed to be orders to withdraw the force, and obeyed accordingly, but no such question can be made against Milroy; in fact, the last order he received was, to prepare to withdraw, *but not to actually withdraw till further orders,*" which further orders never reached him. Thus it will be seen that General Milroy and his army were made the victims of somebody's incompetency other than Milroy's. That the army should have been withdrawn several days before it was, there can be no doubt, and yet, had it not been for the check given Lee's army during the 12th, 13th and 14th of June, the battle fought at Gettysburg would have been fought three days' march further north, and, as General Hooker testified, "Harrisburg, and, perhaps, other cities of the Union, would have been destroyed." General Milroy acted promptly on the orders "to be prepared to withdraw, but not to actually withdraw till further orders."

In a correspondence to the Athens (O.) "Messenger," under date of October 22d, 1863, I summarized the situation, and as this was written at a time when the facts were all accessible, and were fresh in my mind, I here quote liberally from it:

"A great misapprehension has existed in the public mind, and this has been promoted by reckless correspondents to the press, in reference to the amount of public property abandoned and lost at Winchester. 'Millions of dollars' worth' are spoken of, with the appropriate number of exclamation points following the startling announcement. The testimony shows that but a small amount of stores were on hand. *In fact, the men were on half rations when the retreat was ordered.* Ammunition was nearly exhausted for all arms. Under General Milroy's orders, five days' supply of ammunition and subsistence was constantly kept on hand. The last requisition of General Milroy's ordnance officer had not been filled and the supply was scanty, even for ordinary fighting, let alone three or four days' continual firing, as was the case then. *Everything* had been sent out, in accordance with General Schenck's orders, that could be sent, up to Saturday night, a large train having been sent out late in the afternoon of that day, which was followed by rebel cavalry through Chambersburg, and nearly to Carlisle, Penna., but finally arrived safely at Harrisburg. But I am sure the holding of that place as long as we did, and I am convinced that the public now generally believe as I do, gave us information we could not have obtained otherwise, developed the plans and purposes of the enemy, checked and delayed his advance into Maryland and Pennsylvania for three days, and by these means enabled the Army of the Potomac to follow with timely resistance, and to prevent the loss of millions of property, which would otherwise have fallen into the enemy's hands. The inconsiderable loss suffered at Winchester was a trifle compared to these advantages.

"As to the conduct of the retreat, it is in evidence that the disasters which befell the command after it was forced to evacuate Winchester, are attributed in the main either to causes beyond the control of the commanding officer, or the failure, at a critical moment, of Colonel McReynolds to obey General Milroy's orders, the consequences of which disobedience were exceedingly serious. No skill or precaution could have enabled General Milroy to evade the enemy where he met him on Monday morning. He was posted in a position to command both roads, at the point where the one leading to Summit Point diverges from the Martinsburg road about four miles from Winchester. Here we fought him until a signal gun in the direction of Winchester was heard, and the enemy's cavalry and artillery were seen in hot pursuit of us, on the road leading from that place. General Milroy then ordered the march to be continued, and much the larger portion of his command escaped, though the number of the enemy around us was overwhelming. Indeed, the surprise of every one in the engagement was that so many got out of the excellent trap the enemy had set for us. Notwithstanding this attack was made at a most critical moment, and, as it appears in the evidence, important orders from General Milroy were disobeyed by Colonel McReynolds, thus in a great degree thwarting the General's plans, it was found by General Schenck that, of the 6,900 brave fellows who started from Winchester that morning, 6,000 were on duty on the 1st of September. So it will be seen that the terrible 'reports of losses' in circulation just after the retreat, are not sustained by the facts."

As a part of the history of that campaign, and as showing how ignorant the authorities at Washington and Gen. Hooker, of the Army of the Potomac, were of the movements of General Lee, we give below several dispatches taken from the "Report on the Conduct of the War Committee." We call especial attention to the two dispatches of President Lincoln, dated June 14th. The first dispatch in order is the one referred to by General Hooker in his testimony before the Court of Inquiry.

"*Letter to Hon. E. M. Stanton*" "May 28, 1863.

"It is impossible for me to give any information concerning the movements of the enemy at all satisfactory. * Maj. Gen. Stahl should be instructed to look into the Shenandoah Valley and see what is going on over there. * * *

"JOSEPH HOOKER, Major Gen'l Com'd'g."

"WARRENTON JUNCTION, June 12, 1863. 7 P. M.

"*Gen'l S. Williams, A. A. G.*

"A colored boy just captured on (Tuesday) the 9th, states that Ewell's corps passed through Culpepper on Monday last, on their way to the Valley, and that Longstreet's had gone also. A second negro, just across the river, confirms the statement. I send a reconnoisance to find out the truth.

"A. PLEASANTON, Brig. Gen'l."

The following is from Hooker's testimony before the committee:

"Had this information been communicated to Gen. Milroy, probably the disaster might have been averted, as that officer would have had sufficient notice of their approach to have withdrawn his command. In view of the information I had received from Gen. Pleasanton of the presence of an infantry corps at Culpepper, I had, on the 11th, ordered the Third corps to take post on the river, from Rappahannock Station to Beverly Ford; on the 12th for the First corps to proceed to Bealton, and the Eleventh to Catlett's Station."

IN CIPHER.

"WASHINGTON, June 14, 1863.

"*Major Gen'l Hooker:*

"Do you consider it possible that fifteen thousand of Ewell's men can now be at Winchester?

Sent 1:14 P. M. "A. LINCOLN."

Not less than 40,000 men of Lee's army were there then.

"WASHINGTON, D. C., June 14, '63.

"*Maj. Gen. Hooker:*

"So far as we can make out here, the enemy have Milroy surrounded at Winchester, and Tyler at Martinsburg. If they could hold out a few days, could you help them? If the head of Lee's army is at Martinsburg, and the tail of it on the plank road between Fredericksburg and Chancellorsville, the animal must be very slim somewhere; could you not break him?

Sent 5:50 P. M. "A. LINCOLN."

How characteristic is this dispatch of President Lincoln.

"HEADQUARTERS ARMY POTOMAC, }
"DUMFRIES, June 14, 1863.—11:15 P. M. }

"*His Excellency, the President:*

"Has anything further been heard from Winchester? Will the President allow me to inquire if it is his opinion that Winchester is surrounded by rebel forces? * * * I do not feel like making a move unless I be satisfied as to his whereabouts. To proceed to Winchester, and have him make his appearance elsewhere, would subject me to ridicule. With this feeling, unless otherwise directed, I feel it my duty to proceed to execute the movement indicated yesterday. I will not, however, issue my order of march until the last moment, in the hope that further information may be received.

"MAJ. GEN'L HOOKER."

"WAR DEPARTMENT,
"WASHINGTON CITY, June 14, 1863.

"*Maj. Gen'l Hooker, Dumfries:*

"No doubt is entertained here that Milroy is surrounded at Winchester, and so closely invested that no scout or other information has been had from him later than eleven o'clock Saturday night. Tyler was also surrounded to-day at Martinsburg. * *

Sent 12 midnight. "EDWIN M. STANTON."

IN CIPHER.

"HEADQUARTERS OF THE ARMY,
"WASHINGTON, D. C., June 15, 1863.

"*Major Gen'l Hooker, Army of the Potomac:*

"No information of enemy in direction of Winchester and Harper's Ferry as late as that from General Pleasanton. The forces at Martinsburg are arriving at Harper's Ferry.

Sent 12:30 P. M. "H. W. HALLECK, Gen'l-in-Chief."

"HEADQUARTERS OF THE ARMY,
"WASHINGTON, D. C., June 15, '63.

"*Maj. Gen'l Hooker, Army of the Potomac:*

"Garrison of Martinsburg has arrived at Harper's Ferry. Milroy did not obey orders given on the 11th to abandon Winchester, and probably has been or will be captured. Harper's Ferry ought to hold out some time. * *

Sent 2 P. M. "H. W. HALLECK, Gen'l-in-Chief."

"BALTIMORE, MD., June 15, '63.

"*Maj. Gen'l Halleck, Gen'l-in-Chief:*

"Nothing from Milroy since 11 P. M. Saturday. Is it not possible to have a cavalry movement in front as a diversion in his favor?"

"R. C. SCHENCK, Maj. Gen'l."

"BALTIMORE, June 15, 1863.

"*Maj. Gen'l H. W. Halleck:*

"Have not yet received report from Milroy. Gen. Kelley, here on his way, via Harrisburg, to New Creek, says before he left Harper's Ferry, about 1 this P. M., about 2,000 of Milroy's men had arrived. The rebels appeared before Winchester in four divisions, commanded by Ewell, Evans, Early and Rhodes, numbering about 40,000. Milroy fought till 2 this morning, when he determined to evacuate and cut his way out. Spiking his guns, and destroying stores, he marched some distance before his movements were discovered. He was pursued and attacked six miles out of Winchester, and was shelled for several miles. His loss is probably 2,000 men, but that may be exaggerated. Will send, as soon as received, further and more exact report.

"R. C. SCHENCK, Maj. Gen'l."

"BALTIMORE, MD., June 15, 1863.

"*Gen'l Halleck:*

"Gen. Milroy has cut his way through and arrived at Harper's Ferry. His losses reported considerable, with great damage to the enemy. He will telegraph soon. Tyler brought troops from Martinsburg to Maryland Heights, and is in command there. Have sent Kelley around to New Creek to concentrate troops on western portion of railroad. Ordered Averill to concentrate at Grafton, with a view to covering approaches to Wheeling, and to come eastward, perhaps also to New Creek, to hold as much as possible of the railroad eastward towards Martinsburg.

"R. C. SCHENCK, Maj. Gen'l."

Nothing could exceed the injustice of General Halleck's charge that General Milroy disobeyed "orders given on the 11th to abandon Winchester." He, better than any other man living, *knew* that *no* such orders were given Milroy. General Halleck's dispatches were all before the Court of Inquiry, and of them Mr. Lincoln said: "Some question can be made whether some of General Halleck's dispatches *to General Schenck* should not have been construed to be orders to withdraw. But," says Mr. Lincoln, "*no such question can be made against Milroy*," thus showing that Halleck issued no positive order, even to Schenck, to withdraw, and no order, that by any construction could be made to mean so, ever reached Milroy. Nothing ever occurred during the war for which there was so little excuse as allowing Lee's army to escape from the Army of the Potomac, and to throw itself upon Milroy's little force at Winchester, without warning to it, or without the knowledge of Halleck, the General-in-Chief of the Armies of the United States. Then for him to attempt to cast the blame from himself to Milroy, was a heartless and cruel injustice, exceeding anything to be found in the ignoble career of that incompetent and malevolent chief. I take pleasure in thus again putting on record this complete exoneration of General Milroy and his little army. Every word of it has been fully verified by subsequent history, and the brave old General, being shortly afterward restored to command, did gallant service in the Army of the Cumberland, and especially at Murfreesboro, during Hood's disastrous campaign against General Thomas, in December, 1864.

CHAPTER V.

THE FALL AND WINTER AT MARTINSBURG—ALONG THE B. & O. R. R.—PREPARING FOR THE CAMPAIGN OF 1864—REGIMENT ORDERED TO HARPER'S FERRY—BRIGADED ANEW—GENERAL SIGEL TAKES COMMAND—UP THE VALLEY—A SHAM BATTLE—BATTLE OF NEW MARKET.

When we reached Martinsburg, Colonel McReynolds appeared on the ground and assumed command, and among other things, directed the 116th to encamp on the grounds of the rebel Faulkner, and protect that gentleman's house, grounds and property. The 116th went into camp as directed, but Lieutenant Colonel Wildes refused to carry out that part of the order requiring him to "guard Faulkner's grounds, house and property." Colonel McReynolds immediately placed him in arrest. General Kelley, who was in command of the department at the time, with headquarters at Cumberland, on hearing of this, released Lieutenant Colonel Wildes from arrest, and, relieving Colonel McReynolds from command, ordered him to report to Washington for trial by court martial, under charges of disobedience of orders on the retreat from Winchester. The 116th was then removed from the Faulkner grounds to another camp, and that rebel's property allowed thereafter to share the same fortunes of war enjoyed by all other rebels. Colonel McReynolds never returned to his regiment, nor to any other command in the Shenandoah Valley, except the post, just as we were starting out, in April, 1864. What became of the charges against him we never learned. His regiment, the 1st New York cavalry, was one of the best cavalry regiments in the service, made so, not by him, but by the gallant Adams, Quinn, and as fine a lot of company officers as ever rode horses. He was as near being a "rebel sympathizer" as any man ever seen in the Federal Army. During his short stay in Martinsburg the rebel citizens of the place were in high feather, while the Union people were correspondingly depressed. In Colonel McReynolds's absence, Lieutenant Colonel Wildes commanded the post.

In passing from this subject it should be said of Mrs. Faulkner and her family, that they afterwards endeared themselves to the soldiers by their kindness to our sick, especially to Sergeant Patterson, and no special guards were necessary for their protection as soon as the soldiers learned how good and kind they were. Under date of August 5th, 1863, Patterson had Walker write in his diary, he being too sick with fever to write in it himself: "Through to Martinsburg. We are encamped in the lawn in front of Faulkner's house. He was Minister to France, and, for a while, tried to be a Union man, but is now in the rebel army. It is rumored in camp that we are to move to-morrow, for fear we will do some damage to his grounds. If we do go, I hope our boys will destroy everything he has. The lawn contains about eight acres and is ornamented with shade trees of different kinds. A drive extends from the front gate to the house. The plat in front is ornamented with small shrubbery and roses." And, under date of the 6th, Walker again writes for him: "Moved our camp to-day, but instead of going to the woods, only moved across the drive." Under date of the 10th: "Mrs. and Miss Faulkner came to see me to-day noon and brought me some dinner. They seemed very kind and offered to send me anything I wanted." Daily after that, up to the 24th, when he went home on furlough, his diary had some kind mention of them, such as "Mrs Faulkner still visits me daily, and furnishes me everything I need and more. Her ice does me much good. Whatever our feelings may be towards her rebel husband, we cannot help liking her and her daughter, who have been so kind to us. Our men all show their gratitude by their care of everything here." And so many other diaries and letters in my possession speak of Mrs. and Miss Faulkner.

While in command of the post, several orders came to Lieutenant Colonel Wildes from General Kelley to collect assessments from rebels in the vicinity of Shepherdstown, Kearneyville and Charlestown, to indemnify Union citizens for property destroyed by rebel guerrillas. The 116th was often on these "collecting tours," and became quite expert in the business. The following is a sample of numerous receipts in my possession:

"MARTINSBURG, VA., February 28, 1864.

"Received of Lt. Col. Thos. F. Wildes, 116th Reg't Ohio Volunteers, ($1,485.00) fourteen hundred and eighty-five dollars, which sum was collected from rebel citizens in the vicinity of Kearneyville, Va., and paid over to Jacob Williamson, to indemnify him for the loss of a barn burned by the rebels.

(SIGNED) "JACOB WILLIAMSON.

"ATTEST: HORACE KELLOGG, Major 123d O. V. I."

This course of procedure had a very salutary effect. It was well understood that the rebel citizens pointed out the houses of Union men to these rebel marauders, and when it became understood by them that they would have to pay for all property destroyed belonging to Union men, the destruction of such property decreased amazingly.

At the October, 1863, election, the regiment was excused from all ordinary duty. The election passed off quietly and orderly. The vote at the close of the polls stood:

FOR GOVERNOR.

John Brough, . . 398 votes.
C. L. Vallandigham, . . 50 votes.

For some time a great deal of curiosity existed and some indignation was felt over the fifty votes for Vallandigham. But the officers put a stop to political discussions and the excited feeling soon subsided. Before the election, however, not the least restraint was exercised against anyone voting as he pleased.

Martinsburg was headquarters of the regiment until April 29, 1864, though during that time several companies were scattered at various points along the B. & O. Railroad, from Sleepy Creek to Kearneyville. While lying here, Lieutenant Wm. Spriggs of company H was cashiered and dismissed from the service "for using disloyal and treasonable language against the Government of the United States, disrespectful language of the President, and other conduct unbecoming an officer and a gentleman." During September and October there were frequent alarms, occasioned by rumors that Lee was returning again down the Valley. About the 20th of October Lee's left wing was reported at Leesburg, that he was preparing to cross the Potomac, in which event a portion, at least, of his army would pass through Martinsburg. Accordingly, all surplus supplies, Quartermaster's and Commissary stores, except five days' rations, were sent to Harper's Ferry. On the next day sharp cannonading was heard in the direction of Charlestown, and re-enforcements of cavalry, artillery and infantry were dispatched from Martinsburg, but before they arrived, a part of the 9th Maryland regiment stationed there had been captured by Imboden. Imboden was defeated and followed some distance. Some of the 9th Maryland were recaptured, a section of artillery and many prisoners taken. Our orders, on the troops leaving for Charlestown, were to pack up and load and be ready to fight or retreat, as emergency required, and we remained in this condition until their return, when quiet again reigned. About the same time, perhaps a day or two earlier, company E, of the

116th, stationed at North Mountain, together with two companies of cavalry, one of the 1st New York, and one of the 12th Pennsylvania, captured forty of Gilmore's guerrillas and fifty horses. They were concealed in a ravine and were neatly surrounded and surprised, neither side firing a gun. About the same time a passenger train was captured between Kearneyville and Harper's Ferry and the passengers robbed of everything. An iron clad car upon which was placed a piece of artillery, and which was loopholed for infantry, was used in picketing the track from Kearneyville to Sleepy Creek. A great commotion was created one night by some one beating the "long roll" in camp. All the troops were under arms in a moment and awaited developments. Heavy parties of troops were sent out to occupy the roads and certain advantageous points. After waiting some time for the appearance of the enemy, it was ascertained that the alarm had been made by the Colonel of the 12th Pennsylvania cavalry, becoming a little hilarious, beating the "long roll" to show what he could do as a drummer. He was placed in arrest as soon as the discovery was made, and charges preferred against him. They were afterwards withdrawn on his promise to "reform."

The 10th Maryland eastern shore regiment came to Martinsburg one very cold night without their tents or blankets, and the 116th took the whole regiment into their quarters. The Colonel next morning made a neat speech to us, in which he thanked us heartily for our hospitality. Some of our men said it was the prettiest speech they ever heard. When the 18th Connecticut joined us, it camped beside our regiment. The men were short of rations, and they besieged our Sutler for "cookies" and everything else he had to eat. Mr. Armstrong, the Sutler, couldn't make out what they meant by "cookies," and his confusion for a time was very amusing. The 18th Connecticut was always known among us after that as the "cookie regiment."

A notorious rebel spy by the name of Belle Boyd made herself quite conspicuous several times at Martinsburg. She was several times discovered, arrested and sent under guard to Baltimore or Washington. She would there be released under promise to behave herself and keep out of the Union lines. On one occasion she returned on the same train with the guard who had escorted her to Baltimore, dressed as a Union soldier, and representing herself as returning to a Maryland regiment from furlough. She was detected, not by her recent guard, but by some Union citizen, as she alighted from the train at Martinsburg. Upon being searched, she was found to have a great number of letters to rebels and to Confederate soldiers up the Valley, and a Confederate uniform under her outward uniform of blue. She was irrepressible, and a perplexing individual to manage. Doubtless she was often among us in disguise when we knew nothing about it. Once, at least, when captured, she pretended to be insane, and insanity was never better feigned than by her. Finally, she was "let alone," and as soon as importance ceased to be given to her movements, she settled down at her home in Martinsburg and behaved as well as any one. But she was always the same arrant little rebel, and ready at all times for an argument against the Government, and in favor of secession.

The regiment lay at Martinsburg until November 19th, when it was all detailed at different points along the B. & O. Railroad. Some companies had been at points on the road from soon after our arrival in Martinsburg, in the early part of August. Now it all went, and the field and staff officers soon found themselves "more ornamental than useful." Major Morris took charge of the stations west of North Mountain, making his headquarters there. Lieutenant Colonel Wildes was detailed as President of a Court

Martial, and Colonel Washburn was generally in command of some brigade of troops, and looking after the welfare of the regiment as well as he could in its scattered condition. Thus the time was spent until the breaking of winter. As attesting the vigilance and faithfulness of the different companies in the discharge of this unpleasant and responsible service, it can be stated that no raid was successfully made upon, or damage done, to the road during the time they were guarding it. The service was a very severe one, the different companies being almost constantly engaged in scouting and pursuing small parties of rebels. They cleared the whole country for miles of rebel bushwhackers, and captured a large number of prisoners, aggregating more than their own number.

On the 25th of November, Sergeant William Brister, of F, was accidentally shot and killed at Duffield Station by private Stephen Hogue of the same company. It seems that Sergeant Silas King had just returned to camp from a scout on which he had found a number of arms. Among them was an old flintlock musket. Seeing Hogue approaching, Sergeant Brister playfully picked it up and pointed it toward him. Hogue, in the same playful mood, picked up a musket, which he thought unloaded, and pointed it toward the Sergeant and pulled the trigger. It proved to be loaded, and Sergeant Brister was shot through the breast and died in a few minutes. It was a dreadfully unfortunate occurrence and nearly crazed Hogue, as the two men were close neighbors at home, and very warm friends. Hogue soon afterwards wrote to Brister's friends, saying that he "had killed the best friend he had on earth." Brister's remains were sent home.

On the 1st of March, 1864, the regiment was gotten together at Martinsburg, being relieved by the 123d Ohio. Troops were now congregating in considerable force under General Sigel, who had been assigned to the command of the department. Under date of the 3d of March, 1864, General Milroy wrote me from Washington, in which he expressed a hope that he might be assigned to command in the Valley. No one could have been assigned to our command that would have given more general satisfaction to the troops. But General Milroy was under the ban of the ogre General Halleck, and could not expect a command as long as Halleck controlled army affairs. Milroy rejoiced that General Grant had just been appointed Lieutenant General, and that now he had hopes of a command, and it might be remarked that the armies, everywhere, had hopes that newspaper generals, and political considerations in the appointment of army commanders, and public clamor of "on to Richmond," and so forth, had had their day in the conduct of the war, and that henceforth it was to be carried on according to strict military rules and principles. General Grant, in assuming command of the armies of the United States, had, in substance, said to the President and the people of the country what a Roman Consul said to the Roman Senate and people, on his leaving for the seat of war in Macedonia: "If there be any one who conceives himself capable of assisting me with his counsels in the war you have charged me with, let him not refuse to do the Republic that service, but let him go with me into Macedonia. But, if he will not take so much trouble, and prefers the tranquility of the city to the dangers and fatigues of the field, let him not take upon him to hold the helm and continue idle in the port. The city of itself supplies sufficient matter of discourse on other subjects, but as for these, let him be silent on them, and know that we shall pay no regard to any counsels, but such as shall be given us in the camp itself." And General Grant acted upon this policy to the end of the war.

On the 9th of March the 34th Massachusetts arrived at Martinsburg, and Colonel Wells assumed command of the post. In due time we all paid him our respects, generally leaving his presence with a very good opinion of him. His regiment was a very fine one. Having had a great deal of garrison duty about Washington, it was remarkably well drilled and under good discipline. It was so much more neatly dressed and so completely equipped, compared to our own regiment, that it was a sort of curiosity to our "rough Ohio fellers," as its officers and men often spoke of us. But on the third of April, it went back to Harper's Ferry. On the 12th of April, the 116th and 123d followed to Harper's Ferry and encamped on Bolivar Heights. On the 15th we received orders from "Headquarters First Infantry Division," General Sullivan commanding, forming a brigade composed of the 34th Massachusetts, 116th Ohio, 123d Ohio, and the 3d Maryland (Snows) Battery, Colonel Wells, of the 34th Massachusetts, commanding the brigade. Of this brigade, General Lincoln, in his admirable history of the 34th Massachusetts, is moved to remark as follows: "Heaven help us! except the 34th, this infantry is neither drilled nor disciplined; this, however, from no fault of theirs. The bulk of the rank and file of these commands was captured at Milroy's defeat last summer. The men were paroled soon after and have been scattered in small squads along the B. & O. Railroad on picket guard. The officers, however, were retained as prisoners, and many are, in fact, still in rebel hands. It looks as if we were to suffer from the connection." I have looked carefully through General Lincoln's interesting book for verification of the fear that they were to "suffer from the connection." On the contrary, I am led, from his frequent compliments to the 116th, to conclude that his fears were never realized. The fact is, the 34th then very generally regarded itself badly mismated with us. We were looked upon as a lot of barbarians by these well drilled, well disciplined, highly cultured eastern soldiers. They had performed garrison and patrol duty at

Washington, from their enlistment up to July, 1863, since which time they had, with little exception, enjoyed magnificent quarters at Harper's Ferry. At Washington the regiment was the admiration of all beholders, if we are to credit General Lincoln, and we see no reason why we should not. Many of its officers, while brave, good soldiers, were also martinets. But before we separated in 1865 at Richmond, we had learned to respect these martinets as plumed and chivalric knights. It had, withal, a well trained brass band, and was in every way well prepared for serenades, parades and reviews, so much in vogue in Washington early in the war. While we, poor fellows, with constant marching, scouting, picketing, to say nothing of now and then a little fighting, would make a sad display in either of these three ornamental positions. In short, there were no ornaments about us or among us, if we except, perhaps, a few good looking officers, notably the Major, Adjutant, Captain Karr, Lieutenant Frame and one or two others. But before we separated at Richmond in 1865, the 34th Massachusetts regiment felt as much pride in the history the First Brigade had made for itself, as was felt by any regiment in it. It was not then ashamed of the "connection" formed fourteen months before, nor was there an officer or man in it who felt that he had "suffered by the connection."

On the 17th of April we started back to Martinsburg, reaching there the evening of the 18th. The next day Colonel Wells was relieved of the command of the brigade and assigned to the command of the post, and Colonel Washburn was placed in command of the brigade. The congregating of troops at Martinsburg had excited the curiosity of the enemy, and there were a great many small parties scattered about the country annoying us constantly. As we arrived at Martinsburg, we found General Averill just leaving for West Virginia with his cavalry. General

Averil, on leaving, placed Colonel McReynolds, who had made his appearance here again, in command of the post. But Colonel Wells was in *possession* of post headquarters, and so for several days we were receiving orders from both these officers which were often, and in fact generally, in conflict. During this time no one knew whether he "was a-foot or a-horseback. Colonel Wells's orders were, however, very generally obeyed, owing to the utter dislike felt by everybody for McReynolds. It was soon adjusted, however, by Colonel Wells abandoning the contest and going back to his regiment. We were now brigaded anew. Our brigade was composed of the 28th, 116th, 123d Ohio and 18th Connecticut, with Colonel Moore, of the 28th, in command. That is, he would be when he arrived, which he did not do till we reached Winchester, during which time Colonel Washburn commanded. The 34th left us for a short time for duty in another brigade.

On the 20th General Sigel issued an order allowing thirteen teams to a regiment. He told Colonel Washburn, one day, "Turn over your tents and be very ready to march." On the 26th another order came allowing one team for headquarters, and one for every 300 men, each man to carry in his knapsack one extra shirt, one pair of socks, one pair of shoes, and soap and towels. On the 27th we had a "garrison review," and such a time as we had finding our places in the line was never seen before. The brigades had never been in line together before, and all questions of rank had to be settled on the parade ground before any one knew or would take place in the line. After all preliminaries were settled, the review went off very well. Our regiment numbered nearly 800 men and looked like a brigade itself. Colonel Thoburn was in command of the second brigade, ours being known as the first. On the 29th of April we moved out of Martinsburg up the Valley, stopping the first night at Bunker Hill. Generals

Sigel, Stahel and Sullivan were with us. Sigel in command of the army, Stahel of the cavalry, Sullivan of the infantry, the latter being composed of eight regiments. Our cavalry force was not very large, only about 1,500, but we had a good supply of artillery, four batteries. In speaking of the infantry, General Lincoln says: "The 54th Pennsylvania is fair, the 12th West Virginia pretty good; *the rest are barely passable.*" It will be seen that the 34th was deemed *beyond* comparison with any other regiment in the command, and so was not mentioned, while the 116th and the rest were "barely passable." We remained at Bunker Hill until May 1st, when we marched to Winchester, camping about two miles the other side of the place. Much display of the stars and stripes was visible as we passed through, more than we had ever observed before. Little Willie McFielly, the Lieutenant Colonel's boy, was carrying a "marker" at the head of the regiment as it marched through Winchester, when some woman, who was very glad to see us, called out: "That's right, little boy, raise it up high, clear up, and let everybody see it." Colonel Washburn, still in command of the brigade, detailed Quartermaster Williams as Brigade Quartermaster, and Lieutenant W. L. Mosely was detailed to act as Regimental Quartermaster, but only remained one day, when he was returned to his company. Quartermaster Williams had his horse stolen, and looked through all the cavalry for it, finally finding it in the camp of the 1st New York. On the day after our arrival at Winchester our men wandered over the battle grounds of June, 1863, and finding some of our dead but poorly buried by the rebels, selected a nice spot and buried them decently. The cavalry burned a house from which one of their men was shot a few days before our arrival.

On the 4th, the men were ordered to pack all spare clothing in their knapsacks for transportation to Martinsburg, and officers were bereft of almost everything. We were down to our "fighting weight." An order was received for brigade drill on the morrow, and officers were studying Casey diligently. The morrow came, and with it the brigade drill so much looked for and so much dreaded. A whole field full of Generals, Colonels and staff officers were present to witness the performance. General Sigel and Colonel Moore had a lot of Dutchmen on their staffs who could hardly talk English, and who knew nothing about communicating orders on the drill ground. Few of the Colonels knew anything at all about brigade drill, and some of them very little even about battalion drill. One of the first things that was done was to deploy and start out the 34th Massachusetts as skirmishers, and then General Sigel undertook to maneuver the infantry, cavalry and artillery as on a field of battle in their rear. It was the funniest farce ever witnessed anywhere, and can never be forgotten as long as any man who took part in it lives. Our own regiment, for instance, was ordered through something like this: The right wing was ordered to advance, firing, to a fence pointed out, and there to lie down and keep on firing. Then, when it was thought our right wing was out about long enough to be pretty badly cut up, the left was ordered to charge, without instructions how far to go in its wild career, or what to do next. Away we went, "hell bent," with a yell. As soon as we reached the left of the other wing it jumped up and charged, too, the whole regiment yelling like fiends. The "recall" was sounded by General Sigel's bugler, but of course we didn't hear it, and away we went up the Valley, clear out to the picket line. Now came on the gallop three or four leather breeches Dutch staff officers after us, who finally overtook us and ordered a halt. But the 34th Massachusetts skirmishers! What had become of them? Here we had gone to the picket line and had not come up with them. It seemed they had been forgotten in the general muss, and had been allowed to advance some distance beyond the picket line before they were thought of and recalled. It was after dark before the 34th got back to camp that night. "Thus endeth the first lesson," solemnly remarked our Chaplain when we got into camp. "Yes, by God!" responded Colonel Washburn, "and a h—l of a lesson it was, too." At which the Chaplain retired to his "pup tent" in disgust. General Lincoln says the whole thing was a good deal like a "town meeting," no doubt having in mind the meetings held by eastern people, which are noted for nothing so much as for their want of order and decorum. This farce was repeated, with not quite so much blundering, the next day, and then the regiments were given over to their commanders for battalion drill.

Talk about your "corn stalk militia," and "general trainings" of ye olden times! There was never anything seen half so ridiculous, and it bred in everyone the most supreme contempt for General Sigel and his crowd of foreign adventurers. Not an officer or a man retained a spark of respect for, or confidence in, him or any of the leather breeches retinue of staff officers with which he had surrounded himself. So that for all the good that army would or could do under him, it might as well, and better, have returned at once to Martinsburg. Companies F and K were detailed to guard signal posts about seven miles from Winchester, on the 6th, and, when the command moved, were not called in, and did not rejoin the regiment until the second day after we reached Cedar Creek. It was more good luck than good generalship that they were not all captured. Lieutenant Milton A. Ellis was detached to the signal corps, Lieutenant John F. Welch to the pioneer corps, and Lieutenant Ransom Griffin to the ambulance corps. Each of these officers continued so detached during the remainder of their term of service, and each distinguished himself in his respective corps and frequently received high praise and honorable mention in orders, for his efficiency and good conduct.

On the 9th we moved to Strasburg, lying here one day. On the 11th we moved to Woodstock, where we camped in a clover field a mile from water. On our teams coming up, Sergeant Walker took out of a mess pan a little black object, calling out, "Here's the Lieutenant Colonel's baggage." It proved to be a white kitten, which, coming into our camp at Strasburg, the Lieutenant Colonel had fed, and which, on our moving from there, Walker had put into one of the wagons among the sooty mess pans, and now here was kitty, as black as night itself. After being fed and washed white again, it took kitty most of the night to dry herself and be ready for the next day's experience. A citizen came in and told Colonel Washburn that his men were killing his sheep. "Have you taken the oath?" asked the Colonel. "No, but I'm willin' to," was the reply. Upon taking it, a guard was furnished him, but when he got home *no sheep could be found!* Of course the boys all expressed "regrets." Another order, allowing only one Sutler to a brigade, was issued, the rest being ordered to the rear. A neat rebel trick was very near being successful here. A note had been written and handed to the Division Wagon Master, purporting to come from the Chief Quartermaster, and to be in his hand writing, ordering a large train to the rear, with which were also to go the returned Sutlers' wagons. The train had started and was well out on the road *without a guard*, when the Quartermaster discovered what had been done. He dashed off as fast as his horse could carry him to bring it back, which he did in safety. It was afterwards ascertained that Moseby and McNeil were in waiting for the train a few miles down the road. We lay at Woodstock until the 14th, when we moved on to Mount Jackson. That evening some of our troops met Breckenridge with a force of about 4,000 men near New Market, and drove in his pickets, and defeated a small force sent out to reconnoiter our position. The next day the 116th was left with the trains, the first and last time during the war, until about the middle of the afternoon, when some cavalry relieved us, and we were moved to the front on the double quick. Sharp fighting had been going on at the front since noon, which occurred in the midst of heavy thunder storms. The 123d suffered very severely during the afternoon, as did, also, the 34th Massachusetts. We arrived on the field just in time to witness the falling back of our little army. We had moved to the front in a violent rain storm on the double quick, or run, for a distance of about four miles, and to cover the retreat. The 28th and 116th Ohio regiments, with quite a large body of cavalry, were kept in the rear, guarding the immense trains, which were allowed to stand, in the main, stretched out on the road, until the remainder of the army was entirely defeated. Then our regiment was ordered up at the rate of speed spoken of, arriving on the field in an exhausted condition, and too late to do anything, except to cover the retreat of the broken up and defeated regiments. The army fell back across the river to Mount Jackson. The enemy followed us but a short distance, probably because of General Sigel's fame for conducting "masterly retreats." When across the river, some military engineer undertook to blow up the bridge, by exploding kegs of powder on the top of it. After the powder was all exploded, the 116th tore down the bridge in the regular way, with axes and crowbars. The loss of our little army was quite heavy. That of the 116th consisted of a few wounded. Very few of us wanted to fight any more "mit Sigel." His army was beaten in detail. A small force was first sent into the fight, which was allowed to be first beaten, when another small force would be sent in, to be in turn beaten. Had he gotten his army well in hand at first, and given battle with it, he might have been victorious, though the enemy under Breckenridge outnumbered us.

General Sigel himself reported afterwards that, besides his cavalry and artillery, he had only six regiments on the field, while the enemy attacked him with 7,000 men. And he gave as an excuse for this, the extreme length of his trains and the attenuation of his line of march, which prevented him from confronting the enemy with his whole force. It was the height of folly to keep so large a portion of his force with his trains. If properly parked, instead of being allowed to stand stretched out for miles on the road, a very small force would have been sufficient to protect it. When we were ordered to the front, the trains occupied the road, and we were obliged to take to the fields to pass them. As it was, when defeated, his trains were in such bad shape that a portion had to be destroyed to prevent its falling into the hands of the enemy. The defeat was a very bad one. He lost 700 men, six pieces of artillery, about 1,000 small arms, and he abandoned his hospitals to the enemy. The retreat, for some miles, was in great disorder, made so by some bridges breaking down, and others being washed away by the high water, for, be it remembered, we had a real Virginia freshet from the furious rains of the day. We retreated to Cedar Creek, but the enemy did not pursue in force. Reaching Cedar Creek, on the 17th, we at once began reorganization and refitting.

CHAPTER VI.

HUNTER RELIEVES SIGEL — HUNTER'S ORDER ON ASSUMING COMMAND — SHORT OF RATIONS FOR THE FIRST TIME — BATTLE OF PIEDMONT — BRAVERY OF THE REGIMENT — LIST OF CASUALTIES — ONE OR TWO AMUSING INCIDENTS, AND SOME NOT SO AMUSING, CONNECTED WITH THE BATTLE — ON TO STAUNTON.

General Hunter assumed command on the 21st. He found the army in bad shape. A thousand men were without arms and two thousand were without shoes. He at once began the work of fitting out the army and getting it in shape for active service: All stores of every kind were ordered turned over, and a great many other things ordered done, as will be seen from the following order:

HEADQUARTERS DEPT. WEST VIRGINIA,
In the Field, Near Cedar Creek,
May 22d, 1864.

(*General Order No. 29.*)

It is of the utmost importance that this army be placed in a situation for immediate efficiency. We are contending against an enemy who is in earnest, and if we expect success we must be in earnest. We must be willing to suffer for a short time, that a glorious result may crown our efforts. The country is expecting every man to do his duty, and this done, an ever kind Providence will certainly grant us a complete success.

I. Every tent will be immediately turned in for transportation to Martinsburg, and all baggage not expressly allowed by this order will be at once sent to the rear. There will be but *one* wagon allowed to each Regiment; this will only be used to transport spare ammunition, camp kettles, tools and mess pans. Every wagon will have *eight* picked horses or mules, *two* drivers and *two* saddles. One wagon and one ambulance will be allowed to Department Headquarters, and the same to Division and Brigade Headquarters. The other ambulances will be under the immediate order of the Medical Director.

II. For the expedition on hand, the clothes each soldier has on his back, with one pair of extra shoes and socks, are amply sufficient. Everything else in the shape of clothing will be packed to-day and sent to the rear. Each knapsack will contain *one hundred rounds of ammunition*, carefully packed; *four pounds* of hard bread to last *eight days*; *ten rations* of coffee, sugar and salt; one pair of shoes and socks, and nothing else.

III. Brigade and all other commanders will be held strictly responsible that their commands are supplied from the country. Cattle, sheep, hogs, and if necessary horses and mules must be taken and slaughtered. These supplies will be seized under the direction of officers duly authorized, and upon a system which will be hereafter regulated. No straggling or pillaging will be allowed. Brigade and other commanders will be held responsible that there is no waste, and that there is a proper and orderly division amongst their men of the supplies taken for our use.

IV. Commanders will attend personally to the prompt execution of this order, so that we may move to-morrow morning. They will see that in passing through a country in this way, depending upon it for forage and supplies, great additional vigilance is required on the part of every officer in the command of men for the enforcement of discipline.

IV. The commanding General expects from every officer and soldier of the army in the field an earnest and unhesitating support, and relies with confidence upon an ever kind Providence for the result. The Lieutenant General commanding the Armies of the United States, who is now victoriously pressing back the enemy upon their last stronghold, expects much from the army of the Shenandoah, and he must not be disappointed.

VI. In conclusion, the Major General commanding, while holding every officer to the strictest responsibility of his position, and prepared to enforce discipline with severity when necessary, will never cease to urge the prompt promotion of all officers, non-commissioned officers and enlisted men who earn recognition by their gallantry and good conduct.

By order of MAJOR GENERAL HUNTER.

CHAS. G. HALPINE, Assistant Adjutant General.

This order looked like "business." General Sigel had ordered all knapsacks sent to Martinsburg before starting from Winchester, and now Captain Keyes was sent to bring them up, for, among other things, we were to carry 100 rounds of ammunition in our knapsacks. What had not been taken by other regiments before he got to Martinsburg were lost or cut open and destroyed, so we had to draw a new supply. Quartermaster Sergeant Walker, however, hunted up about 200 in other regiments. The Adjutant reporting fifty pairs of shoes wanted, the Quartermaster reported 175 pairs wanted, and so it proved before we were shod. One day while on the march afterwards, some officer riding by asked, "What troops are these?" Jim Hall, of Company A, quickly replied, "Troops! This is Hunter's ammunition train." He asked no more questions, but rode off laughing. The 160th Ohio was now added to our brigade.

We started up the Valley on the 26th of May. The 160th Ohio protested so much against going to the front that it was sent back, on the 30th, from Rude's Hill. On the 1st of June flour was issued to us for the first time, much to our disgust. We reached Harrisonburg on the 3d of June and left on the following day, moving by way of Port Republic. The army crossed the river at Port Republic and camped for the night. Our rear was considerably annoyed by guerrillas, during the last two or three days, and our communications partially destroyed. From a letter written from Staunton, June 8th, by Sergeant Walker, I quote a very clear, detailed account of our movements up to this point:

"We left Cedar Creek May 26th, after having sent back all our tents and everything else that could not be carried on our backs. Passing through Strasburg, General Hunter ordered the men to burn several buildings from which several of our men had been bushwhacked. The folks were allowed to take nothing from the houses. Hunter says 'this bushwhacking has got to be stopped,' and you may depend upon it he will stop it. Many of our men were obliged to march without shoes, and it was really a pitiful sight to see them marching along, leaving marks of blood on the ground. We were put on half rations of bread from the very start, and for several days had been without any. May 29, marched from Woodstock to Mt. Jackson, where we encamped on the same ground on which we fought two weeks ago. Passing through Edinburg we found a great quantity of salt, which we took. Just before leaving the town, one of the men went into a garden to get some onions, and a woman came out and drove him out with rocks. Good! May 31st, went out with Captain Kellogg, of the 123d Ohio, foraging, brought in a great quantity of flour, wheat and salt. This salt is some that has been sent to the counties by the Government, to be sold to the citizens at ten cents per pound, or about $30 a barrel. An order came to-day from General Hunter forbidding us to burn anything but rails; strange order. June 3d, marched from Mt. Jackson to Harrisonburg. The latter is the county seat of Rockingham County, and is a very pretty place. The court house is a very pretty, (rather old) brick building, situated about the center of the town, with a fine yard around it. Just outside the yard is a large spring about twelve feet in diameter, round and walled up several feet, with marble steps going down to the water. The whole is covered with a circular roof supported on pillars, which makes it look very nice. The streets immediately around the court house are of respectable width, but as a general rule they are very narrow. In fact, I have noticed that, in all the Virginia towns we have passed through, the streets are narrow. There are a great many fine residences in and near the town. Our foraging parties searched the houses and stores for flour, meat, etc., taking all they found. They also found some muslin valued by the rebs at $2,000, a bale of batting, valued at $245. We also destroyed three printing offices. June 4th, we expected to go directly up the Valley towards Staunton, but turned off the pike to the left soon after leaving the town, and passed the old Cross Key's battle ground, and so on to Port Republic. It was here Port R. that Fremont came so near capturing Jackson two years ago. You may remember he sent Colonel Carlan to destroy a bridge at this place, but Colonel C. concluded to try to *hold* the bridge, and Jackson drove him from it, and made his escape, and whipped Carlan. As soon as he crossed his army Jackson burned the bridge and so prevented Fremont from following him."

A large portion of our men were now out of rations, except coffee, sugar and salt. After crossing the river at Port Republic, and passing through the village, we went into camp in a piece of woods on the right of the road, and after making coffee, lay down for the night. We were called out early the following morning, June 5th, and took the road without having made even a cup of coffee for breakfast, but with a promise that we should get something to eat very soon. We had marched but a short distance in the direction of Staunton, when we met considerable numbers of the enemy. Before advancing very far we formed line of battle, and advanced behind skirmishers, driving the enemy before us, until we reached Piedmont, where we found the enemy in force, well protected behind rail and log breastworks. The 116th was on the extreme left in this advance, and had several opportunities, of which it availed itself, of enfilading the rebels as they fell back. We reached their lines about 10 A. M. Without waiting for Thoburn, who was, as we understood, coming upon their flank. Moore's and Wynkoop's brigades charged and drove the enemy behind his works. Our men advanced on a charge nearly up to the works, but were there repulsed with severe loss. Re-forming our lines, in a few minutes we made a second charge, meeting with a second repulse and with even greater loss than before. Falling back to a slight cover of a rise of ground, we halted and lay down to await Thoburn's coming, as we ought to have done in the first place. We were still within short rifle range of the enemy's works, and a sharp fire of musketry and artillery was kept up on both sides constantly for over two hours. Colonel Washburn's horse was shot under him in the first charge. A battery of 12-pound pieces came on to the infantry line on the right, shortly after we fell back from the second charge, which did terrible execution, with solid shot thrown into the enemy's rail breastworks. The enemy had once or twice tried to turn our right. The demoralization which every shot created in their ranks could be plainly seen, crowds of the enemy fleeing from the spot where a shot struck the rails, when our infantry would open fire upon them the moment they showed themselves, the guns of the battery also saluting them at the same time with grape and cannister. About 3 p. m. Colonel Thoburn appeared on their right flank, having moved across a ravine by a long and tedious detour. As soon as he was seen charging on their flank, Moore and Wynkoop rose, and with a yell charged across the ground we had charged twice before, and which was covered with our dead and wounded. This time we scaled their works, capturing 1,500 prisoners and completely routing the rest. We captured, besides, three pieces of artillery, about 3,000 stand of small arms and a number of wagons and ambulances. General Jones, the rebel commander, was killed. We saw his body in the woods a short distance behind the works, with a bullet hole through his forehead. This was the most desperate and stubbornly contested battle we were ever engaged in, and tried the mettle of our regiment most thoroughly. The 116th lost 181 men killed and wounded, forty-one being killed and thirteen afterwards dying of their wounds. Every color bearer and every one of the color guard were wounded, some of them very seriously. Our loss was as follows:

KILLED.

COMPANY A—Nathaniel D. Hayden, Ashley Brock, Jacob Zimmerly, Elijah Bennett, Newton Meeks.—5.

COMPANY C—Fred. F. Neptune, John Latchaw, George W. Gannon, Henry Pfeifer, Isaac Barrett, Robert E. Chambers, James B. Mobberly, Corporal Adam Rodecker—8.

COMPANY B—Sylvester C. Shumway—1.

COMPANY D—Corporal Robert Armstrong, John Detwiler, Robert H. H. Dyer, Elias B. Brock, Joseph Scimons, Samuel Alford, Henry B. Hixenbaugh, Richard Mahoney, Washington Bryan, Scott Dixon—10.

COMPANY E—Moses McCulloch, Francis Swartz.—2.

COMPANY F—Corporal William King, Morris Krouse, Garrison Miracle, George W. Johnson, James F. Hughes, Richard Philps, Joshua Mercer, William Sutton. 8.

COMPANY H—Stephen C. McCoy, James Harrison, Solomon Rich.—3.

COMPANY I—Corporal Richard B. Miller, Frederick Warren.—2.

COMPANY K—Edward Henshaw, Nelson B. Clements.—2.

Total killed—41.

WOUNDED.

COMPANY A—Sergeant Mann Smith, knee; Corporal Fred. R. Rose, shoulder; Corporal William Brock, Jacob C. Keyler, hips; James Kimpton, shoulder; David Barcus, wrist; Sergeant Daniel C. Hunt, arm; Cyrus Spriggs, arm; Samuel Tidd, side; Robert McCammon, hand; Corporal Benjamin F. Dye, hip; Robert Smith, arm; John Smythe, arm; John A. Harmon, leg; Albert Gates, leg; James C. Hall, leg.—16.

COMPANY B—Marion Coleman, shoulder; George W. Keyes, shoulder; John Baker, side; John Anderson, face; Sergeant Uriah Hoyt, leg; Sergeant Wm H. Bush, leg; Wells Grubb, arm; Davis Watson, arm; John Deland, leg.—9.

COMPANY C—Sergeant Mathew W. Maris, leg; Sergeant John S. Heald, breast; Sergeant John L. Beach, hip; Color Sergeant David K. Barrett, arm; George Kistner, arm amputated; Thomas South, arm amputated; Wm. Metz, head; Elwood Chambers, foot; John Buchwald, shoulder and neck; Corporal John G. Barrett, leg, (died Aug. 19, 1864,); John J. Montgomery, arm; James A. Preshaw, left shoulder, (died Nov. 3, 1864, at Frederick, Md.); Edward Yockey, leg; Philip Schoupe, leg; Albert Vickers, head; Franklin Barnes, leg; Miles H. Davis, (died Oct. 12, 1864, at Frederick, Md.); Riley Thornburg, hip; Emmon H. Beardmore, wrist.—19.

COMPANY D—Lieutenant Richard T. Chaney, foot; Sergeant James K. Drum, head; William T. Flowers, head, (died at Andersonville, Nov. 5, 1864,); Charles W. Glowers, through breast; Josiah Norris, arm; James C. Headly, hip and ankle, (died at Lynchburg, July 2, 1864,); Henry B. Hixenbaugh, bowels; James A. Sinclair, arm; John H. Windland, arm; John W. Hall, arm; Jacob Hall, side; Eldridge Moffitt, hand; Daniel Bennett, shoulder; Henry Mowder, hip; Hugh Thompson, leg; Samuel Forsyth, hand; Jesse M. Stine, head; Joshua Nixon, shoulder; Peter Hickman, head; Alfred Gray, hip; Peter Schultz, leg; Thomas Rowley, arm; David Conger.—23.

COMPANY E—Corporal Jas. Skiles, groin; Ephraim Henthorn, leg amputated; Madison G. Miller, (died at Staunton, Va., Sept. 12, 1864,); Harrison Cochran, foot; Charles Palmer, leg; William Fisher, shoulder; Corporal Lewis Barcus, leg; Joseph A. Hall, arm; Corporal John J. Atkinson, arm.—9.

COMPANY F—Sergeant Stephen A. Brown, arm; Corporal Robert Martin, arm; William Sutton, leg amputated; James Carson, hip; Elijah Bunting, side; Samuel Stephens, leg; Jacob Dillon, thigh; Joseph Rake, leg; Wesley McGee, side; Thomas Patterson, foot; Emanuel Okey, shoulder; James Piggott, head; Lempenious Efaw, thigh.—13.

COMPANY G—Alexander McFarland, hip; John Rawlings, leg.—2.

COMPANY H—Captain W. B. Teters, leg; Sergeant Joseph Purkey, leg; Sergeant Benjamin C. Drake, leg; Color Sergeant Reese Williams, side; Sergeant William A. Arnold, knee; Corporal Benjamin B. Tilton, ankle; Corporal Jacob Gregg, thigh; Corporal Joseph C. Wilson, leg. Privates, Nathaniel Butler, arm; David Bock, hip; Dighton M. Bates, mouth; William T. Cain, foot; John A. Groves, abdomen; John Wesley James, shoulder; John W. Kockley, foot; John J. Keyser, thigh; Eli T. Kirkbride, ankle; John Larrick, bowels, (died Sept. 12, 1864, at Savannah, Ga.); John

W. Mott, hand; William McBride, thigh and leg; Andrew Powell, wrist; Simon Sechrist, side; Thomas Spear, arm; Reason Baker, hand; Jas. Dudley.—25.

COMPANY I Sergeant John C. Cluck, hip; Joseph Morrison, both legs; Jesse Annon, arm; Bradley P. Barrows, arm; Luther Cayton, head; Samuel P. Fleak, side; Ephraim W. Frost, shoulder and breast, (died at Annapolis, Md., Jan. 13, 1865, of scurvy contracted at Andersonville) ; Consider Frost, both legs, (died at Staunton, Va., June 26, 1864,). Corporal Edwin G. Fuller, through hips; James H. Gilchrist, leg; Jonathan C. S. Gilbert, face, (died Oct. 9th, 1864, at Savannah, Ga.); Nathan Hatch, face and shoulder; Mark W. McAtee, arm; Samuel McCulloch, knee; Elijah Patton, arm; Corporporal Fayette Paugh, leg; Rufus B. Stanley, leg; George W. Tasker, groin.—18.

COMPANY K Lieutenant Gottlieb Sheitley, side; Samuel Spencer, thigh; John Kulow, leg; Thomas Witham, arm; George Lyon, head; Andrew C. Cagg, hand, (died at Andersonville, Ga., Jan. 27, 1865.) 6.

Total wounded.—110.

The following is a list of those who died of wounds:

James C. Headley, James A. Preshaw, Miles H. Davis, William T. Flowers, Madison G. Miller, Emanuel Okey, Corporal Robert Martin, John Larrick, Consider Frost, Jonathan C. S. Gilbert, Andrew C. Cagg, Corporal John G. Barrett, Ephraim W. Frost.—13.

Sergeant Reese Williams, one of the color bearers, was promoted to a lieutenancy for his gallantry. Although shot through the body, the brave fellow would not yield up his colors, and clung to them until he fainted from loss of blood. Being then carried back to the surgeon's, his wound was dressed. Soon recovering consciousness, he rose up from where he had been laid to die and returned to the line, took his colors again and waved them over his head as cheerfully and coolly as though nothing had happened him, and there he held them till the final charge was made. He attempted to advance with the line, but was too weak to do so, and as he gave up the colors to another, he kissed them, and swung his cap and feebly cheered as he saw them carried over the rebel works. For a time after Sergeant Williams was carried from the field, Sergeant Barrett bore bravely both standards with one arm, while the other hung helpless at his side. Captain Mann, on seeing his condition, went forward and took one of the standards from him, and afterward, when the last charge was ordered, the Captain carried the standard which Sergeant Williams was unable to go forward with. Captain Mann was always a hero in battle, and he was especially so in this. His company, C, went into the action with fifty-two men. It came out with just twenty unhurt, having lost thirty-two of its number in killed and wounded. Captain Teters' company, H, lost twenty-eight killed and wounded, more than half the number engaged. Company D lost ten killed and twenty-two wounded. The company was that day in command of Lieutenant Chaney, who, though wounded in the foot, remained in command of his company throughout the engagement. His company lost over half of the men it went into action with. He proved himself on that day to be a brave and gallant officer, and well worthy to command the noble men of company D. He was splendidly supported by his brave Orderly Sergeant, Adam J. Myers, who was next in command. Company F also met with the severe loss of eight killed and thirteen wounded. Captain Brown showed the "white feather," but Lieutenant Martin proved brave, as usual, and all through he and his gallant men behaved splendidly. "Squad I" lost very heavily in proportion to its numbers. Two killed and thirteen wounded was a great sacrifice for it. Lieut. Mosley, as brave a man as we had among us, was in command of the "squad." It will be noticed that the right and center of the regiment suffered more than the left. This was mainly due to their exposed position. Another gallant officer wounded was Captain Teters, of company H, who was struck in the leg by a shell, and very badly hurt. A letter written by me from Staunton, June 8th, thus speaks of this shell: "Just before the last charge a shell struck the ground within two feet of me, plowed the ground up under me, throwing me headlong, and ricochetting out again, passed on and hit Captain Teters in the leg, wounding him quite badly. It didn't explode till it had passed us ten feet or more. Had it exploded where it first struck the ground, the loss of life could not have failed to be great. It was a fortunate escape for us, especially for Captain Teters and myself. I am pretty sore yet and feel a sort of "shook up." I had only one foot on the ground, being in the act of rising from lying down, and the shell passed close under me. My right foot is pretty sore and my abdomen also, but otherwise I am all right, except a bruise from a spent ball on the right knee. It was a stirring time for us. I will write you more fully soon of the splendid conduct of the regiment. This has really been the first battle that thoroughly tested the mettle of our officers and men. You will be proud to know that they stood the terrible test magnificently." I never saw greater bravery than was that day displayed by the color bearers and color guard of the 116th regiment. But to see them all wounded, some we feared mortally, at the close of the battle, brought tears to the eyes of every one who had witnessed their splendid behavior. Nothing could exceed the heroism of the whole regiment in this engagement.

The battle is scarcely more than mentioned in any of the histories of the war, and yet the regiments engaged suffered as terribly and fought as bravely as any equal body of troops in any battle of the war. There were about 8,000 men of all arms engaged on our side, and 6,000 on the other, well fortified. Each side was commanded by brave and skillful officers, and each side had a great deal at stake. If defeated, there would be nothing left for us but retreat, and retreat over so long a distance in the face of a victorious foe, could not be otherwise than very disastrous. On the other hand, if the rebels were defeated, the road to Lynchburg was open and clear to us.

The loss of our army was about 420 killed and wounded. Among the officers killed was Major Schachi, of the 28th Ohio. That gallant regiment lost thirty-three killed and 105 wounded, out of 484 combatants. During its three years term of service the regiment lost ninety-two killed and 180 wounded. Its loss at Piedmont was, therefore, more than one-third its whole number killed and nearly two-thirds its whole number wounded. This shows very clearly the severity of the engagement. General Jones, the rebel commander killed, was in command of the force that surrounded us at Moorefield, January 3d, 1863. His body was found directly in front of the position of the 116th. We saw several men among the prisoners who were in the Moorefield fight. Many of his officers who were among the prisoners gathered about where he lay and wept over his remains. Our officers stood by in respectful and silent sympathy with their grief, for all recognized in him a brave and gallant officer, and felt for him the respect always entertained by one brave man for another, though he be an enemy. Until darkness cut off search and pursuit, both cavalry and infantry were busily engaged in bringing in prisoners from their hiding places. General Vaughan, next in command to Jones, fled to Waynesboro, whence he telegraphed Bragg next day: "Went into the fight yesterday with 5,600. I have not over 3,000 effectives, officers and men, including Imboden's cavalry." Secretary Staunton sent thanks to Hunter for this victory. The next day at Staunton and New Hope, Hunter captured 400 sick and wounded rebels.

One very ludicrous incident occurred while gathering in the prisoners. A very small Irishman by the name of Mike Manning, a member of company I. found hid under the bank of the river close by, a very large and powerful Irishman, whom he brought up as a prisoner of war, with an air of triumph that was truly grand. Mike marched his prisoner ahead of him at the point of the bayonet, abusing him most shamefully for being "a damned rebel and an Irishman, too." The idea of being an Irishman and a rebel was something that Mike could not reconcile. The two would stop every few steps and argue some point involving the Union and secession. This was done in true Irish style, with good strong brogue and both generally talking at once and as loud as they could. Once or twice the rebel Irishman, getting out of patience with his captor's tongue, reached out to catch him, when Mike would "leap to the rear," *a la* zouave, bring his bayonet down to a charge and order his captive to move on. They soon attracted a crowd of amused spectators, who managed to let the reb get hold of Mike and give him a shaking up, and before they got him loose from Mike he had given him good pay for his abuse, but without hurting him any. They were both possessed of the keenest kind of Irish wit, and many a poor wounded soldier forgot his pain in laughing at the comical scene.

Another amusing incident occurred in the midst of the fight, which we must relate, even at the risk of stirring up the memory of Lieutenant Joseph Purkey. He was then Orderly Sergeant of company H. While we were lying down, waiting the coming of Thoburn, he was severely wounded in the leg. He jumped up the instant he was hit, and supporting himself on his gun, doubled up his fist and shaking it at the rebels, exclaimed, "Now, d——n you, I suppose you think you've done it."

The dead were buried, the wounded moved to Staunton, except the very severely wounded. With such of our regiment as could not be moved we left Dr. T. C. Smith, and the next day marched to Staunton.

CHAPTER VII.

DESTRUCTION OF PROPERTY AT STAUNTON — ON THE MOVE, STILL GOING SOUTH — RETURN TO STAUNTON TO MEET A SUPPLY TRAIN — HARD MARCHING TO OVERTAKE THE ARMY — TO LEXINGTON — DESTRUCTION OF REBEL PROPERTY AND WASHINGTON COLLEGE — AND ON WE GO — REGULAR ARMY ENGINEERING SUPERSEDED BY WESTERN IDEAS — LYNCHBURG — BATTLE OF LYNCHBURG — A GALLANT CHARGE — REPORTS — RETREAT TO GAULEY BRIDGE — AT PARKERSBURG — AT MARTINSBURG AGAIN.

The next day after our arrival at Staunton, we were engaged in destroying rebel stores and property of different kinds, including railroad depots and tracks. The following day our regiment was sent out to tear up the railroad track west of Staunton. We did the work effectually. Tobacco warehouses seemed to abound in and around Staunton, and the men will certify that they were filled with a most excellent quality. What the troops did not appropriate was either destroyed or sent to the rear in the train that went back from Staunton. Large quantities of war material were also destroyed, the rebel agent in charge of them estimating their value at $400,000. On the 7th, our regiment started for Buffalo Gap, in which the rebels were holding General Averill. After marching out about five miles, we met his cavalry coming in, the rebels having left the Gap on hearing of the approach of infantry in their rear. We then turned back to Staunton. Quartermaster Williams was now returned to the regiment. Quartermaster Sergeant Walker, though quite unwell much of the time, had performed the duties of Quartermaster to the satisfaction of everybody in Quartermaster Williams' absence. We ought to mention that all the wounded who could be safely moved so far were sent out with the train returning from here, also the prisoners captured at Piedmont. The term of service of the 28th Ohio being nearly expired, that regiment was given charge of the train. The 34th Mass., Colonel Wells commanding, supplied the place of the 28th in our brigade, and Colonel Wells became our brigade commander.

On the 8th General Crook, with his army from the Kanawha Valley, joined us, making now an army of about 18,000 strong. The morning of June 10th, the whole army left Staunton and reached Lexington the 12th. We left about 300 sick and wounded at Staunton, and with them some surgeons and about forty men, all of whom the rebel Colonel E. G. Lee paroled on the 12th. The 116th was the last regiment to leave Staunton, which subsequently proved a little unfortunate for it. After marching seven miles out, the regiment was sent back in haste to meet and guard a supply train, which reached Staunton that morning after our departure. We met the train just coming out of town in charge of the 161st Ohio regiment. It consisted of over 200 wagons, and how it ever got safely to Staunton can only be explained by the fact that all the rebels in the Valley had been concentrated in front of Hunter at Piedmont. We at once turned back, and for the third time that day, traveled over the same piece of road. At dark we stopped for supper. Finding there was hard tack, coffee and sugar in the train, after considerable red tape had been run off we drew some of it, and for the first time in a week, had a good square meal. As we were eating supper, we were told the train had brought up a mail, and after supper found this to be so, for here came the "Post Master" with a load of letters and papers from home. How eagerly their contents were devoured. They were as great a luxury as the supper we had just eaten. After reading our letters and resting an hour, we started with our train to overtake the main column, which was several miles in our advance. It was a dreary, tiresome night march. At two o'clock in the morning we halted, made coffee, and then laid down to sleep. Slept until four, when we took the road again, and after marching four or five miles, came up to the rest of the army, just as it was moving out on the road. General Hunter sent word to us to rest until ten o'clock, and then join him as soon as possible. Towards noon, as we were passing a house by the roadside, quite a number of women stood at the door, who requested us to unfurl our flags, saying they had walked several miles that morning "to get one more look at the old stars and stripes." The flags were unfurled, and the men gave three lusty cheers for these loyal women of Virginia. As the men started up "The Union Forever," the women joined their voices with theirs, which was the first time for several months many of them had heard a woman's voice in the harmony of song.

We reached Lexington just before dark, and just as Crook, who had come in by another road, had captured the place. Lexington was the home of "Stonewall" Jackson and Governor Letcher. Jackson's remains were buried here. By General Hunter's orders the Virginia Military Institute, Washington College, Governor Letcher's residence, and some other fine buildings, including the residences of the professors, were burned. A fine bronze statue of Washington, in front of Washington College, was taken down, and afterwards taken to Wheeling. Four pieces of artillery which belonged to Lafayette were loaded up and taken with us. Two 64-pounders of the same battery were left for want of transportation. There is a slack-water navigation of the James River at Lexington; and a great many canal boats were captured and destroyed, as they were being run off to Richmond, laden with public and private stores of various kinds. Six pieces of artillery were among the cargoes. The young cadets of the Military Institute fought better than any rebels on the field at Lexington. Their bravery and skill was worthy of a better cause.

General Hunter has been severely censured for burning the buildings here, and destroying property, especially for allowing Washington College to be pillaged, and its libraries and apparatus carried off. Generals Crook, Averill and Sullivan protested against the act at the time, and all felt indignant, because they regarded the act as wanton vandalism. The burning of the Military Institute was not so much objected to, and yet its destruction involved the loss of several fine libraries, museums, valuable apparatus, mathematical and astronomical instruments, and rare works of science and art, the destruction of which benefitted nobody, but in which science, art and literature suffered a great and irreparable loss. But for the vandalism in the college, there can be no excuse. Washington College was organized in 1749, was endowed by General George Washington in 1796 with 100 shares in the James River Canal Company, which was afterwards commuted by the Legislature of Virginia to an interest bearing fund of $50,000, at which time it was given its name, it having before that been known as Washington and Lee University, which last name was again given it on the death of General Lee in 1870. At the time it was vandalized, in 1864, it had libraries containing 20,000 volumes, among which were many very old and rare books. To be sure, it and the Institute had educated a great many officers for the rebel army, but West Point had educated a great many more than both of them for the same army. The name and memory of its great founder should have saved it from the vandalism of Turks, and what can be offered in palliation of the act when committed by American soldiers? It will always remain a deep reproach to General Hunter, gallant soldier though he was.

The army moved from Lexington on the 14th, our regiment again being rear guard. The main body reached Buchanan late in the afternoon, where they found a long bridge spanning the James River, destroyed by the rebels the day before, as were all others, great and small, along the road, as they fell back before our cavalry. The citizens of Buchanan had done all they could to prevent the burning of the long bridge across the river, first because firing it would endanger the safety of the town, and second, because the river was everywhere fordable. But McCansland had a mania for burning, and, as anticipated, the town was also set on fire, and a great many fine buildings, including nearly all the stores, were burned. The main body of the troops were across by midnight, but the delays at the front prevented our regiment reaching Buchanan, until 3 o'clock in the morning. We had to remain on the north side of the river until everything was across, and so rested a few hours, but all our cooking utensils were in our wagon, away, somewhere, to the front of the train, and so could cook nothing to eat. Next morning, June 15th, we forded the river and started for Liberty, the other side of the Blue Ridge, over what is called the "Peak Road," taking its name from the fact that it passes the "Peaks of Otter," three very high mountains close together on the other side of the Blue Ridge. On our way across, we were greatly impeded by trees felled across the road, rocks rolled in, and streams of water diverted from their course into the road. At one place we saw the body of a man lying by the roadside. It would shock anyone to repeat the trifling remarks made by the men as they passed him. We passed between two of the Peaks of Otter, and within a mile and a half of the Natural Bridge, but not being on a pleasure excursion, we did not visit this marvelous curiosity of nature. A few of our daring fellows, who never miss anything in any country through which they pass, did visit it, however, and brought away with them relics in proof of their midnight venture. Near the summit of one of the Peaks of Otter is a very large spring, from which flows Otter Creek. We camped a short distance beyond the Peaks, and drank from the cool water of this strange mountain spring. Next day we passed through Liberty, which was at that time almost nothing but a rebel hospital. The houses were nearly all filled with rebel wounded, and, besides, there were four large hospital buildings, erected for the purpose of accommodating the wounded from Lee's army. Every village we entered east of the Blue Ridge, and every one reached by our cavalry on either flank for miles, was in the same situation. Every country house and barn was filled to repletion with wounded men. The Virginia & Tennessee Railroad passes through Liberty, and utter destruction was made of its depots, track, etc., as usual in such cases. Liberty is a very pretty place, and the people, though in the heart of rebeldom, treated us decently. Some of the more ignorant people, who had never seen a "Yank" before, were surprised to see us without horns and all the other traditional appendages of "Old Nick." We had but half rations for two days past, and the Quartermaster said we would have *none* to-morrow. The men told him *he* would suffer if we had none.

June 17th, we left our camp, three miles south of Liberty, for Lynchburg. About 10 A. M. we met the enemy in some force, but drove him before our skirmish line steadily, till between 2 and 3 P. M., when a stand was made at a creek, our crossing of which they disputed. But the advance was sufficient to disperse them, not, however, until they had destroyed the bridge. Its reconstruction delayed the trains and its guard several hours. The rear guard came up while it was yet scarcely begun. All were in haste to cross, but the engineer in charge of its reconstruction was bound to see that it was put up only after the most approved methods of regular army bridge building. But the plans were too elaborate and tedious, and everybody got out of patience, for firing in front was urging everyone forward, especially the artillery. Western expedients came to the rescue. When the 116th came up, Captain John F. Welch, of our regiment, who was in charge of the pioneer corps of our division, was expostulating with the engineer against his plans, which involved too much time. Finally he prevailed on the engineer to let him try his way of building a bridge "in a hurry," and calling for a number of good choppers from the 116th, which it contained in abundance, as he knew, they went into a woods close by and began cutting timbers, which were carried to the ground by the stalwart fellows of the regiment, and in less than an hour the artillery was crossing, on the gallop, to the front. Moving on rapidly now, we arrived at the Quaker Stone Church, in the midst of a sharp engagement, in which the 91st Ohio suffered considerably, Colonel Turley being severely wounded. The 116th took but small part in this affair, being too far to the left, the fighting being more to the right. Crook's division was engaged with the enemy at the church when we came up. The rebels were driven from this point into their entrenchments around Lynchburg. Our division now relieved the second, which went into camp. By this time it was dark, and after our regiment had been moved from one point to another several times, we went on the picket line, quite close up to the rebel entrenchments, and there lay until morning. About 10 o'clock that night, we heard the whistle of a locomotive and the rolling of a train. From that hour till noon next day, we could hear trains arriving, and after daylight could see large bodies of troops moving out of the city towards our position, and hear bands playing, and see movements in all directions, which clearly indicated the arrival of large reinforcements. Early in the morning, we were moved out to the extreme left in support of a battery. The rebels did some of the best artillery firing we ever saw, and our battery had scarcely opened fire, before it was obliged to retire to shelter. Their sharp-shooters were also extremely accurate in their aim, they seemed to know the ground perfectly. About 2 P. M., the rebels made a desperate charge on the right and center of our brigade. We were then a quarter of a mile to the left of it. Our battery pulled out for the right, and we hastened to the support of our brigade. While en route to join the brigade, a column of rebels was seen coming through the woods, directly on our flank. The rebels were making a charge on our center, which they were driving back slowly. Two different regiments went forward in turn to check the rebel advance, but each was repulsed. By this time we had reached a position directly in the course of the regiment that had been last sent in, and was now falling back through us in disorder. Here we halted to stop the further advance of the enemy. We had hardly halted, before Colonel Washburn received an order to "charge with the 116th." We immediately formed for the charge, and went down upon the charging rebels, just as they were ascending a hill. We had the advantage in charging down, as they were charging up the hill, and we not only checked them, but they broke in wild confusion to their breastworks. Clambering over them, we pushed on to their second line, being now reinforced by the 5th West Virginia, under Colonel Enochs. Here we were met by a very heavy force well entrenched, and, lying down, we fought hard against desperate odds, waiting for help, which we felt would surely come, until we were assaulted on both flanks by infantry, and by grape and cannister from a battery, planted not five rods in our front. We then fell back to the first line of works we had taken, and on their face, fought again, until we were struck on our left by a large force which crossed over the works in the woods on that flank. We then fell back to a position in the woods, through which we had charged, where we remained for some time unmolested, and to which we carried most of our wounded. Among our badly wounded was Captain Edwin Keyes and Color Sergeant Fred. E. Humphrey, both of whom we were obliged to leave behind us. We again fell back to the line of the rest of the troops, only to find that the retreat had commenced.

Our regiment was praised without stint for its gallantry on this occasion. It was the only regiment of Hunter's army that entered the rebel works about Lynchburg; its colors were the only colors carried over them, or planted upon them. To show that this is no idle boasting, I quote from several authorities, and first General Hunter says in his report: "The 116th Ohio made a gallant charge, and carried its colors over the enemy's works, but was compelled to retire before superior numbers."

Major Pratt, of the 34th Massachusetts, wrote: "For a moment the stars and stripes, borne by the color bearer of the 116th Ohio, were seen waving from the enemy's breastworks; but the word to withdraw was given, and soon our troops occupied nearly their old position."

George E. Pond, in "The Shenandoah Valley in 1864," says: "During the afternoon, Hunter attacked in force, bringing into action his two divisions of infantry and his artillery in the center, on and near the Bedford turnpike, Duffié along the Forest road, on the left, and a part of Averill's along the Campbell road, on the right. Early's infantry sallied from their works on the Bedford road to meet this attack, but were gallantly driven back by Sullivan, aided by Crook, and the 116th even planted its colors on Early's breastworks."

The second division, under General Crook, moved to the right early in the morning, and reconnoitered the enemy's position in that direction for three or four miles, seeking in vain for an unguarded spot at which to make an attack on the enemy's left.

General Crook says in his report of July 7th, 1864: "I was sent to the right to make a reconnoisance, for the purpose of turning the enemy's left. Found it impracticable, after marching three or four miles, and had just returned with my division and got it in position to support General Sullivan when the enemy made an attack on our lines."

About seven o'clock we moved out, and followed in the rear of the trains all that night. Our loss in the charge was twelve killed, twenty-two wounded and ten prisoners, as follows:

KILLED.

Privates James A. Boyd and Jefferson Gatten, Company A; Charles C. Davis, Company B; Geo. B. Blair, Geo. M. Coulter and Jacob Kernan, Company E; William Fisher, Company F; Gilbert Van Horn, Company I; Moses F. Starr, Micajah Gowdy and Evander B. Hamilton, Company D, and George Lyons, Company K.

WOUNDED.

COMPANY A—Corporal John W. Devore, foot; Henry Harmon, thigh; Daniel P. Hubbard, bowels.

COMPANY B—Captain Edwin Keyes, knee and elbow, (died at Lynchburg, Va., July 19th, 1864,); Color Sergeant Fred. E. Humphrey, shoulder and neck; Royal Danes, side, (died of his wounds after muster out,); Philip Feiger, William E. Lefaver.

COMPANY C—Corporal Walter Tacker, leg; John Egger, leg.

COMPANY D—Corporal Alexander Straight, arm; James G. Dally, leg; Isaiah Mozena.

COMPANY E—Sergeant John G. Reithmiller, side; Joseph Connor, hip.

COMPANY F—William Allen, right arm amputated; Jacob Martin, head.

COMPANY G—Corporal James B. Miller, ankle; David A. Moore, (died at Andersonville, Ga., August 14, 1864.)

COMPANY H—Isaac Russell, side.

COMPANY I—Corporal William Scott, head

COMPANY K—Corporal Carmi Allison, lungs; Corporal John Young, foot; Corporal Perry Gardner, neck; William Hunter, finger.

PRISONERS.

Captain Edwin Keyes, Sergeant Fred. E. Humphrey, Horace McNeal, Wells Grubb, William E. Lefaver, Nelson Watson, Royal Hoyt, Alex C. Warren, all of Company B; Albin Vickers, Company C, and John Vickers, of Company D.

Making a total loss of forty-four killed, wounded and missing.

Color Sergeant Fred. E. Humphrey was wounded while waving his colors over the rebel works. He displayed the greatest gallantry, the whole color guard as gallantly gathering about and following to the last forward step. The entire guard mounted the works beside him, and their dauntless courage inspired the whole regiment to charge over and up to the enemy's second line. As he fell, terribly wounded, one of the guard caught the colors and held them to the front, until we fell back. The Corporals named among the wounded were nearly all of the guard, and when we came out of the fight, it was found necessary to organize a new color guard. Volunteers to carry them were called for, and among the number who stepped forward was private James Logan, of company C, to whom one of the standards was given, and who most honorably, and with the most unflinching bravery, carried it through some of the subsequent battles in the Shenandoah Valley, until he was promoted to the chaplaincy of the regiment, on the 12th of November, 1864, for brave and meritorious conduct as color bearer. He was in very truth a "fighting parson," and, withal, a most exemplary Christian gentleman. Poor, brave Sergeant Humphrey we were compelled to leave behind us, as we were also Captain Keyes. The Captain had a knee and an elbow shattered with musket balls, and he died at Lynchburg on the 19th of July, from the effects of these wounds. He led his company most heroically in the battle, and received his first wound in the knee, at the last moment, in holding his company against the charge made on our left, just before we fell back into the woods from the rebel works, and his second, in the elbow, just as we began to fall back. He was carried back by his men, and when he heard the command to halt given out along the line in the woods, he repeated it to his men, and directed them to form in their places. As soon as it was learned that he was badly wounded, the officers and his men gathered about him to bid him farewell, for it was evident he could not be moved far. The rebels were now shelling the woods with great fury, and being still within range of their grape and cannister, also the rattle of small arms, the hurling and crashing of flying missiles, the explosion of shells, and the yells of the victorious enemy, combined to make one of the wildest battle scenes we ever witnessed. Captain Keyes was now conveyed to the field hospital. His loss was mourned, not alone by his own company, but by the whole regiment.

The march that night was dreary enough. Our men had had but one cracker apiece in two days, had marched all one of these, fought all the other, and stood picket during the intervening night. In this condition, we marched all night quite rapidly, and overtook the train about daylight next morning. We reached our old camp of the night before, about 6 A. M., and stopped to make coffee. The ever faithful colored people now began flocking to our army by the hundreds. Many of them carried heavy loads of provisions, which they gladly divided with the soldiers, and told us where flour, meal, bacon, hogs and other eatables were concealed. A foraging expedition sent out near Liberty, under the guidance of a squad of colored men, returned in a short time with some provisions, which were soon made a meal of. Three good horses were also brought in, taken from the cellar of a "mansion" close by.

Some provisions were saved for another meal. Now, when we say "meal," we do not mean to be understood as having had all we wanted to eat. Not by great odds! Some had none, others a little, and a few lucky fellows, who always had enough, no matter what happened, had an abundance. A letter written by Quartermaster Sergeant Walker to his friends at Athens, upon our arrival at Ganley Bridge, under date of July 1st, 1864, gives such a graphic, faithful history of the retreat from Lynchburg, that with his consent we give it here in full:

"JUNE 18TH. The fighting commenced in good season this morning. Our regiment had been on picket all night, and I had not seen them. After breakfast the hospital steward wanted me to go and help him in the hospital. I started, and was afterwards told I was wanted on the field to assist in the ambulance corps. I went out and reported to Dr. Smith, of our regiment, and remained with him till after the hardest of the fight, which came off between 2 and 3 o'clock P. M. The rebels charged our centre, and drove it. Another regiment then went forward, and were also driven back by the enemy. *Our* regiment then went into the breach, and not only *checked* the rebels, but drove them clear back, and if I am not mistaken in the time, they charged them then, and came near taking another line of works, and would have succeeded had they been properly supported. In the charge Captain Keyes, of company B, was wounded in the left knee and left elbow, and, it is feared, it will be necessary to amputate both the arm and leg; if so, he cannot possibly live. I could not keep from shedding tears when I saw him the first time, and yet he would, while lying there on his back, sing in a cheerful tone, "Rally Round the Flag," and talk to others to cheer them up. He was a *good soldier* and a GOOD CHRISTIAN. This latter accounts for his cheerfulness, even while he knew he must in all probability die. But death had no terrors for him. We also had another "color bearer" wounded, making in all three that have been wounded during this raid. Our flags, too, are beginning to look the worse for wear. Our loss in this fight has not been so great as in the first, but the wounds are of a more serious character. I saw no less than a dozen amputations performed, and there were others that would have to be performed the next day, or as soon as possible. I do hope and pray I may never be called upon to witness the horrors of another battle field. And yet there is no cloud so dark but it may have a silver lining. The poor fellows are so thankful when you do anything for them, it is a pleasure to wait on them. After going to the hospital with Captain Keyes and the Color Sergeant, I did not return to the field, but Lee and I busied ourselves, trying to make the men of our regiment as comfortable as possible. We carried them into a large barn that had been prepared for a hospital, where we made beds of new mown hay. Every man we moved was covered with blood, and by the time we were through we were about as bloody as the wounded men.

* * * * By 6 A. M. Sunday, we reached our old camp near Liberty, where we stopped to get breakfast. Some of the men had foraged a little flour along the road, of which they made batter cakes, but many of the men were obliged to go without bread. About noon we moved forward and stopped about three miles the other side of the town of Liberty, intending to stay all night, but the enemy came up on our rear, and heavy skirmishing ensued. Again we moved forward, and did not stop till Monday morning. The men were so tired that they would go to sleep in the ranks. I went sound asleep quite a number of times, while walking along, and was only awakened by making a wrong step, or something of that sort. While the skirmishing was going on in our rear, Sunday evening, the boys went out and brought in quite a quantity of flour — enough to last a whole day. It was that, and that alone, that enabled the men to make the long march they did Sunday night and Monday morning. It was almost noon when we stopped for breakfast. The men had barely time to bake their flour and fry their meat, when the order was given to 'fall in.' The idea of starting out on another long march without rest was enough to sicken any one, but it must be done. We were out of rations, and in the heart of the enemy's country, and we must move fast or suffer from starvation. Marched all night, and reached Salem early in the day, Tuesday. There was some skirmishing upon our approaching the town, but the enemy were easily driven off. Leaving Salem, we had a rough mountain pass to go through, a place of all others where we might expect danger, and yet the train and artillery were started off without the show of a guard. The train of wagons passed through safely, but just as soon as the artillery had fairly entered the gap, a party of rebs dashed down the side of the mountain, unharnessed the horses, and after cutting the wheels of the artillery wagons, started off over the mountain. As soon as word could be got to General Hunter, a cavalry force was started in pursuit and, I believe, succeeded in bringing back some of the horses. Some of the pieces were not so badly damaged but that we brought them away with us, but we were obliged to burn and destroy eight of the guns. Aside from that disaster, this raid has been a great success, but that leaves a black mark for us to look back upon. This gap, like most others we have passed through, is deep and narrow, mountains rising on either side at an angle of forty-five degrees, very rocky, a small stream winding from one side of the road to the other. It always makes me feel lonely to pass one of them, and yet I am glad when I hear there is one of them on our route. After having marched us three days and three nights, General Hunter concluded to let us rest Tuesday night, and you may be sure the boys were not sorry. After making coffee and frying meat, they laid down and slept soundly till morning. One of our men went out and found a sack of green tea, with over a bushel of tea in it. Wednesday we passed a house where a number of ladies had come together from a distance to get one more look at the old flag they so well loved. Our flag was unfurled, and three cheers given for the flag, and three for the ladies. Our bed that night was the rockiest place you ever saw. Gather together a lot of boulders out of the river, from the size of your fist to that of your head, throw them on the ground till you cannot see anything but stones, cover them with a single blanket, and you are ready to lie down. 'A hard bed,' I think I hear you say, and yet I never slept more sweetly than on that very same pile of stones. Thursday, 23d, we crossed three pretty high mountains, "Sinking Creek," "Spotts" and "Sweet Spring" mountains. While crossing these mountains, many of the teams gave out, making it necessary to burn the wagons. No less than fifty wagons were destroyed in this way in one day, and from 250 to 300 horses and mules gave out, and were shot by the rear guard to prevent them from falling into the enemy's hands. At the base of the "Sweet Spring Mountains" are the Sweet Sulphur Springs. This, though not so noted a place as the White Sulphur Springs, is fast becoming a place of some renown. The buildings, though not quite so extensive, are still sufficient for the accommodation of quite a number of guests. The main building is about 300 feet long, and finished off in very good style. There are two large baths, one for ladies and one for gentlemen, with dressing rooms for each. The water can be graduated from three feet deep to six, at the pleasure of the bathers. I merely tasted the water to see what it was like. It is warm and has a sickish, sulphurish, metallicish, nastyish taste that can not be described. I don't see what folks want to drink such stuff for. If they were compelled to do so, I am sure they would never stop complaining. The Red Sweet Springs are about a mile from the first, but are not much visited. Friday, 24th, marched to White Sulphur Springs. Little did I think, when I started on this raid, I would have an opportunity of visiting this great watering place of America, second only to Saratoga. The buildings are much more extensive, numbering over 100 cottages. I should think the main buildings must be nearly 400 feet long, with porches on either side; the basement story was used for culinary purposes, the first floor contained the dining-room and parlors, the former occupying the central part of the building, the latter the two wings; the dining-hall is about 300 feet long by fifty feet wide, the parlors about seventy-five by fifty; the second and third stories are used as rooms for guests, and, though very small, the rooms are generally finished off in plain style. Everything has been removed since the breaking out of the war, and the whole thing looks desolate indeed. The cottages are divided as a general thing, into four rooms and a bath room, with high ceilings, large windows and doors, with porches in front, and high steps. On the 25th and 26th, marched as rapidly as we could. The men have been without bread for four days. (I have only been out three days.) We are living on fresh beef and coffee; 27th a supply train came up after we got into camp. I never saw such rejoicing. Some of the boys were so weak that they could hardly talk. The 29th, we passed the celebrated "Lover's Leap," and "Hawk's Nest." The latter, particularly, is a grand sight. You stand on an overhanging rock and look down several hundred feet into New River, which seems directly under you, and yet it takes a good man to throw a stone into the water. Looking up the stream, you have a fine view of the river, as it comes leaping and dashing in its wild career over the rocks between the two mountains. We reached this place, (Gauley) June 29th, tired, dirty, worn out, etc., etc."

The enemy's infantry followed us to Bedford Gap, some of his cavalry, under McCausland, to Salem. There is but little to add to the excellent account of Walker. A few incidents of the march only remain to be added. The night before reaching "Sweet Sulphur Springs," companies A and B, through some mistake, were left on picket on the top of Pott's Mountain, and were there attacked. Gilbert G. Webster, of company B, was wounded in the arm. The companies made a good stand, and it was due to this that they escaped capture, for they were largely outnumbered. The companies rejoined the regiment about noon next day, pretty thoroughly exhausted.

Quartermaster Sergeant Walker, under date of June 28th, wrote in his diary: "Found a sack of grain in the train which I took. First we have had since leaving Salem." This shows, as well as more words would do it, how the poor animals of the army fared. A great many of the horses giving out crossing the mountains would, after two or three hours rest and browsing in the woods into which they were turned loose, revive sufficiently to follow along, and were utilized by the men in carrying knapsacks, guns, etc. The poor animals were so hungry they would eat anything, and though the men were half starved themselves, they would cut brush, hunt grass and forage, as much for the horses that were carrying their knapsacks, guns and sick companions as for themselves. In this way a great many abandoned horses were saved and brought through in very good shape. During our halt at Meadow Bluffs, a private soldier—and I wish I knew his name for special mention here—came to our headquarters and gave the Colonel, Lieutenant Colonel and Adjutant each a very large, fresh onion. I do not suppose either of us ever expects again to taste anything half as delicious as those onions were, or to be presented with anything, while we live, that will draw from our hearts such profound thanks. Now and then our men would find among the mountains an "applejack" or illicit distillery. Then there would be "music in the air" for a time. Colonel Washburn's teeth were not very good, and his attempts at "blessing" the tough meat issued to us was a caution to the Chaplain. We did not hear of President Lincoln's re-nomination, which occurred on the 7th of June, at Baltimore, until the day before we reached Gauley Bridge.

The assertion has often been made that we might have captured Lynchburg had we pressed on the night of the 17th. Facts, since developed, show conclusively that we could not. After our victory at Piedmont, Vaughn took up a position in Rock Fish Gap, near Waynesboro. Two brigades of Breckenridge, Wharton's and Echols', were immediately sent there to reinforce Vaughn. As soon as Hunter was far enough up the valley to insure that he did not contemplate approaching Lynchburg by way of Rock Fish Gap, Breckenridge hastened to Lynchburg with the rest of his division, to which he also withdrew Vaughn, Wharton and Echols, and to which he was also able to add quite an army of home guards and convalescents, for Lynchburg and all the country about there was at that time filled with sick and wounded from Lee's army. These forces alone nearly equalled Hunter's army, and they were put behind strong entrenchments and supplied with artillery. But these were not all we met there on the 17th. On the 13th, Lee had sent Ewell's corps, then under Early, from Cold Harbor, to proceed by way of Louisa and Charlottesville, and passing through Brown's Gap, to get in Hunter's rear, who was then supposed to be at Staunton. Striking the railroad at Charlottesville, on the 16th, Early learned of Hunter's near approach to Lynchburg, when, hastily putting his men aboard cars, he pushed them rapidly on to Lynchburg, and on the 17th, half of Early's corps had reached the place and the other half had reached it by noon of the 18th. It was part of Gordon's and Ramseur's divisions that Crook and Averill fought the evening of the 17th. Of the delay at Staunton no one complains, but that at Lexington has been criticised. But there was a sound reason for this. As Hunter started from Staunton he sent Duffié, with his division of cavalry, to demonstrate against Vaughn at Waynesboro, but finding him too strong for him he moved further South, and crossed the Blue Ridge at Tye River Gap. From there he proceeded to Amherst Court House where he broke the Charlottesville & Lynchburg Railroad, and also at Avington Station. Imboden followed him, when Duffié turned on him and gave him a terrible whipping, capturing 100 prisoners, 400 horses, and a part of Imboden's train. He destroyed, beside, some iron furnaces and a large quantity of commissary stores. Hunter sent couriers after him to return to the army and waited at Lexington for his return, which he did not do until the afternoon of the 13th. Duffié was evidently bent on distinguishing himself, though it might be at the expense of the success of the expedition. His destruction of the railroad was not sufficient, as has been seen, to keep Early's troops from being conveyed over the railroad, four days afterward, from Charlottesville to Lynchburg, and he caused a loss of two days at Lexington waiting for him.

The plan of General Grant's campaign comprehended a simultaneous movement, early in May, of Generals Sigel, Crook, Averill, and Burbridge upon Lynchburg, but it failed in the execution as entirely as did that of General Butler's against Petersburg. Sigel was defeated at New Market, and retiring to Cedar Creek was relieved by Hunter. General Crook was the only one successful in the part assigned him. He attacked and defeated Jenkins, at Cloyd's Mountain, on the 9th of May. He then advanced as far as Newbern, on the Virginia & Tennessee Railroad, where he was met by General Morgan, with a superior force, when he decided to give up the attempt to reach Lynchburg and return to Meadow Bluffs. Notwithstanding this first failure, General Grant determined to carry out his original plan, and organized other forces to cut off General Lee's communications by the Virginia & Tennessee Railroad, and, if possible, to occupy Lynchburg. General Hunter was reinforced, General Crook, General Averill and General Sheridan were to join him at Staunton or Charlottesville, and General Burbridge, in the neighborhood of Bonsack's Depot or Liberty. Had this plan not miscarried by the failure of Sheridan to reach us from the one side, and Burbridge from the other, the expedition would doubtless have been a complete success, for it would have been extremely hazardous for Lee to have detached troops enough, from his army confronting Grant, to have checked us.

On the 12th of June, the day that Hunter reached Lexington, Sheridan was forced to retreat from before Gordonsville with Torbert's and Gregg's divisions of cavalry, so that his movement did not even aid Hunter as a diversion, for Early reached Charlottesville on the 16th, about the date of Sheridan's return to White House. General Sheridan was given a lengthy letter of instructions to deliver to General Hunter from Grant, which, of course, never reached him. In it, Grant said: "After the work laid out for General Sheridan and yourself is thoroughly done, proceed to join the Army of the Potomac by the route laid out in General Sheridan's instructions." On the 16th Secretary Stanton wrote to General Stahel as follows: "General Sheridan, who was sent by General Grant to open communications with General Hunter, by way of Charlottesville, has just returned to York River without effecting his object. It is, therefore, very probable that General

Hunter will be compelled to fall back into West Virginia." The "route laid out in General Sheridan's instructions" for joining the Army of the Potomac was the one pursued by Sheridan in his advance to and retreat from Gordonsville. The object of the expedition was plain enough: to destroy Lee's communications with the country and to weaken his lines before Grant. But history shows that the expedition had another quite unlooked for effect, and one much more far-reaching than either of the two objects named.

After the fall of Atlanta, Jefferson Davis told the people of Georgia that "an audacious movement of the enemy, up to the very walls of Lynchburg, had rendered it necessary to cover that vital point with troops otherwise intended for the relief of Atlanta." Burbridge, who was to co-operate with Hunter, was diverted from doing so by "Morgan's raid" into Kentucky, and finally into Ohio, where he and his whole force were captured. Thus it will be seen that "Hunter's raid," as it was termed, proved of very great importance to the Union cause in many ways, that it stirred up the enemy in several directions, and frustrated the plans of Davis and Lee more, perhaps, than anything occurring during the campaign of 1864.

An expedition attended with such important results cannot, in truth, be called a failure. General Hunter, himself, on June 28th, expressed the view, in a dispatch to the Secretary of War, that the expedition had been "extremely successful, inflicting great injury upon the enemy." And in this view the Secretary and General Grant fully coincided, and so did the country, as soon as the true state of facts became known. It was never intended by General Grant that Lynchburg should be held, even should it be captured. In his instructions to Hunter he said: "According to the instructions I sent General Halleck for your guidance, you were to proceed to Lynchburg *for a single day*. But that point is of so much importance to the enemy that in attempting to get it, such resistance may be met as to defeat your getting on to the road or canal at all." But we did get on to both the road and the canal, and destroyed both for long distances, and carried out instructions by remaining at Lynchburg a "single day," and night too.

A letter written to the Athens (Ohio) Messenger by an officer of the 116th, from Gauley Bridge, under date of July 1st, 1864, sums up the results of the expedition as follows: "We destroyed the Virginia Central Railroad from near Waynesboro to its terminus near Covington. The destruction of the Virginia & Tennessee Railroad was almost complete from Lynchburg to Salem, a distance of sixty miles. Every mill, factory, furnace, foundry and shop in the valley, at which anything was ever made, or could be made, for the use of the rebel army, was destroyed. Perhaps $30,000,000 will cover the loss to the rebels though many estimate it much greater. We captured 3,000 prisoners, killed and wounded about 2,000, and broke up entirely the rebel army in the Shenandoah Valley. All the furnaces and iron works of Botetourt county were destroyed. These mainly supplied the rebel manufactories in Richmond with material for cannon, etc. The James River Canal was also badly used up for miles out of Lexington. Our loss will not exceed 1,500 men killed, wounded and missing. All of Hunter's subordinate officers agreed that he had conducted the campaign admirably, and with great skill and energy. And General Crook, speaking of his division, says: The division became a little straightened for provisions, but came out in good shape, thus settling the efforts of some officers of his division to antagonize Crook against Hunter, and at the same time setting at rest the extravagant tales of suffering on the retreat.

Yet still the boys would always sing

"General Hunter, on the Lynchburg raid,
D—d near starved the First Brigade.
Stuval, Stuval, etc."

Reaching Gauley Bridge, on the 29th of June, we rested until the 2d of July, when we marched down to Camp Piatt. At this place we embarked upon steamboats, and made our way tediously down the Kanawha, and up the Ohio to Parkersburg, frequently disembarking and marching by shoals in the river, the water being very low. As rough and uncouth as was our appearance when we first entered Parkersburg, in September 1862, it was far worse now. The clothing of the officers and men was in tatters and dirty, half were barefooted, and all worn down by the hardships of the expedition. To add to their misfortunes, the camp diarrhœa had set in before we left Gauley Bridge, and had prostrated a great many men. We were truly "forlorn and shipwrecked brothers." Getting near their homes on the 4th, many of the men of companies B, I, and G were permitted to visit their friends in Meigs and Athens counties, under a promise to rejoin us at Parkersburg on the 7th, which promise they kept. Colonel Charles G. Halpine, ("Miles O'Reiley,") who was General Hunter's Adjutant General, gave a magnificent dinner to the officers of the 116th Ohio and 5th West Virginia, at Parkersburg, in honor of their charge on the rebel works at Lynchburg. They were so scattered in moving, however, that many of them did not have the pleasure of enjoying the generous hospitality of this brilliant and gallant Irishman.

A great many of our Ohio friends met us here with cordial greetings. On the 9th, we took cars and started for our old home, the Shenandoah Valley. Reaching Cherry Run on the 10th, we found the railroad torn up. From there we marched to Martinsburg, where we camped, and remained one day, the 12th. The men made good use of their time inquiring after their wounded comrades, of whom they found the Union people of the place had taken the best of care. No place in Virginia contained better or truer loyal women than Martinsburg. Many of our men had also left clothes, and other property, in charge of Union people, upon their setting out for Lynchburg, in the spring. It was all safe for them, notwithstanding Early's army had ransacked nearly every house, in search of property they knew had been left and sent back there by the army of Sigel and Hunter. We were, besides, given a fine reception by the citizens of the place, for the 116th was a favorite regiment when stationed there. The officers and men were invited to meals, and many a barefooted lad was shod and given clean under-clothes, gifts that in their needy condition were priceless. Flags were displayed everywhere, and, generally, everything done that could show satisfaction and rejoicing over our return. Several of our convalescent men joined us here, some of whom had been hidden for a long time from the rebel raiders, by the Union people of Martinsburg and the surrounding country.

CHAPTER VIII.

EARLY IN THE VALLEY — HIS ADVANCE INTO MARYLAND, AND UPON WASHINGTON — MARCH TO HARPER'S FERRY TO HILLSBORO — SNICKER'S GAP — BATTLE OF SNICKER'S FERRY — WOUNDING OF COLONEL WASHBURN — HARD FIGHT OF THE REGIMENT ON THE RIGHT — BRAVE CONDUCT OF OFFICERS AND MEN — LIST OF CASUALTIES.

We felt at home, and we *were* at home, and among friends tried and true at Martinsburg, and nothing would have given us so much unalloyed happiness as to have been allowed to remain there until refreshed, clothed and rested, but this could not be, with a rebel army knocking at the gates of the capitol of the Nation, for on that very day, the 12th of July, Early's skirmishers were immediately in front of forts Stevens and De Russey, four miles north of the city of Washington, and as a historian says : "Toward evening their sharpshooters became so annoying, and their audacity so humiliating, that General Augur dispatched a brigade of veterans, by the Seventh street road, to drive them off." So we received orders, in the evening, to be ready to march early next morning, and, as directed, we were early on the road to Harper's Ferry, which we reached on the 14th, and at once crossed over to Sandy Hook. Just as our Quarter Master was about to commence issuing rations on the 15th, we were ordered to march. Most of our men were, by this time, nearly, or entirely bare-footed, and the prospect of entering upon another long march with bare, sore feet, was not calculated to inspire them with any great degree of enthusiasm. Some we had to leave, their feet being in too terrible a condition to move further. At Berlin we forded the Potomac and pushed rapidly up the Loudon valley, camping at Hillsboro.

A strange lack of information seemed to exist on the part of everyone relative to the situation of our own troops or that of the rebels. General Wright, with parts of the Sixth and Nineteenth corps, numbering 15,000 men, arrived at Poolesville, on the evening of the 14th. That night he notified General Hunter of his presence and directed him to join him with his forces as soon as possible, at Leesburg. At 6 P. M. he telegraphed Halleck : " I have not been able to get any intelligence from General Hunter's command." Early the next morning Hunter started his troops under General Sullivan at Leesburg. When we reached Hillsboro we found ourselves on the flank of Early's army, now hastening through Leesburg and Purcelville, but we could get no word of Wright's whereabouts, and so, although we had an excellent opportunity to crush Early's army, if there had been an understanding of the situation, and co-operation between Hunter and Wright, we were obliged to halt and allow the rebel army to pass across our front almost unmolested, for Wright did not proceed to Leesburg at all in pursuit of Lee, but lay at Poolesville until the afternoon of the 16th, when he crossed the Potomac at Edwards' Ferry. " Comparison of dates and places shows that these West Virginia forces were now coming in directly and very fast upon Early's right flank, and that, had it been wise to do so, they might have been thrown exactly across his path ; but the night of the 15th, while Sullivan was at Hillsboro, Wright was at Poolesville, Md., north of the Potomac. Had Wright and Sullivan possessed a common understanding for vigorous action in the best possible way, the former close on Early's heels with 15,000 men, and Ricketts and

Kerby hurrying forward with several thousand more, Sullivan and Duffié would apparently have been able to use their 9,000 men with great effect against Early's line of march from Leesburg to Snicker's Gap." *The Shenandoah Valley in 1864.*

We lay at Hillsboro until the afternoon of the 16th. General Crook came up at noon of that day, and, relieving Sullivan, assumed command. He at once set everthing in motion. His cavalry was sent out to find the enemy, and, hearing there was a rebel train at Waterford, our brigade was sent off, in haste, to that place. Arriving there, we found the rebels gone with their trains in the direction of Snicker's Gap. The soldiers were surprised at the Union sentiment expressed by the people here. It was very hot, and our men called for water as they marched rapidly through the place. Very soon many women and children came along the marching column with buckets and pitchers of water, which they dipped out to the men. Flags were also thickly displayed. Crook's energy soon discovered the fact that Early's columns and trains had been for several hours very close to his command. The infantry was that afternoon moved to Purcelville, where, just before our arrival, Duffié had struck the rebel trains and captured 117 mules and horses, 82 wagons, and 50 or 60 prisoners. That night the forces of Wright and Crook came together just in time to let Early, with all his plunder, slip through between them. Mulligan and Duffié were sent forward to Snicker's Gap that night, where they met the enemy in possession of the Gap, the whole rebel army having crossed into the Shenandoah valley.

We lay at Purcelville during the 17th. On the morning of the 18th, we advanced through Snicker's Gap to the Ferry. About 2 o'clock, General Crook directed Colonel Thoburn to cross the Shenandoah river at Island Ford with his two brigades and the third brigade of the second division. Our brigade was the first to cross, which we did under a severe fire from some rebel skirmishers, who were under cover of bushes skirting the west bank of the river. On crossing we captured a rebel captain and fifteen men. We learned from these prisoners that Early's whole force was close by. The other two brigades soon crossed, and Thoburn forming with the 1st, our brigade, on the left; the 3d in the centre, and the 2d, with about 1,000 cavalry, on the right, moved forward to a position a short distance from the river. Companies B, C, D and K of our regiment were put out as skirmishers, and advanced under Lieutenant Colonel Wildes in search of the enemy. We did not have to search very long. Breckenridge, with two divisions, advanced against Thoburn's left and centre, and Rhodes against his right, pushing the whole line back to the cover of a stone wall along the bank of the river. The 1,000 dismounted cavalry on our right broke in confusion and retreated across the river, when our regiment, on the extreme left, was hurried to the extreme right. We found on our arrival a large body of rebels between the stone wall and the river, bearing down heavily on the right of our position, and the gallant 4th West Virginia fighting to maintain its position against desperate odds. Colonel Washburn fell desperately wounded at the head of the regiment, just as he reached the right. Hurrying forward and assuming command of the regiment, Lieutenant Colonel Wildes stationed two companies under Captain Mallory between the wall and the river. They charged and drove back the rebels, who had been so closely pressing Colonel Vance. Now hastily throwing up a breastwork of stones and logs across this space, the Captain opened a deadly fire upon the rebels in his front, and drove them out. The rest of the regiment as effectually opened on those in front of the stone wall. At this juncture Sergeant Silas King, of Company F, was sent with ten men, still further to the right, to command the opposite side of a stone wall running at right angles with ours, behind which the rebels were gathering to fire on our flank. The gallant sergeant and his men, after a hot contest, cleared the rebels out from behind this wall, killing and wounding some of them almost within the length of some of their guns, the other side of the river wall. Sergeant King's splendid conduct on this occasion won him the praise of his superior officers, and the confidence of everybody in his courage and coolness. He exhibited ability to command and determination and daring bravery not often met with in the rank and file. Thus our front and flank were relieved and we were secure in our position. In a letter I wrote on the 19th of July, 1864, from Snicker's Ferry, I find the following : " Our regiment held the extreme right of the line and successfully resisted several desperate efforts of the rebels to turn it and flank us. Captain Mallory, Lieutenant Moseley, Lieutenant Bidenharn, Lieutenant Martin, and Sergeants King and Humphrey, of the regiment, fought with as much daring bravery as I ever saw. The officers and men of the regiment never behaved better." Soon the rebels returned again to the charge, but we were prepared for them. Every man in the two regiments felt that in driving that column of rebels back depended his life. The river at our back was too deep to more than walk slowly through, and so escape that way was out of the question. Run we could not, if we would. Nothing was left to do but to fight. Every officer and man *but one* met the shock manfully. In the hottest of the fight a portion of Mallory's heroes came to our assistance, and under the fresh volleys they added to ours, the rebels broke over the hill, not to return again while we lay behind that stone wall. The cheer that went up from our men, as they saw the rebels break over the hill, indicated the relief they felt and the value they placed upon the victory they had won. Colonel Thoburn was with us, urging the men to stand their ground. He was the coolest man on the field. The men needed no urging, for every man regarded he was fighting for his life. At the moment the rebels fell back this time, heavy cannonading opened from the other side of the river. Looking around now for the first time since the battle opened, we saw the long lines of the Sixth Corps drawn up on the mountain's side and in the fields at its foot. For some time the enemy had been endeavoring to plant artillery to command our stone wall. Had they succeeded in this, it would have gone hard with us. But ours on the opposite side of the river being on higher ground, soon drove off the guns of the enemy, and now began giving attention to the rebel infantry. The lines were so close to each other that some damage was done to our own men by shells from our batteries. But they kept the rebels discreetly under cover, and from this time, an hour before dark, only desultory firing took place. We dare not retreat, however, as long as that rebel line lay in our front, unless under cover of the darkness. It was long after dark, when we began to cross the river from our position on the right, and we made the crossing without being discovered, or, at least, without being followed or fired upon, while some regiments further to the left, while crossing earlier, met with considerable loss by being followed and fired upon in the river. We carried over all our wounded. I never read of a battle in which so many different regiments claimed to be the "*last to leave the field.*" Lieutenant Keyes, in his history of the 123d Ohio, says : " Our regiment and the 34th Massachusetts, than which there was no braver nor more gallant regiment in the service, were left to protect the rear, and, of course, were the last to effect the crossing." Chaplain W. C. Walker, of the 18th Connecticut, is quoted in " The Military and Civil History of Connecticut in the War of 1861-65 " as saying : " The Eighteenth (Conn.) held its position on the right until flanked, and was the last regiment to recross." Every officer and man in our regiment and in the 4th West Virginia knows that the 18th Connecticut was *not* on that flank when we retired, and they know, further, that our regiment *was* on the extreme right, for over an hour, before the close of the battle, and that the 4th West Virginia was closed on our left all that time, and that when we retired no troops remained on that flank. And we all know, too, that we were *not* flanked, but held our position till we were ordered to retire, after dark. But we leave these various claimants to settle their disputes with the remark that we *all* know the 18th Connecticut was *not* on the right when we fell back across the river, and that, as to the 34th Massachusetts and 123d Ohio, they were on, or towards, the left, and no one on our end of the line can know when they fell back, and, regarding it unimportant which is right, we pass on.

Though the fighting was very desperate, our loss was comparatively small, owing, of course, to the excellent protection afforded us by those friendly stone walls. The following is a list of our killed and wounded in the battle of Snicker's Ferry, which *should* be called the battle of Island Ford:

KILLED.

Samuel L. Hayes, Company B; Joshua Farley, Company G; William Stoneman, Company I; George Lemp, Company H—4.

WOUNDED.

Colonel James Washburn, severely in the head; Sergeant James Hunter, Company A, severely, head; Sergeant Edgar Humphrey, Company I, severely, neck; Privates James Saxton, Company G, severely, neck; Joel B. Cummins, Company G, severely, shoulder; Samuel Dobbins, Company C, severely, side; James McElroy, Company B, severely, thigh; E. S. Clithero, Company D, severely, leg; Leander Eddy, Company A, severely, leg; and Francis M. Byers, Company I, severely, leg—10.

The 4th West Virginia lost one-third its number killed and wounded, mostly, before our arrival. Why the 6th and 19th corps did not come to our assistance, can only be explained on the hypothesis, that it was not thought desirable to bring on a general engagement at that place, and at that time. As we passed through the ranks of the 6th corps, after falling back, the men frequently said to us: "We wanted to go over and help you but they wouldn't let us." "As General Ricketts, commanding the 6th corps, did not think it prudent, under the circumstances, to cross his men, and as the enemy were preparing for another attack on my line, I gave the the order to fall back, which was done in good order." -*General Crook's report, Oct. 12, 1864.*

We again lost several good men killed and wounded. All the killed were choice men. Samuel L. Hayes was a beautiful young boy, only eighteen years of age, whom everybody loved. He was killed on the skirmish line and his body carried back by his comrades. George Lamp, of Company H, was another fine boy of the same age. William Stoneman was one of the very best men of Company I, only 21 years of age. Joshua Farley, of Company G, was but 24 years of age, an excellent soldier and a fine man. His captain, H. L. Karr, writes of him: "Joshua Farley, of Silver Run, Meigs county, was as brave a soldier and as brave a patriot as ever shouldered a musket in defense of his country. His comrades carefully and tenderly laid him in a soldier's grave, a few feet from where he fell, and Company G, officers and men, never had heavier hearts, than when they marched from the grave of that brave soldier."

Sergeant Edgar Humphrey, so badly wounded, came near sacrificing his life, on account of a remark some one had carelessly made derogatory to his personal courage. Several times during the battle he was made to get under cover of the stone wall. He would remain so for only a few minutes, however, when he would rise, and, standing in plain view of the rebel line, load and fire as deliberately and coolly, as if engaged in target practice. I was going to him to make him get down, when he was hit and fell. Kneeling beside him I saw he had received a terrible wound. Recovering soon from the shock he said in a whisper: "Colonel, I guess they won't call me a coward again, will they?" He was too weak then to talk more, but it was afterwards learned that some one had impugned his courage, and here the brave fellow had nearly thrown his life away in order to wipe out the cruel charge. The suffering of his terrible wound, or even death itself, had no pangs compared to what he had silently suffered, till this opportunity came to repel and refute the foul imputation, and, having done it, he was content to die, which he and every one else expected was his fate. A lesson was taught, to the whole regiment, not to be too free in the use of such remarks about any soldier thereafter.

But the most lamentable casualty the regiment met with was the wounding of Colonel Washburn. Just as the regiment reached the right, and before it had been put in position, he was shot in the head, the ball entering the left eye and passing backward and downward through the head, coming out back of and below the right ear. He was struck by a minnie ball at very close range, and the wound was a frightful one. No one expected him to live but a few minutes. He was conveyed across the river during the battle, as we thought, dying. We scarcely hoped to find him alive when we crossed in the evening, but he was, and what was more, fully conscious and able to talk. He inquired anxiously how the regiment had fared, and how it had acquitted itself. And then, after expressing the belief that he could not live, gave his sword and belt, watch, pocket-book, papers, letters, and other small articles, to Lieutenant Colonel Wildes, with the request that they be sent to his family. The surgeons could give no hope of his recovery. The officers and men of the regiment passed by and took his hand gently in theirs, many kissing it and shedding tears as they left his side, for few officers were more sincerely loved by their men than Colonel Washburn was by his. All that night his tent was surrounded by the men, who refused to rest or sleep, while their Colonel, as they supposed, lay dying. Whispered inquiries were made by them of surgeons and attendants as they passed in and out, and as the morning approached, some encouragement was given out of his ultimate recovery. The surgeons claimed to have ascertained that no vital spot had been struck, and in the morning a detail of strong men was made to carefully carry him to Harper's Ferry. There he recovered rapidly, and on the 26th of October he visited the regiment at Cedar Creek, when he was given a royal reception. He had reported by letter to General Crook for duty some time before this; had, in fact, reported for duty within sixty days after he was wounded! He remained several days with the regiment, but did not assume command, having been assigned by General Sheridan as commandant of the Post at Wheeling, West Virginia. During his visit, which was alike pleasant to himself and the regiment, the following circular was issued and read upon the first dress parade the regiment had indulged in since May, and which was held wholly in his honor:

(CIRCULAR.)   HEADQUARTERS 116TH OHIO VOLUNTEER INFANTRY,
           CEDAR CREEK, VA., OCT. 30, 1864.

The Colonel of the regiment embraces this opportunity of tendering his thanks to, and expressing his pride in, the brave officers and men of the 116th regiment. On account of a severe wound he received at Snicker's Ferry in July last, he has not been with you throughout the entire campaign, but he feels proud to say that he belongs to a regiment which has bravely withstood, in the memorable campaign just closed, all the hardships, privations and perils of the march, the bivouac and the battle field. While it was his honored privilege to lead you, he ever found you ready to obey orders; since he has been separated from you he has anxiously and proudly watched your movements. In three of the most stubbornly fought battles of the summer, he has found you always where duty called you, and where good soldiers ought to be, and he has heard only unstinted praise of your conduct. You have made for your regiment a name and a fame that will outlive you all, and to which your children, and your children's children will point with pride in the years of the future.

             JAMES WASHBURN, Colonel.

Officers and men of the 116th:

In your behalf I know I may say that our Colonel's very flattering opinion of his command is reciprocated; that no expression of his esteem for you is too strong to represent your regard for him, and when I assure him that you are as proud of his brave leadership as he is of your prowess. I know I express the honest sentiment of every member of the regiment. He is esteemed by us all as well worthy to be the leader of such men as his pardonable partiality pronounces you to be. It is with sore regret that I have to announce to you that his surgeons and superior officers regard his fearful wound as having unfitted him for active duty with you in the field, and that he is soon to leave us to engage in other less severe and hazardous, though equally honorable and responsible duties. To these duties let us one and all assure him that he carries our love and best wishes, and that he is followed with the earnest hope of a speedy return to his beloved regiment.

WILBERT B. TETERS, Captain Commanding Regiment.

Colonel Washburn never sufficiently recovered to join his regiment, and, of course, he could never entirely recover from such a wound. Its lasting effects are seen in the loss of his left eye, partial paralysis of one side of his face, partial loss of speech, and a general breaking down of his constitution. Doubtless it has shortened his life, which it has made a suffering one, until the end comes. Colonel Washburn possessed great personal courage. He was a leader of men and not a follower. He was bluff, frank and determined, but too kind-hearted to be a good disciplinarian. If an officer or man did anything calling down upon him the penalties of the "Rules and Articles of War," he hardly ever held out until punishment followed, but, as the boys used to say, "the old Colonel would let up." He was a man whom patriotism had made a soldier. His principles were the outgrowth of deep-seated convictions, and his whole army life was alike honorable and creditable to himself and his country. He was in the army, not for the glory or renown of war, but from a sense of duty to his country, and he fought as bravely and suffered as heroically for it as any man ever did.

From the noble Colonel Washburn we recur for a moment to an officer of the regiment who behaved in a most cowardly manner in the battle of Snicker's Ferry. This is the same officer whose misconduct caused the capture of fifty men and a forage train, while we were stationed at Romney. He had acted badly at Piedmont and Lynchburg, and now his peremptory dismissal from the service was recommended by his regimental, brigade, division, corps and army commanders, and on the 9th of August, the order of the War Department arrived dismissing Captain Mathew F. Brown from the service. We had no time for courts-martial in those days, especially when an officer was guilty of cowardice. The captain, himself, explained his dismissal by saying it was because he "couldn't swallow the nigger without grease." The example of such men was intolerably demoralizing, and Secretary Staunton made short work of them, by arbitrarily and peremptorily dismissing them from the service. Captain Brown's dismissal placed company F in command of Lieutenant Wilson F. Martin, a brave and efficient officer, who, it ought to be said for the credit of the company, never faltered himself, nor allowed the company to falter in the presence of the enemy.

A word, before passing on, regarding the characteristic injustice of General Halleck. General Hunter had scarcely returned to the Valley from Lynchburg, before Halleck began a system of persecution and ill-usage toward him, which finally culminated, on the 14th, in Hunter's asking to be relieved from command. Hearing nothing from this request, the next day he wrote to President Lincoln, renewing his request to be relieved, and adding: "When an officer is selected as the scape goat to cover up the blunders of others, the best interests of the country require that he should at once be relieved from command." There had been a disposition at the War Office to cast the whole blame, for all the mischief done by Early, on Hunter. The case was a bad one, and Halleck's instinct for shirking responsibility, and capacity to do any one he did not like an injury, soon selected Hunter as a "scape goat." But the crowd who were bearing down on Hunter, received a most deserving rebuke from General Grant, in a letter he wrote to the War Office on the 15th. Its strong language is unusual for Grant, and for that reason shows the more forcibly the injustice he felt was being done to Hunter, and the directness with which he aimed his rebuke at the authors of the injustice, left no conjecture as to what he meant. He wrote: "I am sorry to see such a disposition to condemn as brave an old soldier as Hunter is known to be, without a hearing. He is known to have advanced into the enemy's country toward their main army, inflicting much greater damage upon them than they have upon us, with double his force, and moving directly away from our main army. Hunter acted, too, in a country where he had no friends. * * * Even the enemy gives him credit for courage, and congratulate themselves that he will yet give them a chance of getting even with him." President Lincoln wrote a conciliatory letter to Hunter, saying, among other things: "General Grant wishes you to remain in command of the Department, and I do not wish to order otherwise." It was a most unfortunate and inopportune time for Halleck to inaugurate one of his quarrels, but it was fortunate that Grant's strong sense of justice was at hand to at once rebuke and stop it. But now Halleck sulked, and it was announced by Dana to Grant: "General Halleck will not give orders, except as he receives them." The result was seen in the blundering and blind pursuit of Early, by Wright from Washington, and Hunter from Harper's Ferry. With the two armies of Wright and Hunter within fifteen miles of each other, the one in Early's rear at Poolesville, and the other on his flank at Hillsboro, neither knew of the other's position during a whole day, and neither would move on the enemy, because Halleck received no orders to move from Grant at City Point. Thus that campaign, ending at Island Ford, was managed. The evil genius of Halleck hovered over it, with an eye single to the defeat and discomfiture of Hunter, whose success would have been his defeat and chagrin, and hence the worst handled and most fruitless campaign of the war.

But still another blunder is to be added to this chapter of blunders. Thinking the 6th, 19th and our corps were in possession of the vicinity of Snicker's Ferry, General Hunter started Colonel R. B. Hayes, with his brigade and two guns, on the 19th, to escort a provision train from Harper's Ferry to the army. Hayes was met at Kabletown with a large body of the enemy, and it was due more to his skill and good management that his train was not delivered to Early, than it was to the knowledge, of any one then in command, of the strength, or whereabouts of either the enemy or our own troops. As it was, Hayes was moving his train in the presence of Early's whole army.

On the next day, the 20th, General Averill and Colonel Duvall met with a victory at Carter's Farm, near Stephenson's Depot, which, according to rebel accounts, was wholly owing to a "blunder" on their part. If it was, it compensated somewhat for the blunders on our side during the past few days. The rebel accounts say that three miles north of Winchester, on Carter's Farm, Ramseur was encountered moving by the flank, intent on capturing Averill. Ramseur supposed, from Vaughn's reconnoisance of the day before, that there were but two or three regiments in his front, which caused him to advance with too little precaution, and thrown into confusion, the troops could not be rallied." The result was a splendid victory for Averill and Duvall, in which they captured 250 prisoners and four pieces of artillery, besides killing and wounding over 200 of the enemy.

CHAPTER IX.

TO WINCHESTER — BATTLE OF KERNTOWN — LIST OF CASUALTIES — RETREAT — REPORT OF GENERAL CROOK — AT HARPER'S FERRY AGAIN — A HOT, HARD MARCH — AT MONOCACY JUNCTION — BACK TO BOLIVAR HEIGHTS — ARRIVAL OF GENERAL P. H. SHERIDAN, 6TH AND 19TH CORPS AND TORBERT'S CAVALRY — DAWN OF A NEW ERA IN THE VALLEY.

On the next day after the battle of Snicker's Ferry, the 6th and 19th corps moved off in the direction of Washington, and the day after their departure, our division crossed the Shenandoah at Snicker's Ferry and went into camp where we remained until the 21st, when we started for Winchester. Arriving there our regiment camped on the same ground we occupied when on our way up the valley in the spring under General Sigel. We here joined the second division under Colonel Duvall. In the forenoon of the 23d our brigade of the first division and Hayes' brigade of the second division went forward on a reconnoisance, advancing about two miles beyond Kerntown. We met but few of the enemy, none till we reached the vicinity of Kerntown. There we encountered a few cavalry, which, without resistance, retired as we advanced. We returned to camp in the afternoon, rather glad the coast was so clear of rebels. General Hayes says in his report of this reconnoisance: "From what was seen of the enemy, as well as what could be learned of citizens, it was believed that the rebel force consisted of about 1,000 cavalry, and two or three pieces of artillery. This was reported to Major General Crook and soon after the brigade was ordered to return." *General Hayes' report, Aug. 8, 1864.*

About 9 o'clock on the 24th, evidence began to thicken that a strong body of the enemy was gathering in our front, and a few brigades were again pushed forward beyond Kerntown. Sharp firing and some cannonading soon ensued, when the whole corps, except a strong train guard, was brought up to the line of battle. As soon as the line was formed it advanced behind a strong skirmish line, and for a time drove the enemy back. But almost as soon as the advance began, the second division was struck on its left flank and rear by an overwhelming force of the enemy, and another large force was detected moving around our right. Our regiment was on the left of our division near the pike and was then near the centre of the line. Orders were at once given to fall back. Early's army of 30,000 was upon our little corps 6,000 or 7,000. The second division was fairly flanked out of its position, by a force far exceeding it in numbers, coming in far to its rear and on its left. Hayes' brigade was on the left, and, when driven back covered the retreat on the right of the pike to Bunker Hill, while ours covered it on the left. Hayes had his horse shot under him and was himself slightly wounded in the head. He displayed great gallantry throughout this engagement and handled his brigade with wonderful skill. In falling back we came upon two pieces of artillery abandoned by our cavalry. The infantry halted and checked the advancing enemy, now close upon us, long enough to haul off the pieces, which was done by hand by a portion of the 36th Ohio, one of Hayes' regiments. Frequently, during the retreat that night, the enemy pushed forward his cavalry with great dash, but it was every time handsomely repulsed. Our regiment behaved splendidly throughout the retreat, scarcely a man straggling from his place. Indeed, the conduct of the whole brigade during the day and night was worthy of all praise. We made a stand between 9 and 10 P. M. at Bunker Hill, where we remained until morning. We had now a large amount of army stores at Martinsburg which must fall into the enemy's hands, unless he was held back long enough to give time to remove them. How it rained that night at Bunker Hill! Before daylight we were under arms, and moving across the creek, soon became engaged in a brisk skirmish with the enemy, who was now pressing us hard with a large force of cavalry, mounted and dismounted, especially on our left flank, which our weak cavalry was unable to cover. We held our position at Bunker Hill until about 9 A. M., when we fell back slowly towards Martinsburg, which we reached about noon, skirmishing all the way, our regiment being rear guard, as the night before. In front of the town, we again drew up in line of battle, and sending out strong skirmish lines, kept up a brisk musketry fire and cannonade until about 4 P. M., when we fell back through the town, where we again halted. The stores had, in the meantime, been all sent out by rail, and our own trains pushed on to Williamsport, under a strong guard. The rebel cavalry occupied Martinsburg as soon as we evacuated it. But we were not yet ready to leave, and while it was yet light, General Crook, with our division and most of the second, charged into the town, giving the rebels a genuine surprise, and drove them pell mell out of the town again, capturing a number of prisoners and horses. Passing through to our former position the other side of town, we lay down in line of battle, and building a long line of camp fires, soon fell back again and retreated to Williamsport, and marched by way of Sharpsburg, Maryland, to Harper's Ferry, where we recrossed the river, and camped at Halltown, four miles south of Harper's Ferry, on the 28th.

Hunter was not on the field, but was at Harper's Ferry. Of the bad conduct of some of the troops, teamsters, etc., General Crook, in his report of the battle, says: "Some of my teamsters got stampeded, and cut loose from their wagons along the road, but their wagons were destroyed, so that nothing fell into the hands of the enemy. I regret to say that the greater portion of my dismounted cavalry, along with some infantry, to the whole number of 3,000 or 4,000, broke to the rear at first fire, and all efforts to stop them proved of no avail. They mostly got into Martinsburg, circulating all manner of reports. A few of them were captured endeavoring to escape my guards. I lost over one-third of my cavalry in this way." *General Crook's report, July 27, 1864.*

This is a sorry picture enough, but it is not overdrawn. This battle settled the question that Early had yet an overwhelming force in the Valley, compared to ours. It also demonstrated that he had largely increased his force of cavalry. Our own teamsters, Dye and McKnight, always cool, took their teams through in good shape. Their example had a good effect upon others. There was no such thing as stampeding them.

General Crook, in his report of the battle, says: "I have the honor to report that on the 24th instant I was attacked by a large force of the enemy at Winchester. I repulsed their force twice, and was driving them, when they partially turned my left, and threw it into some confusion. At the same time a heavy column was moving around my right, and I gave the order to fall back. My left soon reformed, and my whole line re-formed in good order, the enemy pushing both my flanks and center all the time. I got off all my artillery and wagons. * * * I fell back to Bunker Hill, arriving there between 9 and 10 o'clock P. M., part of the enemy's force camping within two miles of me. Next morning the enemy's cavalry pressed my front and commenced turning my flank, and, as I had not sufficient cavalry to ascertain whether his infantry was trying to turn my position, I fell back on Martinsburg. I skirmished with them almost all day, they making demonstrations to turn my flanks. Toward evening I fell back toward Williamsport, when the enemy followed me into town. Supposing they would tell the inhabitants all about their force, intentions, etc., I turned my column back, drove them out of town, and captured a few prisoners. From all the reliable information I could get, the force that attacked me was Early's raiding force, joined by the force left in the Valley when he went into Maryland." * * * "I would also state the enemy has increased his force of cavalry, in the Valley, very materially." *General Crook's report, July 27, 1864.*

The loss of our regiment was one killed — Benjamin G. Patterson, Company B, a few slightly wounded, whose names we have been unable to learn, and eight prisoners, as follows: Corporal Peter Wolf, Company B; William Ball, Company B; John Cole, Company B; Willard Reed, Company B; Corporal Wesley Mickle, Company I; George Bates, Company I; Albert Woodruff, Company I; William Clark, Company K.

The defeat at Kerntown was complete and demoralizing. The dismounted cavalry which broke so shamefully at Snicker's Ferry, repeated the performance here, and some regiments of infantry, and much of the cavalry, did not behave much better, but we are glad to state that none of the troops with Hunter, on the Lynchburg expedition, proved unsteady! Early had sent large bodies of cavalry around our flanks for the purpose of getting in our rear and attacking our trains. The body of cavalry, sent around the left, struck the pike some distance below Winchester, stampeding some of the teamsters, and causing some wagons and caissons to be abandoned and burned. It was here that an artillery officer cut loose his horses and abandoned the two guns mentioned as hauled off by the infantry. "It was owing to the steadiness and good conduct of the infantry which came with us from the Kanawha, that the army was saved from annihilation." *General Hunter's report to General Halleck.*

We were now pretty sick of this sort of campaigning. If the pursuit of Early, in the Loudon Valley, was unskillful, this pursuit, in the Shenandoah, was incautious and reckless. With the knowledge that the 6th and 19th corps had returned to Washington, greater caution should have been exercised in following Early, for, as soon as he learned of their departure, it might reasonably have been expected that he would return down the Valley, unless some of his force had also been sent to Richmond. "Learning, on the 23d, that a large column, sent after him (Early) from Washington, was returning, and that the Army of West Virginia, under Crook, including Hunter's and Sigel's forces, was at Kernstown, he (Early) determined to attack at once." *Jeff Davis' "Rise and Fall of the Confederate Government."*

After relieving Washington, the only purpose, it seemed, of the movement of the 6th and 19th corps toward the Shenandoah Valley, was to follow Early long enough to start him on the retreat, which all seemed to regard as equivalent to his return to Richmond, acting upon which idea they at once fell back to Washington. It was fallacious reasoning, as events proved. Hearing of Crook's defeat, Halleck telegraphed to Grant at 8 P. M. that day: "General Wright, in accordance with your orders, was about to embark for City Point. I have directed him to await your further order. I shall exercise no further discretion in this matter, but shall carry out such orders as you may give." The 6th and 19th corps were immediately ordered back, and part of the 19th united with Crook's corps on the 29th near Halltown. Had there been a better understanding, and more unity of action between Hunter and Wright, there can be no doubt that many of the blunders, from the 14th to the 24 of July, could have been avoided. As it was, no campaign of the war was more disjointed, more fruitless and demoralizing.

In sixteen days we had fought two hard battles, skirmished from Winchester to Martinsburg, much of the time moving in line of battle, and had marched 190 miles. Considering the worn out condition of shoeless men when we reached the Valley on the 12th, their terrible condition now must be left to the reader's imagination, for, even at this distance of time, we have no heart to describe it. We now renewed our requisition for clothing, and, especially, shoes, and lay down to await them, never doubting that now, *surely now*, we would get shoes and clothing for our barefooted, ragged, and dirty men before we were moved again. Before daylight, the morning of the 29th, the Quartermaster and his men were routed out to draw clothing, shoes, etc. Willingly, all hands turned out, and, scarcely stopping to eat during the day, succeeded in getting shoes issued to all in need in the regiment. Over 150 men were barefooted on the recent hard marches. Considerable clothing was also issued, and long after dark the Quartermaster and his men ate their suppers and lay down to rest a few hours, intending to finish issuing early in the morning. The Quartermaster was just ready, on the 30th, with the rest of his stores, including "hard bread," on the ground, when the order to "fall in" was given. In a short time the order to move came, and we took our place on the road. All the corps were on the move. No one on that march will ever forget the fearful heat of that July day, as we marched along side of Maryland Heights. We were started off at a very rapid rate, which was kept up for several miles without a halt. Over 100 of the men of the army died of sun-stroke, and many more than that were seriously affected, and dropped down by the roadside. We passed several by the road who were either dead or dying, and, seeing the effect of such marching, slackened our pace as a mere act of humanity. We thus fell a little to the rear, but soon caught up with the thoroughly exhausted troops resting by the roadside. We marched fifteen miles, and camped near Middletown. The people of this place, on hearing of our coming, set to cooking, and, when we arrived, met us with an abundant meal of everything good. The next day we marched fifteen miles further, the next about the same distance, camping near Wolfesville, and, about noon, on the 3d of August, reached Frederick City, Md. This is a loyal city, true as steel. In the afternoon we moved to within a mile of Monocacy Junction and went into camp. Next day we waded the Monocacy River, and camped near the Junction. We were now on the return trip to the Shenandoah. This marching was to head off Early, from Washington, who was again in Pennsylvania, burning and pillaging. On the 30th, the day we started, he was marching on Chambersburg, which General McCausland wantonly burned late that day. Hearing at Middletown, the next day, that he was retreating, with Averill in pursuit, and another panic occurring in the neighborhood of Frederick, Monocacy and Poolesville, we turned in that direction, to which point the 6th and 19th corps also moved. Here we were greeted with the announcement of another change in commanders. On the 5th of August, General Grant had met Hunter at Monocacy and determined upon a plan of campaign with General Sheridan as commander. On the 6th, General Grant telegraphed to Halleck from Monocacy Junction: "Send Sheridan, by morning train, to Harper's Ferry, calling here, on his way, to see if General Hunter has left. Give him orders to take command of all the troops in the field within his division. General Hunter will turn over to him my letter of instructions." Sheridan arrived at Monocacy that same day, the 6th, and there met Grant and Hunter, and next morning reached Harper's Ferry. Grant returned to Washington the evening of the 6th, and there, next day, caused an order to issue from the War Department, creating the Middle Military Division, out of what then composed the Departments of Pennsylvania, Washington, Maryland and West Virginia, with General Sheridan in command.

The War Department, General Grant, and the government authorities generally, had at last been forced to devote some of its energies to West Virginia and the Shenanhdoah Valley, which, from the beginning of the war, had been treated as though they hardly made a shadow on the troubled field of operations. This Shenandoah Valley, especially, had acquired the soubriquet of "the race ground" in the army and among the people of the country, and Harper's Ferry that of "Harper's Weekly," the title denoting the time of departure and return of armies. Every commander who had entered the Valley had retired "under a cloud" and been labeled "a failure." The troops, whose evil destiny it had been to "occupy it," had been knocked about, whipped, driven and marched up and down it until they had become disheartened, disgusted, and almost demoralized. While they had fought many desperate battles, had won many brilliant victories, and had patiently endured untold hardships, yet they had, withal, suffered so many reverses, had been so thoroughly exhausted by long, fruitless raids and useless campaigns, that they had now arrived at a point where all felt that further endurance "had ceased to be a virtue." "They yearned for a change," and now their hopes began to brighten, and their spirits to revive, as they saw around them ample signs of preparation for another campaign, in which sufficient numbers were to take part to prevent further repetitions of our past disastrous experience. Early had again returned to the Valley, and was now camped at Bunker Hill. It was a satisfaction to us to hear that, on the 7th, Averill had come upon McCausland, at Moorefield, and given him a terrible whipping, capturing 450 prisoners, four pieces of artillery, all he had, all his caissons but one, nearly all his wagons which contained his plunder, over 400 horses, three battle flags, a large number of small arms, killing and wounding a large number, and scattering the rest far and wide through the mountains. Early, in summing up the causes of his misfortunes later in the season, said: "This affair at Moorefield had a very damaging effect upon my cavalry for the rest of the campaign." The infamous act of McCausland, in burning Chambersburg, gave to this annihilating victory over him a peculiar significance, and it earned for General Averill the plaudits of the whole North.

CHAPTER X.

SHERIDAN IN COMMAND — FOR THE FIRST TIME WE ARE PART OF AN ARMY EQUAL TO THE OPPOSING ENEMY — MARCH TO CEDAR CREEK — SKIRMISH ON THREE TOP — MARCH BACK AGAIN — BATTLE OF HALLTOWN, AUGUST 26TH. LIST OF CASUALTIES — BATTLE OF BERRYVILLE, SEPTEMBER 3D. LIST OF CASUALTIES.

A new era had now dawned upon the Valley, and its little army, that had been buffeted about for so long, was now to enter upon a new experience. The 6th and 19th corps were here. Large bodies of cavalry, under the best officers of the army, were arriving from the Potomac Army. Our own men were being well supplied with clothing, well fed, and allowed to rest up thoroughly, without even camp duty to perform. Stragglers, the sick, and the sore and lame from over-marching when barefooted, were flocking to us in large numbers, and we soon showed a good line again. One hundred days men were everywhere relieving veterans from guard and post duty, and our "Army of West Virginia," as Crook's 8th corps was henceforth to be known in history, grew apace in strength and *esprit de corps*. So that when we moved up the Valley, on the 10th of August, Sheridan's army numbered about 40,000 men, of which nearly 10,000 were cavalry, with twenty six-gun batteries. Our corps was on the left, the 6th on the right, and the 19th in the centre. This order was observed throughout the campaign. Our brigade was on the left of the first division, and our regiment on the left of the brigade. The 116th was thus on the extreme left flank of the first line of the army. It occupied this place in every battle of the campaign. Let history tell how it performed the duties of that important position.

On the 10th the whole army moved up the Valley, and we camped that night near Berryville. On the 11th we marched eighteen miles further, much of the time in line of battle, with heavy firing all the afternoon by the cavalry and its artillery in our front. This was a very hot, sultry day, and as we marched, most of the time under cover of woods, where no air was stirring, we suffered terribly from the heat, but our men stood it remarkably well. We were near the Shenandoah River until near the middle of the afternoon and yet our men suffered considerably for want of water, not being allowed to go to the river for it. Sometime before dark, having marched in line of battle for a considerable distance, we were ordered to load. Fred Shofforth, of Company E, had loaded, and, when capping his gun, it was accidentally discharged, killing a fine young soldier of his company named Nathaniel Ady. It was a sad sight to see the poor boy die there from such a careless cause. We buried him decently, and, after prayer by the Chaplain, fired a volley over his grave, at which we placed a head board on which was inscribed his name, company and regiment. We again advanced in line of battle with loaded guns, expecting every minute our cavalry, now hotly engaged close in our front, would open a way for our rifles at the enemy. But as we advanced the carbine firing receded, and ceased altogether at dark, when we went into camp about nine miles from Front Royal. The next morning, the 12th, we changed our line of march, moving off to the right toward Middletown, and going into camp at Cedar Creek, directly under Massanutten Mountain. On the 13th and 14th, the army was engaged in throwing up breastworks,

On the 14th, our pickets advanced and drove the rebels back to Strausburg. We had a good view of the movement from the hill near our right. A signal station we had established on Three Top, the most westerly spur of Massanutten Mountain, was re-enforced. It had been seriously threatened during the day. Next morning, early, the signal station was attacked by the rebels and driven off. Our regiment and the 14th West Virginia were sent out, under Lieutenant Colonel Wildes, to re-establish it, but we found the enemy in too strong force to effect our object. We advanced, skirmishing with the enemy, nearly to the crest of the mountain, but there were met by a large body of rebel infantry, which checked our further progress. The rebels had established a signal station as soon as they drove our men off, and, while we were advancing up the mountain, we could see them signalling their camps below. While we were fighting near the top, the rebels advanced all along the line, and drove our pickets back to the position occupied by them before the advance of the day before. When the rebels advanced on the pickets, a strong body of infantry was sent out from their camps to cut us off. We saw the movement, from our elevated position, and fell back to the foot of the mountain. The officers of the signal corps with us signalled the movement on foot by the rebels to our army, when a force was sent out to intercept it. Upon discovering that we had been re-enforced, the rebel column fell back. We then advanced up the mountain a second time, and our picket line, being strengthened, advanced, and again drove the rebels back to Strasburg. As we were nearing the top again, an order came directing us to fall back to the foot of the mountain, and remain there on picket during the night. That was an exciting night for pickets. Firing was kept up nearly all night. During the night, and again early next morning, brisk cannonading was heard in the direction of Front Royal. Our regiment, and the 14th West Virginia, were relieved from picket about 9 o'clock in the morning, and returned to camp.

But bad news now reached Sheridan, which caused him to make a hasty retreat. On the 16th Custer, Deven and Gibbs, of the cavalry, were confronted at Front Royal with Kershaw's division of infantry, which had taken part in the recent action near Malvern Hill. This explained the artillery firing we had heard the night before. A large force of cavalry also accompanied his division, besides Cutshaw's battallion of artillery. Reliable information showed that Early was now being re-inforced by General R. H. Anderson, commanding the First (Longstreet's) Corps, accompanied by Kershaw's division of infantry, Fitzhugh Lee's division of cavalry, and Cutshaw's battalion of artillery. About the same time McCausland joined him with what was left of his two brigades of cavalry, after his terrible defeat, by Averill, at Moorefield, and also by some scattering commands from the Upper Valley. On the 14th, General Grant sent word to Sheridan that Lee had sent Early "two divisions of infantry, some cavalry, and twenty pieces of artillery," and he requested, "that Sheridan be warned to be cautious, and act on the defensive until movements here, (in the Army of the Potomac), force them to detach to send this way." Again, on the same day, Grant dispatched Sheridan: "The movements on the north side of the James to-day, developed the presence of Field's division of Longstreet's corps, which, I supposed, had gone to the Valley. Picketts' division is also here. * * * It is now positive that Kershaw's division has gone, but no other infantry." Sheridan was thus fully advised of the approaching re-enforcements by Grant himself, but his cavalry had also discovered their approach. Grant further said, in his dispatces to Sheridan. "This re-inforcement to Early, will put him nearer on an equality with you in numbers than I want to see, and will make it necessary for you to observe more caution about attacking." The position then occupied by Sheridan, at Cedar Creek, was a very bad one. It was entirely indefensible. Sheridan saw, and knew this, and so informed Grant as soon as possible after reaching it. And it will be observed, hereafter, that Sheridan never took but two positions, in the Valley, when he deemed it necessary to assume a safe one, viz: the position at Halltown, and the Clifton-Berryville line. On the night of the 15th, the 19th corps fell back to Winchester, and on the night of the 16th, the 6th corps, and ours, followed. On the morning of the 17th, the enemy saw our vacant camps, from Three Top, and followed us at once. Resting a short time at Winchester, we marched to Berryville, where, about 3 P. M., on the 17th, we went into camp. Custer, Devin and Gibbs fell back before Kershaw's infantry; and Lee's cavalry, from Front Royal towards Winchester, following the infantry column, literally destroying, as they fell back, everything upon which man or beast could feed. A Richmond paper of the time said: "With their immense cavalry they extended their lines from Front Royal, in Warren County, to the North Mountains, west of Strasburg, and burnt every bushel of wheat, in stack, barn or mills, in Frederick, Warren, or Clark, as well as oats and hay, they have left absolutely nothing in these three counties. They drove before them every horse, cow, sheep, hog, calf and living animal from the country. What the people are to do, God only knows. General Early, two weeks ago, gave orders not to have a bushel of grain taken from below Strasburg, as hardly enough was left for the citizens."

On the 18th we changed our position, moving about five miles north of Berryville. On the 20th we moved to the vicinity of Clifton, now occupying the Clifton-Berryville line, the enemy closely following us. About 11 P. M., we fell back to the vicinity of Charlestown, the army now stretching from the Shenandoah to beyond Summit Point. We worked all that night throwing up breastworks, and the next day, about 8 A. M., Early came up with Rhodes' and Ramseuer's divisions, and attacked the left of the 6th corps and the right of ours, and fighting continued till dark. During the day, our brigade was sent across to the support of our right, and engaged the enemy, driving him from our front. The 6th corps advanced upon the enemy in its front, driving him back until it came upon his main line, falling back to its original position at dark. Had not Merritt at Berryville, and Wilson at Summit Point, checked Anderson, there would have been a general engagement that day, and probably a hard and doubtful battle fought. It was the purpose of Early and Anderson to have made a combined attack on Sheridan, but the efforts of Merritt and Wilson prevented Anderson joining Early from Winchester, where he had been lying since our retrogade from Cedar Creek. That night Sheridan withdrew Merritt and Wilson, and the army fell back, and took a position on Bolivar Heights at Halltown, its right resting on the Potomac, its left on the Shenandoah. A letter written from Halltown by Quartermaster Sergeant Walker, under date of August 30th, 1864, speaking of the movement of August 21st, says:

"SUNDAY, AUGUST 21ST — Without thinking what I was doing, or intending to do anything wrong, I read a *chapter* in my *Testament* this morning, but the boys said as it was my first offense, and if I promised to reform, they would let the matter drop. About 10 o'clock, the 123d Ohio were ordered out on a foraging expedition. Through some mistake, the whole brigade started, and were not halted till we had gone some distance, when we were turned back, and camped in almost the same place we were in before. Before pitching tents, the men set to work cleaning up the camp, which being done, they were putting up their tents as neatly as they could, as though they expected to remain some time. They had not pitched more than half of them when we were ordered to move immediately. We had heard heavy cannonading for some time in our front, and there seemed to be a pretty severe fight going on. Crook's command, to which we belong, went to the extreme front, our regiment being in front of the brigade. After taking a position on the line, we went to work building breastworks of rails, logs and whatever else was convenient. After they were finished, Colonel Thoburn, commanding the division, rode by and spoke to one of the men, asking him if they had 'got the works so they would turn rebel bullets,' and being answered in the affirmative, he said: 'Well, now, sit down and take it easy, *very easy*, for you may stay here three or four weeks.' Very cool, I thought, considering there was a greatly superior force in our front. At midnight, Sunday, we broke camp and fell back to Halltown, four miles from Harper's Ferry. Passing through Charlestown, our bands played 'John Brown's Body,' etc., much to the annoyance of the citizens of the place."

In Walker's diary, under date of the 22d, I find the following singular entry: "Found our regiment in the extreme front. Got a canteen of whisky and sent out to the officers." After a great deal of inquiry among the officers, I concluded that Walker was mistaken about this. Not an officer had the slightest recollection of such an event. So, thinking he might have some explanation he would wish to make, I wrote him regarding it, and received from him the following terse reply: "*That canteen of whisky was sent to you, if you must know.*" It will be seen that this proved a clear case of too much "cross-examination."

The position of the army here was exceedingly strong, and we immediately set to work making it stronger, by building entrenchments. While our infantry now probably outnumbered that of the enemy, and was daily increasing by accessions from the sick, wounded and those exhausted and straggling from the Lynchburg raid, and the hard marches of July, their cavalry far outnumbered ours, and so roamed the country at will. To meet them in this respect, General Wilson's division of cavalry was brought over from the Army of the Potomac, which joined us at Winchester on the 17th. We had now with us such riders as Torbert, Merritt, Custer, Wilson, Devin, Averill, Powell, Lowell, Gibbs and Duffié, a grand host in themselves, and we heard no more of rebel cavalry raids in our rear. Harper's Ferry, our depot of supplies, was close behind us, and the army was kept daily well supplied.

This retrograde movement had been made for several reasons, but mainly because of the heavy re-enforcements received by Early, and the instructions of Grant to "act on the defensive, until Lee was compelled to detach troops from Early to meet his necessities at Richmond." But now Sheridan was watching every movement of the enemy to detect the very moment any of his troops were sent away. While Early's principal object seemed to be to keep the Baltimore & Ohio Railroad torn up, Sheridan's sole purpose was to destroy Early's army at the first opportunity. Hence active and heavy reconnoisances were sent out from his entrenched position almost daily. A reconnoisance of our brigade on the 24th revealed a change in the enemy's position. We met with no loss. Major Morris, who had been at home since the 9th, on leave of absence on account of sickness in his family, returned to the regiment on the 26th, but in citizen's dress. His resignation had been tendered during his absence, and was a surprise to all. We were sorry to lose him from our numbers. Major Morris was an excellent officer, always prompt in the discharge of every duty, and as a man, was courteous and gentlemanly toward all, officers and men alike.

Cavalry fighting, with varied results, was continuous until the 26th, when, in the afternoon, our brigade was sent out on a reconnoisance in our front, and also to burn some grain and hay stacks, behind which the enemy were sheltered. The 116th had the advance on this occasion, and meeting the enemy's skirmishers soon after starting, it pressed them back to the cover of their artillery, capturing a number of prisoners. The reconnoisance demonstrated the presence of only General Anderson's force, and he did not return to the line from which he was driven, but fell back that night to Stephenson's Depot, where the cavalry found him next day, and where he was confronted by the advance of the 19th corps next day. On the day before, the 25th, Early, with the divisions of Rhodes, Ramseur, Gordon and Wharton, and most of his cavalry, moved past our right to Shepherdstown, leaving Anderson in our front with only Kershaw's division and Cutshaw's artillery. Early attacked our cavalry, under Torbert, between Leetown and Kearneysville, and drove them off the field, nearly all of it returning to Halltown. Custer, however, being cut off, escaped through Shepherdstown. If it was Early's object to draw Sheridan out of his intrenchments, he failed, for all Sheridan did was to send his large body of cavalry across the river into Maryland, there to confront Early and to watch him if he made an attempt to cross into Maryland and Pennsylvania. Whatever Early's purpose was, the next day, the 26th, he marched back to Leetown, and the following day to Bunker Hill.

The loss of the 116th in the affair of the 26th, was as follows:

KILLED.

Private George W. Matchett, Company C.

DIED OF WOUNDS.

Corporal Jacob C. Sidders, Company I; Miles H. Davis, Company C.

WOUNDED.

Sergeant Major William J. Lee, side, slight; Corporal Jerome McVeigh, Company A, right hand, slight; Corporal J. C. Sidders, Company I, died; Private Elza J. Hill, Company A, right arm, slight; Private Emanuel Keylor, Company A, thigh, slight;

Private John A. Harmon, Company A; Corporal Abner G. Carlton, Company C, thigh, severely; Miles H. Davis, Company C, died; Charles D. Watson, Company C, hip, slight; Sergeant A. G. Jackson, Company D, hip, slight; Sergeant James K. Denm, Company D, side, slight; Private Isaac Price, Company D, thigh, slight; Private William L. Morris, Company D, shoulder; Private James D. Ferrill, Company D, knee, slight; Private Charles Dirkus, Company E, knee, severely; Private Christian Miller, Company E, bowels, slight; Private Martin Thoner, Company E, knee, slight; Sergeant Leander Shaae, Company F, head, slight; Sergeant Mathias Rucker, Company F, foot, slight; Corporal Silas King, Company F, very severely; (the ball passed in at mouth and came out between the shoulders;) Private Amos S. Jones, and captured, died in Salisbury prison, March, 1865; Private L. Elaw, Company F, leg, slight; Sergeant Benjamin F. Sammons, Company H, hip slight; Sergeant William A. Arnold, Company H, knee, severely; Private James R. Finley, Company I, leg, slight; Private Charles Watson, Company I, shoulder, slight; Private Jesse Burton, Company I, side, slight.

PRISONER.

Henry King, Company F.

Killed, 3; wounded, 25; prisoner, 1.

Colonel Wells says, in his report of this engagement: "The 116th Ohio and 5th New York were ordered to clear the woods, the 34th Massachusetts to charge across the open field and fire the stacks after the woods should be cleared. The 123d Ohio was held in reserve. The enemy's skirmishers were driven easily from the woods by our skirmish line. After our skirmishers were all in and were formed, Colonel Thoburn directed the skirmishers to charge through the woods. This we did, but as soon as our line entered it, we received a very heavy fire from a line of woods to our right across the pike. Intrenchments having been thrown up along the edge of these woods, and a strong skirmish line firing from these, within easy range, and directly upon our flank, made the small piece we were ordered to hold almost untenable. Our line quickly changed front to the right, and a portion of it charged across the pike, driving the enemy back from the edge of the woods occupied by them. I withdrew them as soon as possible, and formed in the edge of my own woods, parallel with and facing the pike. I sent two companies through to the part of the woods toward Charlestown, and then directed the

34th Massachusetts to move down to burn the stacks. This was soon done. Meanwhile the line in the woods was exchanging fire across the pike with the enemy and losing men fast. After I saw the 34th moving back, I began to withdraw the line from the woods. Just as I was doing this, I received Colonel Thoburn's order to fall back. The 116th Ohio and 34th Massachusetts were steady and gallant as usual. The casualties were nine killed, fifty-six wounded and one missing."— *Colonel Wells' report, August 26th, 1864.*

It will be seen that our loss of twenty-eight killed and wounded was a large share of the whole. It was the right wing of our regiment that drove the rebel skirmishers back from the edge of the woods by a charge across the pike, and it was in this charge we met our greatest loss.

From the appendix to George E. Pond's "Shenandoah Valley," I take the following extract from what purports to be an "Official Diary of First Corps Army Northern Virginia":

"AUGUST 26TH.— Enemy in position, and quiet until afternoon about five o'clock, when he advanced four or five regiments of infantry and one of cavalry to feel our lines. The picket line of the 15th South Carolina regiment, Kershaw's brigade, breaks, and one hundred men of it are captured. The enemy soon retires. During the night we hear of Early, who is at Leetown."

The 1st and 2d brigades of the 2d division attacked the rebel picket line farther to the left on the 26th, at the same time we moved out on the right. General Hayes was in command, and in his report he says: "On the 26th of August, my brigade, in connection with the 2d brigade, attacked the rebel picket line with decided success. My loss was three killed and twenty-one wounded. The loss of the enemy was 104 officers and men captured, and about 150 killed and wounded."

From a letter written August 27th, 1864, I extract the following: "We were in a fight yesterday in which our regiment lost one killed and twenty-six wounded. The 5th New York lost five killed and thirty-seven wounded. We took 103 prisoners, and drove the enemy from his position. This morning there is no enemy visible in our front. There is a movement of the rebels in some direction. The 19th corps is moving out towards Charlestown in pursuit. None of my officers were touched yesterday. The whole regiment behaved gallantly." The prisoners are evidently the same mentioned in General Hayes' report, and in General Anderson's memoranda. On the 28th, the army moved out to our old position of a week before, two miles beyond Charlestown, and then fell back to Charlestown. It must be borne in mind that we never passed through Charlestown without singing:

"John Brown's body lies a moulding in the tomb,
    His soul goes marching on."

On the 1st of September, Corporal Sidders, of company I, thought to be killed in the reconnoisance at Halltown, on the 26th of August, turned up with a broken leg. He had suffered terribly with his broken limb, to which no care had been given, and afterwards died of his wound. Walker's record says of him: "Poor fellow! He was a brave soldier and a good boy, one that will be missed in the company and at home." Sergeant McKinzie, of company G, died in hospital at Sandy Hook, August 26th. These were two fine young soldiers and excellent men, and were a great loss to their companies and the service.

On the 3d of September, the army moved forward to the vicinity of Berryville, where our corps came upon the enemy. It had a very sharp fight. The 116th had four wounded, as follows: Privates Leonard Craig, company H, leg, severe; Benjamin Larrick, company H, hand, severe;

John Harman, company A, nose, slight; George Bates, company I, hand, severe. Benjamin Larrick died of his wounds, October 2d, 1864, at Frederick, Maryland. We had gone into camp, and were cooking supper, when firing was heard on our picket line. Pans and kettles were dropped at once, and we moved up rapidly to the front, and took the position assigned us, where we lay down and sent out skirmishers. Some of our officers then went out to the front to see what was there, as there was no firing in our immediate vicinity. Suddenly a terrible fire opened on the regiments on our right and left, our brigade having been thrown into a gap existing between our second division and the 19th corps. The regiments fired upon stampeded in a panic, which, for the moment, also seized ours, and for the first and only time during its term of service, it fell back without orders. It was rallied by the officers a few rods to the rear, however, when we all had a good laugh, at our own expense, over our "panic." The men were more ashamed of being caught in a "panic," than of any and all the little escapades of their lives, and never quite forgave themselves for it. However, no harm resulted, for the halt was so quickly made that the disaster which might have followed too far a retreat was averted. But we found ourselves alone now, far to the front, without anything for some distance on our right or left, and the rest of the panic-stricken troops not coming back very promptly, we were ordered to fall back to a new line, forming behind a stone wall, some distance to the rear of our first position. Our men went back very reluctantly, for they wanted to wipe out, then and there, what they felt was a stain on their good name. Several of the officers wanted to charge anyhow, before falling back, and the men were as eager for it as they. With the officer who brought the order to fall back, was sent a request to Colonel Thoburn to "bring back the skedaddlers to this line and let us charge," but very soon a peremptory order came, and, reluctantly, the regiment retired to the position assigned it, and as events proved, we were none too soon in making the movement, for the rebels poured after us, close up to the stone wall, and occupied a stone house a short distance from our front. From this we soon dislodged them, taking possession of it ourselves, and we made good use of it in driving the line in the rear of it back a safe distance from our front. We lay in line of battle all that night, and the morning found the army entrenched and ready for what the day might bring forth.

The affair at Berryville was the result of pure accident. It was not brought on by intention on either side. A few days before this, Lee had recalled General Anderson, and the force that came with him to Early on the 16th of August at Fisher's Hill. Grant had been "hammering away" at Lee, and now his necessities compelled him to recall Anderson. Not knowing that an hour before we had moved across the Berryville pike, Anderson, on his way to pass through Ashby's Gap, and thence to Richmond, fairly stumbled upon our corps as some of it was going into camp. The impression given to our commanders was that Early was disputing the ground with us, and had met us there to give us battle, whereas our presence was not known to Early at all, until the head of Anderson's marching column blundered upon our camps. Had the actual situation been known to Sheridan, he could have destroyed Anderson, for Early, with the rest of his army, was several miles away. But it was a complete surprise to both sides, and so each fought shy of the other, and did more feeling and reconnoitering than fighting. Daylight seemed to shed no light on the affair of advantage to either side, and so, after bringing nearly all his force from Winchester to Anderson's assistance, and demonstrating a little towards our now well entrenched line, Early and Anderson both withdrew beyond the Opequan. We were again on the Clifton-Berryville line, and that morning our corps fell back to Clifton, where it went into camp. None of the men of the 116th will ever forget the "lecture" they received on the subject of "panics," and the office of the word "halt" in military matters.

From Walker's record, I take the following account of this affair at Berryville. "About 5 P. M., we moved forward once more, and went into camp on the right of the town. We had not got settled, when an order came to fall in immediately, which we did, and moved out by the right flank about half a mile and formed in line in the woods. Scarcely had we formed, when the enemy opened a severe fire on the left of our brigade, the 123d Ohio, and a regiment on our right, causing both to break and leave the field in some disorder. This left our regiment in danger of being flanked, and a portion began to fall back. The flanking was prevented by the whole regiment falling back to a large house and reforming, when they again went to the front, determined to stay. Lieutenant Colonel Wildes and Captain Teters displayed great gallantry, as indeed they always do. Those of us who had horses in charge fell back as the balls came whistling past us."

We now had a splendid army, and all felt that we could whip the enemy, and were impatient to be at it. Up to this time, from early in the spring, and, for that matter, from June the year before, we had had an almost uninterrupted series of reverses, owing to the undisputed fact that we had invariably been contending with vastly superior numbers.

CHAPTER XI.

AN AMBULANCE TRAIN CAPTURED AND RE-CAPTURED — ACTION TAKEN BY THE OFFICERS, ON HEARING OF THE DEATH OF CAPTAIN KEYES — ANOTHER ACCIDENT IN THE REGIMENT — SHERIDAN'S OPPORTUNITY — GETTING READY FOR A FIGHT — BATTLE OF OPEQUAN, SEPTEMBER 19TH — ANOTHER GALLANT CHARGE — LIST OF CASUALTIES — COLONEL WELLS' REPORT — A MAJOR'S REPORT OF OUR CHARGE.

Before entering upon what followed, we must record some further incidents of our regimental history. On the 5th of September, Moseby attacked and captured our ambulance train, which for some reason had been allowed to depart from Harper's Ferry without a guard. The train was in charge of Lieutenant Ransom Griffin, of the 116th, who had some time before been detached to the ambulance corps. Accompanying it were several officers returning to their commands, among whom was Lieutenant Colonel Kellogg, of the 123d Ohio. They were somewhat in advance of the train when Moseby made his attack upon it. Colonel Kellogg put spurs to his horse, and soon reaching a cavalry post, induced twenty men to follow him back, and attacking Moseby and his gang, they re-captured the train and brought it safely into camp. Colonel Kellogg's dashing act made him the hero of the hour. Next day Lieutentant Griffin made his appearance, not having been released by Colonel Kellogg's dashing act, but having made his escape during the night. It was reported of Lieutenant Griffin, that he charged the rebels with his "stretcher corps," and would have driven them off had all behaved as bravely as he did.

On the morning of the 8th, our corps was moved from the extreme left to the extreme right of the army. We were now not far from Smithfield, and only about five miles from Bunker Hill. The news of the fall of Atlanta was confirmed. Our Sutler came up for the first time since we started for Lynchburg in the spring. We heard to-day for the first time, of the death of Captain Keyes, at Lynchburg, Va., on the 19th of July. On the 10th, the officers met and adopted the following resolutions in respect to him:

"CAMP IN THE FIELD, SEPTEMBER 10TH, 1864.

At a meeting of the officers of the 116th Regiment O. V. I., held in reference to the death of Captain Edwin Keyes, Captain Mallory was called to the Chair, and Lieutenant Wm. Bidenharn was appointed Secretary. The object of the meeting having been stated by Lieutenant Colonel Wildes, on motion, it was voted that a committee of three be appointed by the Chairman to draft resolutions for the occasion. The Chairman appointed Lieutenant Colonel Wildes, Captain W. B. Teters and Captain James P. Mann that committee, who reported the following:

WHEREAS, We hear with unfeigned sorrow and the deepest heart-felt regret, of the death of Captain Edwin Keyes, of Company B, 116th Regiment Ohio Infantry Volunteers, at Lynchburg, Va., July 19th, 1864, Therefore

Resolved, That in the death of Captain Keyes, we are deprived of the society of a fine Christian gentleman, a polished scholar, a brave and gallant officer, and the service and the country of a true, noble and earnest patriot.

Resolved, That in his loss we mourn another sacrifice on the altar of our common country; that the gallant charge in which he received his death wounds, while thus again brought terribly vivid to our minds, is made the more sacred to our memory, because of the precious lives that were there laid down.

Resolved, That we tender his bereaved wife, family and friends our warmest sympathy, and direct them to seek consolation in Him Who holds the destiny of nations in his hands, and Who only can support them under the weight of their great affliction.

Resolved, That a copy of these resolutions be sent to the family of the gallant dead, and to the Pomeroy Telegraph, Athens Messenger, Marietta Register, Spirit of Democracy and Noble County Republican.

On motion of Lieutenant A. W. Williams, Quartermaster of the regiment, the resolutions were adopted after a few pertinent and feeling remarks from Lieutenant Colonel Wildes, reviewing the gallant conduct of the deceased.

THORNTON MALLORY, Chairman.

WILLIAM BIDENHARN, Secretary.

On the 10th of September, Corporal George K. Campbell, of B, who had been for some time on recruiting service in Ohio, was discharged from the 116th and promoted to a captaincy in the 174th Ohio Volunteers, Colonel John S. Jones, of Delaware, Ohio, commanding. Captain Campbell commanded company E in that regiment. Desiring to learn how he sustained the name and fame of his first love, I wrote General Jones and received a long letter in reply, in which he speaks in the most flattering terms of our Corporal. The 174th saw much fighting and severe service, being among the troops which beat off Hood from Murfreesboro in December, 1864, and afterwards was sent with the 20th corps, to Newbern, North Carolina, and joined General Sherman at Goldsboro, after fighting a hard battle at Kingston. The regiment, though a one year's organization, took part in five different engagements, in all of which it reflected credit upon Ohio soldiers. General Jones says of our Corporal: "Captain George K. Campbell was one of the most efficient officers in this gallant regiment. He was with it continually in every march and in every battle, and never omitted, or failed in, a single duty." That Captain Campbell should deserve and sustain, as he did, the character and reputation of one of the most worthy and efficient company commanders in such a regiment was what his old comrades of the 116th would expect of him, and was the fitting close of an honorable and gallant military record.

On the 13th, General McIntosh, of the cavalry, made a dash up the Berryville pike, and captured the whole of the 8th South Carolina regiment of infantry, numbering fourteen officers and ninety-two men. He captured two officers and thirty-five men besides, which, it was said, represented no less than six different Virginia mounted organizations. George E. Pond, Esq., in his "Shenandoah Valley in 1864," gives the number present, for duty, in Terry's brigade of

Gordon's division at this time as 858, and states that the brigade consisted of fourteen Virginia regiments. York's brigade, of the same division, he says, had on August 20th, 1864, present for duty, 614 officers and men, and that the brigade consisted of ten Louisiana regiments. These figures show how depleted were the ranks of many rebel regiments at that time.

On the night of the 13th, another sad occurrence took place in the 116th. It seems that a camp guard, half dreaming, fired his gun, which badly wounded two men of company A. One of them, Private Wilson Danford, had his leg amputated, and afterwards died. The man who fired the gun was subsequently found to be insane.

On the 14th, Lieutenant Gottlieb Sheifley, of company K, obtained leave of absence on the ground of dangerous illness of his wife. Instead of going home, he went straight to Washington, and tendered his resignation *in person* to President Lincoln. The President looked at him a moment, and then sat down and endorsed his resignation as follows:

" To E. M. Stanton, Secretary of War:

"Accept this man's resignation. An officer who will tender his resignation in person to the President, does not know enough to be in the service.
A. LINCOLN."

But Lieutenant Sheifley was out of the service, which was what he most wanted, just at that time of great promise of hard fighting. To say that our officers were indignant, when they heard of his conduct, but faintly expresses their feelings.

On the 14th of September, General Anderson again started for Richmond, taking with him Cutshaw's artillery, and leaving General Fitzhugh Lee's cavalry, this time passing through Chester Gap, thus avoiding the risk of another accidental battle on the way. Sheridan heard of it the evening of the 15th. Now was Sheridan's opportunity, and we will soon see how he improved it. On the 18th, we received orders to be ready to march next morning. That evening surgeon's call was given, with the view of sending all not fit for duty to the rear. Private Charles Fulton, of company E, reported, among others, to be excused and sent back, but the Doctor refused to excuse him. He started for his tent, but before going 100 feet, he fell to the ground dead. It was afterwards ascertained that he died of heart disease, though nothing of the sort was before suspected. His death created a great sensation in the regiment, and a great outcry was made against our Surgeon, Dr. Shannon, but when the true state of the facts were known, the feeling against him at once subsided.

On the 16th of September, the army was visited by General Grant, though few knew it until long afterwards outside of General Sheridan and his staff. Seeing that all Sheridan wanted was permission to attack the enemy, General Grant gave him the laconic order, "Go in," and returned to City Point. Three days afterwards the great battle of Opequan was fought and won.

The 6th and 19th corps took the advance towards Winchester, before daylight on the morning of the 19th. Firing commenced before they were fairly started, and increased in volume until noon, when the steady roar, which indicates the heavy engagement, set in. We were held in reserve where the Berryville pike crosses the Opequan, until about 2 P. M., when we hurriedly pushed to the front. Crossing the creek, we passed rapidly forward, along a narrow gorge skirted by woods. The road was crowded with artillery, caissons, ammunition wagons, ambulances, prisoners, wounded men, field hospitals, and all the debris which indicates a hard battle at the front. With difficulty we made our way through all this, and about 3 o'clock we formed in a ravine behind a piece of woods, in front of which was a brigade of the 19th corps, heavily engaged and fronting the enemy's left wing. Marching forward in two compact lines, we passed through the woods, to the right of the 19th corps' brigade. Our division was on the left in two lines, the second on the right, in the same formation, and the 116th in its accustomed place, on the left in the front line. Before our arrival on the field, the 6th and 19th corps had met with a reverse, the first and second lines having been driven back to the third before a check was given to the enemy. General Sheridan, getting his batteries into a position from which they were enabled to silence the enemy's guns, his lines again advanced, and retook the position from which they had been driven, and held it until the arrival of General Crook. "Then," as a historian remarks, "followed one of the most fiercely contested battles of the war." Large bodies of cavalry were forming to our right for a charge, as we were taking our position, and just as we moved forward, away the great mass went around the rebel left. As soon as the movement began, several bands struck up the liveliest and most soul stirring music. It was a very novel and thrilling scene.

Scarcely were our guns loaded, and our bayonets fixed, before the bugles sounded the charge, which was repeated by every officer in the two lines, and, with a loud cheer, our whole corps threw itself with desperate valor upon the enemy's left wing and flank. For thirty minutes the battle that ensued was perfectly terrific, but then the forces in our front gave way, and in an instant we were over their works, and after them with yells and shouts of victory. The enemy's line still remained intact to our left. All the way across in the charge, the 116th received an enfilading fire from it, which turned back its left to such an extent that when it reached the enemy's works, the left wing went over them almost by the flank. Changing front now to the left, under fire, and without even stopping to adjust our line, or waiting for others to join us, we charged down upon the enemy's flank behind his works, and before he had time to change front to meet us, our bullets were whistling down his line, and we were upon him with the bayonet. We swept his line out from behind his works for a long distance, in fact, clear down to a stone wall which ran at right angles to his first line, a quarter of a mile from where we first charged on his flank. The 10th West Virginia regiment, from the second line, had been sent in on their flank just before we reached the rebel works, but we were only a moment behind it in its support. Driving the rebels out from their works in these woods, and seeing that they were again under good cover behind the stone wall in our front, we were ordered to halt, rest and re-form. Our own fire in front, and the fire of a brigade of the 19th corps, in which was the 116th New York, on their flank, soon drove them away from that part of the wall, but they still held it further to our right. While we lay here, it was with the greatest difficulty the men were restrained from making another charge, so eager were they to finish the work so well begun. As illustrating the ardor and enthusiasm of the men, Corporal Henry T. Johnson, of company H, who was a color bearer that day, did not, and would not halt when the command was given, but ran on several rods to the front, waving his colors, and calling back to the men to "come on." Lieutenant Colonel Wildes ordered him to return, but he would not come. Some of the color guard were then sent forward to bring him and the colors back to the regiment. They returned without him or the colors, but they brought the following message from the Corporal to the Lieutenant Colonel: "Tell Colonel Wildes to come on! We can finish this job just as well as not, and capture those d—d rebel flags." And there he remained, holding his colors aloft, midway between the lines, until they were riddled with balls, and he was severely wounded. When we again received orders to move, we took the gallant wounded Corporal with us, he still clinging to his colors with one arm, the other being disabled. No one had the heart to punish him for disobedience of orders. Moving off to the right, we soon charged the rebel line again, driving it from the stone wall mentioned above. Again advancing, we formed in front of the enemy's inner and last line. In forming the new line, our regiment in the prolongation, was placed on a side hill, facing a rebel battery, which at once opened fire upon us. We were within very close range, and every discharge brought their missles very close to our ranks. Word was sent to Colonel Wells, and permission asked to advance to the rise of ground, on the crest of which the rebel battery was planted, but before a reply could be returned, shells began to drop among us, and the regiment was ordered to advance to a place pointed out, directly under the guns, but protected from them by the formation of the ground. It ran down the hill, and up the next slope until near the top, when the men lay down and crawled along until they got sight of the battery, upon which they now opened a rapid fire, and very soon entirely silenced it, by shooting down some, and keeping the rest of the gunners from the guns. Here, again, the officers had difficulty in holding the men from charging the battery, which they had now silenced by their fire, and which seemed an easy prize. But we had already moved forward several rods without orders, and a second such move might bring down upon us the wrath of our brigade commander, especially should disaster follow our further advance. It is probable we should have charged the battery anyhow, had not Colonel Wells sent an aide up to reprimand us for moving forward without orders, and directing us to advance no further till ordered to do so. At this juncture, Custer came gallantly sweeping down the right, inside the enemy's works. Then it would have required more than orders to keep us from attempting to be the first to reach those guns, and away the regiment dashed in splendid style, the brave young aide joining us, and scaling the parapet, we flung our colors over the guns. Almost at the same instant, the whole of the infantry dashed forward on a furious charge, and the battle of Opequan was won, and, as Sheridan telegraphed to Washington that night, "the enemy was sent whirling through Winchester." Three thousand prisoners, fifteen battle flags, five pieces of artillery, two of those in the works we charged, were the trophies of the victory.

The loss of our army was about 5,000 killed and wounded, that of the rebels about 4,000. They abandoned their dead and wounded, leaving 3,000 of the latter in Winchester, and their dead on the field. The 116th lost six killed, and twenty-nine wounded, as follows:

KILLED.

Orville S. Hetzer, Company B; Lewis C. Secoy, Company B; Charles Schafer, Company E; Corporal Peter Yoho, Company F; John A. McElwee, Company H; George Sigler, Company K.

WOUNDED.

Corporal Jerome McVeigh, Company A, neck, slight; John Drake, Company A, foot, severe; John Hoy, Company A, thigh, severe; James H. Stewart, Company B, stomach, slight; Corporal D. F. Sears, Company C, head, severe; Emmon H. Beardmore, Company C, head, severe; Jacob Mishnack, Company C, thigh, severe; Wm. Montgomery, Company C, thigh, slight; W. W. Wheaton, Company C, groin, slight Second Lieutenant W. H. Moseley, Company H, thigh, severe; Corporal Henry T. Johnson, color bearer, arm, severe; Mathew B. Moore, Company H, leg, severe; John W. Williams, Company H, leg, severe; Isaiah Tribby, Company H, shoulder, severe; Yoho Watson, Company H, head, severe; Israel L. Hamilton, Company D, leg, severe; Peter Beaver, Company D, thigh, severe; Sergeant Mathew Atkinson, Company E, leg, severe; Milton Mozena, Company E, head, severe; Dallas Gillmore, Company E, side, severe; Corporal Lewis W. Mozena, Company E, arm, severe; I. Phelps, Company F, groin, severe; Joshua Mercer, Company F, ankle, severe; Samuel R. Halliday, Company G, leg, severe; J. H. Harman, Company G, finger; John J. Norris, Company I, foot, severe; William McNeil, Company K, arm, severe; Daniel D. Weddle, Company K, knee, severe.

All of these were severely wounded, except four, namely: Jerome McVeigh, James H. Stewart, Wm. Montgomery, and W. W. Wheaton. Lieutenant Moseley was made a cripple for life, from a very severe wound received in the thigh. He was a most excellent officer in every sense. His genial, good natured disposition, made him friends of all who met him, and he was greatly missed ever afterwards by us all. The loss of the 116th would have been very much larger in the first charge, owing to the enfilading fire of the enemy, but for a rail fence on our left, and for the relief given us by the gallant 10th West Virginia. Some of our officers, who went over the field after the battle, to bury the dead and care for the wounded, reported that fence "a paying lead mine." That night we went into camp on the spot near Winchester, upon which we had camped twice before since starting out in the spring.

This battle was a very important one to the Union cause. The President ordered 100 guns to be fired by all the Union armies, in honor of Sheridan and his victorious troops. The feeling of rejoicing among our men, especially in Crook's corps, was almost beyond bounds. It was our first solid victory since the battle of Piedmont, though in that time we had fought seven or eight battles. Early said in his report: "As soon as the firing was heard in rear of our left flank, the infantry commenced falling back along the whole line." President Lincoln telegraphed Sheridan:

> Have just heard of your great victory. God bless you all, officers and men. Strongly inclined to come up and see you.
>
> A. LINCOLN.

The day after the battle, President Lincoln gave to Sheridan the merited appointment of Brigadier General in the regular army.

Colonel Wells says, in his report of the battle of Opequan: "As Colonel Duval's division arrived on our right, we were ordered to charge. This order came so suddenly that I had only time to leave word for the 34th Massachusetts to follow, leap the fence, and go on with the three regiments forming the front line. As we charged through the oblong field, we met a severe enfilading fire from the woods on the left. I asked Colonel Wildes to change front with his regiment, 116th Ohio, and clear the woods. The men were going forward with such enthusiasm, however, that it seemed impossible to make them understand, and I pointed out the danger to the commander of a regiment of the second line, the 10th West Virginia, following close behind. He immediately changed direction, came upon our left, and was soon hotly engaged in the woods. Colonel Wildes also succeeded in turning his regiment under fire, and went to the support of the 10th. Leaving this issue behind us, the balance of my command, strongly re-enforced by a portion of the 3d brigade, passed the woods on our left, and came into the plain. Here I saw that the enemy, driven from his first position, was forming behind a high stone wall which ran across the field at right angles with that of our advancing line. His right was about 1,000 yards from the wood, his left extending toward the Martinsburg pike. Along this line artillery was posted, and in the rear of it, upon a knoll, was an earth-work, with rifle-pits in which were two guns. About 400 yards in front of this line, and parallel with it, was a low stone wall. I immediately threw my men, now thoroughly exhausted by their long run, behind this wall. Soon after, Colonel Wildes came out of the woods, and formed on our left. Here the battle hung, it seemed to me, for hours. The artillery was playing upon our lines from three different directions, one battery being not more than 500 yards distant. The rebels had the advantage in numbers, position and cover, and their fire seemed to increase in intensity every minute. The right flank was, however, wholly exposed, and I was looking every moment for the 6th corps to make its appearance there, and held on. Colonel Thoburn came along the line, and informed me this movement was about to be made, and that General Crook desired our forces to charge, the moment the flanking force should appear. While he was speaking, the 34th Massachusetts, on the right, impatient at their constant and increasing loss, sprang to their feet, and started for the rebel battery alone. Almost the same moment, the long looked for movement was made, and our whole line went forward with a cheer, and the rebels were driven from the wall in utter rout. The battery in the earth-work still remained, and enough of the enemy with it to give us a heavy fire as we advanced to the wall recently held by the enemy. Halting here for a while, I was again ordered forward, and moved the brigade down into the hollow, and within 300 yards of the battery. The 116th Ohio had an excellent position on the left, from which they were enabled to fire directly upon the pieces and horses. We hung here again for some time, the 19th corps forming a line behind the stone wall in our rear, and the 6th corps at some distance to the left. Finally Custer's cavalry made a dashing charge upon the right, sweeping around, almost into the earth-works. Now the whole line went forward again, and the battle was, to all intents and purposes, at an end. * * * Major Pratt, commanding the 34th Massachusetts, and Lieutenant Colonel Wildes, commanding the 116th Ohio, handled their regiments with great courage and skill, and in all the confusion of the charges, kept their commands together and in good order."

Colonel Wells' report, September 20th, 1864.

The 19th corps had suffered terribly up to 3 o'clock. On the right, especially, their loss was fearful. As we passed their right to our position, our regiment came upon the 116th New York. There was a mutual recognition of the regiments on the flags, and some of the officers of the two regiments shook hands. "God bless you! How we have watched for your coming. We'll watch our old number go in, and may victory crown it," said one of its officers, as we passed by.

Major J. W. DeForest, of the 12th Connecticut, whose regiment belonged to the 19th corps, and which lay close by where our division made its charge, gives a very graphic account of it in Harper's Monthly Magazine for January, 1865. I quote from his article as follows: "At 3 o'clock the hour of defeat for Early had come. To our right, where, precisely, I could not see, because of the rolling nature of the ground, but in the direction of the spot where our 1st brigade was forming, those prostrate and bloody ranks which I have mentioned, we heard a mighty battle yell, which never ceased for ten minutes, telling us that Crook and his men were advancing. To meet the yell, there arose from the farthest sweep of the isolated wood, where it rounded away to the rebel rear, the most terrific, continuous wail of musketry that I ever heard. It was not a volley, nor a succession of volleys, but an uninterrupted explosion, without a single break or tremor. As I listened, I despaired of the success of the attack, for it did not seem to me possible that any troops could endure such a fire. The Captain of our right company, who was so placed that he could see the advance, afterwards described it to me as magnificent in its steadiness, the division which accomplished it, moving across the open fields in a single line, without visible supports, in spite of the stream of dead and wounded which dropped to the rear, the pace being ordinary quick-step, and the men firing at will, but rarely." Speaking of the last charge made by us upon the position occupied by the rebels in and around the fort, or earthwork, containing the two guns we captured, the same writer says: "At the distance of half a mile from us, too far away to distinguish the heroism of individuals, but near enough to observe all the grand movements and results, the last scene of the victorious drama was acted out. Crook's column carried the heights and the fort which crowned them. We could see the long, dark line moving up the stony slopes: we could see the smoke and hear the clatter of musketry on the deadly summit; then we could hear our comrades' cheer of victory."

General Crook, in his report of the battle of Opequan, says: "I was instructed by General Sheridan to place my command on the right and rear of the 19th corps, and to look out for my right, as the enemy was reported to be moving in that direction. I directed Colonel Joseph Thoburn, commanding 1st division, to take post nearly on the prolongation of the 19th corps, which was opposite the extreme left of the enemy. Colonel J. H. Duvall, commanding the 2d division, was posted still further to the right, for the purpose of swinging round the left flank of the enemy. Colonel Duvall's right, in thus swinging round, came in sight of the enemy's skirmishers, and finally a portion of the main body of General Torbert's cavalry came sweeping down on the enemy, and protecting my right flank. Just before Colonel Duvall's division got fairly around, Colonel Thoburn's division made a charge, driving the enemy's right back in confusion to their final position. Colonel Duvall, after getting squarely around, charged the enemy in flank, and found him strongly posted behind a stone wall, with his left flank resting on an almost impassable morass named Red Bud Run, which it was necessary for him to cross. The rough and uneven ground, the tangled thickets on the banks of this slough, and the great difficulty experienced by the men in crossing, as it was very deep and miry, broke the lines completely, and mingled the men of the different regiments and brigades into one throng. Without halting to form, after having crossed, the officers and men of the 2d division united with those of the 1st, which had now closed in, sending many prisoners to the rear, and the whole command, cheering as it went, rushed on, heedless of the destructive fire of shot and shell, canister and musketry that thinned their ranks, and which would have driven back in disorder troops less determined, all seemingly intent on one grand object, the total rout of the enemy. In this they were successful, as the enemy gave way in great confusion before their determined assaults, and but for the morass impeding their progress, the 2d division would have captured many more prisoners in this charge. The enemy left two pieces of artillery in our hands when he fled, being so closely pressed that he could not take them off." *General Crook's report, October 17th, 1864.*

CHAPTER XII.

STILL GOING FORWARD—ENEMY AT FISHER'S HILL—BATTLE OF FISHER'S HILL.—ANOTHER CHARGE—LIST OF CASUALTIES—EXTRACTS FROM REPORTS OF COLONEL WELLS, GENERAL SHERIDAN AND GENERAL CROOK, ALSO GENERAL EARLY—TARDY JUSTICE DONE TO CAPTAIN JOHN VARLEY, OF COMPANY E—MARCH TO HARRISONBURG—DEATH OF LIEUTENANT MEIGS—BUILDINGS ORDERED BURNED—ORDER REVOKED AS TO DAYTON.

The morning after the battle, bright and early, we started up the Valley road, over which we had before so often marched. Arriving at Cedar Creek, we found the enemy behind his entrenchments on Fisher's Hill. The army took the position it left on the 16th of August. The position of Early at Fisher's Hill was one of great natural strength. It extended from the north fork of the Shenandoah at Three Top of the Massanutten Mountains to Little North Mountain. The mountains on each flank were apparently inaccessible, and formed a perfect protection to his flanks, while the abrupt heights on which his lines were entrenched seemed to combine to make his position impregnable. But from this strong position, Sheridan made immediate preparations to drive him. After a good deal of maneuvering for position, and a good deal of night marching by our corps, the army, at noon on the 22d, lay as follows: Crook's corps in rear of the 6th corps, and the 19th corps on the left. And now, while the 6th and 19th corps made demonstrations on the left, centre and right, and while Averill drove in the rebel skirmishers and held them close up to the rebel works on the right, Crook moved out to the extreme right, out of sight, under cover of woods and ravines. Here in the woods we threw off and piled up our knapsacks, arranged canteens and bayonet scabbards so that no noise would be made by them, and in the lightest kind of marching order, started up the steep, thickly wooded side of Little North Mountain. Ascending for a half mile or more, we turned abruptly to the left, and silently moved south, along the face of the mountain, each division in two lines, side by side. About 3 P. M., we got squarely on the enemy's flank, with our left past his entrenchments. Now fronting, we started quietly down the mountain side, our division on the left, and the 2d on the right. The 116th, being in its old position, on the extreme left, and in the front line, could now see, through an occasional open space, that we were going in with our left just inside the rebel works. It gave us a fair prospect for some hard fighting, and every man nerved himself for the shock soon to come. But now we were discovered, and the enemy opened on us with shot and shell. *Too late!* The first shot was the signal to charge, and before they could make any, even the slightest, preparations to meet us, we were upon them with the bayonet. Our movement was a complete surprise to them, and they had now only to get out of our way or surrender. "Had the heavens opened," said a rebel officer, "and you been seen descending, no greater consternation would have been created." Their artillery was captured, their left turned and broken, and rushing on, we stripped them out of their works, like the bark from a tree.

Colonel Wells, in his official report of the battle, says: "The 116th Ohio charged the battery in the angle of the rebel works, received its fire when only 100 yards from it, never wavered, but rushing on, captured it in the very smoke of its discharge."—*Colonel Wells' report, September 26th, 1864.*

Thence we went, sweeping down their works like a western cyclone, every man for himself, firing whenever he saw a rebel, and always yelling and cheering to the extent of his ability. Being closest to the works, we were confronted and stopped at several points by small bodies of the enemy, but such stops were only momentary, for as soon as a little sharp firing was heard at any point, the men would, of their own accord, concentrate there, and in a few moments would be rushing on again. At the moment we charged on the flank, the 6th and 19th corps moved on the rebel front, and now, when we had stripped away about a mile of the rebel line, the heavy columns of the 6th corps came on over the works by our side, to the rear and in front of us. Two Ohio regiments with the 6th corps, the 110th and 122d, with which we were once brigaded, came over the works, as the 116th and 123d were running along inside, and partaking at once of our enthusiasm, pressed on with us, after giving the well known "West Virginia yell." The rebel right broke in dire confusion, on the approach of the 19th corps, and, in great disorganization, the enemy fled from all parts of the field towards Woodstock, abandoning artillery, horses, wagons, muskets, knapsacks, canteens and clothing, which the pursuers found covering the roads and fields. Eleven hundred prisoners, sixteen pieces of artillery, a great many caissons and artillery horses, and a large amount of small arms, were captured. The rebel loss at Opequan and Fisher's Hill could not be less than 10,000 men, while Sheridan's did not exceed 5,500. We had taken from them, besides, twenty-one pieces of artillery.

The loss of the 116th at the battle of Fisher's Hill, was one killed and ten wounded, as follows:

KILLED.

Sergeant Edward P. Tiffany, Company B, acting Sergeant Major of the regiment.

WOUNDED.

Corporal James M. Hartley, Company B, head, severely; Corporal James H. Stewart, Company B, arm, severe; John McElroy, Company B, arm, severe; Thomas Smith, Company C, severe; Sergeant James K. Drum, Company D, thigh, severe; Christian Rhines, Company F, foot, severe; Corporal Edward Lowry, Company G, hand, severe; Andrew Powell, Company H, hip, severe; Corporal Joseph Sechrist, Company H, hip, severe; Samuel H. Cramblitt, Company I, elbow, severe.

Sergeant Tiffany was killed by a stray shot at the pike, just at dark, after the battle was all over. He was acting as Sergeant Major of the regiment at the time. It saddened the heart of every man in the regiment to thus lose so fine a soldier. Tiffany was well liked by everybody, and was a very valuable officer at headquarters. He was a very worthy man in every way, well beloved at home, as well as in his regiment. His remains were decently buried where he fell, and were afterwards removed by his friends to his old home in Meigs County. A similar sad occurrence took place in the 34th Massachusetts. That regiment camped near us, and while a group of its officers were standing around a fire, talking over the events of the day, their Major, H. W. Pratt, was mortally wounded by the accidental discharge of a musket. It seemed a terrible fate. He was one of the most gallant officers and perfect gentlemen to be found in the corps, and was loved as few officers ever are by the men of his regiment. These two deaths, occurring as they did, cast a gloom over the camps of our brigade that night, which otherwise would have been so full of rejoicing.

Our regiment captured the Lieutenant Colonel of the 32d Virginia regiment. As he was being escorted to the rear, the 13th West Virginia regiment, in our second line, was passed, when the Confederate officer met his youngest son, who was a private soldier in that regiment. They shook hands, embraced and parted, the father to go to a Northern military prison, the son to continue in the contest, with his Union regiment. A private soldier of company H, Leroy D. Brown, now superintendent of the Union Schools, of Hamilton, Ohio, writes this incident, also: "In this battle," Fisher's Hill, "I had a brother-in-law who belonged to a West Virginia cavalry regiment. He had a brother who belonged to a rebel battery which we captured. After the war closed, it was ascertained that this brother was killed at Fisher's Hill."

Colonel Wells says, in his report of the battle of Fisher's Hill: "The country was a succession of hills, with abrupt sides, and the valleys between of considerable depth. The enemy's line ran directly across these ridges, on each of which was more or less artillery, which had full play on us as we advanced. I directed the 116th and 34th to keep along the left, near the works, and followed myself the same course. The enemy formed along the crest of these ridges, and with musketry and artillery, gave us a hearty fire as we came on. The advance would be stopped, the fire become rapid and heavy, more would come up, and the battle would stand still and increase for a while, when the cheers of the 2d division on our right, could be heard sweeping on behind the enemy's position. Our line would gather force, as men constantly came up, and were directed to the critical point, and the enemy would soon give back to the next crest, to repeat the same efforts, with the same results. Upon all these eminences I found artillery, hot and smoking, which the enemy could not get off. He saved very few of the pieces which were behind the works in the woods. I saw and touched four brass, and more than as many more iron guns, before any, except the men of this corps, had reached them. * * * I cannot speak too highly of the extreme gallantry of the officers and men of the brigade. Colonel Wildes, Major Pratt, Major Urban and Captain Chamberlain, commanding regiments, all did their entire duty. I would especially call attention to the gallant charge of Colonel Wildes' regiment, in the face of the artillery fire."— *Colonel Wells' report, September 20th, 1864.*

General Sheridan says, in his report on the Shenandoah Valley campaign: "At Fisher's Hill it was again the good fortune of Crook's command to start the enemy, and of General Ricket's division, the 6th corps, to first gallantly swing in, and more fully initiate the rout."

General Crook says, of the battle of Fisher's Hill: "The success of my command in this engagement, as well as at Opequan, was mainly owing to the individual bravery of officers and men, who are entitled to much credit. * * * To the color bearers of regiments, I tender my thanks for the example they set their fellow soldiers, both in this action and at Opequan, on the 19th, as the stars and stripes in their hands were ever to be seen waving close upon the rear of the retreating enemy, and in the first line of our advancing forces."—*General Crook's report, October 18th, 1864.*

It was a hurricane battle, and, as General Crook says, "its success was mainly owing to the individual bravery of officers and men." The color bearers, at least of the 116th, well deserve the praise he awarded them.

General Early, in writing to General Lee, three days after the battle, said: "The enemy's immense superiority in cavalry, and the inefficiency of the greater part of mine, have been the cause of all my disasters. In the affair at Fisher's Hill, the cavalry gave way, but it was flanked.

This would have been remedied, if the troops had remained steady, but a panic seized them, at the idea of being flanked, and, without being defeated, they broke, many of them fleeing shamefully. The artillery was not captured by the enemy, but abandoned by the infantry. My troops are very much shattered, the men very much exhausted, and many of them without shoes."

All day the 22d, Ricket's division of the 6th corps had been pushing up closer and closer to the rebel left. About the middle of the afternoon, it finally planted itself in a good position, within half a mile of the enemy's works. The 2d division then closed to it on its left, and the 19th corps worked its way forward to the same line, joining on to the left of the 6th corps. The skirmish lines of both corps being strengthened, pushed the enemy's skirmishers back close up to their works on Fisher's Hill, and there they were held, while our corps was making its silent and secret flank movement. Early said in his report, that when he saw this advance in the afternoon, "orders were given for my troops to retire after dark, as I knew my force was not strong enough to resist a determined assault." But, to use Early's expressive words, he "retired in considerable confusion, an hour before dark," with a "shattered" army.

Our brigade was left to guard the prisoners, collect the captured property, and bury the dead, while the rest of the army moved next morning, in pursuit of the enemy. On the 24th, we started to rejoin the army, now at Harrisonburg, which we reached on the 26th, in charge of a large train.

Just after the battle of Halltown, on the 26th of August, Captain John Varley, company E, tendered his resignation, on account of sickness in his family. It was not accepted, but he was summarily dismissed from the service, for tendering his resignation in the face of the enemy. After reaching Harrisonburg, the following paper was prepared and sent to the Secretary of War:

CAMP 116TH REGIMENT OHIO VOLUNTEER INFANTRY,
NEAR HARRISONBURG, VIRGINIA,
September 26th, 1864.

Hon. E. M. Stanton, Secretary of War:

SIR:—We, the undersigned officers of the 116th Regiment, Ohio Volunteer Infantry, have the honor to submit the request that the order dishonorably dismissing Captain John Varley, of our regiment, from the service of the United States, be so modified as to discharge him honorably. We do this in view of his gallant conduct in the recent battles of Berryville, Opequan and Fisher's Hill, and because it was not cowardice that caused him to tender his resignation before the enemy, but because of a severe family affliction.

Very respectfully your obedient servants,

JOHN HULL, Captain Co. K.
WILLIAM EIDDENHARN, Lieut. Co. C.
W. S. MARTIN, Lieut. Co. F.
R. T. CHANEY, Captain Co. D.
JOHN C. H. COBB, Lieut. Co. G
SAMUEL D. KNIGHT, Lieut. Co. D
PETER DILLON, Lieut. Co. D.
H. L. KARR, Captain Co. G, and A. I. G. 1st Brigade.
THOMAS J. SHANNON, Surgeon.
W. B. TETERS, Captain Co. H.
JAMES P. MANN, Captain Co. C.

Captain Varley was reinstated and honorably discharged, some time after the war, upon all the field officers uniting in a recommendation for his honorable discharge, and afterwards he represented Washington County in the Ohio Legislature. It is unquestionable that his conduct in the battles named, was of the most gallant and daring possible. Some suspicion of bad conduct was raised against him in the battle of Halltown, but that was afterwards clearly and satisfactorily explained, but not in time to prevent the action which resulted in his dishonorable dismissal. It was unfortunate, and very much regretted by all, for no officer had more friends in the regiment than Captain John Varley. But it was a dangerous experiment for an officer to tender his resignation in that army in the summer of 1864, no matter what the reasons were. But justice was finally done him, tardy though it was, and he owed his reinstatement and honorable discharge, mainly to the good opinion of the brave company officers who had served beside him through the most trying period of the regiment's history. It is but just to say of Captain Varley, in view of this unfortunate circumstance in his military history, that he was always accounted a brave and efficient officer. On the 26th of August, he had been sent with his company on the skirmish line. The regiment advanced to the attack through a field of growing corn. Captain Varley mistook the direction in some way, being unable to see the regiment after entering the corn, and did not cover the regiment with his skirmishers. The result was, that the regiment struck the rebel line without warning, on emerging from the corn field, which might have proven very serious, had it been strong. Inasmuch, however, as it broke at our first fire, there was no harm done that time. It mortified him greatly though to be criticised for the error he had committed, and in a hasty moment he tendered his resignation. Tendering it in the face of the enemy was construed to mean cowardice, while nothing could be farther from the real truth. Under other circumstances he would have been at home with his family some time before that, on account of the severe illness of some member of it. That he and his company were selected for the skirmish line, was a sufficient voucher to attest his bravery and skill as an officer, and every comrade rejoiced when the stain put upon him was wiped out in an honorable discharge.

While at Harrisonburg, we were very short of rations much of the time. Officers, especially, had great difficulty in getting provisions. Walker, who had been acting as Sergeant Major since Lee was wounded at Halltown, undertook to provide for headquarters. Foraging trains were sent out daily, and with these Walker and Orderly Webster were sure to go. He writes in his diary:

"SEPTEMBER 27TH — Got among Dunkards to-day. They universally seemed scared almost to death when they saw us coming. One woman begged us not to take her cow or sheep. After we had promised her time and again that we would pay her for everything we got, she would still say: 'Yes, take everything you want, but leave some for the others, or they will be mad, and threaten to shoot us.' Webster and I each got three large loaves of bread, two heads of cabbage, beets, tomatoes, onions, etc. Were near a little village called Dayton. After returning, we learned there had been a skirmish there during the afternoon.

"SEPTEMBER 29th.—Orderly Webster and I went out with a forage train this P. M., intending to go to the same place as on Tuesday, but learned after passing the pickets that a squad of our men had been attacked there, so went off toward the mountains, but got nothing. This evening there is a great light toward Staunton. The 6th and 19th corps went up there this morning, or rather to Mount Crawford.

"SEPTEMBER 30TH.—Orderly Webster and I went with the forage train to-day. After passing the pickets we 'struck out.' It is amusing to hear some of the people talk. One old lady said: 'Are you not going to have a great deal of trouble at your elections this fall?' I told her no, we were going to have the most unanimous and harmonious election ever held in the country. We discussed the respective merits of the United States and Confederate currency, the latter being almost worthless. She seemed sorry I had said anything about it. We returned about 1 P. M. with a bucketfull of honey, one of apple butter, bread, sweet potatoes, cabbage and chickens, a pretty good haul for one day. A great many citizens are preparing to return with us when we go back. The 6th and 19th corps have come back from Mount Crawford."

The general results show that Walker and Webster were good foragers.

Lying at Harrisonburg a couple of days, the 116th was sent out to Dayton to guard some mills engaged in grinding grain for the army. Here we were on the *qui vive* day and night, the rebel cavalry being in strong force in the vicinity, with which our cavalry was constantly engaged. Bushwhackers also infested the roads between there and Harrisonburg, and frequently fired on small parties passing to and fro. But the people of Dayton were as fine and loyal a people as we had met anywhere in the South. They were very kind to our men, and their kindness was reciprocated by them. But neither they nor we knew in what good part these friendly relations were to stand them in a short time.

On the evening of the 3d of October, as Lieutenant Meigs, of General Sheridan's staff, was returning to Harrisonburg from Dayton, he was ambushed by a party of bushwhackers, about midway between the places, and killed. One of his escort galloped back to our camp and notified us of the attack, but he was not aware of the killing of the Lieutenant. A strong detachment of our regiment was sent out on the double quick to the place, where his body was found by the roadside. Shortly afterwards a large body of cavalry came out from Sheridan's headquarters, and placing his body in an ambulance, carried it back to Harrisonburg. The murderers of Lieutenant Meigs were instantly hunted far and wide. He was a son of Quartermaster General Meigs, was a young officer of great merit and high attainments, giving promise of a brilliant career in the army. At the time of his murder he belonged to the engineer corps of the regular army, and occupied the position of chief of engineers on Sheridan's staff. He was greatly loved by Sheridan, and he determined to wreak a terrible vengeance on the country round about in retaliation for his murder. He accordingly issued an order, which was sent to the cavalry about 2 o'clock on the morning of the 5th, and also to us, directing that every house be burned within five miles of the spot where he was murdered. This included the village of Dayton, and the burning of it devolved upon Lieutenant Colonel Wildes. He at once wrote a statement to General Sheridan of the character of the people of the place, and urged and begged him to revoke the order in so far as Dayton was concerned. This he sent in at once by a messenger, with strict injunctions to hand it at once to General Sheridan *in person*. The messenger followed his instructions strictly, though he had hard work at headquarters to pass by staff officers and guards to General Sheridan's private quarters, and probably would not have succeeded, had not the General overheard the wrangle his persistency created. The General read the note and swore, read it again and swore, examined and cross examined the messenger. He was in great grief over the death of his valued staff officer, and terribly determined that the people of the vicinity should suffer for his murder, for he well knew, as we all did, that these bushwhacking murderers were not men of the rebel army, but cowardly citizens who, remaining within our lines, assembled together to commit such dastardly deeds as this at unguarded spots. In the meantime, the citizens of Dayton were notified of the order, and given permission to remove their effects from their houses. Such weeping and wailing as went up from the poor women and children of that town we hope never to hear again. The burning of the place was put off as long as it was possible to do so under the order, and so was fixed for noon. Finally General Sheridan yielded and gave the messenger an order to carry back, revoking his former order as to the village of Dayton. The soldiers had helped the people carry out their goods, which were mostly conveyed to a slight eminence overlooking the town. Every house was now emptied, and the poor people sat among their little piles of household effects, the very picture of despair, awaiting the hour when their houses should be given up to the flames. In the country all about them, the dense smoke now arising in all directions showed them that the vengeful order was being executed. But the messenger finally came with the revoking order. Officers and men went out among the people to announce the good news to them and to help them carry back their goods. When they saw them coming, they thought it was to apply the torch, and the screams of women and children were perfectly heart rending. But the joy that succeeded as soon as their mission was understood, was so sudden and overcoming that many of the poor women fainted, and the clapping of hands and shouts of gladness of the little children over the good news was too much for even the grim and sturdy old soldiers. The sleeve of many a blouse was wet with their tears. All hands turned to and helped to carry everything back to the houses, and the people of Dayton anyhow, if of no other place in the South, believed there were at least *some* Yankees who had some humanity in them. There was not a man in the regiment who would not have faced death in a dozen battles rather than to have burned that village in the presence of those weeping, imploring and helpless women and children. Hearing during the day that we were to move in the morning, a great quantity of provisions and delicacies were prepared by the people and distributed among the officers and men. If a 116th Ohio man ever happens in Dayton, he may depend upon a warm reception. At least he ought to have one.

NOTE—I observe in Pond's "Shenandoah Valley" that it was ascertained after the war that Lieutenant Meigs was killed by an enlisted Confederate soldier of Wickham's brigade engaged in scouting, but the belief at the time was that he was murdered by bushwhackers. This but adds importance to the intercession made by the 116th in behalf of Dayton at the time of Lieutenant Meigs' death.

CHAPTER XIII.

MARCH BACK TO CEDAR CREEK — DESTRUCTION IN THE VALLEY — ELECTION DAY AT CEDAR CREEK — BATTLE OF STICKNEY FARM — DEATH OF COLONEL WELLS — LIST OF CASUALTIES — COLONEL WILDES IN COMMAND OF THE BRIGADE — BATTLE OF CEDAR CREEK, OCTOBER 19TH — DEFEAT OF THE MORNING — SHERIDAN'S ARRIVAL — WE "GO FOR THEM" — A GLORIOUS VICTORY — LIST OF CASUALTIES — REPORTS OF COLONEL WILDES AND GENERAL CROOK — A REST — PROMOTIONS — AT OPEQUAN CROSSING — THANKSGIVING TURKEYS — ORDERED TO THE ARMY OF THE JAMES.

The next morning we moved back to Harrisonburg, where we found the rest of our brigade impatiently, and with some anxiety for our safety, awaiting us, the rest of the army having marched some hours before to the rear. Our brigade being thus in the rear, remained so until we reached Fisher's Hill, on the 9th. This retrograde movement was made for two or three sound reasons: First, because we were so far from our base of supplies that it required a very large force to keep our communications open and our trains properly guarded. Second, because Early had been again re-enforced by Kershaw's division of infantry, Rosser's brigade of cavalry and a battalion of artillery. Third, because it was contemplated sending the 6th corps, and a large portion of the cavalry, to Grant upon reaching Cedar Creek, the Manassas Gap Railroad being in course of repair for the purpose of transporting the infantry to Washington.

Just before our brigade reached Fisher's Hill, the rebel cavalry under General Rosser advanced so far as to get on the left flank of the infantry column, but a mile or more distant, near Round Top, on the back road. Our brigade prepared for action. Our regiment being in the rear, at once faced about, and moving some distance further back, turned in the direction of the rear of Rosser's position, with whom Custer was now hotly engaged. Other bodies of our infantry were brought back and formed on Fisher's Hill. We had approached very close to his rear, when Custer attacked him in full force, and the report spreading among Rosser's men that the infantry was at the same time flanking them, which was a fact, they immediately gave way and broke into a stampede. Custer pursued them for over twenty miles. At the same time Merritt had attacked Lomax on the Valley pike. From our position on Round Top both cavalry fights, which were going on at the same time, were in plain view. The rebels under Lomax and those under Rosser, though fighting independent battles, some distance from each other, broke about the same time, and the pursuit was on parallel roads, that on the pike, especially, being in plain hearing and view of the infantry support. The low, rumbling, steady roll of resounding hoofs, which fairly shook the earth, the reports of artillery, the explosion of shells and the quick thudding sound of heavy carbine firing, added to which were the cheers and shouts of the pursuing host, combined to form the most animating and exciting scene we ever witnessed. In all our experience and observation in the war, nothing approached it in grandeur and sublimity. General Sheridan viewed it from Round Top near us, and it was said at the time that, when he heard of the capture of eleven pieces of artillery, he offered a reward of $500 for the capture of the twelfth. At any rate the pursuit could not have been more spirited, had there been a reward offered for the capture of Rosser himself. Rosser's temerity in pushing onto the flank of the infantry at this time cost him 350 prisoners, eleven pieces of artillery, four caissons, an ammunition train, a great quantity of small arms and a number of wagons, including the headquarters wagons of Rosser, Lomax and others, ambulances and 400 horses, besides many killed and wounded.

General Torbert, speaking of the battle, which is known in history as the battle of Tom's Brook, says: "The cavalry totally covered themselves with glory, and added to their long list of victories the most brilliant one of them all, and the most decisive the country has ever witnessed."

General Sheridan telegraphed Grant concerning it: "I directed Torbert to attack at daylight this morning and finish this 'Savior of the Valley.' * * * The enemy, after being charged by our gallant cavalry, broke and ran. They were followed by our men on the jump twenty-six miles, through Mount Jackson and across North Fork of the Shenandoah. I deemed it best to make this delay of one day here and settle this new cavalry general."

Pond, in his "Shenandoah Valley," says of this battle: "The engagement at Tom's Brook was a fine offset to the check received by Torbert at Millford, for the same two Union divisions had now routed the combined divisions of Lomax and Rosser, inflicting a loss of about 400 men, while Torbert had but nine men killed and forty-eight wounded. Some of the artillery was fresh from the Tredegar Works, and with the five guns taken at Winchester, the sixteen at Fisher's Hill and eleven at Tom's Brook, point was given to the jest that cannon sent from Richmond to the Valley were marked 'P. H. Sheridan, care of General Early.'"

In falling back from Harrisonburg, Sheridan stretched his cavalry clear across the Valley, and destroyed all the hay, grain and forage of every kind beyond what was necessary for his army. This was done in pursuance of orders from the Government. A correspondent, who was present on the march, thus describes some of the scenes witnessed: "The atmosphere from horizon to horizon has been black with a thousand conflagrations, and at night a gleam brighter and more lurid than sunset has shot from every verge. The orders have been to destroy all forage in stacks and barns, and to drive the stock before for the subsistence of the army. The execution of these orders has been perfect: the completeness of the desolation has been awful. This is war; terrible, horrible war. Hundreds of nearly starving people are going North. Our trains are crowded with them. They line the wayside. Hundreds more are coming. Not half the inhabitants of the Valley can subsist on it in its present condition. Absolute want is in mansions used in other days to extravagant living. But in no instance, except in that of the burning of dwellings within five miles in retaliation for the murder of Lieutenant Meigs, have orders been issued for the burning of houses, or have such orders been sanctioned by General Sheridan." And General Sheridan, in a dispatch dated October 7th, says: "The whole country, from the Blue Ridge to the North Mountain, has been made untenable for a rebel army. I have destroyed over 2,000 barns filled with wheat, hay and farming implements, over seventy mills filled with wheat and flour. Four herds of cattle have been driven before the army, and not less than 3,000 sheep have been killed and issued to the troops. This destruction embraces the Luray and Little Fork Valleys, as well as the main Valley."

On the 11th we reached camp at Cedar Creek, where we voted for State and County officers in Ohio, under the law authorizing soldiers to vote in the field. No election anywhere was ever conducted more fairly and honestly than this one. About noon Generals Sheridan and Crook rode down to the polls of the 36th Ohio and voted. When they galloped off to return to their headquarters, they were lustily cheered by the men. The vote of the 116th for Congressman was as follows:

Plants, (Rep.)	220
Morris, (Dem.)	70

Hon. James R. Morris was a brother of our Major, and was very popular with the regiment.

Early followed us down the Valley, and took up his old position on Fisher's Hill on the 13th. We occupied ours along Cedar Creek. The day before, the 11th, Sheridan had started the 6th corps to Washington, and it was now at Front Royal, where Sheridan ordered it to await further orders. The 12th he ordered it to move down the Valley and pass through Ashby's Gap, instead of through Manassas Gap, to Piedmont, fifteen miles beyond, to which point the Manassas Gap Railroad had been repaired.

On the 13th, the enemy appeared on our right, and the front of the 19th corps, the other side of the creek on Hupp's Hill. They opened with artillery on our camps, throwing several shells into that of the 3d brigade, and one or two into ours. The 1st and 3d brigades of Thoburn's division were sent over to feel of the enemy and develop his strength. Between the knoll on which our division was camped and Hupp's Hill, from which the rebel artillery was firing, was a piece of low, open ground, which the batteries swept, but the 116th never moved steadier than it did through this plunging fire of shot and shell, only two men, whom I shall not name here, falling out of ranks and taking shelter behind a friendly log. Crossing this space and the creek, we moved straight towards the saucy batteries, the 3d brigade on the right, ours on the left.

"It became evident to both brigades that Early was in force, but the rage for capturing guns had seized Sheridan's army, and Thoburn's men went forward, through the plunging fire from the brow of Hupp's Hill, until Early was forced to throw out Kershaw's infantry, Conner's brigade leading, to check them." *Shenandoah Valley in 1864.*

Our brigade formed behind a stone wall, and opening fire checked and drove back the enemy. But the 3d brigade was driven back, and there being an intervening space between the brigades, we did not know it, until the enemy advanced on our right flanks. The left wing of our regiment was now thrown forward along a stone wall, running perpendicular to our line of battle, and opening fire across to the right, we checked the advance of Conner, and cleared the front of a body of rebels about making a charge on the brigade. The right of the 34th Massachusetts was broken and driven back. Lieutenant Ballard, in trying to reach our brigade to order us back after the 3d had retired, had his horse shot, and thus the order did not reach us before the enemy struck our right. At this juncture, a large force came down upon the left occupied by the 116th, and the whole brigade was driven back amid a furious shower of balls. We were obliged to retreat across a wide, open field, and the loss of our brigade was very severe for a skirmish, as it was called, being over 200, the 34th Massachusetts alone losing over 100 men. We fell back to a piece of woods, where we re-formed, and the enemy soon withdrawing to Fisher's Hill, we returned to our camp. The loss of the 116th was one killed, seven wounded and five taken prisoners, as follows:

KILLED.

Corporal Dickerson Archer, Company D.

WOUNDED.

Royal Phelps, Company G; Jesse Frazer, Company G, arm shot off; James E. Bullock, Company G; Jehiel Graham, Company G, hip, disabled for life; John W. Hall, Company D, arm; Leroy D. Brown, Company H, knee; John Rush, Company E.

PRISONERS.

Wm. A. Ferrell, Company D; Samuel King, Company F; Orderly Sergeant Charles A. Cline, Company E; George W. Wiley, Company E; Joseph A. Hall, Company, E.

This battle, known by the name of "Stickney Farm," was replete with suprises. Only the day before, the cavalry had gone up the Valley ten or twelve miles without finding any enemy.*

It seems that Powell, in the Luray Valley, had, a day or two before, reported Early at Craig's Creek, between Brown's Gap and Waynesboro. Several reconnoisances of the infantry, one by our brigade, made on the 12th, reported no enemy near. So, to have a lot of big shells dropped into our camps just as we were sitting down to our dinners, when we didn't think there was a Confederate cannon within miles of us, was, to say the least of it, rather sensational. Then, when we went out to see what it was all about, to be met by Kershaw's infantry, batteries in position, and all the rest of Early's army in sight on Hupp's Hill, and to find ourselves repulsed, before we had time to take in the situation, or "view the landscape o'er," was altogether so startling and sudden a visitation as to make us wonder, not only how this surprise happened, but what would be the next thing in order for old Early to treat us to.

Colonel Wells, of the 34th Massachusetts, and Lieutenant Dempsey were killed. The death of Colonel Wells was a severe stroke to his gallant regiment and a great loss to the service. He was one of the very best officers in Crook's corps. He was a natural soldier, and as brave and gallant an officer as there was in our army. By his discipline and incessant drill he had made the 34th Massachusetts one of the very best regiments in the service. It was as steady as a rock in battle, and, as long as any troops could stay on a battle line, they would be found there. Always cool, intelligent, effective and heroically steady and firm, Colonel Wells had the genius, so largely developed in

---

*"October 12th I sent reconnoisances from the 1st and 3d divisions up the Valley pike and the back road for ten or twelve miles, but could find no signs of the enemy."
—*Torbert's Report.*

General Sheridan, of imbuing his men with his own daring and soldierly qualities. He occupied a high position in the esteem of the people of Massachusetts, as he deserved, and his death was deeply mourned in all parts of the State. The day after the battle, his body was obtained under a flag of truce and sent to his home in Massachusetts, accompanied by an escort from his noble regiment. Colonel Wells was brevetted Brigadier General a few days before his death, the commission reaching the army a few days after his death. All felt it a pity that he could not have lived to realize that his services had been appreciated, and, at last, rewarded.

The death of Colonel Wells placed Lieutenant Colonel Wildes in command of the brigade, the 116th thus being left in command of Captain W. B. Teters, a brave and efficient officer, and one thoroughly qualified from his long service to command with credit to himself and honor to the regiment. He commanded it from this time to the close of the war. The brigade at this time consisted of the 34th Massachusetts, the 2d battalion of the 5th New York heavy artillery, the 123d and 116th Ohio.

This demonstration of the enemy satisfying Sheridan that he was being again menaced by Early's re-enforced army, he ordered the 6th corps, now at Ashby's Gap, to return, which it did next day, going into camp to the right and rear of the 19th corps. Up to this time it was supposed that Early was far up the Valley, certainly no nearer than New Market, and some reports located him near Brown's Gap, as before stated. On the 15th Sheridan started for Washington to hold a long deferred conference, taking with him Merritt's division of cavalry, which was to be joined by Powell's at Front Royal, from which point both were to go upon an expedition under General Torbert to destroy the Virginia Central Railroad about Charlottesville and Gordonsville, always a favorite project of General

Grant. Upon Sheridan's arrival at Front Royal, he was overtaken by a messenger from General Wright, whom he had left in command at Cedar Creek, bearing the following dispatch taken from the rebel signal station on Three Top:

To Lieutenant General Early.

Be ready to move as soon as my forces join you, and we will crush Sheridan.

LONGSTREET, Lieutenant General.

While thinking this was a ruse, still General Sheridan, deeming it best to be on the safe side, ordered back the cavalry to Cedar Creek, while he proceeded on his way to Washington, at the same time cautioning General Wright to be on the alert, to "look well to his ground, and be well prepared." It should be borne in mind that from Three Top the rebels could see our whole camp and every movement taking place in it, and from this point it was that Early and Gordon planned for us the surprise of the morning of the 19th, which we are now approaching. It would be difficult to exaggerate the importance of Three Top as a lookout station. It gave a perfect birds-eye view of our entire position and of the whole Valley down as far as Winchester. On the 18th our brigade made a reconnoisance to the left and another brigade of our division made one towards Strasburg and Fisher's Hill, but no sign of any movement on the part of the enemy was discovered.

On the night of the 18th, Sheridan, on his way back, lodged at Winchester. The position of the army was at this time the same as heretofore stated. Behind Crook's left, and at right angles with it, lay Kitching's provisional division, with a view to protect the flank. Thoburn's division lay a half mile in advance of the left of the 19th corps. Hayes' division lay in reserve behind Thoburn's, and half a mile distant from it. To guard against surprise, the North Fork was picketed by Powell's cavalry from Cedar Creek to Front Royal, nine miles distant, on our left.

Artillery was posted on the line of the 19th corps and on ours, one battery being stationed to the right of our brigade, in front of General Harris' 3d brigade. But for some unknown reason the fords on North Fork on our left, and the road and fords at the foot of Massanutten Mountain on our front, were not guarded by the cavalry on the night of the 18th, which left no cavalry on that flank nearer than Buckton Ford, two and a half miles distant from the infantry pickets. But no one believed Early would venture on an attack after so many severe defeats, and it is more than probable that these places had been neglected for some time, and probably never, since our recent occupation, had they been properly guarded. Had they been so guarded before, it is incredible that Early could find out in time to make the move that he did, that on the night of the 18th alone they were left unguarded. The reasonable presumption is that Early had, through his scouts and disloyal citizens, learned of our *habitual neglect* to guard them, and hence his movement on the night of the 18th, which we are about to relate.

Soon after midnight Early, having arranged his troops unperceived at the foot of Massanutten Mountain and at Fisher's Hill, set them in motion toward Sheridan's lines. His cavalry and light artillery advanced against the right of the 6th corps and the cavalry on the right about day light. His infantry marched in three columns, the first of which, composed of Gordon's, Ramseur's and Pegram's divisions, placed themselves before daybreak on the left rear of the whole Federal position. Kershaw got, about the same time, close under the intrenched rising ground, on which lay Crook's corps, and Wharton advanced upon the front of the 19th. Word was sent to General Crook from Kitching's division that his pickets had heard the rustling of underbrush and the tramp of men in their front about 2 o'clock in the morning. Captain John F. Welch, who was then on

Thoburn's staff, heard musket firing at 3 o'clock in the morning, and awakening Thoburn told him what he had heard. Both listened for some time, but heard no more. Captain Welch heard firing again between 4 and 5, immediately followed by a volley and by artillery in their front. This last firing was the opening of the rebel advance upon the first division of Crook's corps. Our brigade was aroused by our camp guard, which we never failed to keep, about 4 o'clock, as the rebel columns struck our pickets in our front, when there occurred enough firing to give the alarm. But the 5th New York heavy artillery battalion was captured almost entire on the picket line in our front, only one officer and twelve men escaping. The pickets were not fired upon, and the rush made upon them was so sudden that their fire was only very scattering. The moment the alarm was given our teams were hitched up, wagons loaded and our headquarters stuff, and much of our camp equipage sent to the rear. Skirmishers were sent out in our front, which soon met the enemy silently advancing through the woods. I at once dispatched Captain Karr to division headquarters. With Lieutenant Dissoway, of my staff, I rode to the brigade on our right, which we found in their beds. Some good, vigorous efforts were made to arouse them. There stood the guns of the battery with only a sentinel over them, and only a man now and then of the infantry or artillery could be roused up enough to ask "What's up?" or "Who the h—l are you?" Seeing we could do nothing with these sleepy fellows, we rode rapidly back to our brigade, which we had scarcely reached before the storm burst in front and on both flanks. The mist and fog was so heavy that you could hardly see the length of a regiment. The enemy came over the works on both flanks unopposed, but we met the rebel advance with so hot a fire that it fell back in our front, which gave us opportunity to move out unmolested. The 34th Massachusetts was on the right of our brigade, and when the rebels came over the works on their right they were struck so suddenly and heavily on the flank that they broke, and becoming involved with the utterly stampeded and broken masses of the surprised brigade and battery on their right, fell back in confusion. The 116th and 123d stuck together and began falling back towards the pike, where it was touched by the 19th corps, about a mile distant. They were hard pressed the entire distance, but kept in good shape, delivering their fire to the rear or either flank as the rebels approached, and checking the pursuit sufficient to get off our trains. We formed a line across the field just after rising out of the ravine, about 1,000 yards in front of Thoburn's headquarters, and facing about opened fire on the enemy, now pouring down the hill on the opposite side. We checked his advance for a short time, but now a heavy line came out of the woods square on our left, and by this force we were pressed to the right off the high ground we were following. Back of Thoburn's headquarters to our rear was a piece of woods in which we intended to make another stand, but it was already occupied by the enemy. The enemy now pressed us hard until we reached the pike, but not a man broke from the ranks, and we rose on to the pike with a firm line.

Lieutenant C. M. Keyes, in his excellent history of the 123d Ohio, says of that morning attack and of the position and action of our brigade. "At half past four on the morning of the 19th of October, the regiment was routed out by a straggling picket fire in our front. The word was passed along that the enemy was advancing, and the men quietly fell into line along the breastworks. The other brigades, however, failed to observe the warning, or were too slow in falling in. The rebels easily turned the right of our corps, getting over the works with little or no opposition, many of the men being still asleep in their tents.

Some resistance, however, was made by our brigade, the only one in the division not surprised. We fell slowly back, the broken ranks of the other brigades rallying upon our line."

General Lincoln, in his history of the 34th Massachusetts, confirms this statement in every particular, saying: "At first sound of the attack our own regiment and brigade fell into line behind our breastworks and made such resistance as was possible."

Upon reaching the pike, we were met by General Emory. The enemy now filled the woods behind us, not over 300 yards from where we struck the pike at the left of General Emory's line, but he had not yet made preparations to protect his flank. We informed him of what was coming, and of the situation of affairs on his left. His reply was an order for our two regiments to charge into the woods. We formed at once for the charge, for which the most we could hope would be time for the 19th corps to turn its line to meet the enemy. Every officer and man in our little band knew he was going to meet overwhelming numbers in those woods, but they never hesitated. Fixing bayonets, we started on the way back down the hill from the pike, and as we started to ascend to the woods, raised the old yell and dashed forward. Just after we started, General Wright rode out in our front and most gallantly led the charge. We advanced close to the edge of the woods, where we met with a terrible fire and a counter charge from ten times our number, which swept us back again to the pike. General Wright was wounded in the face, and came back bleeding freely. He displayed great personal courage, but gallant as he and the men who followed him were, they were obliged to give way before the awful fire they met at the edge of the woods. Falling back again to the pike, we found the 19th corps changing front to the rear along down the pike, and a division of the 6th corps coming up on the double quick.

A correspondent on the ground wrote, at the time, of the action of our brigade up to this point: "Lieutenant Colonel Wildes, of the 116th Ohio, who was in command of a brigade, had his men in line and had sent word to General Wright of the enemy's approach when the storm burst, sweeping away two of his regiments at once, and pushing the rest back in a storm of balls in flank and rear. Failing to find General Crook, he reported the 116th and 123d to General Emory, and was sent into the fight, where he and his noble men made a glorious record."

High praise indeed, but none too high for the two regiments which so nobly stood together that morning, till dashed to pieces against the strong lines of the enemy in this charge, and in the brave stands afterwards made on other parts of the field. Wharton had come up, and was now engaging the 19th corps in front, with Gordon, Ramseur and Pegram coming onto the pike still further to the left, they having routed Kitching and Hayes. Reaching the pike, our broken ranks rallied, and hearing that General Crook had made a stand at a point near Sheridan's headquarters, a short distance beyond the pike, we fell back there. Here were gathered fragments of Crook's corps, and here were Crook and his staff, Hayes and his staff, and a large number of officers striving with might and main to stem the tide of disaster. We had scarcely taken our position here, before the division of the 6th corps we had seen going to the front, and the left of the 19th corps came falling back in considerable confusion. These troops passed mainly to our left, and formed at the new position now being taken by the army, some distance in our rear. Our corps, having formed on favorable ground, now advanced to push back, if possible, or at least to check the rebel advance, until the trains could be got off, and especially until the contents of Sheridan's headquarters could be loaded up and run off. We checked the advance of the enemy, and pushed him back a short distance, and I think the very hardest and most stubborn fighting of the day took place here. We were fighting Kershaw's and Wharton's rebel divisions. The proportion of officers to the number of men in our line was very large. Probably not over 1,500 enlisted men of Crook's whole corps were engaged, while there was fully one-fourth that many line and staff officers. A great many line and staff officers took muskets, and lay down in the ranks of the men, while all mounted officers used their holster revolvers. The position was held for over a half hour, which gave time for the trains to move out of the way and Sheridan's headquarters to be emptied of everything of value, and also for the 6th and 19th corps to form a new line further to the rear. We now fell back to the left of the new line. Our brigade was greatly broken up by this time, but it was re-formed at the new line, where it soon rallied in good shape. Finding the enemy still on our flank near Middletown, we moved forward again to the edge of a piece of woods to check the enemy until another line could be formed by the 6th and 19th corps, still further to the rear beyond Middletown. Here we had another hard struggle for another half hour, finally being driven back by the masses of the enemy in our front and on our flanks. We now fell back again to the position beyond Middletown, the remnant of our little corps still clinging to the left, which it stubbornly refused to yield amid all the dreadful assaults of the morning, the 6th on our right in the center, and the 19th now on the extreme right of the line. Custer's and Merritt's cavalry divisions had been brought over from the right and were now doing valiant service in beating back the enemy from our left. Our left now lay near the pike, beyond which we could see the cavalry driving back the rebel hordes, which was the first ray of hope and grain of encouragement we had received during the morning.

But the day was lost, as all felt, and the army directed its attention to saving its trains and preventing the enemy getting complete possession of the pike and cutting us off from Winchester. A short time, however, served to demonstrate that we had succeeded in placing the enemy squarely in our front. Our camps, lines of works, twenty-four guns and 1800 prisoners were in his hands, and the army, though in a measure re-formed, was in a condition of demoralization that would have justified any commander in withdrawing it from the field. A vast number of stragglers were well on their way to Winchester, and some had already entered that town. But many were now flocking back, and Crook's corps was every moment lengthening its line toward the pike. It was about 9 o'clock by this time, and every exertion was made to bring together the broken commands and strengthen our position. The enemy appeared content with his victory, and was now making no attempts to force us further back. Only straggling skirmish firing was going on, with now and then some artillery firing. We afterwards learned that this time was devoted by Early's men to plundering our camps, which were a rich field for his ragged and half starved army.

We now had time to count our loss. Colonel Thoburn, our division commander, was mortally wounded. General Hayes, commanding the second division, was badly crippled with a broken foot, by his horse, which was shot, falling upon him. Captain Bier, General Crook's Adjutant General, Colonel Hall, of the 13th West Virginia, and a dozen or more other officers were killed. Dr. Thomas J. Shannon, of our regiment, was mortally wounded. Major Kellogg, commanding the 123d, Captain Teters, commanding the 116th, and many more officers of the brigade were wounded; and our loss of men in killed, wounded and missing was very heavy. Our corps had lost seven guns, the 19th corps eleven and the 6th corps six, making twenty-four in all, besides many caissons, ambulances and wagons, our own corps, however, losing but four wagons and two ambulances in all the confusion of the day.

Hearing away in our rear cheer upon cheer, and coming nearer and nearer, we had only a moment to wonder as to the cause, when here came Sheridan galloping across the turnpike to where Crook was standing behind the remnant of his little corps.*

His great black horse, immortalized in song, was covered with flecks of foam and dripping sweat. Throwing the reins from his hand, he jumped to the ground. "Well, Crook, how is it?" he asked. "Bad enough, bad enough," answered Crook, pointing to the hand full left of his corps. "Well, get ready now, we'll lick them out of their boots yet before night," was Sheridan's quick reply, as he nervously and vigorously cut off the tops of weeds and grass with his riding whip. Hardly a minute elapsed before he was in his saddle again and off down the line in a hard gallop, the cheers of the men as he passed along telling just where he was. "We are now going back to our camps, boys." "We'll have all those camps and cannon back." "We'll soon get the tightest twist on them you ever saw." "Get ready, boys, to go for them." "We'll sleep in our old camps to-night." Such are some of the quick, crisp sentences he spoke to the men as he passed down the lines. Presently clouds of stragglers came flocking back to their places, and our corps was moved across the pike. A portion of the 6th corps was some distance in the rear. One staff officer after another was sent to hurry it forward, for

---

*"One thing at once struck me as curious, that the stream of men was now going towards Middletown. Astonished, I left Wheaton and galloped over to the pike, where I learned that Sheridan had just passed up. As well as can be ascertained, it was half past eleven o'clock."—*Colonel Crown-in-shield's Cedar Creek.*

Sheridan determined to stay right where he found the most advanced line. It didn't come quick enough to suit him, and he dashed away for it himself and brought it up on the run. It was not a moment too soon, for just as it moved into its place, about 1 o'clock, the rebel attack which Sheridan had been expecting was made on the 19th corps, and Wheaton's division of the 6th. From the left he had been watching the enemy's movements and knew he was preparing to attack. It was made to our right, and for a moment we trembled with anxiety, for the line at one place broke, but it was at once rallied and rolled back with a ringing cheer, when Sheridan galloped among the men, swinging his cap and calling on them to stand their ground. The attack was repulsed, and Sheridan said: "Thank God for that! Now if they attack you again go for them with the bayonet."*

The demoralization of the morning's defeat was all gone. Everyone felt the tide of disaster had turned, and the men were now only too anxious to move forward to get "those camps and cannon back." About 1 o'clock General Custer, at the head of his cavalry division, moved across behind us from the left to the right. He was cheered, too, for next to Sheridan, Custer was the pride of the army. It was wonderful to see the enthusiasm and confidence the presence of Sheridan inspired. There was real magic in it. Up to 4 o'clock all was silence on both sides, and preparation, or-

---

"The repulse of Early's left told him that fortune had quitted his standard. He thenceforth contented himself with the endeavor to get his prisoners and his captured guns and wagons back to Fisher's Hill." — *The Shenandoah Valley in 1864.*

"So many of our men had stopped in the camps to plunder, (in which I am sorry to say that officers participated) the country was so open and the enemy's cavalry so strong, that I did not deem it prudent to press further, especially as Lomax had not come up. I determined, therefore, to content myself with trying to hold the advantages I had gained until my troops had come up and the captured property was secured." —*Early's report to Lee.*

(General Powell had successfully kept Lomax from coming onto the field and operating on our left, as planned by Early.)

ganization and deep suspense on ours. Sheridan continually rode along the front, studying the ground, encouraging the men, arranging and strengthening the lines. Every minute was adding strength to our lines. There was a growing desire to advance, which Sheridan kept telling the men they would do "as soon as he got a good ready." It was nearly four o'clock when he started "the right wing of the 19th corps to swing towards the left." Getty's and Wheaton's divisions of the 6th corps advanced at the same moment. The left half wheel by General Dwight, of the 19th corps, on the extreme right, was successfully made, while Custer, riding round the right of the wheeling column, made a furious charge on the crumbling ranks of the enemy in the rear. The constant dread of being flanked by the cavalry had caused Early to stretch out his infantry lines until they were made very thin. But it did not after all save him from the dreadful cavalry, while it made it easy for the infantry to crush his distended lines. Now the bugles all along the lines sounded the "advance," and Sheridan's whole army was in motion. The rebels were lodged behind stone walls and rail pens, and in many places on the right made a stubborn resistance. But the strong infantry lines advancing and crowding them back in the front and on the flank, and the clouds of cavalry in their rear, spread consternation all along their lines until one division after another gave way, and as Pond, in "The Shenandoah Valley in 1864," says: "The army that had swept over the field in triumph at dawn, was a mass of fugitives at night. Never was greater rout seen on a battle field since Bull Run."*

---

*"A portion of the enemy had penetrated an interval which was between Evans' brigade on the extreme left and the rest of the line, when the brigade gave way, and Gordon's other brigades soon followed. Every effort was made to stop and rally Kershaw's and Ramseur's men, but the mass of them resisted all appeals and continued to go to the rear. Pegram alone got a portion of his command across Cedar Creek in an organized condition, but this small force soon dissolved."—*Early's report to Lee.*

No stop was made till the embarrassment of crossing Cedar Creek huddled them together in great masses on its bank. Custer and Devin came upon them now, when they broke into utter confusion and fled in all directions. The infantry halted at Cedar Creek, but the cavalry pursued the demoralized enemy towards Strasburg. One division of the 19th corps moved over to Hupp's Hill after dark. Between Strasburg and Fisher's Hill a bridge across a little stream broke down under the weight of a galloping battery, when the road for a long distance became blocked with a mass of guns, caissons, ambulances, wagons and fugitive men. Now Custer and Devin again swooped down upon the tangled mass and gathered it all up. Here is where the great capture of artillery, fifty-seven pieces, and "everything on wheels" that Early had, was made. Scores of wagons, ambulances, etc., were burned. Ten battle flags were among the trophies. The enemy abandoned everything at this last charge of the cavalry and fled in utterly broken up masses. It was well on towards morning before all the captured artillery and other property was brought back, and parked near Sheridan's headquarters. Although tired and hungry, the men stood by the roadside in dense masses and gathered in great crowds around the rebel prisoners and captured property, and about their camp fires, nearly all night. The change from the gloom of disaster that hung over that army in the morning, brought about by the complete and undisputed victory in the evening, can be better imagined than described. What camping we did that night, we did on the *sites* of our camps of the night before. But our tents, blankets, rations, etc., were gone, the rebels having made clean work of our camps, and no rations came up to us until the next morning, when we ate as hearty a breakfast as we ever did in our lives. We found our dead stripped of their clothing, the hyena conduct of which the rebels were almost universally guilty when—

ever by the fortunes of war our dead fell into their hands.

Our large force of cavalry, pursuing the fleeing rout, drove it out of Strasburg, following it to Fisher's Hill that night, and next morning as far up the Valley as Woodstock. Two hours more of daylight, and our infantry would have utterly annihilated Early's army. It was a grand sight to see that army of ours, lately so shattered and stricken, thus re-form its columns and move out on the charge to such a glorious victory! It has no parallel in all the battles of the great rebellion. It was one of the most remarkable battles of modern times. Of all the retrieved battles recorded in history, none equals it. It has often been compared to Napoleon's great battle of Marengo, and some features of both are very much alike. About the same number of men were engaged in each; the losses were about the same; Napoleon's army was defeated in the morning, and returning to the conflict won a decisive victory in the afternoon. As Napoleon rode along his lines after joining his army, he said, "Men, you know I always sleep on the battle field." As Sheridan rode along his lines he said, "We'll sleep in our old camps to-night." And the presence and speech of Napoleon at Marengo inspired his men no less than did the presence and speech of Sheridan at Cedar Creek. But there the parallel ends. Napoleon brought with him to the front 4,000 of the Imperial Guard, the best soldiers in Europe, and a few moments after his arrival, 4,000 of Dessaix's corps of veterans, just arrived from Egypt, came upon the field. Our army, after having sustained a decided defeat, totally routed the victors without receiving any reenforcements, save one man SHERIDAN! It must be remembered, too, that the men had eaten nothing since the night before, that they had lost their canteens and were suffering much from thirst, as well as hunger, and that they had been fighting and maneuvering, often at the double-quick, for nearly twelve hours. To this general condition, our brigade was an exception in one or two respects. Most of the men had their canteens, and many their haversacks, having had more time, as we have shown, to prepare for action in the morning, than most of our corps. Whatever was or may have been the condition of others, our brigade was in line and ready for the onset of the rebels, and it has always been so conceded. We came back to the pike, fighting all the way, with two regiments, and there we went into a charge led by General Wright himself. The stigma of "surprise," therefore, does not, and never did, attach to the 1st brigade.*

---

*Prof. Leroy D. Brown, Superintendent of the Hamilton Union Schools at present, was a private soldier in "H," and on the night of the 18th of October was an orderly at brigade headquarters until midnight, Edward H. Bradley, of "G," then taking his place. Prof. Brown has written a paper of great merit on "Sheridan in the Shenandoah Valley." He has very kindly furnished me with a copy and I am indebted to it for a number of important facts incorporated in this work. But I will let him tell his experience of that night himself: "This night I was orderly at brigade headquarters. General Wildes, now of Akron, then the Lieutenant Colonel of the 116th Ohio, was in command of my brigade. I was on duty till midnight, and it was reported that the enemy was moving towards our left. This was not believed by our commanders. Nevertheless I took the precaution to secure my gun and accoutrements, with the half shelter tent and blanket which I carried before I went to sleep. I was awakened by my comrade Bradley about 2 o'clock, who told me that he had heard the marching of cavalry down by Massanutten. This was confirmed by a captain of the 5th New York, whose regiment was on picket. Still nothing was done to arouse our sleeping army."

In a letter to me Edward H. Bradley says: "I was orderly at brigade headquarters from midnight until the attack was made on the morning of the 19th of October, when I took my gun and went to my company. I heard brisk firing on our front and right about 4 o'clock, and immediately informed you. The brigade was in line fully half an hour before the enemy struck the Virginia brigade (the 3d) on our right. They were asleep, I think, at least they made no stand, and we were flanked out of our works."

The officer of the 5th New York, mentioned by Prof. Brown, came to my headquarters twice during the night, and told of what he had heard at the front and on the left. He was convinced that something more than usual was going on, and he told me that the officer of the day had been notified by him. The regimental commanders of the brigade were ordered about 4 o'clock to have their commands under arms at once. The whole brigade was at the works fully half an hour before the storm burst upon the 8th corps on our left and right. The officer of the day, Lieutenant Colonel Furney, 34th Ohio, was captured about 3 o'clock in the morning. It seems that, being informed of the indications of some movement, he undertook to investigate for himself, and nearing a point at which our cavalry should have been stationed, he saw a body of mounted men up to whom he unsuspectingly rode and was made a prisoner and sent to the rear. This mishap, very likely, combined with other things to make the surprise more complete than it might otherwise have been. Colonel Furney escaped at Mount Jackson and returned to camp in a couple of days after the battle.

Major Karr says in a letter to me: "You sent me to Colonel Thoburn's headquarters a little after 4 o'clock in the morning to notify him of the enemy's approach."

Speaking of the stand made by our corps before falling back beyond Middletown, General Harris, in his report, says: "By this time we had arrested and brought together a sufficient number of officers and men to justify an attack on our part, to aid in checking the enemy's advance, and were directed by the General commanding to a point of the line in the woods. In our advance towards these woods we were aided by Lieutenant Colonel Wildes, commanding the 1st brigade, and Colonel Wells, commanding the 15th West Virginia, each of whom brought a considerable concession to our strength. This force, now numbering three or four thousand men, was pushed forward into the woods until its withdrawal was rendered imperative by the giving way of our lines on our left, as also by a movement of the enemy to turn our right."

The loss of the 116th was as follows:

KILLED.

Dr. Thomas J. Shannon, Surgeon; Francis Caldwell, Company B; Aaron Weekly, Company A; David Bruny, Company E.—4.

WOUNDED.

Lieutenant Colonel Thos. F. Wildes; Captain W. B. Teters, Company H; Lieutenant R. T. Chaney, Company D; Lieutenant J. C. H. Cobb, Company G; Corporal Abraham Strait, Company D; Orlando Griffith, Company K; Pardon C. Hewett, Company K; Abel C. Barnes, Company C; Samuel R. Halliday, Company G; Robert Carpenter, Company F; James Wilson, Company F; Color Sergeant Charles P. Allison, Company K; Milton Mozena, Company C; William S. Parrott, Company I.—14.

PRISONERS.

Corporal James H. Stewart, Company B; William S. Parrott, Company I; John Rawlings, Company G; Daniel Bennett, Company D; Jacob Carpenter, Company H; William B. Seagur, Company G; James Whitman, Company G.—7.

General Sheridan, in his report of the Shenandoah campaign, says: "At Cedar Creek, Getty's division of the 6th corps, and Merritt's and Custer's divisions of cavalry, confronted the enemy from the first attack in the morning, still none behaved more gallantly, or exhibited greater courage than those who returned from the rear, determined to re-occupy their lost camps."

Believing that the reader will be interested in the account they give of this extraordinary battle, I give below in full the official reports of Lieutenant Colonel Wildes and General Crook:

HEADQUARTERS 1ST BRIGADE, 1ST INFANTRY DIVISION, ARMY OF WEST VIRGINIA,
CEDAR CREEK, VIRGINIA, October 24, 1864.

Lieutenant F. L. Ballard, A. A. A. G, 1st Infantry Division, Army West Virginia:

LIEUTENANT:—In compliance with your orders, I have the honor to submit the following report of the part taken by my command in the action of the 19th inst.:

About 4 o'clock on the morning of the 19th of October, 1864, I heard brisk picket firing on the right and left of the position occupied by my command. I immediately ordered the brigade under arms behind its fortifications. In a few minutes afterwards I heard a volley of perhaps twenty rifle shots, and a yell, as though a charge was being made, in the direction of a picket post in front of my left. I at once directed Captain Karr, of my staff, to inform Colonel Thoburn that there was considerable firing along the picket line. I then went to the right of my command to the position occupied by the 3d brigade, 1st division, when I discovered that some of the pickets were coming in. Believing we were about to be attacked, I moved the 123d and 116th Ohio regiments to the right, closing upon the 34th Massachusetts regiment, thus filling up a gap made in my line by the absence of the 5th New York H. A. on picket duty. The line was scarcely closed up when a heavy volley of musketry was fired on my right. Upon going again to the right to learn the cause of it, and the state of affairs there, I found the works of the 3d brigade occupied by the enemy, and that the 34th Massachusetts regiment, being flanked in its position, had left the works in its front. Just at this time I heard brisk firing on my left. Seeing that I was flanked on my right, and apprehending that my left was also threatened, I ordered the 116th and 123d Ohio regiments to move by the left flank and form line of battle in the field on my left, fronting the position lately occupied by the 3d brigade. I had scarcely formed this line when I heard firing in the woods immediately in my rear. I then moved by the left flank of the brigade and formed another line on the hill overlooking the ravine in rear of the works of the 3d brigade. Halting here a moment, I discovered the enemy was in my rear and threatening to cut me off and to surround me. I then moved quickly towards the turn-pike, my command fighting the enemy in my front and on my right until it reached the position occupied by the 19th A. corps. Here it formed a portion of the line under the direction of General Emory, and fought until the line was broken on this part of the field, my command at one time charging the enemy's position under the immediate direction of General Wright. After this the line became so broken that but little could be done in rallying the men until they reached the train of the 6th A. corps in the vicinity of the present headquarters of General Crook. A line was here formed to allow the train to cross the ravine and creek. Considering the broken condition of the ranks, the men of my command fought with great bravery and coolness at this point. When the train had crossed this line gave way, and falling back some distance, scattering portions of my brigade were collected and moved forward under the direction of Colonel Harris to a line formed in the edge of the woods beyond the ravine in which the 6th corps' train had become blocked. When this line fell back, portions of my command formed with the remnant of the 1st division behind a stone wall on the right of the turnpike beyond Middletown. Colonel Harris then directed me to go to the rear and direct all stragglers from the Army of West Virginia to return to their commands. Taking Lieutenant Dissoway of my staff with me, I went to the rear and succeeded in collecting a considerable portion of the stragglers, and shortly after returning, under direction of Colonel Harris, moved the brigade across the turnpike to the support of the batteries situated on that part of the field. It lay there until the advance was made in the afternoon, when it moved forward and encamped near its present position.

I neglected to state in the proper connection that my command was in line of battle fully three-fourths of an hour before the attack was made, and that information of the picket firing was sent to division headquarters a full half hour before the attack was made on my right. My regimental commanders, Major Kellogg, 123d Ohio ; Captain Teters, 116th Ohio ; Captain Potter, 34th Massachusetts, and Captain Wilkie, 5th New York H. A. regiments, did everything in their power with the men, and performed their duties nobly throughout the day.

The members of my staff, Captain Karr and Lieutenant Dissoway, conducted themselves in the most gallant manner throughout the day, and rendered very valuable service in their strenuous efforts to keep the command together. I have heretofore forwarded a list of casualties in my command in the action. I enclose reports of regimental commanders.

I am, Lieutenant, very truly your obedient servant,

THOS. F. WILDES,
Lieutenant Colonel 116th Ohio Volunteers, Commanding Brigade.

HEADQUARTERS DEPARTMENT WEST VIRGINIA,
CEDAR CREEK, VA., November 7, 1864.

Lieutenant Colonel J. W. Forsyth, Chief of Staff, Middle Military Division :

COLONEL :— I have the honor to report that on the morning of the 19th ult. the Army of West Virginia under my command, owing to the heavy details made upon it, did not number over 4,000 bayonets present. The 1st division, Colonel Joseph Thoburn commanding, and batteries B, 5th U. S., and D, 1st Pennsylvania artillery, were encamped further down Cedar Creek and about one mile from the left of the 19th corps, on a high ridge overlooking Cedar Creek and the country in the vicinity of Strasburg, with the right resting close to and fronting down the creek. The general bearing of this ridge was an irregular crescent, running to the rear of and about one-half mile distant from the left of the 19th corps. Battery L, 1st Ohio Artillery, was occupying the works above the bridge across the creek, while the second division, Colonel R. B. Hayes commanding, was held in reserve and camped about one-fourth of a mile in rear of the left of the 19th corps. My pickets were at the usual distance from camp, and connecting with those of other commands. The works in front of the 1st division were being extended on this ridge opposite the 2d division, to be used by other troops in case of emergency, but I had not a sufficient number of men to man them. Subsequent investigation goes to show that the greater part of the enemy, some time during the night previous, crossed the Shenandoah River below the mouth of Cedar Creek and massed just outside of my pickets. At about half past four o'clock A. M., another force of the enemy crossed the creek in front of the first division, and soon after the enemy came rushing in solid lines of battle, without skirmishers, on my pickets, coming to the works with those of the pickets they had not captured, in overwhelming numbers, entered that portion of the works not occupied by our troops and soon were on the flank and in the rear of the first division and the two batteries, compelling them either to retreat or to be captured. The ground to be passed over was one succession of hills and ravines, so that it was impossible for the troops to make a rapid retreat in anything like good order. In the meantime, the 2d division was formed on a ridge parallel to and facing the pike, with its right nearly opposite to the left of the 19th corps. One brigade of the latter was placed in position nearly at right angles to this division and on its extreme right. On the left of the 2d division was Colonel Kitchin's command. This command commenced falling back, when the whole line apparently took it up in a good deal of disorder. In every regiment, however, a considerable number of men contested the advance of the enemy, and so delayed him until the army headquarters and other wagons were enabled to get off safely. Battery L, 1st Ohio artillery, remained in position until compelled to retire, doing good execution in its retreat. The dense smoke which enveloped everywhere tended greatly to create the general confusion that prevailed. After my command was re-formed, General Sheridan placed it on the left of the 6th corps, to be held in reserve. After the general advance was made I followed after, overtaking the other commands before they reached Cedar Creek. Captain H. A. Dupont, with battery B, 5th U. S., and Battery L, 1st Ohio artillery, galloped forward to the skirmish line and did most admirable execution. (See Captain Dupont's report.) The command camped for the night on the grounds occupied before. As the dense fog which prevailed shut from view the operations of most of the army, I respectfully refer you to the enclosed reports of my subaltern commanders for further details of this army's operations.

My loss was as follows: First Division—Killed, 13; wounded, 97; missing, 474; total, 584. Second division—Killed, 26; wounded, 154; missing, 31; total, 211. Artillery Brigade—Killed, 7; wounded, 17; missing, 28; total, 52. Totals—Killed, 46; wounded, 268; missing, 523; total, 847. Seven pieces of artillery, ten caissons, two battery wagons, one forge, four army wagons, and two ambulances.

I am specially indebted to my division and other commanders and to the members of my staff for valuable services rendered on that day. Captain Dupont, chief of artillery, and the officers and men of his batteries are deserving of particular mention for their conspicuous gallantry and the valuable services rendered that day. I am pained to report the death of Colonel Joseph Thoburn, commanding 1st division, and Captain Phillip G. Bier, Assistant Adjutant General on my staff. Both fell mortally wounded while rallying the men. Brave, efficient, and ever conspicuous for their gallantry on the field of battle, in them the country sustained a loss not easily repaired.

I respectfully call your attention to the loss of many brave and valuable officers who fell on that day, as mentioned in the reports of my subaltern commanders. Colonel R. B. Hayes had his horse shot under him, and was slightly injured.

I am, sir, very respectfully your obedient servant,

GEORGE CROOK, Major General.

The loss of the army in killed, wounded and prisoners was about 5,700, of which about 1,400 were prisoners. The loss of our corps was forty-six killed, 268 wounded, and 523 missing, which shows that it did not break to the rear with no attempt to show fight. The 1st brigade lost as follows: 116th Ohio, four killed, thirteen wounded, five prisoners; 123d Ohio, one killed, sixteen wounded, thirteen prisoners; 34th Massachusetts, two killed, seven wounded, thirty-four prisoners; 5th New York H. A., one killed, seven wounded, 153 prisoners, making a total of seven killed, forty-two wounded and 205 prisoners, which shows a very large proportion of the loss of the corps, and a still greater proportion of the loss of the division, which was thirteen killed, ninety-seven wounded, and 474 prisoners.

This battle ended the campaign in the Shenandoah Valley, and effectually destroyed the fine army, among which were the choice troops of the South, with which General Early had entered the Valley, and threatened Washington in July. Among the rebel killed was General Ramseur. When the news of this great battle reached the North, it rang with the praises of Sheridan. General Grant ordered salutes of 100 guns fired by the armies in Sheridan's honor, and he wrote the President as follows:

"Turning what had bid fair to be a disaster into a glorious victory, stamps Sheridan what I always thought him, one of the ablest of Generals."

President Lincoln telegraphed Sheridan:

"With great pleasure I tender you and your brave army the thanks of the Nation and my own personal congratulations and gratitude for the month's operations in the Shenandoah Valley, and, especially, for the splendid work on October 19th, 1864."

And, a few weeks later, the President appointed him a Major General in the regular army; and a few months later still, Congress passed a resolution thanking "Major General Philip H. Sheridan and the officers and men under his command, for the gallantry, military skill and courage displayed in the Valley of the Shenandoah, and especially for their services at Cedar Run on the 19th day of October, 1864, which retrieved the fortunes of the day, and thus averted a great disaster."

The greatest loss we met was in the death of Colonel Thoburn. No better or braver officer ever lived. Every man in his division fairly loved him. Firm, yet kind hearted as a child, he impressed every one who met him as an honest, patriotic, Christian gentleman. As a man he drew around him a pleasant circle of friends, constant and affectionate, who deeply and inconsolably mourned his loss. In disposition he was frank, manly, kind, and always cheerful. He was the soul of kindness to those he commanded, and the very soul of honor itself in all the relations of army life. He did not possess an impulsive nature. He was not a thunder-bolt on the field. He was a rock, rather. Fiery floods might break upon him, and yet he was always the same, always cool, strong, intrepid, brave and firm. While he was the soldier, every inch, he never forgot that he was also a citizen and a gentleman, and that he was simply engaged in war because duty and patriotism called him there. Hence he took no interest or pride in the pomps or forms of military life. He was too sincere, too deeply in earnest in the cause of his country to give a thought to anything that did not point directly toward the unity of the Nation, and its restoration from the fell powers of treason and disunion. His young State of West Virginia and the Nation could ill afford to lose such a man as General Thoburn. After the battles ending with Fisher's Hill, he was asked by General Crook to furnish the names of the officers of his division most conspicuous for gallantry and efficient conduct, and who were most deserving of promotion. A few days before his death he sent me a copy of his reply to this request. I here publish it, possibly for the first time it has been published anywhere, as a part of the history of our regiment. It will doubtless be gratifying to the officers named in it to know now, if they never did before, of the esteem in which their dead friend held them.

HEADQUARTERS 1ST INFANTRY DIVISION, ARMY WEST VIRGINIA,
September 27, 1864.

CAPTAIN:—In answer to your request to furnish you with the names of the officers of the 1st division most conspicuous for gallantry and efficient conduct in the late battles of Winchester and Fisher's Hill, and who are most deserving of promotion, I have the honor to report that with few exceptions all were brave and efficient, and deserving of all praise, and it is very difficult to avoid making the list too long, and thus defeat the object at which you aim. Among the bravest and most efficient I have the honor to present you with the following names: Colonel T. M. Harris, 10th West Virginia Volunteers, commanding 3d brigade; Lieutenant Colonel Thos. F. Wildes, commanding 116th Ohio Volunteers; Major H. W. Potter, commanding 34th Massachusetts Volunteers; Lieutenant Colonel J. P. Linton, commanding 5th Pennsylvania Volunteers; Adjutant Baughman, 10th West Virginia Volunteers; Lieutenant Geo. McComber, 34th Massachusetts Volunteers; Lieutenant H. H. Hornbrook, 1st West Virginia Volunteers; the last two, members of my staff. These officers were most conspicuous for gallantry, and are all highly deserving of promotion.

I have the honor to be very respectfully your obedient servant,

J. THOBURN, Colonel.

CAPTAIN P. G. BIER, A. A. Gen'l, A. W. Va.

I write of him as General Thoburn, at times, from the fact that he was promoted to Brigadier General, and his commission reached the headquarters of General Crook a few days after his death. No man in the army more meritoriously deserved high rank than he did. It was sorely regretted by all that he did not live to enjoy and wear the star he had so well earned, and so richly merited. It will, I know, be considered pardonable pride to have won the confidence and esteem of this noble man, otherwise I would not have published this highly prized paper.

A great many promotions in the army followed this battle, which was the effectual wiping out of the rebel army in the Shenandoah Valley. Serenading was the order of nearly every evening. The band of the 34th Massachusetts was one of the best in the army, and was in constant demand. On the 21st of October, General B. R. Cowen, then Adjutant General of Ohio, wrote to us: "I congratulate you on the gallant bearing of your command during the past campaign. You have reflected honor on the State by your actions, and will not be forgotten." On the 26th we received a visit from Colonel Washburn, to whom we gave a royal greeting. Tuesday, the 8th of November, the regiment voted for President, casting 374 votes for Lincoln, and eighty-one for McClellan.

On the 16th of November, at Kernstown, to which place we had fallen back on the 9th, the regiments of our brigade held the first dress parade they had had since early spring, except the 116th, on the occasion of Colonel Washburn's visit. Over six months had been so crowded with marches, battles and hard field service that there was no room for drills or parades, except in maneuvers on bloody battle fields.

Our Chaplain, Rev. E. W. Brady, resigned on the 18th, and left for his home. Before leaving he talked a few moments to the men and offered prayer, the first for five months. The last few months had been hard ones for a Chaplain, but Chaplain Brady always did the best he could. He was always ready to do anything he could, as well as officiate as Chaplain. He was exceedingly kind and attentive to the sick and wounded, and did a great deal of good work in the hospitals. During the whole time he was with the regiment he acted as postmaster, and was very faithful in the discharge of the important duties of that position. Both officers and men paid him the highest respect whenever he engaged in the duties of his calling, but when off duty and among the men, he was as jolly and as fond of sport as any of them in their efforts to break the *ennui* of camp life. He left the regiment with the good wishes of every officer and soldier in it. Rev. James Logan a private soldier in company C, was promoted to Chaplain and commissioned by the Governor at the request of the regiment. He had distinguished himself in several engagements in carrying the colors of the regiment after the color bearers had been disabled, coming forward at Lynchburg at the call for volunteers to carry the colors after the whole color guard had been wounded. His bravery was so noted, and his Christian character so marked, withal, that the private soldiers unanimously requested his appointment to the chaplaincy on the resignation of Reverend Brady. On the 28th we were paid off, and the men of company I raised a subscription, and sent it to Mrs. Matilda Secoy, whose husband had been killed in the battle of Opequan, on the 19th of September.

On the 18th of November, our brigade was ordered to Opequan bridge to guard the railroad at that point. On the 24th we received our share of the 10,000 Thanksgiving turkeys sent to "Little Phil's" army by the loyal people of Ohio and New York City, which, together with such chickens, pigs, turkeys, sheep, etc., as the "enemy's country" afforded, were served up at a Thanksgiving dinner, that, could our friends at home have seen, would have dispelled many a story to be found in the press and in old letters about the "sufferings of the boys in the field." Of the turkeys sent to the army at this time, Sergeant Walker wrote in his diary, under date of November 24th, 1864: "The train stopped at our depot to-day and put off 1,000 pounds of turkeys for this brigade, our share of 36,000 pounds sent to the Army of the Shenandoah by the citizens of New York City. All honor to the noble State that could thus remember the soldiers in the field. I will venture to say this is the first instance on record of turkeys being furnished to an entire army. American citizens against the world." Great boxes of all sorts of good things came at the same time from Massachusetts for the 34th, from which Lieutenant Ripley selected many a toothsome morsel for the table at headquarters. It now rained nearly every day, and was very cold and disagreeable, but very comfortable log huts were speedily built and "winter quarters" established on a grand scale. But, as was the constant fate of the soldier, we were doomed not to enjoy them very long. On the 17th of December a grand salute was fired in honor of General Thomas' victory over Hood.

On the 18th orders came to be ready to move next day for the Army of the James, in front of Richmond. The 6th corps had preceded us to the Army of the Potomac, going about the 1st of December. An order had come from General Grant for "the best division in Crook's corps," and in compliance with the order the 1st was selected. We were now to bid good-bye to the Shenandoah Valley! What recollections the thought revived

> "The echoes that start
> While memory plays its old tune on the heart."

What hardships the men of this division had endured in this Valley of Virginia. How often had its soil been baptized in the blood of its bravest and its best. What severe defeats they had sustained and what glorious victories they had achieved upon its soil. Scores of its best men were to be left behind in sanctified graves. From the Heights of Bolivar to the environs of Lynchburg, the roadsides, fields and forests were dotted with the burial places of its noble dead. In the hospitals of the army, lay hundreds of its maimed and disabled, and Oh, how many languished, worse than dead, in Southern prisons! How faithfully had its men fought for the success of the great cause of Liberty and Union in this bloody Valley. Is it any wonder, then, that protests were entered to its removal? Not from its officers or men, but from army commanders and the authorities of West Virginia. Strong protests against its removal from the field upon which it had achieved its renown were sent to General Grant and the authorities at Washington. It was urged that this division was more familiar with the Valley than any troops in it, was better acquainted with its people and their character, had become identified with it in every sense more closely than any troops that ever occupied it. But this was all in vain, and on the day designated in our orders, we started for our new field of operations. How well we maintained the good name of the "Army of West Virginia" alongside the veterans of the Potomac and the James, let history tell.

CHAPTER XIV.

GOOD-BYE SHENANDOAH VALLEY — ON THE CARS TO WASHINGTON — RIDE ON THE WATER — ARRIVAL AT DEEP-BOTTOM — PROMOTIONS — DRILLING AND INSPECTIONS — HIGH STANDING OF THE REGIMENT IN THE 24TH ARMY CORPS — REBEL RAMS AND GUNBOATS CREATE AN EXCITEMENT — MORE PROMOTIONS.

On the 19th of December, 1864, we took cars at Harper's Ferry. There was considerable anxiety among the men as to which course we would take, east or west, but this was soon settled by the train moving out toward Washington. Captain Mallory, having received a leave of absence, left us at the Ferry for his home in Meigs County. Owing to several hindrances, we did not get started until nearly dark. That night ride will be remembered as the most disagreeable ever experienced by the men. They were in box cars without any fire, and many in open cattle cars. It had rained all day and did not cease until dark, when it turned very cold and windy. The men suffered terribly with the cold. The entire 1st division of the Army of West Virginia followed us, our brigade being in the advance. We reached Washington about daylight and at once marched through the city to the Potomac River landing, where we took transports in waiting for us. The 116th boarded the "Lizzie Baker," the 123d and brigade headquarters the "Keyport," and the 34th Massachusetts the "Massachusetts," all sidewheel steamers. Without any delay all moved down the river, and at night anchored off Point Lookout. It was blowing a hurricane in the morning, and was very cold, and we did not start out until nearly noon. We were scarcely under way before the wind became furious again. Our vessel rolled terribly, and to us landsmen the experience was far from pleasant. The men were soon nearly all "seasick." The "Keyport" was an old vessel, and even the captain and crew were a little afraid of her, to say nothing of the rest of us, who saw nothing but destruction in the wild wind and waves. The wind continuing, toward night, we put into the mouth of a creek below Rappahanock. A gunboat on picket there, on seeing us approach, saluted us with a shot across our bow, which was another surprise to us. After we had hove to and anchored, the gunboat came out to us, and its officers invited brigade headquarters to take supper with them, which they gladly did. We started early next morning. We had proceeded but a short distance before we struck high wind and waves, rougher by far than the day before. The "Massachusetts," with the 34th Massachusetts regiment on board, had disappeared from our fleet. The "Keyport" was in real danger of foundering several times, and all felt great relief when we passed out of the breakers into smoother waters, and Fortress Monroe appeared in the distance. We anchored that night five miles below City Point, and next day moved up to James Landing, where we disembarked, and crossing the James River on pontoons, marched out to "Camp Holly," at Deep Bottom, on the Libby estate, and we were in the Army of the James. The 34th Massachusetts had not yet come up nor been heard from, and considerable anxiety was felt about it. Captains Dillon, Mann and Hull, of our regiment, by some mistake were left to come up on their boat. The mortars and Howlett's batteries kept roaring all night. General Butler was absent, trying to take Fort Fisher when we arrived, and General Ord was in command of the army.

Our first night was a very cold one, and we were furthermore obliged to sleep on the ground without tents and but little wood for fires. Since leaving our comfortable quarters at Opequan Bridge, on the 19th, until now, the 24th, we had a rough, hard time of it. The next morning found us all in pretty bad humor, and quartermasters and commissaries were hurried around as lively as ever they were. The 34th was now heard from. Their vessel was driven into Cherry Stone Inlet, where it was obliged to lie for two days. The regiment arrived on the 25th, and with it several of our officers and men. The men busied themselves building quarters, and having theirs well under way on the arrival of the 34th, turned out in force to help them build theirs. The Massachusetts men were not so handy with the axe, shovel and trowel as our western troops, and made the erection of quarters irksome work. Our men were always ready to help them on such work, for they were good fighters, and for that our men liked them. We were quartered on Libby's plantation, he of Libby prison fame, and our quartermaster erected his quarters in the Libby door yard, but the "door" and the house and all other buildings were long since gone the way of war.

The rebels came round to greet our coming, and considerable picket firing took place the night of the 25th, and the brigade was in line of battle behind the works most of the night. The next morning we went out a short distance on a reconnoisance, but the rebels had retired in the early morning. On the 26th, we received the news of General Sherman's capture of Savannah, and his presentation of it to President Lincoln as a Christmas gift. Salutes were ordered fired, and this brought on an angry cannonade which continued all day and nearly all night, and kept us under arms another night. Several of our officers received New Years gifts in the shape of well earned commissions:

>Captain W. B. Teters was promoted to Major.
>First Lieutenant J. C. H. Cobb was promoted to Captain.
>First Lieutenant A. B. Frame was promoted to Captain.
>Second Lieutenant Ransom Griffin was promoted to First Lieutenant.
>Second Lieutenant Wm. F. Boldenhorn was promoted to First Lieutenant

Their commissions were all dated December 27th, 1864. Captain Mallory returned to the regiment on the 9th of January from a leave of absence he received in the Shenandoah Valley, and the same day his company, "A," was detailed as provost guard at division headquarters, he to act as Provost Marshal. About this time an order was issued allowing furloughs to one-tenth of the command, and the scramble became quite exciting. In a few days, however, it was revoked. Road making was the "fatigue" work here, and we did our share of it. On the 18th, a dispatch was sent round announcing the capture of Fort Fisher on the 15th, and the regiment was called out and it read amid the wildest cheering. Many had just finished reading a long and labored letter published by General Seymour in the New York Times on the 16th, the day after the capture of Fort Fisher, but before the news reached the North, in which he conclusively demonstrated that it was impossible to capture the Fort. It was fine sport to turn from this dispatch to this able article. General Seymour "put his foot in it" badly.

Dr. James A. Sampsell joined us on the 19th, having been assigned to our regiment as Assistant Surgeon. For some time past very rigid inspections had been an almost daily occurrence. Under a corps order, our brigade had been competing for the first place in the corps in everything pertaining to the soldier. Major General Gibbon, a fine disciplinarian and splendid soldier, was now in command of the 24th Army Corps, to which our division was temporarily attached as a "provisional division." General Gibbon had already visited us on an inspecting tour, and he and his staff and the division commanders accompanying him spoke in high terms of praise of our camps and the soldierly bearing of officers and men, not only of the 116th, but of the 1st brigade. At an inspection held on the 22d, under the supervision of Captain Chas. W. Elwell, Inspector General of the brigade, the 116th was pronounced the best in the brigade, and excused from fatigue and picket duty for one week. Corporal James M. Stout, of company B, was pronounced the "best soldier in the regiment," and a little Irishman by the name of Hogan, in the 34th Massachusetts, the "best soldier in the brigade." He had the prettiest gun I ever saw, and had everything belonging to it and himself in the most complete order possible. He was, moreover, the perfect soldier in every respect. He was sent forward to division and corps headquarters, there to compete with others similarly selected from all the brigades in the corps. He came back in the evening pronounced the "best man in the 24th Army corps," and, under a provision of the inspection order, with a furlough in his belt for thirty days, and written permission to take his gun and accoutrements home with him. This was "first blood" for the 1st brigade.

At a very early hour on the morning of the 24th, a rebel fleet composed of the ironclads "Virginia," "Richmond" and "Fredericksburg," each carrying four guns, the wooden vessels "Drewry," "Nansemond" and "Hampton," each with two guns, the "Bedford," with one gun, the steamer "Torpedo" and three torpedo boats, dropped down from their anchorage above the Howlett batteries, ran past Fort Brady in the fog without being observed and attempted to pass the obstructions in the river and get down to City Point. The attention of the fort was, however, soon drawn to the vessels, and a lively cannonading followed for some time. It terminated in a hundred-pound gun being dismounted in the fort and the rebel vessels getting out of range. At length the enemy succeeded in cutting the chain in front of the obstructions beyond the lower end of Dutch Gap Canal, and the Fredericksburg got through under full head of steam; but the Richmond, Virginia and Drewry grounded, and the Fredericksburg had to return to their assistance. The Drewry could not be got off and was abandoned. A shell from Battery Parsons subsequently falling into her magazine, she blew up. It was now approaching daylight, and as the rebel fleet was in range of of the battery, and the gunboats on the river had recovered from their demoralization and were coming into action, the whole fleet retired up the river and escaped. It was a close call for the Army of the James, for had the rebel ironclads not grounded, the entire fleet of transports at City Point might have been sunk and the base of operations there destroyed, in which event the Army of the James and Fort Harrison would have been isolated from the forces on the south side and greatly endangered. Our army was all under arms from the moment the first gun was fired in the morning, and fearing a repetition of the experiment the next night, the whole army lay behind its works. A large force of rebel infantry lay waiting in our front to attack and "wipe us off the map," had the ironclad expedition been successful. It failing, all soon became quiet on the James.

On the 25th, General Harris inspected our brigade very minutely. We all thought him specially exacting and scrutinizing with the 116th. The next day he promulgated an order to the effect that the 116th was the best regiment in the division, "and would therefore be excused from fatigue and picket duty for two weeks." This created great excitement in camp, and as showing the good natured rivalry existing among the regiments of the brigade, the officers of the 34th and 123d, accompanied by the 34th band, went over and gave the 116th officers a serenade. Commissions arrived on the 28th for Sergeant Major Wm. J. Lee, to Second Lieutenant; Sergeant Joseph Purkey, to Second Lieutenant; Sergeant Jacob Wyckoff, to Second Lieutenant. On the same day we received notice of Lieutenant Sibley's resignation. He had but shortly before been exchanged in broken health. Captain Dillon resigned January 29th; Captain Chaney, February 1st; Adjutant Ballard, February 3d; and Captain Cochran, February 9th, which created several vacancies. On the 10th, Lieutenant Wm. B. Henry was promoted to First Lieutenant; Second Lieutenant Edward Muhleman, to First Lieutenant; Q. M. Sergeant Ezra L. Walker, to Second Lieutenant. On the 15th, First Lieutenant W. S. Martin was promoted to Captain; Second Lieutenant Rees Williams, to First Lieutenant; Sergeant Wm. H. Bush, to Second Lieutenant; Sergeant John S. Heald, to Second Lieutenant; Sergeant Charles A. Cline, to Second Lieutenant.

About the 3d of February, we received the news of the submission of the Thirteenth Amendment to the States for their ratification. There was universal rejoicing all through the army. None of the bad feeling seen everywhere when in January, 1863, the President issued the Emancipation Proclamation, existed anywhere now. Everyone was ready to adopt measures that would forever put an end to American slavery, and was glad steps to that end were being taken. Salutes were fired, and officers and men cheered, shook hands, pulled and jerked each other about and fairly danced for joy. As the news passed from one regiment to another, you could hear the cheers and shouts of men rolling along, and echoing and re-echoing, until it seemed as though the whole army was uniting in one grand effort to all cheer at once, and mingled with it all was the tremendous roar of artillery from the forts and artillery parks off to our left, and the gunboats and mortars on the river in our rear. Of course all this exasperated the enemy, and that night there was a great deal of picket firing, and we stood at arms most of the night.

At the Sunday inspection, January 29th, Corporal James M. Stout, who stood first in the regiment and second in the brigade at the previous inspection, was first in the brigade and first in the division and corps, and received a furlough for thirty days and written permission to take his gun and accoutrements home with him. The 1st brigade was announced, in an order from corps headquarters, as in the best order in the division, and the 34th Massachusetts the best in order in the brigade. Lieutenant Colonel Wildes, as brigade commander, now became entitled to a leave of absence under the inspection orders, and on the 6th left for home. Q. M. Sergeant Walker, now acting as Sergeant Major, also obtained a furlough. Captain Dillon, who had resigned on the 29th ult., on account of disability, went home now, and also Major Teters on leave of absence. We thus had a pleasant party. John A. Dennis, of company I, was accidentally killed at Chapin's Farm by the falling of a tree, on the 10th of February. It was a sad affair. He was a good soldier, had always done his duty well, and it seemed hard to thus lose his life after passing through all the great battles of the Shenandoah Valley safely. About the 12th, it grew very cold and windy. Among other capers of the wind, was the blowing down of our chapel, which had been built about a month before at the request of the Chaplain, and a great many chimneys. On the 15th, a great many prisoners were exchanged at Aiken's Landing, among them several of our regiment. They met with a royal reception when they came out to our camp. For several nights along between the 15th and 23d there was a great deal of disturbance on the picket lines. On the 21st, we received news of Sherman's capture of Charleston, Columbia, etc., and more salutes were fired, again exasperating the rebels. The old flag was again floating over Fort Sumter.

On the 23d, a commission as Assistant Surgeon was received for Hospital Steward James T. Moran, but the regiment had not men enough to allow him to be mustered. No more faithful, industrious and competent man for his position could be found in the service than Dr. Moran, and his failure to enjoy his well earned promotion was deeply regretted. No officer or man in the regiment performed his duty more faithfully, throughout the service, than Jas. T. Moran. Major Teters returned on the 27th. News to-day of the fall of Wilmington. More salutes, and the rebels are mad again. Orders to move at an hour's notice have been in existence for several days. On the 28th, Corporal John M. Mitchell, of company I, and Sergeant Uriah Hoyt, of company B, received orders from the War Department to report at Columbus for promotion in a new regiment, the 186th, of which Lieutenant Colonel Wildes was made Colonel. Desertions from the rebels were very numerous along about this time, and the deserters say that shooting at them as they cross the lines explains much of the picket firing heard every night. February 26th. Lieutenant Colonel Wildes was appointed Colonel of the 186th O. V. I., and Major Teters was promoted to Lieutenant Colonel of the 116th. Quartermaster Sergeant Ezra L. Walker, who had performed so long such valuable services in the Quartermaster's department of the 116th, was appointed Quartermaster of the 186th. Commissary Sergeant W. T. Patterson was appointed Quartermaster Sergeant, *vice* Walker, promoted, and Frank O. Pickering was appointed Commissary Sergeant. Captain John Hull was promoted to Major. Major Hull resigned and went home on the 16th of February. He was an old man, too old for active field service, but he had endured the hardships of the service remarkably well, always bravely did his duty as an officer, and he now left the regiment for his home with the kind wishes of both officers and men, and with the esteem and respect of all. On the 18th the following promotions took place:

    First Lieutenant John C. Heathorn, to Captain.
    First Lieutenant Wm. Mosely, to Captain.
    First Lieutenant John S. Manning, to Captain.
    Second Lieutenant Charles P. Allison, to First Lieutenant.
    Second Lieutenant Wm. J. Lee, to First Lieutenant.
    Second Lieutenant Joseph Parkey, to First Lieutenant.

General Grant and the Secretary of War reviewed the Army of the James on the 18th. It was a grand affair, and the whole army appeared in admirable condition. General Gibbon, in command of the 24th army corps, is one of the very best officers in the army, and General Ord, in command of the Army of the James, well deserves the confidence which General Grant seems to repose in him. On the 22d, Brevet Major General Turner assumed command of the division, which was now designated the 2d division of the 24th army corps, relieving General Harris, who returned to the command of his old brigade, the 3d. The troops are marching and counter-marching, and all are under orders to march to-morrow morning. Instead of marching on the 23d, we had another inspection.

CHAPTER XV.

OFF FOR PETERSBURG — CONTINUOUS HARD MARCHING — HATCHER'S RUN — SKIRMISHING — LIST OF CASUALTIES — A NARROW ESCAPE FOR CAPTAIN MANN AND FORTY MEN — FORT GREGG CARRIED BY ASSAULT — SOME INCIDENTS CONNECTED WITH THE CHARGE — REPORT OF LIEUTENANT COLONEL POTTER — CASUALTIES OF THE REGIMENT — AFTER LEE — FARMVILLE AND RICE'S STATION — LIST OF CASUALTIES — A GOOD DAY'S MARCH — LEE'S RETREAT CUT OFF — APPOMATTOX — THE WHITE FLAGS — SURRENDER — GENERAL GIBBON'S ORDER.

Finally, on the morning of the 25th, our division started on the march with a pontoon train and entrenching tools. Leaving Camp Holly to our left, our division moved out on the White House road, through a dense evergreen forest among the Chickahominy swamps. Our anticipations were that we were going out to meet Sheridan, on his way to join the Army of the Potomac from White House, which he had reached from the Shenandoah Valley on the 19th. After moving out some distance, we took the Charles City road. Cavalry was posted all along. We soon came to some of McClellan's battle fields covered with fortifications and the debris of battle. We halted at noon near the Chickahominy, and the pontoon corps began the construction of a pontoon bridge across the river. The bridge was scarcely laid before some of Sheridan's troopers made their appearance and crossed over, but Sheridan himself, with the main part of his cavalry, had crossed further down, and were now well on their way to James' Landing, on the James. It was a great disappointment to our old division of the Army of West Virginia not to meet our old commanders, Sheridan and Crook. Next morning we counter-marched for the James. Coming within sight of our old camp, we filed to the left, and went into camp at Deep Bottom Landing. We found Sheridan crossing to the south side of the James at James' Landing, a little below us. Monday, March 27th, we stripped for battle, casting aside everything not absolutely necessary. We never before marched so light. Just after sundown we crossed the James on pontoons, wound along the river bank some distance, and then turning to the right entered the dense evergreen forest. Were it not for fires at intervals, we could not have made much headway in the darkness and splashing mud. Crossed the Appomattox below the Point of Rocks, and filing to the right took the Petersburg road. Halted at 4 A. M. opposite the Petersburg front. Picket firing was very lively in front. We slept about three hours, and then marched very rapidly along the lines to the left. Large bodies of troops were everywhere, forts and earthworks on all sides. Everything was on the move. On our march to-day we passed Sheridan's cavalry taking a rest. Also passed General Mead's headquarters. Marched fifteen miles, and went into camp after crossing the Weldon and Grant's military railroads. The next morning we moved at daylight. Going a short distance, we relieved the 2d corps, taking their quarters at Humphrey's Station. Grant, Sheridan, Meade and Crook passed us on their way to the front. On the 29th, Captain Hamilton L. Karr was promoted to Major, First Lieutenant Richmond O. Knowles to Captain, and Second Lieutenant Wm. H. Bush to First Lieutenant.

At 5 o'clock the morning of the 30th, our division crossed Hatcher's Run, the left connecting with the right of the 2d corps, and the right resting near Hatcher's Run, our brigade being on the right. During the day we moved forward in conjunction with the 2d corps, our brigade, at night, connecting on the right with Foster's 2d division. General Harris' brigade was on the left, and Colonel Curtis' being in reserve. Skirmishing was lively all day, our regiment having a few wounded. Early in the morning of the 31st, our brigade was ordered to drive in the enemy's picket line in our front, in order to develop the position of the enemy. This was very gallantly done. The enemy's entire picket line was either captured or driven within his works, and our own picket line established within 400 yards of the enemy's works, enabling us to completely silence his artillery on this part of his line, and giving us a very important advantage. Lieutenant Colonel Kellogg, of the 123d Ohio, had charge of our skirmish line, and he is very highly praised by General Turner for his gallantry on this occasion. After this advance we fortified, and during the remainder of that day and the 1st of April we were engaged in strengthening our position. The loss of our regiment on the 30th and 31st was two killed and nine wounded, as follows:

KILLED.

John E. Smith, Company E; Emanuel Byers, Company C. 2.

WOUNDED.

Erastus H. White, Company B; Corporal Abner G. Carlton, Company C; John M. Carlton, Company C; Andrew J. Morris, Company C; Jos. S. Johnson, Company C; James Agin, Company D; James A. Strong, Company G; Miner Starkey, Company F; George Beach, Company I.—9.

Sheridan had, early in the morning of the 30th of March, connected his right with the left of the 5th corps near the Boydton plank road. The enemy were found to have constructed a very strong line of entrenchments to cover the position known as Five Forks, of great strategic value, where five roads meet in the woods, three of which led back to the South Side Railroad, and the possession of which would be equivalent to turning the enemy's right flank.

To give a more complete outline of the position, it might be recapitulated that Sheridan, with the cavalry, occupied the extreme left, and was working round to get beyond the enemy's right. Next toward the right in order lay the 5th, the 2d, the 24th, the 6th, the 9th corps, with a division of the 25th in reserve. Early on the morning of 31st, Warren began to move the 5th corps. At Gravelly Run, it was met by the enemy in strong force and driven back, and the attack was not checked until met by Miles' division of the 2d corps. Towards noon Sheridan had been also attacked on the left and portions of his cavalry driven back. About 5 o'clock the 5th corps, having rallied, advanced its lines again. During all the 31st of March, the 9th and 25th corps were not engaged, but about 10 o'clock at night the 6th, 9th and 24th opened a general cannonade, which was continued till four o'clock on the following morning. The great events of the first of April were inaugurated by the enemy at 4 o'clock in the morning, by an attack on Foster's division of the 24th corps. The onset was so sudden and impetuous that the enemy planted their colors on the fortifications held by Damby's brigade, and was near routing the entire division. Our division instantly came to its support, the 116th charging the rebels in possession of Damby's works, and they were driven out almost as suddenly as they came in. A musketry and artillery fire broke out along the center and right of the line, but it was soon over, with little loss on either side. The rebels captured a few prisoners in their charge, but we captured a great many more from them when we drove them out. Seven slightly wounded was the result in our regiment, and a number of prisoners passed to the rear through our ranks.

An exciting incident occurred to Captain Mann and forty men of our regiment. On the evening of the 31st, the Captain was summoned to division headquarters by General Turner, who advised him that he had been selected to take charge of forty select men, to be supplied with axes, whose duty it would be to advance in the morning, in advance of the skirmish line, and cut away the abatis in front of the rebel works, so that his troops, who were to make an assault at daylight, could pass through. At 12 o'clock, the Captain and his men moved out in front of our works, and lay down to await the time of the movement in the morning. But the enemy, probably anticipating our tactics, made an assault upon our works a little before the time fixed for our assault upon theirs. The battle raged right over the prostrate forms of the Captain's detail, many rebels being killed and wounded right among his men. They hugged the ground closely throughout the struggle, and when the rebels were repulsed, the Captain and his forty brave pioneers came within our works, where they were greeted as if they had risen from the dead. Nobody expected to see one of them alive again, and probably had they gone on the mission assigned them the night before, but few, if any, of them would have escaped alive. The assault contemplated by General Turner was not made, the assault of the enemy, just described, disarranging his plans, and besides because other plans were at once conceived.

But all day on the 1st, the most desperate and decisive fighting had been going on about Five Forks on the left. The day before, Sheridan had met with some reverses in his efforts to flank the rebel right. At night General Grant had placed Sheridan in command, not only of all the cavalry, but of the 5th corps under Warren, determined that the disasters of the day before should not be repeated. Sheridan now controlled four divisions of cavalry and three of infantry, aggregating not far from 30,000 strong, and double that which the enemy could concentrate against him at Five Forks, while the rebel lines, all the way from Dinwiddie Court House to Petersburg, were threatened by forces largely superior to theirs. At daybreak, Sheridan put his whole cavalry force in motion to accomplish his mission of getting round the rebel right. Five Forks was the strategic point of the whole rebel position. That taken, and the position would be completely turned and rendered untenable. Sheridan worked his way steadily up to the entrenchments on all sides, while the enemy fell back, fighting fiercely. Finally a division of the cavalry got well round on the enemy's flank and rear. About 3 o'clock, the 5th corps was ordered up to support the cavalry. As soon as it arrived, Ayres' and Crawford's divisions were swung in on the left, Ayres' striking the flank of the enemy's works. Crawford, advancing, found himself in the rebel rear.

"The Great Civil War," speaks of the battle from this point as follows: "The enemy had steadily fallen back at first, fighting obstinately, however, till 5 o'clock, when they made a decisive stand, and then for two hours raged one of the most fearful contests of the war. Riding to all parts of the field, Sheridan cheered, urged and drove on his men, and at length they nearly surrounded the enemy's position, swarmed over the parapets, and the rebel troops, exhausted with their great efforts, and much weakened by the havoc which had been made in their ranks, and seeing it useless longer to resist the overwhelming force pouring in upon them, broke and rushed to the rear, seeking to escape by the only outlet still open. There was another fierce struggle, but by half-past seven the battle was over."

Thus Five Forks fell into our hands, and that night Custer's and McKenzie's divisions of cavalry pressed on in pursuit of the fugitives. The 2d corps had all day been swinging forward so as to connect with the 5th, fighting hard all the way, and in the evening Miles' division pushed on to Sheridan at Five Forks.

We thus give a brief account of the movements on the left on the 1st, so that a clearer idea may be had of the importance of our own movements on the right on the 2d.

As before stated, a furious cannonade was kept up all along the front of the 6th, 9th and 24th corps, until 4 o'clock on the morning of the 2d. At that hour, these several corps were massed for a charge, the 6th in front of Forts Welch and Fisher, and Turner's and Foster's divisions of the 24th on both sides of Hatcher's Run, in front of Fort Gregg, Turner's division in support of Foster's. At 4 o'clock, the 6th moved on the double quick across the intervening space of 800 yards, and after several hours of hard fighting captured the two forts in their front. The 24th had further to move, but it also was successful in capturing Fort Gregg, a very formidable work in its front. The 116th won great praise for its gallantry in its charge on Fort Gregg. In the assault on Fort Gregg, the 116th was in the third line of the assaulting column. The first line was checked, the second also. When our line came up, it was also checked by the troops lying in front of us, extending back from the ditch around the fort four or five rods. In the final rush, our line was first on their feet and charged over and through the other troops, many of them joining in the charge. Our colors, with the colors of the 10th Connecticut, were the first planted upon the parapet of the fort. These two stands of colors, it was claimed at the time, were planted simultaneously. The 116th colors were carried by Corporal Francis J. Stout, of company C, who took them up at Cedar Creek, after they had been shot down several times, and he carried them to the close of the war. The record of modern warfare hardly furnishes a parallel to the desperate encounter which took place on the parapet of Fort Gregg. Thirteen rebels were found inside the fort killed by bayonet thrusts, while scores were wounded by the same weapon. Union and rebel soldiers lay dead on the parapet and inside the fort in each other's grasps. Nor were officers the only brave ones. There was scarcely a private soldier of our regiment who was not worthy of special mention and praise for his gallantry. Sergeant E. C. King, of company F, is said to have been among the first to scale the enemy's works. He was promised a Medal of Honor, but for some reason never received it. There were numerous noted acts of bravery on the part of officers and men. A party of men, privates Williams and Reusser of E, Samuel Forsythe of D, Joseph Van Meter of G, and Corporal Thompson of F, advanced in a squad by themselves under the lead of Sergeant Reithmiller of E, to a bank close up to the fort, and lay down, watching for a chance to dash forward. Seeing the chance, all rose together to start, but that instant the brave Sergeant was killed. The rest of the party ran on, and digging holes in its side with their bayonets, climbed on to the parapet of the fort. In a moment they were joined by Corporal Stout bearing the colors, and the rest of the regiment. Then followed the most desperate fighting, the rebels trying to capture the colors and kill its bearers. The men clustered around their colors, and here we met our most serious loss in killed and wounded. As the men drove the rebels back, and were jumping from the parapet into the fort, a rebel Captain cried out: "Never surrender to the d——d Yankees." The words were scarcely out of his mouth, before John Cole of B, and Ephraim Williams of E, clubbed their guns, and he soon paid for the remark with his life. At the same moment, a rebel and John W. Reusser of E, leveled their guns upon each other. They each fired at the same instant, the rebel's ball grazing Reusser's ear, and Reusser's ball going through the breast of the rebel. Forsythe was attacked by two big burly rebels. He bayonetted one, and was himself bayonetted in the leg by the other, just as the surrender was made. Corporal Freeman C. Thompson of F, and Joseph Van Meter of G, were conspicuous for their bravery from first to last in the attack and capture of Fort Gregg, and were each awarded a "Medal of Honor" by the Secretary of War. Corporal Thompson was knocked off the parapet into the ditch twice by clubbed muskets. A third time he mounted it, and lying down beside Van Meter, they two fired directly into the fort, while others, unable to get up, handed up loaded guns, and re-loaded those handed down to them by these two gallant soldiers. Finally, the men covering the parapet on all sides, the rebels who had been in partial cover under the walls, rose up and made a last desperate effort to drive our men down. Then our men rose, and rushing down into the fort, engaged in a hand to hand struggle, and forced a surrender in a short time. In the final struggle, Van Meter wrenched a rebel flag from the hands of its bearer. Thirteen men in the division were awarded "Medals of Honor," and all accompanied General Gibbon in charge of rebel flags to Washington, after the surrender of Lee. Joseph Gerolds, of H, seized a rebel officer on the parapet, and after a desperate struggle, compelled him to surrender his sword. Colonel Teters was, as usual, conspicuous for his great gallantry, and led the regiment throughout the attack with the utmost fearlessness and bravery. All the officers behaved splendidly, and where all did so nobly, it seems invidious to single out any for special mention. All, however, concede that Lieutenant Wm. H. Bush, who was killed in the charge, and Captain Mann, Lieutenant Wm. Biddenharn, and Lieutenant Reese Williams greatly distinguished themselves, and added fresh laurels to their former reputations as gallant officers.

Lieutenant Colonel Potter, in command of the brigade, says in his report of the battle of Fort Gregg: "I moved with the 116th Ohio and 34th Massachusetts from Hatcher's Run. About 8 A. M. came onto the field in front of Fort Gregg, a very strong position held by the enemy. My command supported General Foster's division of the 24th A. C., advancing with him. As we advanced, I found some rebel pickets behind an entrenched line, who annoyed my flank at first. I advanced by an oblique movement to the right, and then by a left half wheel, succeeded in placing one regiment of my command, the 116th Ohio, on the southern front of the fort. This gave me a direct fire on this front and an enfilading fire on the westerly front. We advanced rapidly without firing till we reached a road some fifty yards from the fort, where we lay down and poured in a rapid and accurate fire. We suffered severely in reaching this point, but once there we had the best of it. After lying here some twenty-five minutes, and succeeding in a great measure in silencing the enemy's fire, we charged the work and placed our colors on the fort among the first. The attack was gallantly made and most stubbornly resisted. The enemy refused to yield till we were fairly within his works. My loss was one commissioned officer and sixteen men killed, and sixty-three wounded." *Colonel Potter's report, April 2, 1865.*

In this movement the 34th Massachusetts was on the right, the 116th on the left, and when the "left half wheel" mentioned by Colonel Potter was made, the 116th bore the brunt of the movement and suffered great loss. Colonel Potter reports seventeen killed and sixty-three wounded, including one commissioned officer killed, Lieutenant Bush, of the 116th. It will be seen that our killed was fifteen and wounded thirty-three. General Lincoln, in his history of the 34th Massachusetts, gives the loss of his regiment as five killed and thirty-two wounded. Consolidating these losses makes the loss of the two regiments twenty killed and sixty-five wounded. It is probable that the severely wounded in our regiment on the 1st of April are included in our report for the 2d, and that the discrepancy in the number killed is accounted for by including a few who, being mortally wounded, died after Colonel Potter's report of casualties was made, which seems to have been made on the evening after the battle. The loss of the 116th in the charge exceeded that of any other regiment engaged, being fifteen killed and thirty-three wounded. It is given in full below:

KILLED.

Lieutenant William H. Bush, Company B; Sergeant Fred. E. Humphrey, Company B; Sergeant Myron R. Hitchcock, Company B; Corporal James M. Hartley, Company B; Privates William Hall, Company C; William H. Mobberly, Company C; Sergeant John G. Reithmiller, Company E; Corporal Louis W. Mozena, Company E; Robert S. Hutcheson, Company E; Gilbert McCoy, Company E; Samuel Rubener, Company E; Martin Hysell, Company G; James Irwin Rogers, Company H; James Lindsay, Company K; David G. Groce, Company K. Total killed, 15.

WOUNDED.

John P. Kibble, Company B; Otis P. Henry, Company B; Benj. F. McLain, Company B; Philip Feiger, Company B; John Truax, Company C; Geo. W. Sampson, Company C; Sergeant Wm O. Belt, Company D; Corporal Samuel Forsythe, Company D; Eli Whitlatch, Company D; John M. Bougher, Company E; Frederick Stephens, Company E; Levi Howell, Company E; Jacob S. Hurd, Company E; Andrew J. Curtis, Company E; John Schappa, Company E; David Amos, Company F; Corporal Edward King, Company F; Valentine Mahl, Company F; Henry Dillon, Company F; George Ray, Company F; Corporal David Longstreth, Company G; Corporal Edward Lowry, Company G; Samuel Barrett, Company G; Sergeant B. F. Sammons, Company H; Henry C. Mathews, Company H, right foot shot off by a shell; Corporal Jeremiah Swain, Company H; Joseph Smith, Company H; James R. P. Keyser, Company H; Nathaniel Butler, Company H; Corporal Armstrong Johnson, Company H; Isaac Yoho, Company H; Sergeant Geo. H. Bean, Company I; Charles Andrews, Company K. Total wounded, 33.

Company A was not engaged in this or any of the battles of this campaign, being detached as Provost Guard at Division Headquarters.

In a letter to the Athens Messenger, published April 20th, 1865, Quartermaster Sergeant Wm. T. Pattersen says: "To render Petersburg untenable and its evacuation and capture certain, Fort Gregg, a formidable work. defended by men *selected* for its defense, must be taken. It was situated near General A. P. Hill's headquarters. The 116th was one of the regiments selected to assault and take this fort. It did its part nobly. Never did men display greater bravery. Lieutenant Colonel Teters was conspicuous for gallantry. Every officer and man did all that brave men could do. Out of 350 engaged, the 116th lost fifteen killed and thirty-five wounded. It was a desperate charge, and one of the few instances in the war where bayonets were used. Many of the prisoners bore bayonet wounds. The rebel General A. P. Hill was killed here."

The loss of our regiment on the 2d was cause of great mourning. Company B was fearfully stricken in the death of four of its finest men. Lieutenant Bush was a brave man, a most worthy and exemplary citizen, and in every way that a man could be, was a true soldier and noble officer. He was wounded at the battle of Piedmont. Sergeant Humphrey was very severely wounded in the battle of Lynchburg, in the shoulder and neck, while most gallantly bearing the colors of the regiment, as before stated, and remained a prisoner for several months. He was First Sergeant of his company at the time of his death. No man in the company made a better record as a soldier than Sergeant Humphrey. Sergeant Hitchcock was a finely educated, brave and courteous gentleman, and was always to be found at his post of duty. He was chief of Division Orderlies at Division Headquarters, and was in discharge of his duty delivering orders on the field when he received a mortal wound, of which he soon after died. In the Athens (O.) Messenger of March 16th, 1861, appears an account of the closing exercises of the "Third Term of Tupper's Plains Seminary," from which is taken the following mention of Sergeant Hitchcock, then a student at the Seminary: "The music selected for the occasion was most appropriate and beautiful, and gave evidence of the ability of Prof. M. R. Hitchcock." He was a musician of very high order, and often relieved the monotony and dullness of camp life with his sweet singing. He organized a quartette in company B which was not easily excelled. Few men had more friends in the regiment or at home than Sergeant Hitchcock. Corporal James M. Hartley had been wounded quite severely in the head at Fisher's Hill. He was a fine man and a brave and efficient soldier. Sergeant John G. Reithmiller was a splendid soldier and highly esteemed man. At the time of his death he was the Orderly Sergeant of company E, and his loss was a great one to his company and his friends. He, too, was quite severely wounded at Lynchburg. Our very best men seemed fated to fall that day. This record shows that these men were always in the fore front of battle. By a little comparison, the reader will find many more names among our list of killed and wounded of that day that were on our lists of wounded in battles before.

General Turner, in his report of the battle of Fort Gregg, says: "During the night of the 1st and morning of the 2d, in obedience to orders received direct from Major General Ord, I massed Colonel Curtis' and Colonel Potter's brigades on the right of Colonel Damby's brigade of the 1st division in preparation for an assault, which, however, was countermanded by Major General Gibbon. Shortly after daybreak, I directed General Harris to advance a strong skirmish line up to the enemy's works to ascertain if he was not leaving, of which I had strong suspicions, which was accordingly done. Lieutenant Colonel Kellogg of the 123d Ohio, of the 1st brigade, who had been left on the skirmish line with his regiment under General Harris' order, when Lieutenant Colonel Potter's brigade was moved off during the night, advanced with his regiment with General Harris' line. This line, after some slight resistance, carried the enemy's works, capturing two guns, three battle flags and some prisoners. Before General Harris had reached the enemy's line, I received an order to send two brigades to our signal tower near Fort Gregg in support of the 6th corps, which, I was then informed, had broken the enemy's line. I accompanied these two brigades (the 1st and 2d) and subsequently, in the afternoon, I found them in support of Foster's division, which, immediately after my arrival, moved to the assault of Fort Gregg, an important out-work of the enemy's defenses around Petersburg. Colonel Curtis and Colonel Potter moved in close support to the 1st division, and joined hands with Foster's troops in the desperate struggle which took place for the possession of Fort Gregg. After nearly half an hour of desperate fighting, this work was carried, but with the loss of many brave officers and men. Immediately after the capture of Fort Gregg, an adjoining work of the enemy was carried by General Harris, who reported to me shortly after with its garrison, some sixty in number, including its commander." *General J. W. Turner's report, April 26, 1865.*

Two of the cannon here captured were taken from General Milroy at Winchester, in June, 1863.

The night of the 2d, the 116th was placed on picket in front of another fort close by, into which it advanced its skirmishers about 4 o'clock on the morning of the 3d, the enemy abandoning it during the night. In a report made on the 4th, Colonel Potter says: "I have the honor to report that on the night of the 2d, I placed the 116th regiment O. V. I. on picket in front of my brigade. I instructed Lieutenant Colonel Teters commanding to post his videttes well up to the enemy's works. He reports that about 4 A. M., finding that the enemy had abandoned the works, he advanced a portion of his skirmish line into the fort. He found about sixty stand of arms and a small quantity of tobacco." The fort thus occupied was Fort Lee.

On the morning of the 3d, we found the enemy gone. Fort Gregg is about two miles from Petersburg, in a southwesterly direction, but with it and the works taken by the

6th and 9th corps the day before, Petersburg must easily
fall, and so, without awaiting our coming, the rebels evacuated it during the night. Early in the morning, we received
the news of the fall of Richmond also, and very soon both
Richmond and Petersburg were occupied by Federal troops
without opposition. O, what rejoicing! What cheering
and what gladness among the troops! General Deven's division occupied Richmond. But the work was not yet finished. Lee was making a desperate effort to escape, and
pursuit was begun early on the morning of the 31st.*

The column of the Army of the James under General
Ord accompanied by General Grant, pushed on that day
fifteen miles, our division in the advance, the purpose of our
march being to get between Lee and Danville. Jefferson
Davis again says: "This was done, and thus Lee was prevented from carrying out his original purpose, and directed
his course toward Lynchburg." Our column marched
along the Cox road to Sutherland Station, ten miles west of
Petersburg, and from that point, leaving the main line of
march of the body of the army, marched along the railroad
to Wilson's Station, where we encamped for the night.
Still following the railroad on the 5th, our division in the
advance, reached Blacks and Whites about 2 o'clock.
Thence, the roads being very good, we pushed on briskly
to Nottaway, nine miles from Burkesville. At this point,
having marched twenty miles, it was proposed to stop and
rest. But at half-past 6, Sheridan's dispatch reached Grant
informing him of the state of things, and the two divisions
of the 24th corps were pushed on to Burkesville, which we
reached at 11 P. M. At the same hour Grant joined
Sheridan at Jettersville. The 2d and 6th corps had, during

---

*"At nightfall, April 2d, Lee's army commenced crossing the Appomattox, and
before dawn was far on its way to Amelia Court House, Lee's purpose being, as previously agreed upon in a conference with me, to march to Danville, Virginia." Jefferson
Davis in "Rise and Fall of the Confederate Government."

the day, attacked Lee's retreating army near Dratonville and driven it across Sailor's Creek, where General Sheridan met it with the cavalry. The head of Lee's army was directed towards Farmville. After a hard fight at Sailor's Creek about 10,000 of the enemy surrendered, among the prisoners being Generals Ewell, Kershaw, Curtis Lee and several other prominent officers. Lee, with the remainder of his force, made his way toward Farmville. Early on the morning of the same day, the two divisions of our corps took up the line of march for Farmville, intending to head off Lee in his retreat. It was a tight race between us. We met the head of the enemy's column at Rice's Station, where our regiment was engaged with considerable loss, and drove them back upon Farmville.

Early on the morning of the 6th, the 123d Ohio, 54th Pennsylvania, a squadron of the 4th Massachusetts cavalry, and a large pioneer corps, all under command of General Read, were hastened forward to either possess themselves of the bridges near Farmville, or destroy them. This small force met the enemy crossing the bridges to the south side of the Appomattox. General Read at once attacked. The enemy fell back in his front, only to allow large bodies to fall upon his flanks and rear, when, being surrounded by an overwhelming force, Lieutenant Colonel Kellogg was obliged to surrender, the gallant General Read having been killed. But a delay was thus occasioned, which enabled General Ord to get up with the remainder of his force and place himself across Lee's path southward. Both sides immediately entrenched. We held Lee there during the night of the 6th. Early on the morning of the 7th, the 2d corps and Crook's division of cavalry came up and attacked the rebels. A sharp engagement followed, in which our army suffered considerable loss, and Lee was driven across to the north side of the Appomattox, and so closely was he followed, that he could not destroy the bridges, and the 2d and

6th corps and a division of cavalry crossed in pursuit. Only the left wing of our regiment was engaged, the right wing having been sent down the Danville Railroad, the morning of the 6th, from Burkesville Junction. Our loss in the engagement on the evening of the 6th and morning of the 7th was all from the skirmish line, as follows:

KILLED.

Robert S. Hutcheson, Company E.—1.

WOUNDED.

William B. McFarland, Company E; Isaac Littleton, Company E; Samuel McConnell, Company E; Thomas Berry, Company K.—4.

At High Bridge the following, who were pioneers, were captured upon the surrender of the 123d Ohio and 54th Pennsylvania:

Uriah Reldin, Company E; John Baker, Company B; John J. Walters, Company E; William H. Bassett, Company C; Jacob Dudley, Company B; John C. Bailey, Company I; John E. Ewers, Company I; Hopson L. Sherman, Company I; Perry Gardner, Company K; James Lafever, Company A.—10.

Colonel Potter reports the loss of the brigade in the engagement at Rice's Station as one killed and five wounded, so it will be seen that all the loss fell upon the 116th. He makes no mention of the prisoners we lost at High Bridge.

Early on the morning of the 7th, the enemy was found to have abandoned his position, and we moved on to Farmville, where we remained until 5 o'clock the morning of the 8th, when we moved out on the Lynchburg road, and following General Sheridan's cavalry all day, went into camp near Appomattox Station, about 11 P. M. General Grant passed us on the road serenely smoking a cigar and pushing liesurely to the front on a small black horse. No one would think such momentous events were transpiring under his direction. He appeared as cool and calm as if on a pleasure trip. The roads were terrible. Rain fairly poured nearly all the time, yet, notwithstanding, the army moved with incredible speed. It was the hardest and best day's march, taking the state of the weather and condition of the roads into consideration, that was made by any troops during the war, the distance made from 5 A. M. to 11 P. M. being about thirty-eight miles. The march was in a southwesterly direction till about noon, when it turned abruptly in a northwestwardly direction. Every soldier felt that the object of our movement was to keep south of Lee, and when we turned to the northwest all seemed to realize that the end was near, and with renewed energies the men pushed on. The firing of the 2d and 6th corps pursuing Lee became more and more distinct as we advanced, and the eagerness of the men to get across Lee's track knew no bounds. The cavalry, under Sheridan, pushed directly for Appomattox Station. Late in the evening, Sheridan struck the railroad at Appomattox Station, drove the rebels from that point, and captured twenty-five pieces of artillery and a large amount of other war material, including a hospital train and four trains loaded with provisions for Lee's army. At 3 o'clock the morning of the 9th, we were again on the move, and after marching four or five miles, the last half of the distance at nearly a double quick, we went into line of battle on the right of the road leading from Appomattox Court House to Lynchburg, the 1st division taking position on the left of the road. Sheridan's cavalry was in our front dismounted, fighting with all their might to hold the enemy until the infantry should come up. The rebels were pressing on hard and rapidly, hoping to break through before the arrival of the infantry, and before their furious attacks the cavalry was stubbornly falling back. As the cavalry met our infantry lines rapidly advancing, they sent up a cheer which spoke the relief they felt and their gladness at seeing us there. We were square across Lee's track and in the very front of the head of his retreating and escaping army. The enemy advanced eagerly on the charge as the cavalry fell back and around our flanks, evidently resolved now to break through, when lo! at the edge of the woods appeared the long, strong lines of our infantry coming out with a yell. They recoiled and shrank back as if paralyzed! The infantry pushed on, and, as it advanced to the open ground, before it, could be seen, in the valley about the Court House below, the broken fragments of a once great and proud army. We knew the 2d and 6th corps were beyond in the rear of Lee, for we could hear them firing, and that now, anyhow, Lee and his army were surrounded!

Before advancing into the open ground, the lines were halted, aligned and prepared for the onset. Starting again after but a moment's delay, our corps moved steadily forward to the attack, every man as eager for the fray as though fresh from a night's rest and his morning's coffee. It was to be a charge, and the front line was fixing bayonets as it advanced. What was present of the 116th was on the skirmish line well on in the advance, when on a sudden "out from the enemy's line comes a rider, bound on bound, "bearing a white flag of truce, to ask for time to consum- "mate surrender." "Halt!" "Halt!" "Halt!" "Cease firing," rang out all along our hot pressing lines. Reluctantly the eager troops stopped, and leaning on their rifles watched the approach of the horseman bearing the white flag. As he neared the middle of the space between the lines, he was met by an officer from our side, and at the same time the white flag appeared at different points along the enemy's lines. The meaning of this was soon spread among the troops. The men mechanically, and without orders, stacked arms. Grant now soon came riding, rather faster than usual, up to Sheridan, held a brief conversation, and then rode forward to where Lee was said to be awaiting him. In a very brief time he returned. For a few moments there was a deathlike stillness, as though everyone was trying to comprehend and take in the full import of the scene before him. But soon some one screamed out in a cheer, and the spell was broken. Instantly the whole army broke out in continuous, thundering, long-drawn-out cheering, yelling, screaming, which, beyond doubt, was the happiest, heartiest, gladdest ever listened to by mortal man. Officers and men threw up their caps and as they came down caught them on their swords or bayonets or stamped them into the ground. As soon as exhaustion shut off the longest winded and collapsed the strongest lungs, our ears were greeted with tumultuous cheering over among the rebels. It seemed as though both sides were overjoyed and would never cease their noisy demonstrations.

As remarked above, the left wing of the 116th, at the moment the white flag appeared, *was advancing on the skirmish line.* The satisfaction which this fact afforded that wing of the regiment may be seen in the entry each company made upon its "pay roll" on the 30th of April, 1865. In the "record of events" made at that date, we find on each company's roll the following memoranda: "This company was engaged in the recent campaign of General Grant which resulted in the capture of Richmond and Lee's whole army. Broke camp north of the James, March 25, 1865, marched to Hatcher's Run, distance twenty-five miles, there, 31st, engaged the enemy with success. April 2d took part in the capture of Fort Gregg, and then engaged in the pursuit and capture of Lee and his army at Appomattox, Virginia, April 9, 1865, *this company being on the skirmish line at the time of his surrender.*" This was a final record well earned, and one of which the regiment was justly very proud. It paid it well for all its hard fighting, and the hardships it had so patiently endured.

The last shell fired by the enemy injured James Davis, company G. A comrade of his, Orderly Sergeant Francis A. Bartley, writes of the incident as follows: "The last cannon Lee's army fired at us threw a shell into the woods as we were advancing. As it exploded, a piece of it knocked down James Davis, of company G, merely stunning him, however, as he came up in ranks again in a few minutes afterward."

Of course no one need stop to further describe the joy of that victorious army over the surrender of Lee and his army, nor recount the details, so often told, of the surrender. These became long ago the history of the Nation, as well as the proud history of the regiments there present. Our lines were again re-formed upon the restoration of order, and moving forward halted, stacked arms and went into camp a short distance from the surrendered rebel army. How sweet was the rest that followed! How tired that infantry was, no one can understand who was not on that memorable march from Fort Gregg to Appomattox, a march which has no parallel in modern history.

Toward evening of the 9th, the 123d Ohio, 54th Pennsylvania, and also those of our regiment captured at High Bridge, came in. They gave us many particulars occurring inside the rebel lines prior to and at the time of the surrender. They reported that generally the rebels manifested as much satisfaction over the surrender as our own men did, and that the cheering we heard came from the rebels. Some of those closely identified with the rebellion were, however, dreadfully broken down, and a few such shed tears. Shortly after the white flags were raised, General Crook came by where our division was standing behind its stacked arms. The men cheered him lustily and gathered about him to shake hands. He spoke a few kind words to them, among other things saying: "There is not much use for my cavalry while this old West Virginia division is here." The division was in the advance nearly all the time from Petersburg until Lee was headed off and brought to bay at Appomattox, and no better marching was ever done by any army than it led the 24th and 5th corps to do during that time. The following is General Gibbon's order issued on the march, relating to the 24th corps:

HEADQUARTERS 24TH ARMY CORPS,
BEFORE RICHMOND, April 3d, 1865.

(*General Order No. 11.*)

With great satisfaction the Major General commanding congratulates his gallant command upon the successful operations of the past few days. The 24th Army Corps has demonstrated that with a well organized and disciplined force no military achievement is impossible. The marching has been superior to anything of the kind heretofore witnessed, while the desperate assault upon Fort Gregg, the last of the enemy's strongholds around Petersburg, entitles this command to a place alongside their late gallant comrades of Fort Fisher. Your commander is proud of you.

By command of
MAJOR GENERAL JOHN GIBBON.

EDWARD MEADE, Lieutenant Colonel and A. D. C.

General Gibbon's command, the 5th corps under General Griffin, and MacKenzie's cavalry, were designated to remain at Appomattox Court House till the paroling of the surrendered army was completed, and to take charge of the public property. The remainder of the army returned immediately to the vicinity of Burkesville. During the next two days the work of paroling prisoners and gathering in public property continued. It was said that fifty cannon were found buried. Our soldiers and the rebels were as sociable and jolly together as could be. No one would have thought them ever to have been enemies. They were constantly passing back and forth between town and their camps, and making arrangements to go to their homes, which they all seemed very anxious to reach.

Of the last few days of marching, General Devens, of the 3d division of the Army of the James, said: "On the morning of the 9th of April, by a march unprecedented in the annals of warfare, the Army of the James had placed itself across the Lynchburg road and closed the avenue of escape. On that morning Lieutenant General Gordon, of Georgia, who commanded the advance, said to General Lee that his way was barred. 'It can be nothing but cavalry,' said General Lee, 'brush them away; no cavalry can stand against infantry.' It was done as General Lee ordered, but as the cavalry fell back, they revealed the long and gleaming line of steel which marked the line of infantry of the Army of the James. There were Ord and Gibbon, there were Turner and R. S. Foster at the head of their divisions. To throw his exhausted troops upon that wall of steel was a madness of which the rebel chieftain was not capable, and the sword of Lee was laid in the conquering hand of Grant."

In General Lincoln's history of the 34th Massachusetts we find an extract from a Richmond paper of April, 1865, evidently in charge of a Union editor then, which we reproduce here: "The 1st and 2d divisions of the 24th army corps, who were engaged in the pursuit of Lee to Appomattox Court House, after the fall of Petersburg, returned to this city on Tuesday morning. It is reported by military men that General Lee's surrender was necessitated in consequence of the severe marching and skillful maneuvering of these forces. Their marching will compare with any on record. For four successive days they marched respectively eighteen, twenty-three, twenty-seven and thirty-eight miles. By this rapid marching they were enabled to overtake and surround the Confederate forces. Had these two divisions been later in getting round to the right of General Lee, it is confidently believed that he would have made his escape. It was owing to General Ord's energy that his troops marched thirty-eight miles from 3 o'clock in the morning of April 8th to 11 o'clock the following night, when they quietly threw themselves down upon the ground to rest, in front of Lee's army, without the enemy's suspecting, as acknowledged on the following morning, that there was an infantry soldier within ten miles of them, and by four o'clock on the following morning in line of battle, and fighting until a flag of truce was sent from the enemy for a conference. The march certainly has no parallel in the history of the rebellion, or, any war in Europe."*

But the great, controlling, overpowering, conquering genius of this last and decisive campaign was General Philip H. Sheridan. To him was assigned the work of turning the enemy's right at Five Forks. After accomplishing this he took up the task of cutting off Lee's escape. The 5th and 24th corps were hurried on after his cavalry. At one time, while Sheridan was north of the Appomattox, Lee was very near making his escape at Farmville, and but for the unparalleled marching of our corps, which met and stopped him at Rice's Station, he would most certainly have succeeded in getting away with a large portion of his army. But at this point he was driven back across to the north side of the Appomattox River, and from that time till he reached Appomattox Court House, kept on that side of the river by the 5th and 24th corps, whose line of march was on the south side of the river. He was followed vigorously by the 2d and 6th corps, and so pushed to his best. His escape was assured if he reached there ahead of the 5th and 24th corps, for although Sheridan could and did reach it before him with his cavalry, yet, as Lee remarked, "no cavalry can stand against infantry," and he could "brush them away." But the terrible energy of Sheridan was equal to the task, and these two corps were thrown across the track of Lee just in time, and with not a half hour to spare. As our infantry went into line of battle on the run in the rear of the exhausted cavalry, Lee was at the very same moment engaged in the easy work of "brush-

---

Jefferson Davis says of Lee's last hope and of his purpose in directing his course toward Lynchburg when turned from Danville at Farmville: "Lee had never contemplated surrender. He had long before, in language similar to that employed by Washington during the revolution, expressed to me the belief that in the mountains of Virginia he could carry on the war for twenty years, and in directing his march toward Lynchburg, it may be that as an alternative he hoped to reach those mountains, and with the advantage which the topography would give, yet to baffle the hosts which were following him."—*Rise and Fall of the Confederate Government.* Volume II, Page 656.

ing them away" with his infantry. A few minutes more, and he would have been through, and by the night of that day would have occupied the fortifications of Lynchburg with his army, and the struggle have been prolonged.

General Sheridan was never measured correctly by the people of the country. The estimate put upon him that he was a fiery, hot-headed, dashing fellow, a sort of torrent or cyclone, without genius to plan or power to execute, does him great injustice. In my judgment, no officer in the army combined in such harmony the bravery of the soldier with the calm and cool penetration of the General. While he possessed daring resolution, he also possessed moderation and most excellent judgment. Possessing the wild ardor of the warrior, the havoc, roar and excitement of the battle field only quickened his naturally keen perceptions and made him capable of executing at the most critical moments, the most unexpected and unlooked-for movements. His heroic and successful exploits on every battle field, from Stone River to Cedar Creek, to Five Forks, to Appomattox, show him to be a man of not only great personal bravery, but a man of genius, judgment, great resources, inexhaustible expedients and wonderful executive powers. In the days of chivalry he would have been a knight of uncommon renown. Few men ever lived who were greater leaders, who were greater commanders, or who possessed in an equal degree his power to inspire others with his own fire, dash and daring. No officer in our army could be compared with him in this important respect. When the impartial history of that war comes to be written, this will be the future estimate of General Sheridan.

CHAPTER XVI.

MARCH TO LYNCHBURG — BACK TO RICHMOND — TRIUMPHAL ENTRY OF THE REBEL CAPITAL — PREPARING FOR HOME — MUSTERED OUT — TRANSFERS TO THE 62D OHIO — OFF FOR HOME — HOME.

At noon on the 12th, our division started for Lynchburg, marched sixteen miles and halted for the night within seven miles of the place. Rebel officers and soldiers were all along the road, making for home. There were nearly as many of them as of us. Companies, squads and large and small parties of them were everywhere in the roads, fields, woods and houses. Negroes in great numbers were shouting around us all along the road. It was a strange sight. At night the rebels camped with us, ate with us, slept with us, and told camp stories with us. With scarce an exception they were glad the war was over, and they on their way to their homes. There was not half the rancorous feeling among them that we found among the citizens who had not been in the army. At 5 the next morning, we were on the road. Had not gone more than two miles before we came to a creek, where we found the bridges burned. The troops crossed some distance below on a canal bridge. The railroad bridge across the James River Canal was also burned. Bridges had to be built for the trains, which delayed us till after noon, and we did not reach Lynchburg until about 4 P. M. The rebels had laid out extensive fortifications about Lynchburg, with the intention of making a stand there, and thousands of negroes had recently been at work upon them. Great quantities of artillery had been thrown into the canal, a lot lay here and there spiked, with the carriages either cut down or burned, the canal, roads, streets, yards and houses were full of sabres, muskets, carbines and all kinds of war material. No such sight was ever before witnessed as we beheld as we marched through the city. Thousands of negroes thronged the way, clapping their hands, shouting and singing, and praying, and thanking God that they were *free!* They were frantic with delight, did all sorts of peculiar, novel and extremely ludicrous things. Their joy seemed unspeakable, which they tried to express by actions the most peculiar and singular, and which, among themselves, seemed to be full of meaning and expression. Such looks of gladness; such shouts of joy; such blessings; such prayers! Those poor people will never be happier in Heaven than they were on the evening of the 13th of April, A. D. 1865. We halted in the streets, and then the rush they made for us nearly took us off our feet. It seemed impossible for their joy to exhaust itself. Being short of rations, we were hungry. On learning this, they rushed off, soon returning on the run with everything they could find that was eatable, corn bread and bacon largely predominating. In all this scarcely a citizen was to be seen, none, in fact, save of the poorer classes. As we again took up the line of march through the city, we were followed by thousands of negroes with songs, prayers and thanksgivings. The men were by this time all well fed, and were carrying abundance for another meal. We have no doubt that many an aristocratic larder and cellar was scarce of provisions that night. Our regiment finally went into camp about a mile beyond the city, and near our battle ground of June 18, 1864.

General Turner, of our division, assumed command of the post, and at once issued very strict orders forbidding men entering houses or committing depredations of any kind upon citizens, or public and private property. On the next day, many of our officers and men visited the battle ground of 1864 and made search for the graves of our fallen heroes, especially for that of our lamented Captain Keyes. We were unsuccessful. Inquiry finally led us to the records of the undertakers of the city, from which we readily found his and other graves. We found Captain Keyes' grave on the Seminary Hill, west of the Seminary, and in front of the rebel breastworks thrown up against Hunter. It was to this Seminary, which was used as a hospital, that the Captain was taken by the rebels, and here he lay till he died, on the 19th of July. A large number of Union dead are buried in this cemetery, which is now known as "The Poplar Grove National Cemetery." Captain Keyes is buried in "grave 333, section E, division E." The burial place of others of the 116th at Lynchburg will be found in the list, given elsewhere, of names of men of our regiment buried in Southern cemeteries. General Harris made a speech to the negroes in the afternoon, giving them good advice in the exercise of their freedom. Rations were issued to the poor, and to the paroled prisoners on their way home. The rebel soldiers were surprised at our kindness to them, and at the leniency of the Government.

At 3 P. M. on the 15th, our regiment, with its division, started back toward Richmond. Camped that night about seven miles out. Next morning we started at 6. After going six or seven miles, a train on the South Side Railroad took most of the 3d brigade on board. Ours marched on some distance beyond Appomattox Station and camped. The news of the assassination of President Lincoln reached us that night. It was not credited, and hence created very little excitement. We reached Farmville on the 18th, where we received newspapers which confirmed the sad news of the assassination of the President. The revulsion of feeling and the terrible depression it caused among the soldiers has never been, and can never be, described. President Lincoln was regarded by the army in the light of an exceedingly kind and indulgent father, and the mourning his death created is indescribable. A little way beyond Burkesville Junction, on the 20th, that part of the regiment which had been on the Danville Railroad since the 6th joined us, bringing with it a large number of prisoners, horses and mules.

It is now in place to mention the services of the right wing, which had been sent down the Danville Railroad from Burkesville Junction, under Captain Mann, on the 6th. The Captain was ordered to go hastily down the road and take a position, with a view to capturing any supply or other trains which it was supposed Jeff Davis, who had passed down just before we reached the Junction, would send up to Lee. The Captain proceeded down the road, capturing many prisoners as he advanced. Reaching Meherrin Station, he found a lot of corn, to which a squad of rebel cavalry was helping itself. His skirmishers soon drove them off. The whole neighborhood was alarmed by the firing, and the presence of Union troops caused great excitement. Breaking the road was the work of but a few moments. He then stationed his men in a good position, well under cover and out of sight of any approaching trains. Very soon they heard the rumbling of a train, and then the whistle of an engine, evidently at the first station below. They waited anxiously for its approach. But all at once there was heard sharp whistling to put on brakes. The noise of the moving train ceased for a moment, "off brakes" was whistled in a manner that indicated an excited engineer was in the cab, and then as the rumbling noise of the train began to grow fainter and fainter, they saw that their game had escaped them, information of their whereabouts having doubtless been conveyed to those in charge of the train by the cavalry driven from Meherrin. In the evening, the

Captain observed rebel cavalry hovering about and watching his movements. Anticipating a night attack, he prepared himself by fortifying his position. Chaplain Logan accompanied this wing of the regiment, and observing the threatening appearance of things, went to the Captain and said to him: "Captain, we will no doubt be attacked during the night, and as John ——— never does us much good in a fight, I will esteem it a favor if you will give me his gun." This was just like Chaplain Logan, who was a "fighting parson," in the true and patriotic sense of the term. But the Captain and his men were not attacked that night, and saw no more rebels until they came streaming through on their way home from Appomattox. The command was actively engaged in scouting and preventing foraging parties, of our own and the rebels, from pillaging, and in gathering up prisoners, horses, mules and other rebel property. The citizens about Meherrin soon recovered from their alarm, and treated our men with great kindness, furnishing them cheerfully with plenty of provisions. They expressed regrets when the Captain and his men were ordered to rejoin their regiment, for they were thus left without protection from the gangs of marauders with which the country was at that stage of proceedings overrun.

We lay at Burkesville during the 20th and 21st. On the 22d we started direct for Richmond, keeping on the railroad most of the time. Passed through Jennings, Jettersville and Section House, and camped within a couple miles of Amelia Court House. The 23d, we marched twenty miles, and on the 24th thirteen miles, camping within two miles of Richmond. The next day at 8 A. M., we passed through Manchester, and crossed the James River on pontoons, just one month from our leaving Camp Holly. On striking Main Street, the 3d division of our corps, which had been in possession of Richmond since its evacuation, the night of the 2d of April, was drawn up to receive us, cheering, presenting arms, and bands playing. It was a befitting welcome to troops returning from a campaign so fruitful of results. We were cheered everywhere as the "heroes of Appomattox." We passed directly through Richmond, and went into camp about two miles out on the Lynchburg pike. Here we lay, with some changes of camp, until the 14th of June, when the regiment was mustered out.

On the 30th of May, Lieutenant Colonel Teters received his commission as Brevet Lieutenant Colonel, and Lieutenant Wm. Biddenharn as Brevet Captain. These officers were recommended for promotion to these brevet ranks just after the battle of Cedar Creek, October 19th, 1864, for gallant and meritorious conduct in the battles of the Shenandoah campaign. Lieutenant Colonel Teters was then a Captain, and Captain Biddenharn a Second Lieutenant. The promotions came tardily, many months after they were earned, but they were none the less deserving. At the time Captain Biddenharn was recommended for promotion, he was an aide on the staff of Lieutenant Colonel Wildes, then commanding the 1st brigade, 1st division, Army of West Virginia.

On the first day of June, orders were received to prepare rolls for muster out. The order excepted companies F and K, and some recruits of other companies, whose term of service did not expire prior to October 1st. This was regarded by all as particularly unjust and unfortunate, and was the occasion for a great deal of bad feeling throughout the regiment. The fact is that these two companies, although not mustered in at the same time with the others, were in every action, and on every march and service in which the rest of the regiment was engaged, and the recruits were in every battle, save Moorefield and Winchester, in 1863. These men were transferred to the 62d Ohio regiment, and afterwards, when the 62d and 67th were consolidated, they formed a part of the latter organization, under command of Colonel and Brevet Major General A. C. Voris, of Akron, Ohio. The non-commissioned officers, thus transferred, were mustered out June 20th, and the privates August 8, 1865. This has rendered it impossible to get the rolls of these two companies into proper shape. I have done the very best I could with them, but I am not at all satisfied with their condition. I am greatly indebted to Sergeant Silas King, of company F, for the assistance he has given me in preparing the rolls of that company, and to Major Hull and Captain John F. Welch, of company K, for their aid in preparing those of company K.

Whilst waiting for muster out at Richmond, Quartermaster Sergeant W. T. Patterson wrote for Whitelaw Reid's "Ohio in the War," the sketch of the regiment which appears in that work. Mr. Patterson contemplated writing the history of the regiment upon his return home, and with that view kept a very full and accurate daily memoranda of events from the beginning to the end of its service. After his muster out he graduated from the Ohio University at Athens, and began the study of the law, which he soon abandoned, and entered upon a theological course at Waynesburg, Pa., and afterwards went to Andover, Mass., to continue his theological studies. He had just finished his studies when he was stricken down with fever, and died July 2d, 1869. His friends have very kindly placed in my hands his manuscript and memoranda. He had begun to write the history of the regiment, and had covered the time up to our arrival at Winchester in March, 1863. He and his companion and friend in the Quartermaster's department, Quartermaster Sergeant Ezra L. Walker, kept very full diaries of passing events. Sergeant Walker was a matter-of-fact man in everything. Sergeant Patterson was very different. While he noted all the facts passing before his eye, he found pleasant society also in noting everything of the country through which he passed. The blue edges and gleaming caps of the mountains of Virginia, its beautiful Valleys, clear streams, virgin forests, winding mountain roads, with their display of magnificent scenery, furnished him never-ending subjects for pleasant comment and enthusiastic description. His memoranda and writings are replete with pictures of the country. Even when returning from the Lynchburg raid in 1864, when we were all more than half starved, and all the enthusiasm and inspiration was worn out of everybody else, he found heart to describe the enchanting scenery along that dreadful march. In one place, we see him in ecstacies over the beauties of Sinking Creek, Potts and Sweet Spring Mountains. At another, we have interesting descriptions of Sweet Sulphur Springs and vicinity, then of Big and Little Sewel Mountains, Meadow Bluffs and New River, and even the night march we made through that rocky gorge before reaching White Sulphur Springs had romance and grandeur in it to him. Nothing could dampen his enthusiasm, nothing could drench his ardor. Patterson with nature was like a youth with the maiden he loves. He lived closer to nature than any man I ever knew. Desert places, dreary regions, desperate mountain passes ribbed with barren ridges, had charms to him and gave play to the imagery of his poetic mind, when they were casting nothing but gloomy shadows and discouragement over the sore and weary footsteps of all others. Every object, when he looked upon it, seemed to revolve about and exhibit its bright side. As Theodore Winthrop says of John Brent, so it might be said of Will Patterson: "She (nature) was always his love, whatever she could do; however dressed, whether in clouds or sunshine, unchanging fair; in whatever mood, weeping or smiling, at her sweetest; grand, beautiful for her grandeur; tender, beautiful for her tenderness; simple, lovely for her simplicity; careless, prettier than if she were trim and artful; rough, patient and impressive, a barbaric queen."

On the evening of the 2d of April, after the charge of our regiment on Fort Gregg, he got lost in the darkness in returning to the train, but he could not help putting down his impressions of the grandeur of that night search for the "look out" near which the train had been parked. On the 12th of April, as the regiment was approaching Lynchburg, he writes: "The red clay hills and oak forests about us remind one of dear old Ohio." And so he saw and noted everything, and everything pleased him. His powers of description, too, were boundless, and did I not feel constrained to eliminate everything from this little book not closely connected with the personal history of the regiment, I would take great pleasure in making use of much more than I have of his beautiful descriptions of the country through which we passed. I know many would feel a keen interest in the panorama, which his pen has drawn, of our long and tiresome marches. It would afford them, as it has me, great pleasure to look back over the routes they traveled, and as they saw them pictured anew, to note the beautiful things they missed seeing as they passed along, too footsore or too weary to observe them. But he loved the 116th, as every line of his copious memoranda verifies. He grew prouder and prouder of its career as he wrote down its daily record, and it will ever remain a source of deep regret to us all that his young life was not spared to finish the pleasant task of writing out and publishing the record he had so religiously kept, and in which he felt such deep concern and pride.

On the 10th of June, General Gibbon issued the following farewell order to his corps:

HEADQUARTERS 24TH A. C. REVIEW GROUND,
RICHMOND, VA., June 10th, 1865.

Soldiers of the 24th Corps:

This, probably, is the last occasion upon which you, as a corps, will be assembled. Many of you are about to re-enter civil life, to resume those domestic duties which by your service in the great cause of your country have been so long neglected. Before we separate, I desire to thank you, in the name of a grateful country, for the service you have rendered her. By your discipline, long marches, and hard fighting, you have established for yourselves a name second to none in the army. Your badge has become an emblem of energy, valor and patriotism, and is a source of just pride to all who wear it. Those of you who are entering civil life should still wear it on all occasions as an evidence to your brothers who remain in the service, of your pride in a badge made sacred by the blood of so many brave men, and of your disposition, should your country ever again call you to arms, to again assemble under that proud emblem and revive the glory of the 24th corps. To our comrades who are leaving the service, we pledge a kind farewell, and a wish that their career in civil life may be as successful and prosperous as their military life has been honorable to themselves and valuable to their country.

JOHN GIBBON, Major General Volunteers, Commanding Corps.

The regiment was mustered out just before noon, June 14th, and forming it in a hollow square, Lieutenant Colonel Teters delivered the following farewell address:

HEADQUARTERS 116TH O. V. I.,
RICHMOND, VA., June 14, 1865.

Officers and Soldiers:

In bidding you farewell to-day, I desire to tender you my thanks for the kindness, co-operation and support I have received from you since assuming command of the old regiment. Since putting on the soldier's garb you have endured untold hardships without a murmur. You have toiled through one of the most trying raids of the war. You have engaged in some of the most desperate battles of the war. You have never disgraced your colors. You have honored your State and have won the esteem and praise of every commander of every army in which you have served. Now that you are returning to your homes crowned with honors, now that the smoke of battle has been dispelled by the rays of the glorious Sun of Peace, and you are about to enter again upon the duties of civil life as citizens of our restored Republic, that your brave brothers in arms, and the people to whom you return, may always be proud of you and will feel it a solemn duty to honor you and your posterity, be as peaceful and honorable in civil life as you have been brave and glorious in battle. Let us not forget to cherish the memory of our brave comrades who have fallen from our sides in battle, died in hospitals, or who have been tortured to death in rebel prisons. Here at the rebel capital let us pledge our fealty to the widows and orphans of our dead comrades, and be ready to stretch out to them, wherever we meet them, the hand of a comrade and of charity.

And now a word to those who remain behind for a short time. Comrades, let me beseech you to be good, obedient soldiers, as you have always been in the past. I am sorry from the bottom of my heart that it is not your fortune to go home with us. You have my heartfelt sympathy, and if my influence can effect your discharge, you may rest assured you shall not remain behind. God bless you, comrades! You will always in the future, as in the past, find me your firm friend.

W. B. TETERS, Lieutenant Colonel Commanding Regiment.

Here is the language and sentiment of the true soldier, and farewell was never bidden to brave men by a braver man.

But little remains to be done to close the record of the 116th. The next morning at daylight, the regiment marched down to the wharf and took the "M. Martin," General Grant's old boat, and steamed down the James. It was interesting now to pass Forts Darling and Brady, the Howlett House batteries, Dutch Gap Canal, Butler's Lookout, Deep Bottom, Camp Holly and the great fortifications of both sides. No thundering of artillery or mortars now, no pickets or picket firing, and no troops holding forts or fortifications. We could see Camp Holly from our vessel, and the forts and lines of earthworks we had watched with such vigilance so long. There were our log huts yet, but no smoke arose from their chimneys, and none of the signs of busy camp life were anywhere visible in the company streets or on the well trodden parade ground. It was a "deserted village," indeed. It was hard to think that only a few weeks before, these opposing lines of works we were passing were held by hostile armies, striving their very best to destroy each other. As we passed the spot, where we crossed the James in the early evening of the 27th of March, to commence the wonderful campaign which ended so gloriously thirteen days afterwards at Appomattox, many an one thought of the brave fellows who crossed with us, but were not now on this happy journey home.

The regiment reached Columbus on the evening of the 19th, where we took supper at Tod Barracks, and at 10 P. M. again took the cars and started for Camp Dennison, which we reached next morning at daylight, and where we were paid off on the 23d, and the next day we started for our homes. As soon as we reached the Athens County line, squads began to leave us at every stopping place. Crowds were everywhere waiting to greet friends, and such welcomes as they met with on every hand was enough to turn the heads of these brave fellows. But still another greeting awaited them in their homes, a greeting that no other should witness. To that sacred and precious greeting they were remitted, and our work is done.

The Spartan mother who sent her son to battle, bade him to return with his shield in honor, or on his shield in death. Here came a mere remnant of a regiment, bearing their shields in honor, but how many of their brave comrades had returned before them on their shields in death!

On the 20th of June, quite a number of promotions were made in the regiment, which were, of course, not to fill vacancies for further service, but to do honor to a number of worthy men, who had long since earned promotion but could not be mustered, because of the reduced condition of the regiment. The promotions were as follows:

First Lieutenant Samuel D. Knight, to Captain.
First Lieutenant Ransom Griffin, to Captain.
Second Lieutenant Jacob Wyckoff, to First Lieutenant.
Second Lieutenant John S. Heald, to First Lieutenant.
Second Lieutenant Charles A. Cline, to First Lieutenant.
Sergeant Mann Smith, to Second Lieutenant.
Sergeant Peter D. Wolf, to Second Lieutenant.
Sergeant John L. Beach, to Second Lieutenant.
Sergeant Adam J. Myers, to Second Lieutenant.
Sergeant Samuel Atkinson, to Second Lieutenant.
Sergeant Francis A. Bartley, to Second Lieutenant.
Sergeant Benjamin F. Sammons, to Second Lieutenant.
Sergeant John C. Chick, to Second Lieutenant.
Sergeant Leander Shane, to Second Lieutenant.
Sergeant Benjamin Sheffield, to Second Lieutenant.
Sergeant Andrew W. Henthorn, to Second Lieutenant.

Thus closes the history of the 116th Regiment of Ohio Volunteers. We have only to add the rosters of the field and staff and the various companies, following which is the list of those who died in Southern prisons, or on Southern battle fields.

CHAPTER XVII.

PRISON LIFE — THE CRUELTY OF REBELS TO PRISONERS — BARBARITIES OF PRISON KEEPERS — THE EXPERIENCES OF SEVERAL OF OUR OFFICERS AND MEN — THE DEATH ROLL.

ELMER ARMSTRONG,
Sutler of the Regiment.

It was on the morning of June 15th, 1863, after holding Lee's whole army at bay for three whole days, that Milroy had at last given the order to retreat, and his little command, that had done such gallant service, started along the Winchester and Martinsburg turnpike for Martinsburg. Our guns had been spiked and with our wagons and ambulances left behind. Thus unencumbered, we had gone about five miles, when we came across the enemy in strong force, just where the road to Harper's Ferry branched off from the turnpike. While our first line was engaging the enemy, the second line, consisting of the larger part of the command, filed to the right and escaped to Harper's Ferry. The order had been given the night before, that if we were attacked on the retreat, those having horses in charge were to make their escape as best they could. I had my horses with me, and attempted to escape to the left with the troops that afterward struck the railroad at Sir John's Run, but was captured before leaving the pike. In obedience to orders, I had left my wagon at Winchester with about $6,000 worth of goods. The regiment had been paid off a few days before, and I had considerable money about me, some two thousand dollars. I also had two hundred dollars of Adjutant Ballard's money, which he had given me before he went into battle, saying, "I may never come out of this; if I don't, send this to my wife if you get out." Well, that money I put in a place that I had ripped in my shoe and then stitched up again, and I carried it safely through all my prison experience.

The first thing I thought of when I found that we were cornered, was to hide the rest of the money. I stuck it around in different places. I remember I put $750 between the lining and seat of my pants, where it escaped the three searchings I got at Libby. I was placed under guard until morning, when I was sent to General Gordon's headquarters, where I was given breakfast in his tent. I was then sent back to our old fort at Winchester. About a thousand of our fellows were there. I was in Winchester about two weeks before being sent south. Dr. Brown, our assistant surgeon, and I got leave to go on our parole to Staunton, so I hired a man to take us over in a stage, and paid him $50 in rebel money. We were not guarded, and when we arrived at Staunton we hunted lodgings where we could and registered our names as if we were not prisoners. Next day, right after breakfast, we reported and were sent down to Richmond. Dr. Sweet's wife, Colonel Washburn's wife and Chaplain Brady were on the same train, but in another car. On our way down, we heard of the capture, just ahead of us, of Fitzhugh Lee and a son of General Winder. This made them cautious, and we were run back on a siding until dark and then run into Richmond. We were treated well on our journey, except that nothing was given us to eat.

On our arrival at Richmond, Dr. Brown and I were put into the union cell down in the basement of Castle Thunder. The first person I saw there was a man named Parker, who had been an engineer on the Baltimore & Ohio Railroad, and whom I had known when I was shipping stock to Baltimore. There was with him a brakeman from the same road. Both these men remembered me and were very kind to me. Till now I had kept my spirits up, but meeting these acquaintances in such a place, and the kindness they showed me, completely broke me up. I tell you I felt pretty sick. Brown and I laid down, but Parker came to us and said if we stayed there the lice would drop down on us from the rebels above. He also offered to get us something to eat, but I had no appetite in that place, though I had not tasted food since morning. The only person in the cell beside these I have mentioned was a crazy southerner, whom the rebels had picked up and taken for a Yankee spy playing off. The fellow was, however, as much a rebel at heart as his captors. He had evidently been a preacher, for he wandered on, telling us if Jeff Davis and General Winder would humble themselves before God they would get their independence. The fellow stammered when he spoke. Said he to Parker: "These f-f-friends of of yours s-s-seem to be n-n-nice men, I should l-l-like to p-p-pray with them." So he went on, while Parker paced up and down the cell. The surroundings were so terrible, and the earnestness of the poor man so impressed me, that I felt very much humbled, and especially when he began to pray very devoutly. But when he began to pray for the success of the Southern Confederacy, it fired Parker, who, though used to his insane chatter, would not listen to anything like that, even from a crazy man, but began to pelt the old fellow on the head with some bullets he had in his pocket, saying, "I will teach you better than to pray for the Southern Confederacy in the presence of Union prisoners, you d——d old reprobate." That prayer was cut off pretty short, I can tell you.

After a couple of days, they moved us up into the third story, part of which was a temporary hospital. Brown was taken away from me here, and I supposed that he had gone home. In the third story we could buy a few things to eat of the hospital steward. I thus became acquainted with Bullock, the hospital steward. He told me that Captain Alexander, who was in command of Castle Thunder, was from Baltimore and was a Union man at heart. I knew Baltimore pretty well, and determined to make the most of this to get into his good graces, so whenever the Captain was about I talked loud about Baltimore. I had kept this up about two months, and was beginning to think that it was no go, when, one day, he came up to me and said: "Mr. Armstrong, didn't I hear you say you were raised in Baltimore?" "No, sir," I said, "I am a native of Ohio, but I own property in Baltimore. Were you ever there?" "Oh, yes," he answered, "I was born and raised there. I came down here before the war and married here, and so, you see, am a Southerner." A few days after this, he came in and gave me a peach; he also gave me the privilege of walking through some of the halls because I was sick. I knew I had made a point. One day, as I was taking my walk through the halls, I came to the Captain's room. A guard stood at the door and halted me. I told him who I was, and asked to see the Captain. He went in and told what I wanted. Captain Alexander came out, took me into his room, and introduced me to his wife, and then asked me what I wanted. I told him that I had come to beg a favor. "I want you to send a guard out with me and let me get some fresh air and buy something to eat." He said he wouldn't send an armed guard, but took me down stairs to the outer door, and ordered the guard there to let me go out every day and buy what I wanted, and said I was not to be molested. He sent a young boy with me to show me the way. Almost the first man I met when I got out was old Kephardt, a rebel detective. "Where are you from, and what are you doing?" he asked. I told him as politely as I could, that Captain Alexander had kindly permitted me to go out and get some refreshments. This seemed to anger the old fellow, and he said: "They had no right to do it, G—d d—n you; they ought to make breastworks of all such Yankees as you are." By making good use of my guide, and spending a good deal of rebel money, I managed to get everything I wanted. Whenever I wanted any money for these trips, I would take a five dollar bill and buy rebel currency. I could get forty of their dollars for five of ours. But I was always careful never to appear to have more than five dollars at a time.

After the news came of the battle of Gettysburg, and the fall of Vicksburg, a hundred of the prisoners were taken from the third story, where I was, and held as hostages. They were kept by themselves in a room above ours, and we could hear them every night praying for the safety of the Government, and for a blessing on their families. Parker was one of the hundred, and he sent down to see if Bullock, the steward, couldn't get something for them to eat. Bullock said that he did not dare to, but that Armstrong could, as he was free to go in and out, and that he would be careful not to be looking when these things were going on. We punched a pine knot out of the floor above, and at night they let down a large bandana handkerchief through the hole, into which I would put such things as I had for them, and then they would let down a string from the window above and draw up the bundle. Bullock would draw rations and give them to me, which were sent to the men above in the same way. They would then draw up the string and put the knot back in its place. Bullock was very kind to me all the time. I remember that when a brother of his was sick, his wife would send him wine and other delicacies for him, and a good share of these fell to my lot.

I was afraid that I could not be exchanged regularly, as I was not a soldier, and when I saw some of our boys go, and I was left, I tell you my heart sank. The way I was finally exchanged was this: I had written home of my sorry plight and ill-health, and had said that I never expected to live through it. My wife wrote me how she and the children felt, and on the back of one letter she wrote to the officers, asking if she might come and care for me, or, if I was already dead, take back my remains. When the officers got this letter, I was sent for, and went down to Major Carrington's room. He was an officer of Castle Thunder. He handed me the letter, and said to me: "You have not disobeyed us in any particular, you are away from your family, and Captain Alexander and I have determined to send you home." When Bullock found that I was going to be sent away, he came to me and asked whether, if he could get into our lines, our officers would give him back to the rebels if he came as a deserter. I told him if he could get to our lines and show himself with a white flag, he would be well treated. He seemed much pleased to know this. Before I was sent away, I went around to bid Major Carrington and Captain Alexander good-bye. They had done everything they could for me. I thanked them from the bottom of my heart, and told them that, although I trusted they would never be so unfortunate as to be captured, yet if they were, I could wish them nothing better than that they should fall in with friends as kind and helping as they had been to me. Captain Alexander said, "don't speak of kindness, I would have done a great deal more if I had dared." I then told them that I belonged to the military committee, and gave them my address, and told them to write to me if they were ever taken prisoners.

Mrs. Alexander said: "If you and he both live, you will see him in your lines a prisoner, and have a chance to do something for him, for I am sure he will be captured."

On the 12th of September I was transferred to "Libby," and there I saw some of the men of our own regiment. Dr. Brown, Dr. Smith, Lieutenant Sibley, Lieutenant Knowles, the Chaplain of the 87th Pennsylvania, and others of different regiments of our command. Castle Thunder was truly a palace compared to this place, and the treatment we received in the two places was altogether different. Here I was searched three times for money. Once they found twelve dollars and eighty-seven cents, which was taken from me. They also took my account books, but gave them all back but one. They promised to give back the money, but as I did not believe them, I was not disappointed. I found some acquaintances among the prisoners on the lower floor, but most of the men that I knew were up stairs. The first man I saw from our regiment was Dr. Smith. He cut a little hole through the floor, and sent a note down to ask if there wasn't a man there named Armstrong, and if there was, to tell him Dr. Smith wanted to see him. I went and showed myself, and he slipped down another note asking if I had any money, or whether they had taken it. I told him I had plenty, and sent him, I think, twenty-five dollars. Then I went up to the head of the stairs, to another room, and looked through the key-hole, and saw Lieutenant Sibley. He was nearly starved to death. I told him I had plenty of money. He said if I would let him have some he would give me his note for it. I put one hundred dollars through the key-hole to him. I also let Lieutenant R. O. Knowles have one hundred dollars, and they sent back their notes. I was afraid the notes would be found on me, and their names would let the rebels know that they had the money, so I told them I would tear their names off the notes, and if they ever got out, and could pay me, all well and good, and if not, all right. So I tore off the names. I also sent Eberhardt, Chaplain of the 87th Pennsylvania, and Dr. Brown fifty dollars. We were all in one box, and didn't care much for money. Now, I want to say right here that every dollar I lent these men in " Libby " was paid back to me. After being there twelve days, I was ordered to be exchanged. We had been nearly starved, for we had but little to eat. Sibley and Knowles, in the other room, had bribed the guard and got a little food in that way. The treatment we received here was brutal. Turner, who was said to be a nephew of General Winder, made us stand up to be counted every day, and, when I would lean against a post, because I was so sick and weak, he would swear at me and tell me to stand up straight. I didn't expect to live to get away from there. I found out afterwards that Captain Alexander had protested when they sent me to Libby, and said I was too old and sick, and that he would keep me in the Castle till I could be exchanged, and then put me on the boat, but Winder would hear nothing of it, and had me sent to Libby with the rest. The time for my release came at last. With others I was sent to City Point, where we were put on a boat and taken to Fortress Monroe and exchanged, after which I was not long in getting home.

One more little incident will end my story. Bullock, the steward who had been so kind to me, was taken prisoner. I wrote to some one at Washington about how kindly he had treated me and others, but before my letter arrived, he was put on the exchange list and sent south. He got a thirty days' furlough, and after visiting his family, made his way into our lines and showed himself with a white flag. He got the soldiers to give him a certificate that he had surrendered voluntarily, so that he would not again be sent back. He wrote to me and I went to Judge Morris for advice. He wrote out a statement of the facts I gave him, and sent it to Postmaster General Dennison, who secured his release, gave him a pass and sent him to Ohio. He hunted me up, and remained with me till the close of the war, when he returned to his family.

CAPTAIN R. O. KNOWLES,

Who was captured at Winchester, June 15th, 1863, was confined in various Rebel prisons before he finally found himself at Columbia, South Carolina. After a confinement of twenty days there, he and others began to lay plans for escape. How they did it and how they fared afterwards is told by the Captain in a letter from him to Captain A. B. Frame, under date of Deland, Florida, September 10th, 1882. We let the Captain tell the story himself:

"I escaped from Columbia Rebel Prison October 26th, 1864. After being there about twenty days we began to watch for a chance to escape. We finally approached a guard whom we found willing to aid us in case some greenbacks were forthcoming. We soon arranged with him to let three or four of us pass his post the next time he came on duty, which was the 26th of October. We had prepared for it by cooking every thing we could find and making maps of the route we would take.

The night arriving, we went to the spot our man was to occupy, about nine o'clock in the evening. There were three other Ohio officers besides myself, and two Wisconsin officers in our crowd, all of whom had bribed the same guard. We found our man after some difficulty. I walked up to the guard, and he let me pass. One of the other officers had the greenbacks. I called to the other officers to come on, when a guard close by fired his gun. I jumped pretty high at this and ran as fast as I could; the other officers started with me. The guards fired six or seven shots at us, and of course alarmed everybody. We ran as hard as we could, falling several times over stumps and into holes. Two officers were ahead of me, they thinking I was a Johnny, ran for dear life. After eighteen months of captivity, you may well imagine that we ran well. We soon got into a swamp, with mud and water up to our knees. Getting out of this after awhile, we took our planned route, as near as we could guess. After about an hour, we came near a house, where we were seen by some persons who started after us with some dogs. We took the back track for about two hundred yards, when we climbed a fence and took across a field, the dogs keeping on our old tracks and passing where we crossed the fence. We heard their barking all night. Striking a piece of woods, we lay by all the rest of the night and next day. When night came again, we started on our journey, keeping our eye on the North Star. Some time in the night we struck a road, and concluded to follow it, although it was not our direct course. When morning came, we took to the woods, and lay by all day, taking turns in keeping watch. This we did every day and night. I think it was our third night and about three o'clock in the morning, that I gave out, and lay down by the roadside, saying I could go no further. I was sick and weak, and had been so for some days past. We were out of provisions, hungry and exhausted, and something had to be done, so we dragged ourselves into the edge of a woods, and watched for a colored man to pass. During the day we hailed one, who, after seeing our condition and learning who we were, left us to return at dark in company with his wife, with a good supply of victuals. They put us on the right road and gave us directions for several days travel, telling us, at the same time, that whenever we got out of provisions, to let the 'cullud people know it.' After this if we missed our way or got out of provisions, we applied to the Negroes, who never failed to help us or to be true to us. We had many narrow escapes from capture, often meeting parties on the roads, but fortunately were never molested. After travelling together nearly across

North Carolina, our party separated, I going in a squad by myself. The next night I went to a house, and telling the man who I was, he gave me half a loaf of corn bread and started me on the right way over the mountains. That night I waded a wide, cold river. I was two nights crossing the mountains into Tennessee. I called at a house about two o'clock in the morning of the second day, and asked an old lady the way. She told me, but had to tell me too, what a pity it was to send so many souls to Hell in this war. She was firmly of the conviction that there was where all engaged in it were going. After getting into East Tennessee, I travelled in the day time, and after twenty-one days, or rather nights, I reached Knoxville, and was within the Union lines once more, thank God! I tell you I was never happier in my life! I went to a paymaster there, who paid me two months' pay, and in a few days I was at home, sweet home in Coolville."

CAPTAIN ALEXANDER COCHRAN,

WHO was so badly wounded at Bunker Hill, June 13th, 1863, and there made a prisoner, often spoke of the great kindness of J. B. T. Reed, of Winchester, a brother Mason. This man deserved the gratitude of every Union soldier for his kindness to them when in hospital and prisoners. When Captain Cochran was well enough to move, Mr. Reed secured his escape.

JOSEPH PURKEY,
First Sergeant, Company H.,

WAS captured at Winchester, June 14th, 1863, and escaped to the Union lines at New Creek, Virginia, June 30th, 1863. He was afterwards severely wounded at Piedmont, Virginia, and promoted to Second and First Lieutenant.

CORPORAL HARRISON COCHRANE,
Corporal of Company E.,

WAS severely wounded in the right foot at Piedmont, Virginia, June 5th, 1864, and taken prisoner at Staunton upon our army advancing from that place. He was taken to Andersonville, Georgia. He escaped from there January 27th, 1865, and reached Cedar Keys, Florida, April 27th, 1865, being just three months a wanderer within the rebel lines. During all this time he never saw the face of a white man, but was taken care of and guided by colored people. An account of his experience would be exceedingly interesting, but we have been unable to obtain it.

LIEUTENANT JOHN S. HEALD,

Who was wounded, as all thought fatally, through the body, at Piedmont, and captured at Staunton the same time with Corporal Cochrane, has kindly given me some of his experience, from which I make liberal quotations. Lieutenant Heald says: "The next day after our troops left Staunton for Lynchburg, we who were left there in hospital were prisoners under the rebel, Colonel Lee. He promised us that as soon as we could be moved, we would be sent through the lines to our own friends. I occupied a cot from which I could see the operating table and the spice of life with me for several days was to watch the process of amputating legs and arms, which would, in itself, be quite a history, had I the heart to write it. On the 28th of June, orders were given for all who were able to get into line to go to our own hospitals, to do so. I was on hand, but was told that the trip would be likely to kill me, and that I couldn't go; but my anxiety to get within our lines was so great, that I begged to go and they let me. We were marched four miles out of town to where the railroad had not been torn up. Here sixty-four wounded men were put into each box-car, and the train moved on. After a day of weary plodding along and suffering, we were landed at Lynchburg. We were unloaded and marched part way through town and halted in front of what was called the Commandant's headquarters, where we were ordered to throw away the sticks with which many had helped themselves to hobble along. Then they tried to form us in ranks. I, with others, could not stand without help. Explanations were of no avail, and the brutes in charge took clubs and went along the line, beating, kicking and calling us 'd——d lousy Yanks,' and pushing us here and there. All this time these ruffians were cheered by the citizens. We were finally put into a small, dirty slave pen in the rear of headquarters, for the night, and each given a small piece of bread and fat pork. As mean as the diet was, we ate it with a relish, for we were very hungry. That was a hard night for most of us. Next morning we were taken a short distance out of town and placed in a deep ravine, where we were kept for two days with a strong guard around us. It was very warm weather, but we had access to a small stream of water, which was a great relief to us in washing and dressing our wounds. I can never forget Edward Yockey and James Preshaw, of my company, who, though suffering from wounds themselves, were so kind to me. On July 1st, all who could walk were placed in ranks again, along with about 1200 able bodied men, recently captured from our armies, and we were started on the march for Danville, Virginia, distant seventy or eighty miles. The suffering endured on this march by the wounded it is impossible to describe. A great many died on the way from sun-stroke and exhaustion. Not as much as one day's rations was issued to us on the whole trip, and we suffered terribly for water to drink and to dress our wounds with. As we passed along the road, old men and boys would come out with shot guns, and go a certain distance as guards when they would be relieved by others. All believed that General Lee was going to 'take Pennsylvania.' 'Let's see, that's in Maryland, isn't it?' inquired an old citizen one day. We begged, time and again, to rest, and for water to drink and to bathe our wounds, but the only answer we got was,

'Keep up, you d——d Yanks, or I'll run my sword through you and leave you by the roadside for the hogs to eat.' We arrived at Danville about sun down, the fourth day, and were quartered in the upper stories of two ware houses. The floors were covered with filth and vermin. About ten o'clock they distributed rations, consisting only of corn bread. The stock provided for us went only about two-thirds around. I was in the last third and got nothing. It was the first time in my life that I was brought to tears from hunger. Next morning we received rations for two days, most of which was eaten by some of us for breakfast. We inquired if there was not some mistake, as there was not enough left for another meal. Our answer was, ' No, that's all that was intended for you, and it is better than you deserve.' In the morning we were loaded, sixty or seventy in box stock cars, for Andersonville, to be bumped and jolted for four days in the most inhuman manner, over terrible roads. I cannot describe our sufferings from hunger, thirst and every ill-treatment that could be heaped upon us. Among the many inhuman wretches who had charge of us, there were a few who were as kind to us as they dare be. Some of our guards fairly shuddered at the cruel way in which we were treated, but they were powerless to relieve our suffering. For miles the very bad condition of the railroad prevented us going faster than a man could walk, but every time a stop or a start was made, it was done with such bumps and jerks as to almost kill the sore and wounded men on the train; the seeming purpose being to punish us as much as possible. A number died on the way in the cars. At places we stopped, our men traded their shoes, knives, combs and blouses for something to eat. I think it was at Charlotte, North Carolina, that we had information that we were to remain on the side track for about two hours. I had almost given up being able to live through the journey. I beckoned a Lieutenant to the car door, and showing him my wound as politely as I knew how, asked to be let out on the ground for a short time. He picked up a stick, and striking me with it, told me to 'get back there, or I'll wound you a d——d sight worse than you are.' The blow he gave me, which was on the head, rendered me insensible for awhile. One of the guards finally, for a two dollar confederate note, obtained me a cup of water and a sweet potato. I learned the name of the officer who struck me, and tried to remember it, but have long since forgotten it. Many of our men had similar experiences of cruel treatment. On the 10th of July, all but the dead and dying were marched into Andersonville, and past the demon Wirz' headquarters. We were then divided into detachments of 270, and grouped into squads of ninety. One of our men who stepped from ranks to place a blouse under a dying man's head, was struck by an officer with his sword, and sent reeling back into ranks. Finally we were started off for the south gate of the stockade, which resembled butchers driving hogs into the slaughter pens more than anything else. This was the most awful hell-hole ever seen on earth. Men were not only starved to death, but they were inhumanly shot down and tortured to death in a hundred untold ways. Here were once strong men in every stage of idiocy and imbecility, the result of cruelty, the most barbarous ever witnessed. When weak, sickly men would vomit up the filthy food furnished them; others would struggle with each other to get and eat it, and even quarrel over it. The villain Wirz deserved not only one, but a thousand deaths. He was a cruel monster, such as only could be bred in the red fires of that hellish rebellion. Andersonville under his charge was worse than any picture ever yet written of hell. But the horrors of Andersonville, as often as they have been described, have never been half told, because no human power can do it. About the middle of September, Yockey and myself were taken out of the pen, as we were told, for exchange, but instead were sent off to Florence, Alabama. Preshaw was sick and soon after died. (Preshaw died November 3d, 1864, at Andersonville, and is buried there in grave No. 11779). Barrett, the keeper at Florence, we found to be as great a brute as Wirz. Indeed, the results of neglect and cruelty were here seen in more horrible shapes than at Andersonville. Men's limbs rotted off with gangrene; men died by inches of starvation; fell victims to that dread disease, scurvy; great numbers were insane from hardship, privation, exposure and starvation. Seasoned and hardened soldiers wandered restlessly about the camp in despair, and utterly, hopelessly insane from melancholy and privation. The sight was terribly distressing and painful. The guards were anxious, and sought excuses to shoot down men at the 'dead line,' and many men in their desperation, rushed upon death and begged to be shot as a relief from their unendurable misery. Escaping prisoners were chased by blood-hounds. The 'stockade' at Florence was not completed, and a strong guard was placed around the field in which the prisoners were placed. Soon after our arrival, between four and five hundred prisoners made their escape in open daylight, by breaking through the guard; some were killed, others wounded, others were recaptured, but a great many made their escape and reached our lines at different points. A soldier of an Illinois regiment, one from a Maine regiment, and myself had got about seventeen miles from Florence, when we were overtaken by blood-hounds in the night, and we climbed trees. Horsemen came up to the hounds very soon and ordered us down. We came down, and, contrary to our expectations, they treated us kindly. We spent most of the next day, Sunday, in the jail at Darlington, South Carolina, with about fifteen others who had been re-captured. Men, women and children came to see us. Some kind Samaritans, pitying our condition, brought us provisions, and we really had a feast. After getting a good meal and washing up well, we started back for Florence, which we reached that night. We expected rough treatment for our attempt to escape, but to our surprise, we received no punishment. About the middle of December we were told that the sick would that day be taken out for exchange. I managed to be pretty sick, and went out, leaving my trusty friend Yockey behind, who could not even play sick, and so had to remain for several weeks longer. We were taken to Charleston and delivered aboard our transports, and, I think, on the 17th of December, landed at Annapolis, Md. I would like to describe our feelings and actions on first getting sight of the old flag, but I have not the power to do it. Oh, how we cheered, yelled and cried! At Annapolis we were again in God's country, and were washed, clothed, fed, and taken the kindest possible care of. I spent Christmas at my home in Malaga, Ohio, and soon after went to Columbus to await exchange, which occurred the latter part of February, 1865. I rejoined my regiment near Appomattox in time to see the surrender, and afterwards went with it to Lynchburg, and looked for that rebel commander of the post and some of the citizens who cruelly cheered when the brutes beat and insulted us there, but they were all 'out of town.'"

HORACE M'NEIL,
Of Company B,

WAS captured at Lynchburg, Virginia, July 18, 1864, and was confined at Andersonville, Georgia, and Blackshire, Georgia; escaped from the latter place, December 14, 1864, and reached the coast and was rescued by a blockading ship, December 18, 1864. I have been unable to obtain the particulars of his escape.

LIEUTENANT MANNING,

WAS a prisoner from June 14, 1863, to March 5, 1865, and during this time made the tour of nearly all the rebel prison pens of the South. But he returned in time to witness the final surrender at Appomattox.

LIEUTENANT SIBLEY

REMAINED a prisoner from June 15, 1863, to December 10, 1864, when he was exchanged at Charleston Harbor. In response to my request for his experience as a prisoner of war, he sends me an article published in the Cleveland Herald, June 2, 1881. It is so important, and at the same time develops so interesting and startling a feature of his prison life, that I give it here entire. It is befitting, also, that so important a fact as it relates be placed in some more enduring form than in the files of a newspaper, and as it so nearly concerned several of our own officers, at the time confined in Libby Prison, it is entirely appropriate that it appear in the history of the regiment:

"When all the unpublished records of the war are brought forth to the light of day, a much worse showing will be made for the slave-driving prosecutors of the secession war than even now is thought possible. We know of some of the horrors of Andersonville and Libby prisons, but those who could have told the worst were not permitted to speak. They were "dismissed" from their horrible places of confinement even as the Nihilists of to-day dismiss their recreant members—through the gateway of death. Nothing more fully demonstrates the condition of a people than the treatment they bestow upon helpless prisoners of war. The North, with its fuller and better civilization and broader culture, cared for the Southern prisoners as though they were brothers in captivity. In return, the barbarous Southerners devised all the horrors of an inquisition, and placed the volunteers of the Northern army into the midst of them. Hunger and starvation were hastened on in their ghastly work by the lack of proper clothing and constant exposure to a climate which was new to the victims. Men were shot and bayoneted for trivial offences, and there was a constant failure to exchange at the proper time. In short, the Southern heart, brutalized by generations of human slavery, contemplated, with a coolness that we can scarcely understand, the proposition of starving to death thousands of regular prisoners of war. Much of this has already been known, and the apologists of this inhumanity have urged that it was done by irresponsible parties largely, and by those who were far removed from the seat of the secession Government. This cannot be said of the atrocities of Libby prison, which were enacted right in the shadow of the secession capital, and there is little doubt but the soured old man, who should have been hanged at the close of the war, but has lived and now has the effrontery to write his recollections of the time and justify in a dull dogged way the actions for which he should have been executed, was the man who planned them.

But of all that has been said, it would seem to me that the manuscript given below, and published now for the first time, betrays the most damnable and cold-blooded plan of all. It was nothing less than a plan to blow up the prison in case of a contingency by which the prisoners were likely to escape or by which they might be rescued by their friends.

I have been permitted to copy this from a manuscript in possession of H. L. Sibley, Esq., a prominent attorney of this city, who was a lieutenant in company B, 116th O. V. I. and was confined in Libby prison at the time this manuscript was written, and himself made a copy of it from the manuscript of Colonel Nichols, of Connecticut, the author. The paper was written and the copy made, of course, in Libby prison:

(COPY.)

"LIBBY PRISON, RICHMOND, VA., }
FRIDAY, March 4th, 1864. }

"This morning the rebel sergeant called me to the office of Major Turner. There I met Dr. William A. Smith, president of Randolph Macon College. Under a mistaken idea as to who he was, I had asked his assistance in procuring for me a special exchange. I knew by the papers that he was a man of large influence — a champion upon the rostrum of the Confederate cause. I thought it was another Smith — a graduate of the Wesleyan University of Connecticut, a man of the same college lodge as myself, and though personally unknown to me, I felt justified in addressing him. Last —— he called, apologizing for delaying so long to see me, saying it was the first time he had visited the city since receiving my note. I perceived I had mistaken the man, and duly excused my error. But he seemed rather pleased to meet me, although a stranger, and we conversed about noted Methodists of the North, with whom we were both acquainted. He was an old man, seventy-five, perhaps, and had been president of Macon College seventeen years. He spoke of the divisions of the M. E. church, of Dr. Olin, the first president of R. and M. College, and various other topics. I stated why I was desirous of an exchange, and he thought without a doubt he could bring it about, and would be pleased to do so. He referred to the war, its causes, its purposes, etc., eulogizing Southern bravery, determination, and declaring that a conquest would not bring peace, that he himself 'would never live again under the common flag.' 'Old as I am,' said he, 'and a cripple, I will leave forever my native land.' The

South would, however, never yield. He left, after various incidental remarks having passed between us, saying he would write to me, or call and see me soon.

"This evening at sunset he sent for me. Had seen, in a long interview, Judge Ould, and learned from him that through the *cartel*, and that alone, would he consent to make exchanges. They only deferred a general exchange, and if our Government wanted me, or all, it could have us by living up to its sworn treaty, as by the *cartel*, and not otherwise.

"Various remarks passed between us. I said I thought that to be the Judge's idea, but still he had varied the rule in some instances, and thought he continued to occasionally. He had urged my case strongly, he said, and was sorry he could not obtain my release. I thanked him warmly, for I felt that he had acted kindly in so interesting himself in a stranger. I perceived that he desired to talk upon general matters, and he even said that Judge Ould requested him to say to me that the officers here owed it to themselves that they express some dissent to the action of the United States Government in thus leaving us here, by violating its own pledges in the *cartel*, which stipulated for a paroling and exchanging of all, or words to that effect. The doctor thought I ought to write to my Government, and that the officers generally should, in their letters to their friends, express their disappointment at such a course and such neglect. He also said that the late *raid* had been characterized by much brutality and atrocity — private property destroyed and general plundering permitted. That on the body of Colonel Dahlgren were found instructions from our Government, saying that three columns were to advance upon the city, which was to be taken, plundered, sacked and burnt, the prisoners rescued and the place abandoned. Accordingly, he said, the authorities (Mr. Davis and Cabinet) were now in session, deliberating on the course to be taken in view of this state of affairs; this was upon private rights, so ruthless and so contrary to legal warfare. He said, moreover and here I make a record of it, that I may make no mistake hereafter through lack of memory *that the prison was ~~so~~ undermined, and powder placed beneath, so that in case of an attempt that was likely to be successful by an expedition thus carried on, the prisoners in Libby would be blown to atoms.* This he stated as though he had been asked to, that the prisoners, through me, might know how dangerous would be an effort on their part, or on the part of their friends, to rescue us. To all his remarks I made, as I thought, moderate but fitting replies. But to my direct question, whether or not he approved of such a resort, he made no definite answer. I asked him if any parallel in the annals of war would justify it, or to that effect. He remarked generally that only as a retaliatory measure could anything of the kind be justified. He asked me if the officers were aware of it. I told him we had sufficient evidence to believe it so, and had had for two days. But the proceeding was so horrible to think of that we rejected all evidence, and said it could not be that the authorities here would resort to a measure so murderous, and even so impolitic. I remarked that I regarded such proceedings as a high crime, not against the United States Government only, but against humanity. I told him that the officers, as a body, had shown themselves reasonable men. They had never in a single instance resorted to desperate measures, nor had they proposed to. They would respect, and had respected, a sufficient guard. Such a guard the Confederate authorities were bound to furnish, and not a guard sufficient only by holding *intersorum* certain destruction *en masse*, as well in case our friends were able to release us, as in case we rise up ourselves for our liberty. In any event I pronounced it unjustifiable, barbarous and murderous. The old gentleman was full of anxiety, evidently, and expressed what I supposed to be the fact, that this raid had greatly exasperated the people. He thought we might all soon leave for a more interior place of confinement. He shuddered to forecast the probabilities of severe measures that would yet be necessary; said Mr. Davis held back public sentiment, for he was a wise and God-fearing man — so unlike President Lincoln, who had violated the Constitution, and diverted the war from its originally proposed objects, etc., etc.; said that Mr. Davis was a praying man. I asked him if he did not think it a significant circumstance that in the last Presidential election not a word did the bitterest opponent utter against the honesty and general character of Mr. Lincoln.

"Other remarks were passed between us. But mainly I write this to put freshly on record what no one of these thousand officers but myself knows — that we are moving, sleeping, living over a torpedo, a magazine — which is designed to 'blow them to atoms,' to use Dr. Smith's own words.

"MONROE NICHOLS,
"Lieut. Col. 18th Conn. V. I."

NOTE. I copied the original of the above in Libby Prison the day following. Colonel N. was then my messmate, and read it to me immediately it was written by him. I sat by him as he wrote, seeing that something of importance was in hand.

HIRAM L. SIBLEY,
Lieut. Co. "B," 116th O. V. I.

Monday morning, March 7th, 1864, the Richmond Daily Enquirer of that date had the following editorial remarks, viz:

"LIBBY PRISON. The commandant of this prison, we learn, has made very satisfactory arrangements to secure the Yankee officers now under his charge, in case of a successful inroad into Richmond by the Yankee raiders. The nature of these arrangements need not be mentioned."

The following is an extract from a work entitled "A Rebel War Clerk's Diary at the Confederate States Capital, by J. B. Jones, clerk in the War Department of the Confederate States Government, author of 'Wild Western Scenes,' etc., etc." Published by J. B. Lippincott & Co., Philadelphia, 1866. Under date of "March 2d, 1864," on page 164, the Diary says:

"Last night, when it was supposed probable that the prisoners of war at the Libby might make an attempt to break out, General Winder ordered that a large amount of powder *be placed under the building*, with instructions to *blow them up* if the attempt were made. He was persuaded, however, to consult the Secretary of War first, and get his approbation. The Secretary would give no such order, but said the *prisoners must not be permitted to escape under any circumstances, which was considered sanction enough*. Captain —— obtained an order for, and procured several hundred pounds of powder, which were *placed in readiness*. Whether the prisoners were advised of this, I know not."

What Colonel Nichols refers to in his statement to Dr. Smith, that the prisoners had *evidence* of this "gunpowder plot," is the hints, and finally the open assertions of the colored men who "policed" our quarters. They were our friends, and were evidently horrified at the thought of what had been done. In hasty sentences, given when not watched by the rebel who had them in charge, they had, for a couple of days before Colonel Nichols saw Dr. Smith in the conversation he reports, given us warning, at first vaguely, as of some terrible impending calamity, and at last the *fact* that powder was under the prison to blow us up.

HIRAM L. SIBLEY.

In a private note to your correspondent Mr. Sibley says: "I hand you a copy of the document you desire, and also an extract from a book published by an ex-rebel (Jones) since the war, corroborating all that Colonel Nichols states as to the atrocious schemes to 'blow us to atoms,' rather than suffer our rescue.

"The whole affair comes very vividly to my memory in going over the paper. Besides, the night following, we could at times hear the boom of cannon which told that the raiders were in the vicinity of Richmond, and if they got in, I with the three others who alone knew the facts which Dr. Smith gave Colonel N. (being Generals Neal Dow and Scammouth, *four*) expected the springing of the mine. A more uneasy night I never yet have passed.

"Colonel N., after reading the paper to me, went to these two Generals, they being the only general officers then in prison, and privately read the statement to them, asking their judgment as to keeping it secret, or letting the prisoners generally know the facts. The former was deemed the wiser course, lest in a frenzy the attempt be made by some to force the guard, and we all thereby become involved in destruction by setting off the mine.

"Colonel Nichols was a Christian scholar and gentleman. He was educated at the Wesleyan University of Middletown, Conn. Later he was specially exchanged, but not until he had contracted a disease from which he died in 1867, I believe. No nobler or truer man perished from the wounds or hardships of the war.

"I was a lieutenant in Company 'B' 116th O. V. I. Resigned the County Common Pleas clerk's office, in Meigs County, O., to go into service, under the second call for 300,000 men in 1862. Was captured with part of General R. H. Milroy's command, near Winchester, Va., June 15th, 1863, by the advance (Ewell's corps) of Lee's army. June 22d I went to Libby. May 7, 1864, I went out, going to Danville, Va., about a week, and thence to Moscow, Ga., where I stayed till July 30th, when I was taken to Savannah. There I was kept till September 13th, when I was carried to Charleston, S. C., and put 'under fire' (from our bombardment of the city) until October 5th, when I was taken to what came to be known as 'Camp Sorghum,' about three miles from Columbia, S. C. There I stayed until December 9th, 1864, when, as one of the "sick or wounded," I was taken back to Charleston, and the next day (the 10th) was exchanged, being a prisoner eighteen months, lacking five days."

But what account shall we give of the the poor fellows who entered the prison pens of the South, never again to come out alive? Their story of prison life is briefly told in their death! The rolls tell the end of many and many a gallant boy and man who "died at Andersonville," "died at Salisbury," and so on. No pen can ever paint black enough the horrible treatment given our prisoners by rebel prison-keepers. Humanity through all time will shudder at the story of the wrongs they inflicted upon the men who, through the fortunes of war, fell into their hands.

In his report to the War Department, dated October 31, 1865, on the findings of the court which tried the inhuman monster Wirz, Judge Advocate General Holt says:

"Language fails in an attempt to denounce, even in faint terms, the diabolical combination for the destruction and death, by cruel and fiendishly ingenious processes, of helpless prisoners of war who might fall into their hands, which this record shows was plotted and deliberately entered upon, and, as far as time permitted, accomplished by the rebel authorities and their brutal underlings at Andersonville prison. Criminal history presents no parallel to this monstrous conspiracy, and from the whole catalogue of infamous devices within reach of human hands, a system for the murder of men more revolting in its details could not have been planned. Upon the heads of those named by the court in its findings, the guilt of this immeasurable crime is fixed, a guilt so fearfully black and horrible that the civilized world must be appalled by the spectacle."

* * * * * * * * *

"The annals of our race present nowhere and at no time a darker field of crime than that of Andersonville, and it is fortunate for the interests, alike of public justice and of historic truth, that from this field the veil has been so faithfully and so completely lifted. All the horrors of this pandemonium of the rebellion are laid bare to us in the broad, steady light of the testimony of some 150 witnesses, who spoke what they had seen and heard and suffered, and whose evidence, given under oath and subjected to cross-examination, and to every other test which human experience has devised for the ascertainment of truth, must be accepted as affording an immovable foundation for the sentence pronounced."

"The proof under the second charge shows that some of our soldiers, for mere attempts to escape from their oppressors, were given to ferocious dogs to be torn in pieces; that others were confined in stocks and chains till life yielded to the torture, and that others were wantonly shot down at Wirz's bidding or by his own hand. Here in the presence of these pitiless murders of unarmed and helpless men, so distinctly alleged and proved, justice might well claim the prisoner's life. There remain, however, to be contemplated, crimes yet more revolting, for which he and his co-conspirators must be held responsible. The Andersonville prison records (made exhibits in this case) contain a roster of over thirteen thousand (13,000) dead, buried naked, maimed and putrid, in one vast sepulchre. Of these, a surgeon of the rebel army who was on duty at this prison, testifies that at least three-fourths died of the treatment inflicted on them while in confinement, and a surgeon of our own army who was a prisoner there, states that four-fifths died from this cause. Under this proof, which has not been assailed, nearly 10,000, if not more of these deaths must be charged directly to the account of Wirz and his associates. This widespread sacrifice of life was not made suddenly or under the influence of wild, ungovernable passion, but was accomplished slowly and deliberately, by packing upwards of 30,000 men, like cattle, into a fetid pen, a mere cesspool, there to die for need of air to breathe; for want of ground on which to lie; from lack of shelter from sun and rain, and from the slow, agonizing process of starvation; when air and space and shelter and food were all within the ready gift of their tormentors. This work of death seems to have been a saturnalia of enjoyment for the prisoner, who, among these savage orgies evidenced such exultation, and mingled with them such nameless blasphemy and ribald jests, as at times to exhibit him rather as a demon than a man. It was his continual boast that by these barbarities he was destroying more Union soldiers than rebel generals were butchering on the battle-field. He claimed to be doing the work of the rebellion, and faithfully, in all his murderous cruelty and baseness, did he represent its spirit. It is by looking upon the cemeteries which have been filled from Libby, Belle Isle, Salisbury, Florence and Andersonville, and other rebel prisons, and recalling the prolonged sufferings of the patriots who are sleeping there, that we can best understand the inner and real life of the rebellion, and the hellish criminality and brutality of the traitors who maintained it. For such crimes human power is absolutely impotent to enforce any adequate atonement."

This is the horrible story of Andersonville, one of the many hellish prison pens of the South, while of those less notorious prisons, such as Libby, Belle Isle, Cahawba, Blackshire, Millen, Tyler, Florence, Salisbury, Macon and Charleston, almost nothing is known, save the reports given by those escaping from them with their lives. These reports make them but a little more humane than Andersonville.

We have endeavored to obtain a full list of our men who died in rebel prisons. We have succeeded in making it more complete than we dared to hope, and here give the result of our efforts. It will be a consolation, though a sad one, to many, to know where lie the remains of their dead hero friends. The following list also contains the burial places of many who were killed in battle, many who died of wounds and of disease. I have taken great pains to make it as complete and accurate as possible, yet there may be some errors in it, and some names may be omitted which ought to be included in it. But it is as correct as I could make it after a great deal of care and searching of records, together with the kind assistance of the Quartermaster General of the Army and the Adjutant General of Ohio:

List of Names of 116th O. V. I., Buried in Southern Cemeteries.

DATE OF DEATH.	NAMES.	RANK.	CO.	PLACE OF BURIAL.
October 13, 1864	Archer, Dickerson	Corporal	E	National Cemetery, Winchester, Va., Lot 11.
June 14, 1863	Arckeron, F. H	Captain	C	National Cemetery, Winchester, Va., Lot 20.
July 16, 1864	Alford, Samuel	Private	D	Staunton, Va.
June 5, 1864	Armstrong, Robert	...	B	Piedmont, Va.
July 16, 1864	Bryan, Washington	...	D	National Cemetery, Staunton, Va.
May 27, 1865	Byers, Emmanuel	...	C	National Cemetery, Hampton, Va.
August 18, 1864	Barrett, John G	Corporal	C	Annapolis, Md., U. S. G. Hospital, Division No. 1.
July 11, 1864	Barrett, Isaac	Private	E	National Cemetery, Staunton, Va.
June 18, 1864	Blair, George	...	E	National Cemetery, Lynchburg, Va.
April 1, 1863	Baker, Stephen	...	E	National Cemetery, Antietam, Md.
October 19, 1864	Bruny, David	...	B	National Cemetery, Winchester, Va., Lot 28.
June 5, 1864	Bruck, Elias G	...	E	National Cemetery, Staunton, Va.
September 17, 1864	Birch, Josephus	...	D	Loudon Park Cemetery, Baltimore, Md.
June 18, 1864	Boyd, James A	Private	A	National Cemetery, Lynchburg, Va.
...	Brock, Cody	...	E	National Cemetery, Staunton, Va.
November 8, 1864	Conley, Leonard J	...	A	National Cemetery, Annapolis, Md.
October 14, 1864	Cregg, Moses	...	E	Mt. Olivet Cemetery, Frederick, Md.
June 18, 1864	Coulter, George M	...	B	National Cemetery, Lynchburg, Va.
...	Comstock, Josephus	...	...	National Cemetery, Antietam, Md., Sec. 1, Lot B, No. 30
June 20, 1864	Chambers, Robert E	...	...	Beverly, West Virginia
June 27, 1865	Cagg, A. C	...	K	Andersonville, Ga.
July 9, 1865	Clark, Jacob	...	B	City Cemetery, Gallipolis, O., Grave No. 134.
October 21, 1864	Caldwell, Francis	Private	E	National Cemetery, Winchester, Va.
...	Cline, Henry M	...	A	National Cemetery, Winchester, Va.
June 20, 1864	Davis, Charles	...	...	Lynchburg, Va.
June 5, 1864	Dyer, Robert H. H	...	C	National Cemetery, Staunton, Va.
June 5, 1864	Detwiler, John	...	C	National Cemetery, Staunton, Va.
October 12, 1864	Davis, Miles H	...	E	National Cemetery, Antietam, Md., Sec. 1, Range F, Grave No. 290.
September 25, 1864	Dipkas, Charles	...	C	National Cemetery, Antietam, Md., Sec. 1, Range F, Grave 301.
February 10, 1865	Dennis, John A	...	...	National Cemetery, Fort Harrison, Va., Sec. D, Grave 22.
June 20, 1864	Dickson, Scott	...	D	Lynchburg, Va.
July 24, 1864	Eoff, Leander	...	D	National Cemetery, Antietam, Md., Sec. 1, Lot A, Grave 26.
March 30, 1863	Erskin, Lewis	...	D	National Cemetery, Antietam, Md., Sec. 1, Lot A, Grave 14.
July 18, 1864	Farley, Benjamin	...	E	National Cemetery, Winchester, Va., Lot 19.
November 5, 1864	Flowers, W. F	...	E	National Cemetery, Andersonville, Ga., Grave 11,819.
September —, 1864	Forshay, Asa	...	...	National Cemetery, Andersonville, Ga., Grave 10,045.
June 26, 1864	Frost, Consider	...	...	National Cemetery, Staunton, Va.

Since removed to Frost's Church, Carthage Township, Athens County, Ohio.

List of Names of 116th O. V. I. Buried in Southern Cemeteries.—(CONTINUED.)

DATE OF DEATH.	NAMES.	RANK.	CO.	PLACE OF BURIAL.
June 18, 1864	Fisher, William	Private	F	National Cemetery, Lynchburg, Va.
September 28, 1864	Fulton, Charles	....	E	National Cemetery, Winchester, Va., Lot 28.
January 13, 1865	Frost, Ephraim W	....	H	Annapolis, Md.
April 23, 1865	Giver, Jacob	Corporal	A	Camp Parole Hospital, Annapolis, Md.
July 20, 1864	Gatten, Jefferson	Private	F	National Cemetery, Lynchburg, Va., Sec. E, Division E, Grave 167.
October 9, 1864	Gilbert, J. C. S	....	..	Savannah, Ga.
April 2, 1865	Grave, David L.	....	K	National Cemetery, Lynchburg, Va., Sec. C, Division C, Grave 24.
June 16, 1864	Gannon, George W.	....	C	National Cemetery, Staunton, Va., Grave 104.
June 3, 1864	Hayden, Nathaniel D	....	A	National Cemetery, Staunton, Va.
September 13, 1864	Hoyt, Royal	....	B	National Cemetery, Andersonville, Ga., Grave 8,189.
April 2, 1865	Hall, William	....	C	National Cemetery, Petersburg, Va.
March 4, 1865	Hill, Hezekiah	....	..	National Cemetery, Hampton, Va., Sec. E, Row H, Grave 4.
July 22, 1864	Headley, James C	....	C	National Cemetery, Staunton, Va.
January 13, 1865	Hunt, D. W	....	D	Annapolis, Md., U. S. G. Hospital, Division No. 2.
April 12, 1865	Hutchinson, Robert S	....	E	National Cemetery, Farmville, Va.
July 24, 1864	Hamilton, E. B	....	E	Lynchburg, Va.
April 2, 1865	Hysell, Martin	....	G	National Cemetery, Petersburg, Va.
December 20, 1864	Hall, Jacob	....	D	National Cemetery, Salisbury, N. C.
July 18, 1864	Hayes, Samuel L	....	D	National Cemetery, Winchester, Va.
August 6, 1863	Harbine, John M	Corporal	B	National Cemetery, Antietam, Md., Lot D, Sec. 1, Grave 179.
April 2, 1865	Hartley, James M	Private	G	National Cemetery, Petersburg, Va.
September 6, 1864	Hill, Eliza J	....	H	National Cemetery, Antietam, Md., Lot C, Sec. 1, Grave 163.
October 10, 1864	Henshaw, Edward	Private	K	Andersonville, Ga.
August 4, 1864	Hill, Samuel H.	....	H	National Cemetery, Antietam, Md., Lot F, Sec. 1, Grave 349.
September 19, 1864	Hetzer, Orville S	....	B	National Cemetery, Winchester, Va.
March 2, 1864	Hennael, Thomas	....	C	National Cemetery, Winchester, Va., Lot 28.
April 2, 1865	Hall, William	....	C	National Cemetery, Petersburg, Va.
April 22, 1865	Hitchcock, M. R.	Sergeant	A	National Cemetery, City Point, Va., Sec. A, Lot 1, Grave 11.
June 3, 1864	Hayden, Nathaniel D	....	H	Piedmont, Va.
June 6, 1864	Harrison, James	....	B	National Cemetery, Staunton, Va.
June 14, 1865	Heck, Oswald	Sergeant	..	Winchester, Va.
July 13, 1864	Hughes, James F	Private	F	National Cemetery, Staunton, Va.
August 9, 1862	Johnson, G. W	....	F	National Cemetery, Staunton, Va., Sec. B, Grave 63.
March —, 1865	Jackson, W. S	....	..	Cumberland, Md.
July 13, 1864	Jones, Amos S	Captain	H	Salisbury, N. C.
....	Keyes, Edwin	Private	E	Poplar Grove National Cemetery, Lynchburg, Va.
....	Kerfuah, Jacob	Corporal	E	Poplar Grove National Cemetery, Lynchburg, Va.
June 5, 1864	King, William	....	F	National Cemetery, Staunton, Va.

ONE HUNDRED AND SIXTEENTH O. V. I.

Date	Name	Rank	Co.	Burial
June 5, 1864	Krouse, Morris	Private	F	National Cemetery, Staunton, Va.
October 3, 1864	Larrick, Benjamin	"	H	Mt. Olivet, Frederick, Md., Area O.
June 5, 1864	Latshaw, John	"	C	National Cemetery, Staunton, Va.
September 12, 1864	Lampton, Levi	"	E	Race Course Cemetery, Charleston, S. C.
September 19, 1864	Lathey, Samuel	Lieut.	H	National Cemetery, Winchester, Va.
October 2, 1864	Larrick, John	Private	H	Savannah, Ga.
July 8, 1864	Larrick, Benjamin	"	K	National Cemetery, Antietam, Md., Sec. 1, Lot C, Grave 112.
June 18, 1864	Light, Mathias	"	K	National Cemetery, Antietam, Md., Sec. C, Grave 12, Division C.
April 2, 1865	Lyon, George	"	H	Lynchburg, Va.
July 18, 1864	Lindsay, James	"	C	National Cemetery, Poplar Grave, Va., Sec. C, Division C, Grave 45.
June 5, 1864	Lamp, George	"	L	Island Ford, Va., (Snicker's Ferry.)
April 18, 1865	McCoy, Stephen C.	Corporal	H	National Cemetery, Hampton, Va.
June 5, 1864	McCoy, Gilbert	Private	H	National Cemetery, Hampton, Va., Sec. L, Row 20, Grave 1
July 21, 1863	Moluarly, William H.	"	D	National Cemetery, Staunton, Va.
September 12, 1864	Madourey, Richard	Corporal	E	National Cemetery, Staunton, Va., Sec. B, Grave 64.
July 12, 1864	Mozena, Lewis W.	Private	E	National Cemetery, Petersburg, Va.
June 15, 1863	Miller, Madison G.	"	C	National Cemetery, Staunton, Va.
January 2, 1865	Motharty, J. B.	"	D	National Cemetery, Staunton, Va., Sec. B, Grave 57.
	Matthew, Theodore	"	D	National Cemetery, Winchester, Va.
	Morris, Augustic	"	F	Salisbury, N. C.
September 19, 1864	McCain, John C.	Private	C	National Cemetery, Winchester, Va., Lot 25.
June 20, 1864	McElwee, John A.	"	C	National Cemetery, Winchester, Va., Lot 25.
August 20, 1864	McCullouth, Moses	"	C	National Cemetery, Staunton, Va.
June 3, 1864	Matchett, G. W.	"	C	National Cemetery, Winchester, Va., Lot 28.
June 3, 1864	Metzger, Joshua	"	B	National Cemetery, Staunton, Va.
	Miller, R. B.	"	I	National Cemetery, Staunton, Va., Sec. B, Grave 31.
August 15, 1864	McCoy, Stephen	Corporal	H	Piedmont, Va.
August 3, 1864	Moore, David A.	"	G	Andersonville, Ga.
June 3, 1864	Martin, Robert	Private	C	Andersonville, Ga.
October 2, 1864	Neptune, Fred F.	"	F	London Park Cemetery, Baltimore, Md.
	Oliver, James W.	"	C	Andersonville, Ga.
November 4, 1864	Okey, Emmanuel	Private	A	Andersonville, Ga., Grave 11,579.
May 25, 1864	Predmow, J. A.	"	C	National Cemetery, Andersonville, Ga., Grave 11,579.
July 1, 1864	Pether, Robert	"	H	National Cemetery, Winchester, Va.
June 3, 1864	Pitch, Soloman	Corporal	C	National Cemetery, Staunton, Va., Sec. C, Grave 13.
April 22, 1865	Rodecker, Adam	Sergeant	E	National Cemetery, Staunton, Va., Sec. C, Grave 2.
April 7, 1865	Reiboutler, John G.	Private	C	National Cemetery, Poplar Grave, Va., Sec. B, Grave 32, Division A.
April 2, 1865	Entfleure, Samuel	"	E	National Cemetery, Hampton, Va., Sec. E, Row 22, Grave 24.
August 10, 1864	Rodgers, James	"	H	Petersburg, Va.
September 25, 1864	Russell, John C.	"	H	Andersonville, Ga.
November 30, 1862	Schatter, Charles	"	G	National Cemetery, Winchester, Va.
September 11, 1864	Stoncking, J. A.	"	E	National Cemetery, Antietam, Md., Sec. 1, Grave 1
	Sidener, Jacob C.	Corporal	I	National Cemetery, Antietam, Md.

Since removed to Milford Cemetery, Hunterdon County, New Jersey.

List of Names of 116th O. V. I. Buried in Southern Cemeteries.—(Continued.)

DATE OF DEATH.	NAMES.	RANK.	CO.	PLACE OF BURIAL.
July 18, 1864	Stoneman, William	Private	I	National Cemetery, Winchester, Va., Lot 19.
June 7, 1864	Simmons, Joseph		D	National Cemetery, Staunton, Va.
June 6, 1864	Shumway, S. C		B	National Cemetery, Staunton, Va., Sec. A, Grave 16.
June 19, 1864	Starr, Moses F		D	Lynchburg, Va.
September 19, 1864	Secoy, Lewis C		B	National Cemetery, Winchester, Va.
March 31, 1865	Smith, John		E	National Cemetery, Petersburg, Va.
June 5, 1864	Swartz, Francis		B	National Cemetery, Staunton, Va.
	Trilley, Isaiah		H	National Cemetery, Winchester, Va., Lot 20.
June 18, 1864	Van Horn, Gilbert		I	National Cemetery, Lynchburg, Va.
December 6, 1864	Winland, John H		D	National Cemetery, Antietam, Md., Sec. 1, Lot A, Grave 3.
June 30, 1864	Warren, Frederick		B	National Cemetery, Staunton, Va.
October 22, 1864	Yohn, Peter		F	Philadelphia, Pa.
March 31, 1865	Yohn, Reuben		H	National Cemetery, Winchester, Va., Lot 27.
July 7, 1864	Zimmerly, Jacob	Private	A	National Cemetery, Staunton, Va., Sec. B, Grave 34.

CHAPTER XVIII.

SKETCHES OF DECEASED OFFICERS — CAPTAIN F. H. ARCKENOE — CAPTAIN E. KEYES — LIEUTENANT ROBERT WILSON — LIEUTENANT LEVI LUPTON — SURGEON THOMAS J. SHANNON — CAPTAIN ALEXANDER COCHRAN — CAPTAIN EDWARD FULLER — CAPTAIN WILLIAM MYERS — SURGEON WALTER R. GILKEY — HOSPITAL STEWARD JAMES T. MORAN — LIEUTENANT M. A. ELLIS — MAJOR JOHN HULL.

IN MEMORIAM.

It has been thought best to add this chapter in commemoration of the noble men who surrendered their lives to their country. Included in the following pages are those officers who died in the service, as well as those who have since died from wounds received or disease contracted in the service.

CAPTAIN FREDERICK H. ARCKENOE.

The first officer killed in action was Captain Arckenoe, who fell at the battle of Winchester, June 14, 1863. He was a Prussian by birth, and had been in this country but a few years before the breaking out of the war. He was a finely educated gentleman, had learned the art of war in the military schools and armies of his fatherland, and gave early promise of great distinction in the service of his adopted country. A large portion of his company consisted of Germans, and no happier military family existed in the regiment than he and his officers and men made of company C. A man of noble presence and martial bearing, he was the beau ideal of a soldier. He was kind to his men, courteous and dignified at all times, an excellent disciplinarian, of spotless character and refined culture, and in the broadest and fullest sense, a soldier "without fear and without reproach." He was as graceful and attractive as he was manly and dignified; possessing unbending integrity, and strict conscientiousness, and the highest sense of honor, he was the very personation of true chivalry, and of the highest type of manhood. The 116th never had a truer gentleman, a finer officer, or a braver man, and never met a more serious loss than in his death.

CAPTAIN EDWIN KEYES.

The following sketch is taken from " Marietta College, in the War of Secession."

The subject of this sketch was born in Windsor Township, Morgan County, Ohio, July 21, 1828, the child of poor but upright Christian parents. At an early age he showed a studious disposition, and while young became a school teacher in the neighborhood of his birth. Compelled to support himself by work on the farm or in school, young Keyes struggled for more of an education than his home opportunities afforded. Accordingly, in 1848, he became a student in the preparatory department of Marietta College. Passing regularly through, in 1850 he entered college a freshman. Adverse circumstances, however, prevented his going further in the course than to the junior year of his class. April 13th, 1854, he was married to Sybil Sargent, by whom he had a son, Charles Edwin, now iving. His attachment to his family was remarkably strong and deep.

About 1860, Mr. Keyes removed to Tuppers Plains, Meigs County, Ohio. This is a pleasant village, finely located on a plateau, the center of a prosperous farming community. The point was selected for the site of a school he wished to establish. Teaching was then his chosen vocation. Devoted to his work, and a natural leader among men, he so aroused the people of this village and vicinity in the cause of education, as to secure the erection of an academy building, wherein he founded a flourishing school known as the Tuppers Plains Seminary. Young men and women from a distance, as well as of the country immediately around the Plains, were attracted to this school by the success and growing fame of the teacher, and by the high character he bore as a man. The specific aim of the institution was to train its pupils for teaching, and prepare young men for college. The close of the first year showed the enterprise triumphantly successful. Even the excitements and anxieties of civil war did not prevent a steady increase in the attedance upon the school, and of interest in the work it was doing. Truly, a master was at its head. The summer of 1862 came, with its disasters to the Union armies in the terrible conflict with rebellion. Still the school on the Plains was full. A large number of young people was gathered there, enthusiastic in study, under the inspiring direction of a teacher they had learned both to love and respect. But the appeals of that dark year to Northern patriotism rang in the ears of the master, and met a warm response from his heart. At this time Mr. Keyes was in the clear road of assured success in his profession. The field for a great and good work was open in peace before him. Moreover, he was bound to home by ties which, with a nature such as his, were at once among the tenderest and most powerful in life. But he was a patriot who loves liberty and the Union of his fathers, and to whom the trumpet call of duty never was sounded in vain. Around him, also, was a body of young men who would follow him as their leader to the field of battle, or remain under his guidance in the pursuit of knowledge at home. The struggle, the writer knows, was exceedingly severe. But a clear sense of duty—the vital principle of all his actions—was, as it ever had been with him, decisive; and August 12th, 1862, he accepted, after enlistment, a Captain's commission in the volunteer service of the United States for "three years, or during the war." The young men of his school rallied around him in the country's service, almost to a man. Such was his influence, indeed, and so profound the confidence which his abilities and character inspired, that in less than one week from his appointment, he was in camp at Marietta, Ohio, followed by a dozen more men than could be mustered into his company.

His became company B of the 116th O. V. I. While Captain Keyes remained with his men, they served chiefly in West Virginia and in the war-famed Valley of Virginia. He participated in all the important battles of this valley, from the opening of 1863 until he was made a prisoner of war. On the 18th of June, 1864, near Lynchburg, Va., with his men, he was engaged in a desperate and bloody charge upon the enemy's works. While leading his command amid a storm of bullets, he was hit and severely wounded in the knee. Our forces being driven back, one of his men was helping him along when another shot was received in the arm, inflicting a painful wound. Unable further to proceed, he was unavoidably left, with others disabled by wounds, to fall into the hands of the enemy. To the last, however, he was undismayed, and showed the resignation of the Christian with the fortitude of a soldier.

Finally, July 19th, 1864, in hospital at Lynchburg, Va., of the wounds received as stated above, he died. He faced the last enemy surrounded by strangers and in prison. Before his death, Marietta College had conferred upon him the honorary degree of Master of Arts.

Captain Keyes stood full six feet, with a well proportioned frame, and a presence which always commanded respect. He was a man of refined sensibilities and feelings of child-like tenderness. His life was pure, blameless, of exalted aim and purpose. He was possessed of a vigorous mind, well disciplined, and marked by a peculiarly sound and comprehensive understanding. As a teacher he greatly excelled; and as a soldier he leaves a proud record for personal bravery, and the able, prompt discharge of every duty which the service cast upon him. But the crowning glory of his character was his moral symmetry and power. In the regiment his was styled the "religious company." Twice a day, when circumstances permitted, he led his men in prayer, and in one instance, it is known, these services resulted in a soldier's conversion. A few words from a letter to his father, in January, 1863, give an insight into the real life of the man, which justifies their insertion here. Thus he wrote: "I meet with the sorest trials and endure the keenest temptations. But through all these my Savior sustains me. Indeed, I feel while leaning on His powerful arm that nothing can harm me. These are my feelings in scenes of danger. * * * I know not but sorer trials are in store for me. My country may demand the poor offering of my life, and my dear wife and darling boy be left without their earthly stay and support. But if the bitter cup must be drained, trusting in my Savior, I hope to be sustained as life is laid upon the altar."

Heroic Christian soldier! You drank this cup to the dregs. No life more sublimely pure and noble in purpose and work was given, a sacrifice for the Nation's life, in the war against rebellion. Of all who thus fell we can truly say:

> Beautiful is the death-sleep
> Of those who bravely fight
> In their country's holy quarrel,
> And perish for the right.

LIEUTENANT ROBERT WILSON.

While lying at Buchanan, Lieutenant Robert Wilson was stricken down with fever. Realizing that he was dangerously sick, he asked and obtained leave to go to his home in Woodsfield, where he died on the 19th of November, 1862. The regiment had scarcely become acquainted with him, but among those with whom he came in contact, he was regarded as one of the best officers in the regiment. He was a well educated man, and when Colonel Washburn detached Adjutant Ballard to act as A. A. General of the brigade, he was selected to act as Adjutant of the regiment. He was then sick and never assumed the position. He gave bright promise of making an efficient and valuable officer. His was among the first deaths, if it was not the very first, in the regiment, and being so good an officer and excellent a man, his loss was greatly felt, and the sorrow at his death was deep and universal.

LIEUTENANT LEVI LUPTON.

Lieutenant Lupton, as before shown, was captured on the 14th of June, 1863, at Winchester. He, too, was a brave and efficient officer and an excellent man. His capture was due to his unflinching courage and his aversion to turning his back to the enemy. He never had any conception of what fear was. He suffered the untold horrors of Libby, Salisbury and Charleston. At the latter place he was among the Union officers placed under the fire of the forts and gunboats in the bombardment of that hot-bed of treason. He endured untold hardships, privations and dangers. The officers of our regiment sent him, and others of the regiment who were prisoners, a great amount of everything for their relief, but we have the best reasons for believing that they never received a tithe of it. Among papers in my possession I find a subscription paper prepared at Martinsburg in the winter of 1863-4, which reads as follows: "We, the undersigned officers, promise to pay the sums set opposite our respective names for the relief of Lieutenants Lupton, Sibley, Knowles and Manning, of the 116th regiment, now in Prison at Richmond, Virginia, said money to be sent to them through C. C. Fulton, Esq., of the Baltimore American." To this paper is subscribed, in the aggregate, $130. It is in the hand writing of Captain Karr, and its possession affords me the signature of all the officers of the regiment present. A great many well filled boxes were also sent them. Among letters I find brief acknowledgements from Lieutenant Sibley, dated "Libby Prison, Richmond, Va."

Lieutenant Lupton was a zealous patriot. It was patriotism made a soldier of him, not a love for military life. But nothing could excel the conscientiousness with which he discharged every duty assigned him. He was in downright earnest always, and never took part in the fun or frolic of camp life. But though of so serious a turn of mind, he was never morose or gloomy, but was very kindhearted, obliging and thoughtful to every want and comfort of his men. As a result, he was well liked and held in very high esteem by officers and men alike. At Charleston, in the fall of 1864, he was taken down with fever and died September 12. He was buried in Race Course Cemetery, near the City of Charleston. Every effort was made by the officers of the regiment to secure the exchange of the officers captured at Winchester and Bunker Hill, but all efforts were in vain. The rebel authorities seemed to have a special pique at General Milroy's officers. This spirit of hate for them is shown in all rebel works, and especially in Jeff Davis' "Rise and Fall."

SURGEON THOMAS J. SHANNON.

Among our killed at Cedar Creek was our Surgeon, Major Thomas J. Shannon. Of the manner of his death, Captain John F. Welch, of the 116th, then on Thoburn's staff, writes: "When I had reached Middletown with the trains, I found Thoburn there and reported to him. Dr. Shannon, Surgeon of the 116th, and Medical Purveyor of the division, was with him. Dr. Shannon had charge of several wagon loads of medical stores. Thoburn ordered Dr. Shannon and myself to go beyond Middletown with our wagons, and there try to form a line of the straggling soldiers, which by this time were numerous. Shannon's wagons were on the pike leading to Winchester, and mine on a street west of the pike. I was to drive my teams to the pike and get them together. While I was after my wagons, and before I got back to the pike, and when not over two or three hundred yards from it, Thoburn and Shannon were both shot and mortally wounded. They were shot by sharpshooters who had succeeded in getting within our lines. As I neared the pike several shots were fired at me, two of them striking my horse." Thoburn lingered during the day and died that evening. Dr. Shannon died at Winchester on the 21st. Dr. Shannon was one of the most skillful, pains-taking, hard-working and faithful surgeons in the army. He never had a thought of anything but duty, which he discharged with a zeal and fidelity that made him not only trusted and esteemed, but remarkably successful and valuable. He was too good a surgeon among the great number of indifferent ones in the service, to be kept with his regiment. His services were in con-

stant demand in wider fields of labor. But he was a
worker, and being fond of his regiment, he found time to
look after it daily. His loss to our regiment and to the service was irreparable. He was withal an exceedingly brave
and fearless man, and too often exposed himself to the perils
of the battle field in his anxious care for the wounded. He
could easily have escaped harm the morning he was shot,
but in his charge was a train loaded with several thousands
of dollars worth of medical stores, and to save it he exposed
his own life, and gave it up a sacrifice to duty and to principle. Dr. Shannon's sense of honor was sensitively acute,
and while he was often hurt by adverse criticisms of his
severe treatment of "hospital bummers," he was as kind as
a mother to the really sick and wounded. The regiment
owed its good standing and effectiveness as much to him as
to any officer connected with it. He held a "dead beat"
in the greatest aversion, but attended upon a good soldier
with the greatest pleasure and most assiduous care. He
was a quiet, still, unpretending, plain man, but he possessed
the courage, dignity, faith and manliness which devotion to
principle, a conscientious discharge of life's duties, and an
unfaltering purpose to do right, lend to character. His remains were sent to his home, accompanied by an escort in
charge of Lieutenant Cobb, who was slightly wounded in
the battle. But the greatest disaster to us all was the loss
of Colonel Thoburn.

CAPTAIN ALEXANDER COCHRAN.

Captain Alexander Cochran was born in Bridgeton,
Bucks County, Pennsylvania, in 1818. Both of his parents
died when he was a mere child, and leaving no property for
his support, he was at once thrown upon the world to make
his own way through it, and to carve out his own fortune.
When a boy he learned the shoemaker's trade, which he followed with few interruptions ever afterwards, and through

industry and good management he acquired considerable property. He was married in Bridgeton in 1840 to Miss Rebecca Butler, with whom he had five children, all of whom died in childhood, except Sarah Jane, the wife of Prof. George E. Blair. His first wife died in 1850, and in 1853 he was married to Miss Emma Robeson, who survives him. Of this union he had seven children, five of whom are still living. Captain Cochran removed from Bridgeton, Pennsylvania, to Athens in 1853, where he resided up to his death, April 25th, 1872. In the fall of 1862 he entered the service of the United States and was appointed First Lieutenant of Company I, 116th Regiment Ohio Volunteers. He served in this capacity until January 31st, 1863, when he was promoted to Captain. During nearly all the time of his Lieutenancy, he acted as Quartermaster of his regiment, and no more faithful or competent officer ever held that position in the 116th, and no Quartermaster was ever more popular with men and officers, because none were more efficient. At the battle of Bunker Hill, on the 13th of June, 1863, Captain Cochran was wounded in the elbow of the right arm and taken prisoner. As he was unfit to be moved, he was left there, and had the good fortune to fall into the hands of a noble hostess and fraternal brother by name of John B. T. Reed, who, as soon as the Captain could be moved, pointed out a way of escape for him and sent him within the Union lines. In the fall of 1863 he returned to his company with his arm in a sling and reported for duty. The Surgeon, however, pronounced him unfit for active duty, and he was ordered to Concord, New Hampshire, on recruiting duty, where he remained until he resigned, February 9th, 1865. Captain Cochran was a brave man, and upon the field of battle was cool and collected as when moving among his friends and business acquaintances at home. As Regimental Quartermaster the men had in him a true friend, as their wants were never neglected when it was possible to supply them. His kind heart would not suffer him to retire at night until he knew that everything was done that could be done for the comfort of his men.

CAPTAIN EDWARD FULLER.

Edward Fuller, late Captain Company I, 116th Regiment O. V. I., was born April 12, 1832, near Coolville, Athens County, Ohio. He was the son of Jedediah Fuller, who was one of the earliest settlers of Athens County. He opened up a large farm and was during his lifetime one of the leading farmers of Athens County. He gave his children a liberal education. Edward, while not in school, spent his time on the farm, which finally fell into his possession. He was widely known, and was noted for his generosity. He was a strong Republican, and at the breaking out of the war, his time, money and services were at the service of his country. He was largely instrumental in raising volunteers, and finally took a company and went into the 116th regiment as Captain; was assigned to company "I." The hardships and severe weather of the winter of 1862-3 preyed heavily upon his health, so much so that he was compelled to resign his position in the army and seek for restoration of health, which he never found. He gradually went down until April 10th, 1872, when he died. Captain Fuller possessed a magnetism which drew around him a large circle of friends and his death made a vacuum which has not been filled.

There were only fifteen days between the deaths of Fuller and Cochran. Both were buried under the auspices of the Masonic Order.

CAPTAIN WILLIAM MYERS.

Captain William Myers was born in Monongahala County, Virginia, June 14, 1809, and moved with his parents to Monroe County, Ohio, in 1822, where he was married, in 1832, to Miss Hannah Mitchell. He engaged in farming, and took great interest in stock raising. He brought the first herd of short horn Durhams into Monroe County. He was a man of sterling integrity, and by his conscientious, upright life, won the confidence of all who knew him, as was shown by his being chosen to serve as justice of the peace for some eighteen or twenty years, and being twice elected treasurer of his county. When Fort Sumter was fired upon and the permanency of our Government was threatened, he with others felt called upon to do all within his power to put down the rebellion that had so defiantly reared its head, and as one call after another was made for troops he aided and encouraged enlistments among the younger men around him. But when Governor Tod issued his call, July 9th, 1862, for two full regiments from his district, he felt that the time had come for *him* to go forth, and bidding adieu to home and friends, and having received a recruiting commission from Governor Tod, he called upon his neighbors to "come." So successful was he, that in about one week his company was ready to go into camp. As an officer, Captain Myers had everything to learn, but he applied himself diligently to the task and soon became quite proficient in the art of war, remarkably so considering the peaceful surroundings of his former life. He was prompt in the performance of every known duty, and though one of the oldest men in the command, endured unflinchingly the weary marches and exposures of soldier life. His life in the army, as at home, was without blame; he governed his men by love rather than by virtue of his office. But he had arrived at the time of life when so much exposure could not fail to have a damaging effect upon his health, and in September, 1864, he resigned his commission on account of failing health, and returned home carrying with him the respect and best wishes of the entire regiment. In October, 1865, he removed from Ohio to Polk County, Missouri, where he died December 10th, 1878, at the advanced age of 69 years.

SURGEON WALTER R. GILKEY.

The subject of this sketch, Dr. Walter R. Gilkey, entered the service early in 1862 and was commissioned examining surgeon for Ashtabula County, being assigned Surgeon to the 116th regiment in September following. While holding the position of examining surgeon he performed the difficult duties of that important office conscientiously and fearlessly. His duties in the field, camp and hospital were never slighted or neglected. Cultured, genial and courteous, Surgeon Gilkey occupied a warm place in the hearts of his comrades. He contracted rheumatism in the spring of 1863, while the regiment was in Western Virginia, which terminated in typhus fever, his death occurring on the 4th of June of the same year at Winchester, Virginia. His remains were conveyed home by a loving wife and brother, E. H. Gilkey, and laid to rest in Kinsman.

Surgeon Gilkey was born in Trumbull County, Ohio, in 1827. His early education was confined to the narrow limits of the common schools of those days. After acquiring his majority he took up the study of medicine, teaching in winter and studying in summer, filling in the vacations by working in the harvest fields. In 1854, he entered the office of Drs. Peter and Dudley Allan, of Kinsman, Ohio, where he remained four years with alternate courses of study at the Cleveland Medical College, where he graduated in 1858 and soon after commenced the practice of medicine. He was married, in 1859, to Miss Kate Frame, of Poland, Ohio, locating at Jefferson, the county seat of Ashtabula County, where he was at the breaking out of the civil war. Dr. Gilkey was an untiring student and deep thinker. Seeking a high place in the medical profession, he soon occupied an enviable position among his brother physicians.

DR. JAMES T. MORAN.

James T. Moran was born in Leitrim County, Ireland, August 26th, 1831. He lived with his parents, who gave him a good education, until the age of 20, when he came to this country. He engaged as a clerk in a dry goods store for a time, and afterwards held a position in the auditor's office of Trumbull County, Ohio. In 1856 he began the study of medicine at Williamsfield, Ashtabula County, Ohio, and in 1859 attended Burlington Medical College in Vermont. Returning to Williamsfield in 1860, he entered upon the practice of his profession, which he continued till the time of his enlistment in the 116th O. V. I.

We will venture the assertion that no regiment in the service was blessed with a better, more competent, faithful and kind hospital steward than was the 116th O. V. I. He was neat and careful in the preparation of all prescriptions, and as tender and kind in his treatment of patients as a woman. Conscientious in a high degree, the charge of misappropriation of hospital stores, so common at that time among different commands, was never uttered against him. As one after another of our surgeons or assistant surgeons resigned or was taken away by disease or death, it was confidently expected that Dr. Moran would be appointed to fill the vacancy, but there were so many brave, patriotic citizens of Ohio at home desirous of showing their love to their country by serving her in positions where they could draw handsome salaries and be out of the way of danger, that no sooner was a position made vacant than scores of these high priced patriots (?) stood ready to urge their claims to the appointment, so that the *true* patriot, who had responded to the call of his country and was serving faithfully in the field, receiving almost nothing for his valuable services, was overlooked, ignored. It was not till February 15th, 1865, that justice was done to Dr. Moran, his claims to promotion were recognized and he was appointed to fill the place of assistant surgeon of the regiment, then vacant; but it was then too late. The regiment had sustained such heavy losses during the campaign of 1864 that it was no longer entitled to a full corps of surgeons, and James T. Moran, after having served faithfully his country for three years, much of the time doing double duty as hospital steward and assistant surgeon of the regiment, was mustered out of the service as *Hospital Steward* of the 116th O. V. I. He resumed the practice of medicine in Ashtabula County, Ohio, where he continued till the time of his death, July 11th, 1882. He left a wife and five children to mourn his death.

MAJOR MILTON A. ELLIS.

At 6:30 P. M., Friday, November 9, 1883, in his 43d year, Major Milton A. Ellis died quite suddenly at the home of his parents in Racine, Ohio, of heart disease, from which he had been suffering for over a year. He was apparently in good health an hour before his death. Major Ellis was well known in Meigs County as a man of generous impulses and unusually fine business qualifications. In 1862 he enlisted in the 116th O. V. I., where he was successively made Orderly Sergeant, Sergeant Major and Second Lieutenant of company F. He was then promoted to a First Lieutenantcy and assigned to General Sheridan's staff as chief of his signal corps, which position he filled with much ability until the close of the war, when he was brevetted Major. His superior officers speak only in terms of praise of his military record. He was brave, earnest, reliable, and never grumbled. His superior social gifts won him the friendship of many of the high officers of the army. After the war he became an agent for the Charter Oak

Life Insurance Company. He subsequently connected himself with the business of W. A. Ellis & Co., at Racine, where he continued until disease incapacitated him for work. His remains were interred with Masonic honors at Letart, Ohio.

MAJOR JOHN HULL.

Major John Hull was born May 12th, 1814, in the State of Connecticut. His parents moved to Ohio when he was about six years of age, and settled near Cincinnati. His father died in 1822, and soon after his mother moved to the vicinity of Nelsonville, in Athens County, where the subject of this sketch continued to reside till his death. At an early age he began to learn the trade of shoemaking, but afterwards served an apprenticeship to the trade of house carpenter and became a competent and skillful workman. At the outbreak of the rebellion his impulse was to join the ranks of those who took up arms to maintain the integrity of the Government, but was restrained by the care of a large family dependent upon him. In the summer of 1862, however, he received authority to recruit a company for the 116th regiment O. V. I., and was subsequently chosen Captain. He participated in every campaign the regiment made, was in every battle in which it was engaged, and could always be found at his post of duty. At the battle of Piedmont, Virginia, June 5th, 1864, he received an injury from the concussion of a shell that afterwards resulted in the loss of his left eye. During the winter of 1863-4, while the regiment was doing guard duty along the B. & O. Railroad, Captain Hull was stationed with his company at Back Creek. While here his skill as a mechanic was called into requisition in the construction of a block-house to be used in defense of that point. His oft-repeated assertion that he was a "good carpenter" was fully verified in the manner in which this work was done.

February 26th, 1865, he was commissioned Major of his regiment, but owing to the death of a member of his family and his inability to secure a leave of absence, he resigned, and was mustered out of the service as Captain of his company. Returning home, he resumed his former calling. He died August 15th, 1883, respected by all for his honesty, integrity and many other good qualities. As a soldier he was brave and prompt in the discharge of every duty.

Roster of the Field and Staff of the 116th Regiment O. V. I.

NAME.	WHEN ENROLLED.	RANK	GENERAL HISTORY.
James Washburn	Aug. 22, 1862	Colonel	Wounded at Snicker's Ferry, Va., July 18, 1864, through the head; mustered out at close of the war.
Thomas F. Wildes	Aug. 18, 1862	Lt. Colonel	Discharged February 28, 1865, by order of Secretary of War, to accept Colonelcy 186th O. V. I.; appointed Brigadier General by brevet, March 11, 1865.
Wilbert B. Teeters	Aug. 17, 1862	Lt. Colonel	Enrolled as Capt. B; promoted to Major, December 27, 1864; to Lieutenant Colonel, February 26, 1865; mustered out with the regiment at the close of the war.
Wm Thomas Morris	Aug. 19, 1862	Major	Resigned, August 24, 1864.
John Hull	Aug. 18, 1862	Major	Enrolled as Captain of Co. K; commissioned as Major, February 26, 1865; resigned and mustered out as Captain, February, 1865.
Hamilton L. Karr	Sept. 13, 1862	Major	Enrolled as First Lieutenant Co. G; promoted to Captain Co. G, January 21, 1865; to Major, March 29, 1865; mustered out with regiment as Captain at close of the war.
Walter R. Gilkey	Sept. 4, 1862	Surgeon	Died of disease at Winchester, Va., June 4, 1864.
Thomas J. Shannon	Aug. 11, 1864	Surgeon	Killed in battle of Cedar Creek, Va., Oct. 19, 1864.
Thomas C. Smith	Aug. 27, 1862	Surgeon	Enrolled as Assistant Surgeon; promoted to Surgeon, December 19, 1864.
J. Q. A. Hudson	Aug. 19, 1862	Ass't Surgeon	Resigned March 24, 1863.
James Johnson	Aug. 22, 1862	Ass't Surgeon	Resigned February 19, 1863.
Josiah L. Brown	Jan. 14, 1864	Ass't Surgeon	Resigned October 28, 1864.
James A. Sampsell	Jan. 4, 1865	Ass't Surgeon	Mustered out with the regiment at close of the war.
James T. Moran	Nov. 15, 1864	Ass't Surgeon	Enrolled as Hospital Steward; commissioned Assistant Surgeon, February 15, 1865; mustered out with the regiment at close of the war as Hospital Steward.
Frederick L. Ballard	Sept. 8, 1862	Adjutant	Resigned February 3, 1865.
Artemas W. Williams	Sept. 3, 1862	Qr. Master	Mustered out with the regiment at close of the war.
Ebenezer W. Brady	Sept. 29, 1862	Chaplain	Discharged October 18, 1864, by order Major General Crook.
James Logan	Jan. 2, 1864	Chaplain	Enrolled as private in Co. C; promoted to Chaplain, November 18, 1864.

NON-COMMISSIONED STAFF.

NAME.	WHEN ENROLLED.	RANK	GENERAL HISTORY.
Milton A. Ellis	Sept. 4, 1862	Serg't Major	Discharged to receive promotion, April 1, 1865.
Edward Muhleman	Aug. 13, 1862	Serg't Major	Discharged for promotion, March 16 1864.
William J. Lee	Sept. 4, 1862	Serg't Major	Discharged for promotion, February 28, 1865.
John B. Ritchey	Aug. 14, 1862	Serg't Major	Enrolled as Corporal Co. B; promoted to Sergeant Major, March 1, 1865; mustered out with regiment at close of the war.
Ezra L. Walker	Sept. 4, 1862	Q. M. Serg't	Enrolled as private Co. G; appointed Commissary Sergeant, September 19, 1862; Q. M. Sergeant, April 16, 1864; Commissioned Second Lieutenant, February 10, 1865; discharged as Q. M. Sergeant for promotion in 168th O. V. I., February 28, 1865
William T. Patterson	Aug. 22, 1862	Q. M. Serg't	Enrolled as private Co. I; appointed Commissary Sergeant, March 16, 1864, and Q. M. Sergeant, March 1, 1865; mustered out with the regiment at close of the war.
Frank O. Pickering	Aug. 22, 1862	Com'y Serg't	Enrolled as private Co. I; appointed Commissary Sergeant, March 1, 1865; mustered out with regiment, at close of the war.
David G. Frost	Aug. 12, 1862	Prin. Musician	Enrolled as private in Co. E; transferred to non-commissioned staff, April 1, 1865; mustered out with regiment at close of the war.
Joel B. Lowther	Aug. 14, 1862	Prin. Musician	Enrolled as private in Co. G; transferred to non-commissioned staff, September 19, 1862; mustered out with regiment at close of the war.

Record of Company A, 116th Regiment O. V. I., in the Service of the United States.

NAME	AGE	RANK	DATE OF ENLISTMENT	GENERAL HISTORY AND FINAL RECORD
Charles W. Ridgeway		Captain	Aug. 11, '62	Resigned March 17, 1863
Thornton Mallary		Captain	Aug. 11, '62	First Lieutenant of Co. B till May 11, 1863; mustered out with regiment at close of the war
Robert Wilson		1st Lieutenant	Aug. 11, '62	Died November 19, 1862
William M. Kerr		1st Lieutenant	Aug. 12, '62	Second Lieutenant till April 1, 1863; dismissed by order Secretary of War, November 27, 1864; re-mustered and honorably discharged
John S. Manning		1st Lieutenant	Aug. 11, '62	Enrolled as First Sergeant; promoted to Second Lieutenant, April 1, 1863; promoted to First Lieutenant, April 1, 1865; captured at Winchester, Va., June 13, 1863; confined in "Libby Prison, Columbia, Macon, etc., till March 5, 1865; mustered out with regiment at close of the war.

PRESENT TO BE MUSTERED OUT WITH THE REGIMENT AT CLOSE OF THE WAR.

NAME	AGE	RANK	DATE OF ENLISTMENT	GENERAL HISTORY AND FINAL RECORD
Manz Smith	28	1st Sergeant	Aug. 11, '62	Prisoner of war from June 13, 1863, till July 1, 1863; also from June 5, 1864, till December 1, 1864, at Andersonville, Ga.; commissioned Second Lieutenant, June 20, 1865; not mustered.
George A. Way	21	Sergeant	Aug. 22, '62	Promoted from Corporal April 1, 1864
James H. Wonder	30	Sergeant	Aug. 29, '62	Prisoner of war from June 13, 1863, till July 1, 1863, at Belle Isle, Va.
James Hunter	23	Sergeant	Aug. 15, '62	Wounded in hand at Snicker's Ferry, July 18, 1864
Lionel C. Hare		Sergeant	Aug. 16, '62	Prisoner of war from June 13, 1863, till July 1, 1863, at Belle Island, Va.; wounded at Piedmont, Va., June 5, 1864
Benjamin F. Dye	31	Corporal	Aug. 29, '62	Prisoner of war from June 13, 1863, till July 1, 1863, at Belle Island, Va.; wounded at Piedmont, Va., June 5, 1864
Jesse Keyser	25	Corporal	Aug. 13, '62	Prisoner of war from June 13, 1863, till July 1, 1863, at Belle Island, Va.
John W. Devore	23	Corporal	Aug. 16, '62	Promoted to Corporal, April 1, 1864, wounded at Lynchburg, Va., June 18, 1864
George Rice	23	Corporal	Aug. 14, '62	Promoted to Corporal, September 1st, 1863
Jerome McVeigh	26	Corporal	Aug. 14, '62	Promoted to Corporal, March 1, 1864; wounded at Halltown, August 26, 1864; also at Opequan
Williams Breck	23	Corporal	Aug. 15, '62	Prisoner of war from June 13, 1863, to July 1, 1863, at Belle Island, Va.; wounded at Piedmont, Va., June 5, 1864
Albert Gates	21	Musician	Aug. 14, '62	Prisoner of war from June 13, 1863, till July 1st, 1863, at Andersonville, Ga.; also prisoner from June 5, 1864, till February 1, 1865
William Ronam	21	Musician	Aug. 16, '62	Wounded at Piedmont, Va., June 5, 1864
Hazzel Dye	30	Wagoner	Aug. 14, '62	Prisoner of war from June 13, 1863, till July 1, 1863, at Belle Island, Va.
David Burcus	21	Private	Aug. 15, '62	Prisoner of war from June 13, 1863, till July 1, 1863, at Belle Island, Va.
John C. Bean	29	Private	Aug. 15, '62	Prisoner of war from June 13, 1863, till July 1, 1863, at Belle Island, Va.
Joseph R. Brock	28	Private	Aug. 11, '62	Prisoner of war from June 13, 1863, till July 1, 1863, at Belle Island, Va.
Samuel H. Clare	41	Private	Aug. 11, '62	
Jesse Coulter	24	Private	Aug. 15, '62	Prisoner of war from June 13, 1863, till July 1, 1863, at Belle Island, Va.

Record of Company A, 116th Regiment O. V. I. in the Service of the United States.—(CONTINUED.)

NAME.	AGE	RANK.	DATE OF ENLISTMENT	GENERAL HISTORY AND FINAL RECORD.
Abraham Coulter	22	Private	Aug. 15, '62	Prisoner of War from June 13, 1863, till July 1, 1863, at Belle Island, Va.
John Drake	41	Private	Aug. 22, '62	Wounded at Opequan, Va., Sept. 19, 1864; discharged June 10, 1865.
William S. Dyer	29	Private	Aug. 20, '62	Prisoner of war from June 13, 1863, till July 1, 1863, at Belle Island, Va.
Frederick Edge	34	Private	Aug. 16, '62	Prisoner of war from June 13, 1863, till July 1, 1863, at Belle Island, Va.
Samuel Gates	22	Private	Aug. 14, '62	Prisoner of war from June 13, 1863, till July 1, 1863, at Belle Island, Va.
James C. Hall	23	Private	Aug. 16, '62	Wounded at Piedmont, Va., June 5, 1864.
Cheeseman Haney	24	Private	Aug. 14, '62	
Henry Hartman	29	Private	Aug. 22, '62	Wounded at Bunker Hill, Va., June 13, 1863, and prisoner of war from June 13, 1863, till July 1, 1863; wounded at Piedmont, Va., June 5, 1864.
Alexander Hartman	22	Private	Aug. 22, '62	
Aaron Hendly	33	Private	Aug. 20, '62	
Joseph W. Hill	26	Private	Aug. 13, '62	
Isaiel P. Hubbard	22	Private	Aug. 18, '62	Wounded at Bunker Hill, Va., June 13, 1863, and prisoner of war from June 13, 1863, till July 1, 1863; wounded at Piedmont, Va., June 5, 1864.
Israel Keylor	26	Private	Aug. 15, '62	
Emanuel Keylor	24	Private	Aug. 13, '62	Wounded at Halltown, Va., August 26, 1864.
Jacob C. Keylor	20	Private	Aug. 15, '62	Wounded at Piedmont, Va., June 5, 1864.
William Loy	22	Private	Aug. 15, '62	
Archibald Maidey	31	Private	Aug. 15, '62	
Meshack Morris	25	Private	Aug. 15, '62	
William C. Montgomery	37	Private	Aug. 22, '62	Prisoner of war from June 10, 1864, till August 1, 1864, at Belle Island Va.; wounded at Piedmont, Va., June 5, 1864.
George McCammon	44	Private	Aug. 15, '62	
Joseph Paith	22	Private	Aug. 13, '62	Prisoner of war from June 13, 1863, to July 1, 1863, at Belle Island, Va.
Michael Palmer	29	Private	Aug. 20, '62	
Henry Palmer	29	Private	Aug. 20, '62	
Jacob Ring	37	Private	Aug. 14, '62	Prisoner of war from June 13, 1863, till July 1, 1863, at Belle Island, Va.; wounded June 14, 1863, at Bunker Hill, Va.
Benjamin King	39	Private	Aug. 15, '62	Wounded and taken prisoner at Bunker Hill, Va., June 13, 1863; prisoner at Belle Island, Va., till July 1, 1863.
Robert Smith	22	Private	Aug. 15, '62	Wounded at Piedmont, Va., June 5, 1864.
Cyrus Spriggs	22	Private	Aug. 22, '62	Wounded in action, and prisoner at Bunker Hill from June 13, 1863, till July 1, 1863, at Richmond, Va., also prisoner from June 5, 1864, to August 1, 1864; also at Piedmont, Va., June 5, 1864.
Samuel Steel	19	Private	Aug. 15, '62	Wounded at Bunker Hill, Va., June 13, 1863; also at Piedmont, Va., June 5, 1864.
Alfred E. Steel	29	Private	Aug. 15, '62	
Samuel Tidd	24	Private	Aug. 15, '62	Wounded at Bunker Hill, and prisoner from June 13, 1863, till July 1, 1863, at Belle Island, Va.; wounded at Piedmont, Va., June 5, 1864.
Samuel Tschappat	22	Private	Aug. 22, '62	

ABSENT TO BE MUSTERED OUT.

Leonard Chro	25	Private	Aug. 14, '62 In hospital at Baltimore, Md.
James Lafever	24	Private	Aug. 15, '62 Prisoner of war from June 13, 1864, till July 1, 1865; also from April 6, 1865, till April 9, 1865; wounded at Bunker Hill, June 13, 1863.
Samuel H. McHugh	15	Private	Aug. 22, '62 Prisoner of war from June 13, 1863, till July 1, 1864, at Belle Island, Va.
George C. Williamson	30	Private	Aug. 24, '62 Wounded at Bunker Hill, Va., and prisoner of war from June 13, 1863, till July 1, 1863, at Belle Island, Va.; in hospital at Annapolis, Md., September 15, 1863.

DISCHARGED.

Isaac Adams	31	Private	Aug. 15, '62 Honorably discharged, April 17, 1863.
Abraham Blue	42	Private	Aug. 22, '62 Honorably discharged, April 17, 1863.
Amos Cord	30	Private	Aug. 16, '62 Honorably discharged, April 17, 1863.
Isaac N. Cline	20	Private	Aug. 14, '62 Honorably discharged, February 14, 1863.
William Dillon	35	Private	Aug. 22, '62 Honorably discharged, February 14, 1863.
Stephen P. Ford	25	Private	Aug. 22, '62 Honorably discharged, February 11, 1864.
John Kallotsch	26	Private	Aug. 22, '62 Honorably discharged, May 15, 1865, on account of wound received at Bunker Hill, Va., June 13, 1863.
John Ruble	34	Private	Aug. 11, '62 Honorably discharged, February 14, 1864.
Hiram Shafer	29	Private	Aug. 15, '62 Honorably discharged, February 14, 1865, on account of wounds.
Newton Meek	22	Corporal	Aug. 15, '62 Prisoner at battle of Bunker Hill, June 13, 1863; honorably discharged on account of wounds received at Piedmont, Va., June 5, 1864.

TRANSFERRED.

Frederick R. Rose	22	Corporal	Aug. 16, '62 Wounded in shoulder at Piedmont, Va., June 5, 1864; transferred to veteran reserve corps, date not known.
Solomon Shafer	41	Private	Aug. 16, '62 Sent to Norfolk, Va., two years hard labor, by order general court martial, March 11, 1865; wounded at Bunker Hill, Va., June 13, 1863.

DIED.

Simpson Smith	28	Corporal	Aug. 15, '62 Killed in action at Bunker Hill, Va., June 13, 1863.
Levi Beck	21	Private	Aug. 22, '62 Died at Winchester, Va., April 27, 1863.
James A. Boyd	21	Private	Aug. 11, '62 Killed in action at Lynchburg, Va., June 18, 1864.
Elijah Bennet	35	Private	Aug. 22, '62 Died at Grafton, Va., June 22, 1864, of wounds received in action at Piedmont, Va., June 5, 1864.
Henry M. C. Cline	26	Private	Aug. 11, '62 Died at Martinsburg, Va., December 15, 1863.
Wilson Dunford	19	Private	Aug. 15, '62 Died of wounds received by accident, September 13, 1864.

Record of Company A, 116th Regiment O. V. I., in the Service of the United States. —(CONTINUED.)

NAME	AGE	RANK	DATE OF ENLISTMENT	GENERAL HISTORY AND FINAL RECORD
Nathaniel D. Hayden	33	Private	Aug. 18, '62	Killed in action at Piedmont, Va., June 5, 1864.
Hezekiah Hill	36	Private	Aug. 14, '61	Died March 4, 1865, at Fortress Monroe, Va.
Elzy J. Hill	18	Private	Feb. 15, '64	Died of wounds received in action at Halltown, Va., August 31, 1864.
John D. Kerr	44	Private	Aug. 15, '62	Died August 22, 1863.
Samuel Morris	27	Private	Aug. 15, '62	Died April 13, 1863.
James W. Oliver	33	Private	Aug. 12, '62	Wounded at Bunker Hill, June 13, 1863; died October 2, 1864.
Lewis C. Ring	18	Private	Aug. 14, '62	Died June 11, 1864.
Aaron Woskly	22	Private	Aug. 15, '62	Wounded at Cedar Creek, Va., October 19, 1864; died of wounds October 31, 1864.
Addy Brock	35	Private	Aug. 15, '62	Died of wounds received in action at Piedmont, Va., June 5, 1864.
Joan A. Bowman	25	Private	Aug. 15, '62	Killed in action June 13, 1863, at Bunker Hill, Va.
Jefferson Guthen	18	Private	Aug. 22, '62	Died of wounds received in action at Lynchburg, Va., June 18, 1864.
John Welch	18	Private	Aug. 15, '62	Killed in action at Bunker Hill, Va., June 13, 1863.
Jacob Zimmerly	21	Private	Aug. 15, '62	Wounded at Bunker Hill, Va., June 13, 1863; also at Piedmont, Va., June 5, 1864; died July 1, 1864.

DESERTERS.

John D. Brown	27	Private	Aug. 15, '62	Deserted at Lynchburg, Va., June 18, 1864.
Isaac Elliott	30	Private	Aug. 15, '62	Deserted at Parkersburg, Va., October 24, 1862.

TRANSFERRED TO 62D REGIMENT O. V. I.

John Smythe	30	Private	Jan. 4, '64	Wounded at Piedmont, Va., June 5, 1864; deserted at Letart, O., July 5, 1864; joined Co. April 27, 1865, under President's proclamation to deserters.
George Drake	21	Private	Jan. 4, '64	
Alfred M. Earley	36	Private	Jan. 4, '64	
Abel Hall	26	Private	Aug. 16, '62	Wounded in action, in both legs, June 13, 1861; sent home on surgeon's certificate, August 15, 1864.
John A. Harmon	20	Private	Feb. 27, '64	Wounded at Piedmont, Va., June 5, 1864; also at Halltown, Va., August 26, 1864.
John Hoy	19	Private	Jan. 4, '64	Wounded at Opequan, Va., September 19, 1864.
James Kimpton	20	Private	Dec. 15, '63	Wounded at Piedmont, Va., June 5, 1864.
Robert McCammon	20	Private	Jan. 4, '64	Wounded at Piedmont, Va., June 5, 1864.
Abraham Myers	20	Private	Feb. 15, '64	In Hospital at Frederick, Md., September 15, 1864.
Emmanuel Path	21	Private	Dec. 24, '63	
John Rake	29	Private	Aug. 20, '62	Detailed to brigade headquarters, November 24, 1864.
Joseph Smythe	23	Private	Dec. 19, '63	

ONE HUNDRED AND SIXTEENTH O. V. I. 327

Record of Company B, 116th Regiment O. V. I., in the Service of the United States.

NAME.	AGE.	RANK.	DATE OF ENLISTMENT	GENERAL HISTORY AND FINAL RECORD.
Edwin Keyes		Captain	Sept. 15, '62	Wounded and captured at Lynchburg, Virginia, June 18, 1864; died July 19, 1864, at Lynchburg, Virginia.
John F. Welch		Captain	Aug. 18, '62	Promoted from First Lieutenant, Co. K., November 14, 1864; mustered out with Regiment at close of the war.
Thornton Mallory		1st. Lieutenant	Aug. 14, '62	Promoted to Captain May 11, 1863, and assigned to Co. A
Hiram L. Sibley		2d. Lieutenant	Sept. 18, '62	Captured at Winchester, June 15, 1863; First Lieutenant from February 1, 1864; Resigned January 11, 1865.
William B. Henry		1st. Lieutenant	Aug. 12, '62	First Sergeant till February 26, 1864; Second Lieutenant from February 26, 1864 until February 10, 1865; mustered out with regiment at close of the war.
William H. Bush		2d. Lieutenant	Aug. 11, '62	Promoted to Second Lieutenant from Sergeant February 15th, 1865; wounded at Piedmont, Virginia, June 5, 1864; killed at Fort Gregg, Virginia, April 2, 1865.
Charles A. Cline		2d. Lieutenant	Aug. 11, '62	Promoted from First Sergeant of Co. E, April 5, 1865; mustered out with regiment at close of the war.

PRESENT TO BE MUSTERED OUT WITH THE REGIMENT AT CLOSE OF THE WAR.

NAME.	AGE.	RANK.	DATE OF ENLISTMENT	GENERAL HISTORY AND FINAL RECORD.
Peter D. Wolfe	26	1st Sergeant	Aug. 15, '62	Promoted from Corporal September 28, 1864; prisoner of war at Winchester, Virginia, July 24, 1864; commissioned Second Lieutenant June 20, 1865; not mustered.
Gilbert W. Bradshaw	22	Sergeant	Aug. 14, '62	Promoted from Corporal, March 4, 1865.
Warrick M. Knowles	26	Sergeant	Aug. 12, '62	Promoted from Corporal, March 4, 1865.
Joseph Fisher	28	Sergeant	Aug. 14, '62	Promoted from Corporal, March 4, 1865.
James M. Stout	19	Sergeant	Aug. 12, '62	Promoted to Corporal, March 16, 1864; promoted to Sergeant, April 3, 1865.
Marion Coleman	21	Corporal	Aug. 12, '62	Promoted to Corporal September 16, 1861; Promoted to Sergeant, April 22, 1865.
Abraham Kelb	18	Corporal	Aug. 12, '62	Promoted to Corporal, January 1, 1865; wounded and captured at battle of Piedmont, Virginia, June 5, 1864.
Royal James	17	Corporal	Aug. 15, '62	Promoted to Corporal, March 4, 1865.
Phil D. Faeger	24	Corporal	Aug. 14, '62	Wounded and captured at Lynchburg, Virginia, June 18, 1864; was prisoner at Andersonville, Georgia, till September 1, 1864.
John M. Boyd	23	Corporal	Aug. 14, '62	Promoted April 3, 1865; wounded at Lynchburg, Virginia, June 18, 1864; at Fort Gregg, April 2, 1865.
Thomas C. Burston	21	Corporal	Aug. 11, '62	Promoted April 3, 1865.
John Anderson	23	Private	Aug. 15, '62	Promoted September 28, 1864.
Charles Ball	18	Private	Aug. 15, '62	Wounded at Piedmont, June 5, 1864
William Ball	26	Private	Aug. 15, '62	
Alvin P. Bodwell	22	Private	Aug. 12, '62	Prisoner of war at Winchester, Virginia, July 24, 1864.
George F. Brown	23	Private	Aug. 12, '62	Detached as teamster at brigade headquarters, since May 5, 1864.
George H. Baumgardner	23	Private	Aug. 11, '62	
John M. Campbell	18	Private	Aug. 14, '62	
Leander Chirteher	21	Private	Aug. 11, '62	Prisoner of war at Winchester, Virginia, June 15, 1863.

Record of Company B, 116th Regiment O. V. I., in the Service of the United States. —(CONTINUED.)

NAME	AGE	RANK	DATE OF ENLISTMENT	GENERAL HISTORY AND FINAL RECORD.
Charles Chevalier	24	Private	Aug. 14, '62	
James M. Cochran	20	Private	Aug. 14, '62	
John Cole	23	Private	Aug. 12, '62	Prisoner of war, Winchester, Virginia, July 21, 1864.
Milton Cooper	20	Private	Aug. 11, '62	Detached to division ambulance corps since May 27, 1864.
John Curry	24	Private	Aug. 12, '62	
Samuel P. Dinsmore	19	Private	Aug. 13, '62	
John Doland	18	Private	Aug. 15, '62	
Samuel T. Dougherty	28	Private	Aug. 12, '62	Wounded at Piedmont, Virginia, June 5, 1864.
Timothy S. Gilmore	18	Private	Aug. 15, '62	
John Goldsberry	34	Private	Aug. 15, '62	
Thomas Greene	22	Private	Aug. 12, '62	Detached to quartermaster's department since May 27, 1864.
Otis P. Henry	16	Private	Aug. 14, '62	
James R. Hostoter	30	Private	Aug. 14, '62	At hospital July and August 1864.
Henry Jennings	28	Private	Aug. 12, '62	Prisoner of war, Winchester, Virginia, June 15, 1864; exchanged October 16, 1864.
Hewitt C. Law	32	Private	Aug. 12, '62	
Joseph Lau	26	Private	Aug. 14, '62	
William J. Lovett	25	Private	Aug. 12, '62	
John M. McElroy	45	Private	Aug. 11, '62	Wounded at Fisher Hill, Virginia, September 22, 1864; returned to duty Jan. 14, 1865.
Benjamin McLane	15	Private	Aug. 12, '62	Prisoner of war, Winchester, Virginia, June 15, 1864; exchanged October 16, 1864.
Horace McNeil	32	Private	Aug. 12, '62	Prisoner of war, Lynchburg, Virginia, June 18, 1864; escaped from Andersonville, Georgia, December 18, 1864.
Daniel Myers	23	Private	Aug. 15, '62	
John Newland	19	Private	Aug. 15, '62	Detached to division pioneer corps, March 23, 1864.
William J. Odlum	22	Private	Aug. 15, '62	
Simeon L. Pettit	31	Private	Aug. 12, '62	Teamster from May 24, 1864, till May 1, 1865, at division.
Willard Reed	21	Private	Aug. 12, '62	Prisoner of war, Winchester, Virginia, July 24, 1864.
Daniel Rose	16	Private	Aug. 15, '62	Prisoner of war, Winchester, Virginia, June 15, 1864; exchanged October 16, 1864; detached to division pioneer corps, May 1, '64.
Dennis Savoy	21	Private	Aug. 13, '62	
George Shumway	22	Private	Aug. 12, '62	
James F. Springer	45	Private	Aug. 12, '62	
William Wakeley	19	Private	Aug. 12, '62	Detached to ambulance corps, April 24, 1864.
Isaac B. Watson	23	Private	Aug. 11, '62	
Nelson Watson	20	Private	Aug. 13, '62	Wounded at Piedmont, Virginia, June 5, 1864; escaped from Andersonville, Georgia, November 30, 1864.
Isaac S. Watson	20	Private	Aug. 12, '62	
Aurelius P. Wiley	22	Private	Aug. 12, '62	Detached in office of Chief Engineers, Department West Virginia, as surveyor, from April 3, 1864, till May 10, 1865; taken prisoner at Winchester, Virginia, June 15, 1864.

ONE HUNDRED AND SIXTEENTH O. V. I.

ABSENT TO BE MUSTERED OUT.

Name	Rank	Date	Remarks
James H. Stewart	22 Corporal	Aug. 14, '62	Promoted to Corporal, April 23, 1865; wounded at Fisher Hill, September 22, 1864; prisoner of war at Cedar Creek, Virginia, October 19, 1864.
Thomas C. Barston	21 Corporal	Aug. 15, '62	Promoted to Corporal, September 28, 1864.
George Ritchey	18 Corporal	Aug. 12, '62	Promoted to Corporal, March 1, 1865.
John Baker	18 Private	Aug. 14, '62	Wounded at Piedmont, June 5, 1864; taken prisoner April 6, 1865.
Martin Green	21 Private	Aug. 14, '62	At hospital, Cumberland, Maryland, since October 13, 1864.
Wells Grubb	42 Private	Aug. 13, '62	Wounded at Piedmont, Virginia, June 5, 1864; taken prisoner at Lynchburg, Virginia, June 18, 1864.
John A. Johnson	21 Private	Aug. 13, '62	Wounded at Piedmont, Virginia, June 5, 1864; in hospital at Annapolis, Maryland.
George W. Keyser	30 Private	Aug. 15, '62	Wounded and taken prisoner at Piedmont, Virginia, June 5, 1864; was prisoner at Andersonville.
William E. Letavor	19 Private	Aug. 14, '62	Wounded and taken prisoner at Lynchburg, Virginia, June 18, 1864.
John Mayer	37 Private	Aug. 15, '62	Detached as army taker since September 16, 1861.
Benjamin G. Patterson	25 Private	Aug. 14, '62	Captured at battle of Winchester, July 24, 1864; (died at Andersonville, Georgia.)
Walter S. Reynolds	20 Private	Aug. 14, '62	At hospital, Martinsburg, Virginia, since November 12, 1864.
Joseph L. Roler	17 Private	Aug. 15, '62	At hospital, Portsmouth, Virginia, since March 27, 1865.
Jonn Rose	24 Private	Aug. 15, '62	At hospital, Annapolis, Maryland, since April 29.
Albert Walton	21 Private	Aug. 15, '62	At hospital in Cumberland, Maryland, since July, 1864.
Haddock L. Warren	31 Private	Aug. 12, '62	Captured in battle at Lynchburg, June 18, 1864.
Gilbert G. Webster	30 Private	Aug. 13, '62	Wounded at Fott's Mountain, on retreat from Lynchburg, Virginia; in hospital at Gallipolis, since July 4, 1864.
Charles Winley	28 Private	Aug. 13, '62	At hospital, Cumberland, Maryland.
Erastus H. White	19 Private	Aug. 14, '62	Wounded at Hatcher's Run, Virginia, March 31, 1865; sent to hospital at Fortress Monroe, Virginia.

DISCHARGED.

Name	Rank	Date	Remarks
Uriah Hoyt	21 Sergeant	Aug. 12, '62	Wounded at Piedmont, Virginia, June 5, 1864; discharged for promotion, March 3, 1865, and transferred to 186th O. V. I.
George K. Campbell	28 Corporal	Aug. 15, '62	Discharged for promotion, September 9, 1864.
Spencer Beatty	24 Private	Aug. 14, '62	Discharged on surgeon's certificate at Gallipolis, Ohio.
Christopher Cooper	22 Private	Aug. 14, '62	Discharged on surgeon's certificate at Gallipolis, Ohio.
John P. Kibble	19 Private	Aug. 15, '62	Discharged on surgeon's certificate at Fortress Monroe, Virginia; wounded at Ford George, Virginia, April 2, 1865.
John Lobdill	43 Private	Aug. 15, '62	Discharged on surgeon's certificate at Columbus, Ohio, June 16, 1865.
Samuel McElroy	26 Private	Aug. 14, '62	Wounded in battle at Snicker's Ferry, Virginia, July 18, 1864; discharged on surgeon's certificate at Chester hospital, Pennsylvania, May 16, 1865.
William L. Oakley	22 Private	Aug. 12, '62	Discharged on surgeon's certificate at Winchester, Virginia, May 3, 1864.
Aaron Sinclair	25 Private	Aug. 14, '62	Discharged on surgeon's certificate at Columbus, Ohio, June 25, 1863.
Ross Smith	21 Private	F'b'y 1, '64	Discharged on surgeon's certificate at Baltimore, Maryland, May 19, 1865.
Marion A. Starling	18 Private	M'ch 31, '65	

Record of Company B, 116th Regiment O. V. I., in the Service of the United States.—(CONTINUED.)

TRANSFERRED.

NAME.	AGE.	RANK.	DATE OF ENLISTMENT	GENERAL HISTORY AND FINAL RECORD.
John B. Ritchey	22	Corporal	Aug. 14, '62	Transferred to non-commissioned staff, as Sergeant Major, March 1, 1863.
David G. Frost	31	Musician	Aug. 12, '62	Transferred to non-commissioned staff, as Drum Major, April 1, 1863.

DIED.

NAME.	AGE.	RANK.	DATE OF ENLISTMENT	GENERAL HISTORY AND FINAL RECORD.
Frederick E. Humphrey	31	1st. Sergeant	Aug. 11, '62	Was Corporal till March 16, 1864; Sergeant till promoted to First Sergeant, March 1, 1865; wounded at Lynchburg, June 18, 1864; killed at Fort Gregg, Virginia, April 2, 1865.
Edmond P. Tiffany	24	Sergeant	Aug. 11, '62	Killed in battle at Fisher Hill, September 22, 1864.
Myron R. Hitchcock	23	Sergeant	Aug. 11, '62	Promoted from Corporal, September 16, 1861; Wounded in battle at Fort Gregg, Virginia, April 2, 1865; died in hospital at Point of Rock, Virginia, April 23, 1865.
James M. Hartley	24	Corporal	Aug. 11, '62	Promoted to Corporal September 16, 1864; Wounded at Fisher Hill, September 22, 1864; killed in action at Fort Gregg, Virginia, April 2, 1865.
Francis Caldwell	29	Private	Aug. 12, '62	Killed in action at Cedar Creek, Virginia, October 19, 1864.
Leonard J. Cooley	41	Private	Aug. 16, '62	Captured at battle of Winchester, June 15, 1863; died in hospital at Annapolis, Maryland, November 9, 1863.
John M. Cooper	18	Private	Dec. 31, '63	Died in hospital at Martinsburg, Virginia, of measles, March 7, 1864.
Charles C. Irwin	39	Private	Aug. 12, '62	Killed in battle of Lynchburg, Virginia, June 18, 1864.
Orville S. Hetzer	18	Private	Aug. 13, '62	Killed in battle of Opequon, Virginia, September 19, 1864.
Samuel L. Hayes	18	Private	Dec. 25, '63	Killed in battle of Snickers Ferry, July 18, 1864.
James H. Kinnamon	19	Private	Feb. 8, '64	Died in Meigs County, Ohio, of disease, May 29, 1864.
Lewis C. Scoy	38	Private	Aug. 13, '62	Killed in battle of Opequan, Virginia, September 19, 1864.
Sylvester C. Shumway	26	Private	Aug. 12, '62	Killed in battle of Piedmont, Virginia, June 5, 1864.
Royal Hoyt	23	Wagoner	Aug. 12, '62	Captured at Lynchburg, Virginia, June 18, 1864; died at Andersonville, Georgia, August 16, 1864.

DESERTED.—TRANSFERRED.

NAME.	AGE.	RANK.	DATE OF ENLISTMENT	GENERAL HISTORY AND FINAL RECORD.
Marion Smith	18	Private	Aug. 12, '62	Deserted at Gallipolis, Ohio, November 15, 1862; court martialed at Harper's Ferry, Virginia; sentenced to two years hard labor; confined in military prison at Wheeling, Virginia; returned to regiment June 13, 1865; transferred to 62d regiment O. V. I., June 12, 1865.

RECRUITS TRANSFERRED TO 62D REGIMENT O. V. I.

NAME.	AGE.	RANK.	DATE OF ENLISTMENT	GENERAL HISTORY AND FINAL RECORD.
Clemens Bruker	18	Private	Jan. 1, '64	Detached to headquarters Independent Division, 24th Army Corps, June 6, 1865; order Major General Turner.
Charles H. Collins	18	Private	Aug. 12, '62	Discharged on surgeon's certificate dated June —, 1865.
William H. Clark	38	Private	Feb. 4, '64	
Benjamin N. Flowers	38	Private	Jan. 5, '64	Discharged on surgeon's certificate dated June —, 1865.
Sidney P. White	18	Private	M'ch 31, '64	Detached to headquarters Independent Division, 24th Army Corps, December 28, 1864; order General Harris.

Record of Company C, 116th Regiment, O. V. I., in the Service of the United States.

NAME.	AGE.	RANK.	DATE OF ENLISTMENT	GENERAL HISTORY AND FINAL RECORD.
Frederick H. Archeson		Captain	Sept. 19, '62	Killed in action at Winchester, Va., June 14, 1863.
James P. Mann		Captain	Aug. 19, '62	Enrolled as First Lieutenant; promoted to Captain June 15, 1863.
Levi Lupton		1st Lieutenant	July 25, '62	Enrolled as Second Lieutenant; promoted to First Lieutenant June 15, 1863; taken prisoner at Winchester, Va., June 14, 1863; died in prison at Charleston, S. C., September 12, 1864.

PRESENT TO BE MUSTERED OUT AT CLOSE OF WAR.

NAME.	AGE.	RANK.	DATE OF ENLISTMENT	GENERAL HISTORY AND FINAL RECORD.
William T. Boldenbaru		1st Lieutenant	Sept. 19, '62	Enrolled as First Sergeant; promoted to Second Lieutenant June 15, 1863; to First Lieutenant January 2, 1865.
John S. Heath		2d. Lieutenant	Sept. 19, '62	Enrolled as Sergeant; promoted to First Sergeant June 15, 1863; to Second Lieutenant March 26, 1865; wounded in battle at Piedmont, Va., June 5, 1864; prisoner at Andersonville, Ga., and Florence, S. C., from June 5, 1864, till December 10, 1864.
John L. Reach	26	1st Sergeant	Aug. 11, '62	Enrolled as Sergeant; promoted to First Sergeant March 26, 1865; commissioned Second Lieutenant June 20, 1865; not mustered.
Oliver A. Hackety	21	Sergeant	Aug. 11, '62	Enrolled as Corporal; promoted to Sergeant June 15, 1864; prisoner at Winchester, Va., June 15, 1863; confined at Libby Prison; exchanged November 6, 1863.
David T. Sears	22	Sergeant	Aug. 14, '62	Promoted from Corporal March 26, 1865; wounded in head at Opequan, Va., September 19, 1864.
Martin L. Slasher	21	Corporal	Aug. 8, '62	Promoted to Corporal June 15, 1863.
Walter Tucker	19	Corporal	Aug. 16, '62	Promoted to Corporal June 5, 1864; wounded at Lynchburg, Va., June 18, 1864, and prisoner till September 14, 1864.
Lewis Sulzberger	21	Corporal	Aug. 15, '62	Promoted to Corporal August 19, 1864.
Francs A. Stout	21	Corporal	Aug. 11, '62	Promoted to Corporal March 26, 1865.
John W. Inmann	19	Corporal	Aug. 13, '62	Promoted to Corporal January 1, 1865.
Clarkson W. Adams	24	Musician	July 30, '62	Taken prisoner at Winchester, Va., June 15, 1863; confined in Libby Prison; exchanged November 6, 1863.
John Sill	36	Wagoner	July 30, '62	
James Barrett	30	Private	Aug. 11, '62	
Abel B. Barnes	28	Private	Aug. 4, '62	
Franklin Barnes	18	Private	Aug. 8, '62	Wounded at Piedmont, Va., June 5, 1864.
Miller Booth	20	Private	Aug. 11, '62	Taken prisoner at Winchester, Va., June 14, 1863; confined at Libby Prison.
William Bush	30	Private	July 26, '62	Taken prisoner at Winchester, Va., June 14, 1863; confined at Libby Prison.
Adam Barkhart	18	Private	Sept. 18, '62	
Henry C. Clme	22	Private	Aug. 6, '62	
Jacob Diehl	19	Private	Aug. 15, '62	
Samuel Loslons	23	Private	Aug. 8, '62	Taken prisoner at Winchester, Va., June 14, 1863; exchanged November 2, 1863; wounded at Snicker's Ferry, Va., July 18, 1864.

Record of Company C, 116th Regiment O. V. I., in the Service of the United States.—(CONTINUED.)

NAME	AGE	RANK	DATE OF ENLISTMENT	GENERAL HISTORY AND FINAL RECORD
Charles L. Eberle	21	Private	Aug. 11, '62	Taken prisoner at Winchester, Va., June 15, 1863; exchanged and returned to regiment November 3, 1863.
Moses W. Edgar	27	Private	Aug. 11, '62	Captured at Winchester, Va., June 14, 1863; confined in Libby Prison; exchanged and returned to regiment, November 2, 1863.
Eli Evans	38	Private	Aug. 12, '62	
Henry Flushman	32	Private	Aug. 11, '62	Captured at Winchester, Va., June 15, 1863; confined in Libby Prison; exchanged and returned to regiment, November 3, 1863.
George Greenbank	29	Private	Aug. 11, '62	Wounded in the arm at Winchester, Va., June 14, 1863.
John H. Lang	19	Private	Aug. 15, '62	
William A. Mann	18	Private	Aug. 11, '62	
Alfred A. Mann	25	Private	Aug. 15, '62	
John Mahony	18	Private	Aug. 11, '62	Captured at Winchester, Va., June 14, 1863; confined in Libby Prison; exchanged and returned to regiment, November 11, 1863.
William Montgomery	41	Private	Aug. 8, '62	Wounded and taken prisoner at Winchester, Va., June 14, 1863; confined in Libby Prison; exchanged and returned to regiment, November 2, 1863.
Alexander Robbins	29	Private	Aug. 11, '62	Taken prisoner at Winchester, Va., June 15, 1863; confined in Libby Prison; exchanged October 2, 1863.
Ivan Stephens	22	Private	Aug. 11, '62	Captured at Winchester, Va., June 14, 1863; confined in Libby Prison; exchanged and returned to regiment, November 3, 1863.
Lewis Steuber	29	Private	Aug. 15, '62	
Reily Thornberry	24	Private	Aug. 13, '62	Wounded in right shoulder and captured at Winchester, Va., June 14, 1863; exchanged and returned to regiment, November 2, 1863; was confined in Libby Prison.
John B. Truax	30	Private	Aug. 8, '62	
Charles B. Watson	15	Private	Aug. 11, '62	
Jacob Walter	25	Private	Aug. 11, '62	Captured at Winchester, Va., June 14, 1864; confined in Libby Prison; exchanged and returned to regiment, December 11, 1863.
John F. Wheaton	21	Private	Aug. 11, '62	Was wounded in leg and prisoner at Piedmont, Va., June 5, 1864; confined in prisons at Andersonville, Ga., and Florence, S. C., from June 5, 1864, till February 24, 1865.
Christian Yockey	20	Private	Aug. 11, '62	
Edward Yockey	24	Private	Aug. 11, '62	

ABSENT TO BE MUSTERED OUT.

David K. Barrett	22	Sergeant	Aug. 11, '62	Wounded at Piedmont, Va., June 5, 1864; in hospital at Gallipolis, O., since June 15, 1864.
Matthew W. Maric	23	Sergeant	Aug. 8, '62	Wounded in leg at Piedmont, Va., June 5, 1864; taken prisoner, exchanged and in hospital at Annapolis, Md., since November 25, 1864; was Corporal till June 15, 1863.
Abner G. Carlton	23	Corporal	Aug. 6, '62	Wounded in hip at Piedmont, Va., June 5, 1864; at Halltown in thigh, August 26, 1864; at Hatcher's Run in foot, March 31, 1865; in hospital at Fortress Monroe since April 1, 1865; was private till December 12, 1862.

Name	Age	Rank	Date of Enlistment	Remarks
William R. Hardesty	24	Musician	Aug. 8, '62	In hospital at Clayville, Md., since December 11, 1862.
Abel C. Barnes	21	Private	Aug. 8, '62	Wounded at Cedar Creek, Va., October 19, 1864; in hospital Wheeling, Va., since that time.
William H. Bassel	24	Private	Aug. 4, '62	Taken prisoner at High Bridge, Va.; paroled prisoner at Camp Chase since April 6, 1865.
Emon H. Beardmore	21	Private	Aug. 12, '62	Was Corporal till December 12, 1862; taken prisoner at Winchester, Va., June 15, 1863; exchanged and returned to regiment, November 2, 1863; wounded and in hospital at Frederick, Md., since September 23, 1864.
Henry Bitz	25	Private	Aug. 15, '62	Detailed at Washington, D. C. since May 2, 1864; by order of Gen. Sigel.
David Brulach	25	Private	Aug. 15, '62	Wounded at Hatcher's Run. March 31, 1865; in hospital at Point of Rocks since April 1, 1865.
John M. Carlton	22	Private	Aug. 20, '62	
Benjamin Coffield	20	Private	Aug. 12, '62	Paroled prisoner at Camp Chase, O., since April 6, 1865.
Joseph Knowlton	21	Private	Aug. 11, '62	In hospital at Cumberland, Md., since October 14, 1864.
Wilson S. Mann	20	Private	Aug. 15, '62	Taken prisoner at Winchester, Va., June 14, 1863; exchanged and returned to regiment November 9, 1863.
Andrew J. Morris	22	Private	Aug. 11, '62	Wounded in forearm at Hatcher's Run, Va., April 1, 1865; in hospital at Fortress Monroe since that time.
John Paul	21	Private	Aug. 12, '62	On detail service at Winchester, Va., since August 16, 1864, order Col. Tholarn.
George W. Sampson	18	Private	Aug. 8, '62	Taken prisoner at Winchester, Va., June 5, 1863; confined in Libby Prison; exchanged and returned to regiment, October 2, 1863; wounded at Hatcher's Run, Va., March 31, 1865; in hospital at Point of Rocks since April 1, 1865.
Samuel Stonebraker	25	Private	Aug. 15, '62	Captured at Winchester, Va., June 14, 1863; in hospital at Annapolis, Md.
Lewis A. Thompson	20	Private	Aug. 11, '62	On detail service at Columbus, O., since February 10, 1864, order Gen. Kelly.
John Walters	32	Private	Aug. 13, '62	Captured at High Bridge, Va., April 6, 1865; paroled prisoner at Camp Chase, O., since then.
William W. Wheaton	27	Private	Aug. 7, '62	Captured at Winchester, Va., June 14, 1863; exchanged and returned to regiment November 18, 1863; was confined in Libby Prison; absent on furlough since May 28, 1865; was wounded.

TRANSFERRED.

Name	Age	Rank	Date of Enlistment	Remarks
Eli Hill	25	Private	Aug. 8, '62	Taken prisoner at Winchester, Va., June 15, 1863; was exchanged; transferred to veteran reserve corps February, 1864, by order Provost Marshal General.
John Egger	30	Private	Aug. 11, '62	Captured at Winchester, Va., June 14, 1863; exchanged and returned to regiment, November 6, 1863; wounded at Lynchburg, Va., June 18, 1864; transferred to veteran reserve corps, February 2, 1865.

DISCHARGED.

Name	Age	Rank	Date of Enlistment	Remarks
Walter S. Hardesty	19	Private	Aug. 8, '62	Discharged for disability by order Gen. Kelly, Cumberland, Md., February 24, 1864.
Thomas L. Tipton	18	Private	Aug. 12, '62	Discharged for disability by order Gen. Kelly, Cumberland, Md., February 25, 1863.
John T. Mayberry	26	Private	Aug. 11, '62	Discharged for disability by order Gen. Kelly, Cumberland, Md., March 23, 1863.
David Truax	31	Private	Aug. 2, '62	Discharged for disability by order Gen. Kelly, Martinsburg, Va.
James Logan	34	Private	Jan. 2, '64	Discharged to receive promotion, November 17, 1864, order General Crook.
George Kisner	21	Private	Aug. 15, '62	Discharged for disability. (Wounded at Piedmont, Va., June 5, 1864, and arm amputated), March 7, 1865, at Annapolis.

Record of Company C, 116th Regiment O. V. I., in the Service of the United States.—(CONTINUED.)

NAME.	AGE	RANK.	DATE OF ENLISTMENT	GENERAL HISTORY AND FINAL RECORD.
Thomas South	18	Private	Aug. 11, '62	Discharged on account of wounds, January 16, 1865. Wounded at Fisher's Hill, September 22, 1864.
Reinhard Straub	27	Private	Aug. 11, '62	Discharged May 17, 1865, by order of War Department; captured at Winchester, Va., June 14, 1863; exchanged November 11, 1863.
Jacob. Michnack	22	Private	Jan. 5, '64	Discharged May 17, 1865, on account of wounds.
Daniel Ludwig	32	Private	Jan. 4, '64	Mustered out by order of War Department, May 14, 1865.

DEATHS.

NAME.	AGE	RANK.	DATE OF ENLISTMENT	GENERAL HISTORY AND FINAL RECORD.
Amos Byers	26	Private	Aug. 11, '62	Accidentally shot while in the line of duty, at Romney, Va., February 17, 1864.
Emanuel Byers	24	Private	Aug. 11, '62	Died at Fortress Monroe, Va., May 27, 1865, of wounds received at Hatcher's Run, Va., March 31, 1865.
Thomas C. Booth	18	Private	Aug. 12, '62	Died of disease at Winchester, Va., May 17, 1863.
Jacob Butt	21	Private	Aug. 15, '62	Died of disease at Miltonsburg, O., November 7, 1863.
Isaac Barrett	23	Private	Jan. 4, '64	Died at Staunton, Va., July 10, 1864, of wounds received at Piedmont, Va., June 5, 1864.
John G. Barrett	28	Corporal	Jan. 12, '62	Died at Annapolis, Md., August 19, 1864, of wounds received at Piedmont, Va., June 5, 1864.
Josephus Bush	21	Private	Feb. 2, '64	Died of disease at Baltimore, Md., September 17, 1864.
Robert E. Chambers	20	Private	Aug. 12, '62	Died at Beverly, Va., June 26, 1864, of wounds received in action at Piedmont, Va., June 5, 1864.
Miles H. Davis	18	Private	April 2, '63	Died at Lundy, Md. October 12, 1864, of wounds received in action at Halltown, Va., August 26, 1864.
George W. Gannon	24	Private	Aug. 12, '62	Captured at Winchester, Va., June 14, 1863; exchanged and returned to regiment December 11, 1863; killed in action at Piedmont, Va., June 5, 1864.
Oswald Heck	24	Sergeant	Aug. 8, '62	Died at ———, of wounds received in action at Winchester, Va., June 13, 1863; date of death not known.
John W. Harten	22	Private	Aug. 12, '62	Died of disease at Sharpsburg, Md., August 6, 1863.
Citizen H. Hudson	20	Private	Aug. 13, '62	Died of disease at Beallsville, O., September 13, 1863.
William Hall	19	Private	Aug. 11, '62	Killed in action at Fort Gregg, Va., April 2, 1865.
Abram Jeffries	19	Private	Aug. 11, '62	Died of disease at Harper's Ferry, Va., July 23, 1863.
John Latchan	18	Private	Aug. 11, '62	Captured at Winchester, Va., June 15, 1863; exchanged and returned to regiment November 6, 1863; killed in action at Piedmont, Va., June 5, 1864.
David A. Mann	25	Private	Aug. 11, '62	Died of typhoid fever at Martinsburg, Va., March 24, 1864; taken prisoner at Winchester, Va., June 14, 1863.
James Moherly	24	Private	Feb. 29, '64	Died at Staunton, Va., July 12, 1864, of wounds received at Piedmont, Va., June 5, 1864.
George W. Matchett	39	Private	Aug. 15, '62	Prisoner at Winchester, Va., June 14, 1863; exchanged October 2, 1863; killed in action at Halltown, Va., August 26, 1864.

ONE HUNDRED AND SIXTEENTH O. V. I.   335

William H. Mobberly	30	Corporal	Aug. 11, '62	Died at Fortress Monroe, April 18, 1865, of wounds received at Fort Gregg, Va., April 2, 1865.
Frederick F. Neptune	18	Private	Aug. 11, '62	Killed in action at Piedmont, Va., June 5, 1864.
Henry Pfeifer	29	Private	Aug. 15, '62	Killed in action at Piedmont, Va., June 5, 1864.
James A. Preslaw	19	Private	Aug. 16, '62	Captured at Winchester, Va., June 15, 1863; exchanged and returned to regiment, November 2, 1863; wounded and taken prisoner at Piedmont, Va., June 5, 1864; died in Andersonville, Ga., prison, November 3, 1864.
Adam Rodecker	26	Corporal	Aug. 11, '62	Killed in action at Piedmont, Va., June 5, 1864.

DESERTER.

Gilbert Johnson	34	Private	Aug. 9, '62	Deserted March 17, 1863, while the regiment was on the march from Romney to Winchester, Va.

RECRUITS TRANSFERRED TO 62D REGIMENT O. V. I.

Joseph S. Johnson	12	Corporal	Aug. 9, '62	Original enlistment. Not a recruit, wounded at Hatcher's Run, Va., March 31, 1865.
William M. Barnes	34	Private	Jan. 4, '64	
John E. Buchwald	32	Private	Jan. 5, '64	
Daniel Conger	31	Private	Jan. 4, '64	
Alfred W. Davis	18	Private	July 30, '62	
John I. Montgomery	29	Private	Mar. 30, '64	
William Metz	25	Private	Dec. 30, '63	Wounded in the head at Piedmont, Va., June 5, 1864.
Christian Schlapp	34	Private	Dec. 30, '63	
Philip Schank	24	Private	Dec. 31, '63	
Isaac W. Tomlinson	19	Private	Aug. 12, '62	
Albin Vickers	29	Private	Jan. 29, '64	In hospital at Baltimore since November 25, 1864.

Record of Company D, 116th Regiment O. V. I. in the Service of the United States.

NAME.	RANK.	DATE OF ENLISTMENT	GENERAL HISTORY AND FINAL RECORD.
William Myers	Captain	Aug. 11, '62	Resigned August 24, 1864; mustered out September 1, 1864.
R. T. Chaney	Captain	Aug. 12, '62	Enrolled as Second Lieutenant; promoted to First Lieutenant, September 1, 1863; promoted to Captain, September 22, 1864; resigned February 1, 1865.
Henry Obey	1st. Lieutenant	Aug. 11, '62	Taken prisoner at Moorefield, Va., January 3, 1864; resigned January 2, 1865.
Samuel D. Knight	1st. Lieutenant	Aug. —, '62	Enrolled as First Sergeant; promoted to Second Lieutenant April 1, 1864, to First Lieutenant, December 8, 1864; mustered out with regiment at close of war.
Jacob Wycoff	2d. Lieutenant	Aug. 18, '62	Promoted from First Sergeant to K. March 5, 1865; acting R. Q. M. from May 13, 1865; mustered out with regiment at close of war.

PRESENT TO BE MUSTERED OUT WITH THE REGIMENT AT CLOSE OF THE WAR.

NAME.	RANK.	DATE OF ENLISTMENT	GENERAL HISTORY AND FINAL RECORD.
Adam J. Myers	1st. Sergeant	Aug. 12, '62	Wounded at Lynchburg, Va., June 18, 1864; commissioned Second Lieutenant June 29, 1865; but not mustered.
John B. Brum	Sergeant	Aug. 16, '62	Promoted from Corporal Jan. 1, 1865.
William M. Detwiler	Sergeant	Aug. 14, '62	Promoted from private, April 25, 1863.
Simon P. Piatt	Corporal	Aug. 19, '62	Promoted from private, April 25, 1864.
Madison Smith	Corporal	Aug. 18, '62	Promoted from private, Sept. 22, 1864.
William L. Norris	Corporal	Aug. 19, '62	Promoted from private, July 1, 1865.
Josephus Cox	Corporal	Aug. 13, '62	
Owen Penn	Wagoner	Aug. 14, '62	
Thomas B. Brock	Private	Aug. 15, '62	Wounded at Piedmont, Va., June 5, 1864; taken prisoner at Cedar Creek, Va., Oct. 19, 1864; at Andersonville, Ga., from Oct. 19, 1864, till Feb. 22, 1865.
Daniel Bennett	Private	Aug. 14, '62	
Roseberry M. Cline	Private	Aug. 12, '62	Wounded at Piedmont, Va., June 5, 1864.
David Cooger	Private	Aug. 19, '62	Prisoner of war at Belle Island, Va., from June 15, 1863, till Oct. 29, 1863.
John Couger	Private	Aug. 18, '62	
John Cox	Private	Aug. 13, '62	
Edward Daugherty	Private	Aug. 14, '62	Wounded in leg at Lynchburg, Va., June 18, 1864.
James G. Daily	Private	Aug. 16, '62	Wounded at Piedmont, Va., June 5, 1864; also at Fisher's Hill, Sept. 22, 1864.
James K. Drum	Private	Aug. 16, '62	
George W. Evans	Private	Aug. 12, '62	Wounded at Piedmont, Va., June 5, 1864; also at Fort Gregg, Va., April 2, 1865.
George L. Emmons	Private	Aug. 13, '62	
Samuel Forsyth	Private	Aug. 15, '62	
Merriman Gray	Private	Aug. 13, '62	Taken prisoner at Winchester, Va., June 15, 1863; exchanged Aug. 1, 1863.
Alfred Gray	Private	Aug. 13, '62	Prisoner of war at Libby Prison from June 15, 1863, to Aug. 1, 1863; taken prisoner at Winchester, Va., June 15, 1863.
John J. Goudy	Private	Aug. 16, '62	
Thomas Haslem	Private	Aug. 12, '62	

Name	Rank	Age	Enlisted	Remarks
Peter Hickman	Private	31	Aug. 15, '62	Wounded at Piedmont, Va., June 5, 1864.
David Hickman	Private	18	Aug. 12, '62	
John Jackson	Private	20	Aug. 11, '62	
Bruce Jackson	Private	35	Aug. 16, '62	
Leonard A. Jackson	Private	21	Aug. 18, '62	Taken prisoner at Winchester, Va., June 15, 1863; prisoner at Belle Island, Va., till July 19, 1863; exchanged Nov. 26, 1863. Was prisoner of war in Libby Prison from June 15 to Oct. 20, 1863; taken at Winchester; exchanged Oct. 3, 1863.
Henry Moore	Private	26	Aug. 22, '62	Wounded at Piedmont, Va., June 5, 1864.
Eldridge Maffet	Private	27	Aug. 14, '62	Taken prisoner at Winchester, Va., June 15, 1863; returned Oct. 8, 1863.
Alexander McWilliams	Private	25	Aug. 14, '62	
John Nixon	Private	37	Aug. 12, '62	
Joshua Nixon	Private	19	Aug. 13, '62	Wounded in leg at Piedmont, Va., June 5, 1864.
Josiah Norris	Private	21	Aug. 16, '62	Wounded in arm at Piedmont, Va., June 5, 1864.
Henry Owens	Private	18	Aug. 13, '62	
Levera O. Okey	Private	21	Aug. 16, '62	
John W. Reeser	Private	21	Aug. 13, '62	Wounded in head at Piedmont, Va., June 5, 1864.
Peter Shutts	Private	18	Aug. 16, '62	Taken prisoner at Winchester, Va., June 15, 1863; exchanged Nov. 1, 1863; wounded in arm at Piedmont, Va., June 5, 1864.
Jesse M. Stine	Private	21	Aug. 15, '62	
James A. Sinclair	Private			Taken prisoner at Winchester, Va., June 15, 1864, in prison at Belle Island, Va., from June 15 till July 19, 1863; exchanged and joined Company Nov. 12, 1863.
John Truex	Private	29	Aug. 18, '62	Taken prisoner at Lynchburg, Va., June 18, 1864.
John W. Vicker	Private	21	Aug. 19, '62	
Walter T. Wilcox	Private	21	Aug. 12, '62	

ABSENT TO BE MUSTERED OUT AT CLOSE OF WAR.

Name	Rank	Age	Enlisted	Remarks
Abraham G. Jackson	Sergeant	21	Aug. 11, '62	Enrolled as Corporal; promoted to Sergeant, Aug. 2, 1863; wounded in hip at Halltown, Va., Aug. 26, 1864; in hospital from that time.
Alexander Strait	Corporal	21	Aug. 22, '62	Promoted to Corporal, December 25, 1862; wounded at Lynchburg, Va., June 18, 1864, also at Cedar Creek, Va., Oct. 19, 1864; in hospital since Oct. 19, 1864; was prisoner of war.
Eli Whitlatch	Corporal	21	Aug. 14, '62	Promoted to Corporal, March 15, 1864; wounded at Fort Gregg, April 2, 1865; in hospital since that time.
James Agin	Corporal	24	Aug. 13, '62	Promoted to Corporal, September 22, 1864; wounded at Hatcher's Run, April 1, 1865; was prisoner of war.
Edward S. Clothero	Private	22	Aug. 16, '62	Wounded at Snicker's Ferry, Va., July 18, 1864; in hospital since that time.
Henry B. Huxenbaugh	Private	26	Aug. 11, '62	Wounded at Piedmont, Va., June 5, 1864; prisoner from hospital at Staunton since June 11, 1864.
Isaac Price	Private	38	Aug. 12, '62	Taken prisoner of war at Winchester, Va., June 15, 1863; exchanged and joined company, Oct. 3, 1864; wounded at Halltown, Va., Aug. 26, 1864, in right thigh; in hospital since Aug. 26, 1864.

ONE HUNDRED AND SIXTEENTH O. V. I.

Record of Company D, 116th Regiment O. V. I., in the Service of the United States.—(CONTINUED.)

TRANSFERRED.

NAME.	AGE.	RANK.	DATE OF ENLISTMENT	GENERAL HISTORY AND FINAL RECORD.
Charles M. Bowers	22	Private	Aug. 16, '62	Wounded at Piedmont, Va., June 5, 1864, through breast; transferred to Veteran Reserve Corps, March 22, 1865.
Jackson Cox	26	Private	Aug. 13, '62	Taken prisoner at Winchester, Va., June 15, 1863; transferred to Veteran Reserve Corps, Nov 4, 1864.

DISCHARGED.

William O. Belt	22	Sergeant	Aug. 12, '62	Wounded at Fort Gregg, April 2, 1865; discharged on account of wound, May 30, 1865.
David Clark	25	Private	Aug. 12, '62	Discharged March 27, 1863.
Leander A. Eddy	22	Private	Aug. 14, '62	Taken prisoner at Winchester, June 15, 1863; exchanged and rejoined Company, Nov. 11, 1863; discharged April 4 1865, on account of wound received at Snicker's Ferry, July 18, 1864.
John W. Hall	22	Private	Aug. 11, '62	Discharged May 23, 1865, on account of wound received at Cedar Creek, Oct. 13, 1864.
George W. Kenny	25	Private	Aug. 12, '62	Discharged April 2, 1863.
Henry Mowder	38	Private	Aug. 16, '62	Taken prisoner at Winchester Va., June 15, 1863; exchanged and rejoined Company, Nov. 1, 1863; discharged Jan. 7, 1865, on account of wounds received at Piedmont, Va., June 5, 1864.
Willoughby Morgan	44	Private	Aug. 16, '62	Discharged April 7, 1865, for disability.
John Winland	40	Private	Jan. 4, '64	Discharged Feb. 2, 1865.
Thomas Rowley		Private	Aug. 16, '62	Taken prisoner at Winchester, Va., June 15, 1863; exchanged and rejoined Company, Oct. 3d, 1863; discharged May 8, 1865.

DEATHS.

Samson Patterson		Sergeant	Aug. 12, '62	Taken prisoner at Winchester, Va., June 15, 1863; exchanged and sent to Harrisburg; died Aug. 9, 1863, at Chambersburg, Pa., of typhoid fever.
Robert Armstrong		Corporal	Aug. 26, '62	Taken prisoner at Winchester, Va., June 15, 1863; killed in action at Piedmont, Va., June 5, 1864.
Henry Barnard	38	Corporal	Aug. 13, '62	Died Dec. 22, 1862, of chronic diarrhoea, at Cumberland, Md.
Archer Dickerson		Corporal		Killed at Cedar Creek, Oct. 13, 1864.
Samuel Alford	20	Private	Aug. 12, '62	Died June 15, 1864, of wounds received in action at Piedmont, Va., June 5, 1864.
Charles W. Bennett	19	Private	Aug. 16, '62	Died Dec. 12, 1862, of fever, at Cumberland, Md.
Elias G. Brock	36	Private	Jan. 4, '64	Killed in action, June 5, 1864, at Piedmont, Va.
Washington Bryan	22	Private	Aug. 13, '62	Died July 16, 1864, of wounds received in action at Piedmont, Va., June 5, 1864.
Jacob Clark	24	Private	Aug. 12, '62	Died July 9, 1861, of typhoid fever, at Gallipolis hospital, Ohio.
Scott Dickson	25	Private	Aug. 14, '62	Died (date not known) at Lynchburg, Va., of wounds received at Piedmont, Va., June 5, 1864.

ONE HUNDRED AND SIXTEENTH O. V. I.

Name	Rank	Date		Remarks
John Detwiler	27 Private	Dec. 26, '63	Killed in action at Piedmont, Va., June 5, 1864.
Robert H. B. Dyer	19 Private	Jan. 4, '64	Killed in action June 5, 1864, at Piedmont, Va.
William T. Flowers	Private	Aug. 13, '62	Wounded at Piedmont, Va., June 5, 1864; prisoner of war since June 11, 1864; died at Andersonville, Ga., Nov. 5, 1864.
Micajah Gowdy	23 Private	Aug. 16, '62	Missing in action June 18, 1864, at Lynchburg, Va.; prisoner of war; died at Lynchburg, Va.; date of death not known.
James G. Headly	18 Private	Aug. 15, '62	Wounded at Piedmont, Va., June 5, 1864; prisoner June 11, 1864; killed at Lynchburg, Va., June 18, 1864.
Evander B. Hamilton	30 Private	Aug. 14, '62	Wounded and prisoner at Lynchburg, Va., June 18, 1864.
Jacob Hal	34 Private	Aug. 13, '62	Died Dec. 19, 1864, of chronic diarrhœa, at Salisbury, N. C., while prisoner of war.
Thomas Hunnel	25 Private	Aug. 16, '62	Died March 2, 1864, of remittent fever, at Martinsburg, Va.
Wilson S. Jackson	20 Private	Aug. 15, '62	Died Aug. 9, 1864, of consumption, at Cumberland, Md.
Jacob Mathews	18 Private	Jan. 4, '64	Died Feb. 12, 1864, of pneumonia, at Martinsburg, Va.
Richard Mahoney	20 Private	Aug. 22, '62	Died June 15, 1864, of wounds received in action at Piedmont, Va., June 5, 1864.
Moses F. Starr	25 Private	Aug. 16, '62	Killed in action at Lynchburg, Va., June 18, 1864.
Joseph Simmons	19 Private	Aug. 16, '62	Taken prisoner at Winchester, Va., June 15, 1863; exchanged and rejoined Company Oct. 22, 1863; killed in action at Piedmont, Va., June 5, 1864.
Hugh Thompson	21 Private	Aug. 12, '62	Taken prisoner at Winchester, Va., June 15, 1863; exchanged and rejoined Company Nov. 1, 1863; died Sept. 9, 1864, of chronic diarrhœa, at Parkersburg, Va.
John H. Winland	20 Private	Aug. 16, '62	Died Dec. 6, 1864, of typhoid fever, at Cumberland, Md.
Stephen K. Wright	18 Private	Aug. 19, '62	Died April 8, 1864, of scrofula.

DESERTED.

| James K. Harvey | 18 Private | Aug. 18, '62 | Deserted Oct. 8, 1862, at Gallipolis, O. |

RECRUITS TRANSFERRED TO 62D REGIMENT O. V. I.

Name	Rank	Date		Remarks
William A. Ferrel	22 Corporal	Aug. 12, '62	Sick in hospital, Columbus, O.; was prisoner of war.
James A. Brady	19 Private	Jan. 25, '64	
Joseph F. Beaver	35 Private	Dec. 25, '63	
Peter Beaver	18 Private	Dec. 2, '64	
Andrew C. Boyd	18 Private	M'ch 2, '64	Wounded in action at Opequan, Va., Sept. 19, 1864.
William G. Cumming	Private	Jan. 4, '64	
James D. Ferrel	20 Private	Aug. 28, '64	Sick at Sandy Hook, Md., since Sept., 1864.
David Gray	25 Private	M'ch 8, '64	Wounded at Halltown, Va., Aug. 26, 1864; in hospital Cumberland, Md., since Jan. 29, 1865.
Judson Gates	32 Private	Nov. 18, '63	
Israel L. Hamilton	18 Private	Jan. 4, '64	
Samuel Jones	30 Private	Jan. 25, '64	
Absolom Pattman	27 Private	Oct. 5, '62	
George W. Smith	17 Private	April 1, '65	
Thomas Swadell	34 Private	Dec. 22, '63	
Asa Truex	36 Private	Aug. 22, '62	Sick in hospital, Cumberland, Md., since March 15, 1865.
George W. Murphy	Private	Aug. 22, '62	Transferred to Company F, 116th O. V. I., by order Colonel commanding regiment.

339

Record of Company E, 116th Regiment O. V. I., in the Service of the United States.

NAME.	AGE.	RANK.	DATE OF ENLISTMENT	GENERAL HISTORY AND FINAL RECORD.
John Varley		Captain	Aug. 11, '62	Dismissed by order of General Sheridan, September 15, 1864; reinstated and honorably discharged.
Peter Dillon		Captain	Aug. —, '62	Enrolled as First Lieutenant; promoted to Captain, December 7, 1864; discharged by order General Ord, January 29, 1865.
John C. Henthorn	32	Captain	Aug. 11, '62	Enrolled as Second Lieutenant; promoted to First Lieutenant, February 20, 1864; promoted to Captain, March 25, 1865; mustered out with regiment at close of war.
Edward Muhleman	18	2d. Lieutenant	Aug. —, '62	Enrolled as First Sergeant; promoted to Sergeant Major, September 1, 1863; to Second Lieutenant, March 16, 1864; to First Lieutenant, February 10, 1865; resigned, date not known.
William J. Lee	21	1st. Lieutenant		Enrolled as Quartermaster Sergeant; promoted to Sergeant Major, March 16, 1864; to Second Lieutenant, March 1, 1865; to First Lieutenant, March 25, 1865; wounded at Hallitown, Va., August 26, 1864; mustered out with regiment at close of war.

PRESENT TO BE MUSTERED OUT WITH THE REGIMENT AT CLOSE OF THE WAR.

NAME.	AGE.	RANK.	DATE OF ENLISTMENT	GENERAL HISTORY AND FINAL RECORD.
Andrew W. Henthorn	32	1st. Sergeant	Aug. 16, '62	Appointed Corporal, October 10, 1862; promoted to Sergeant, September 1, 1863; taken prisoner at Moorefield, Va., January 3, 1863; commissioned Second Lieutenant, June 20, 1865; not mustered.
Samuel S. Atkinson	28	Sergeant	Aug. 22, '62	Commissioned Second Lieutenant, June 20, 1865; not mustered.
Mathew Akinson	28	Sergeant	Aug. 18, '62	
Joseph J. Spears	2	Sergeant	Aug. 28, '62	Appointed Corporal, November 1, 1862; promoted to Sergeant, May 1, 1865.
Joseph Muhleman	18	Corporal	Aug. 15, '62	Appointed Corporal, July 1, 1864.
Joseph Gillespie	15	Corporal	Aug. 19, '62	Appointed Corporal, October 15, 1864.
Dallas Gillmore	18	Corporal	Aug. 12, '62	Appointed Corporal, May 1, 1865.
Lewis Barcus	21	Corporal	Aug. 19, '62	Appointed Corporal, May 1, 1865; wounded at Piedmont, Va., June 5, 1864; prisoner from June 10, 1864, till September 21, 1864.
Isaiah Mezeca	21	Corporal	Aug. 13, '62	Appointed Corporal, May 1, 1865; wounded at Lynchburg, Va., June 18, 1864.
Oregon Boughner	18	Corporal	Aug. 18, '62	Appointed Corporal, October 15, 1864.
Levi M. McKnight	28	Wagoner	Aug. 14, '62	
Abel M. Atkinson	18	Private	Aug. 30, '62	
Enoch Barcus	18	Private	Aug. 19, '62	
William Blair	25	Private	Aug. 19, '62	
Jacob Byers	27	Private	Aug. 13, '62	
Joseph Conner	20	Private	Aug. 24, '62	Wounded to hip at Lynchburg, Va., June 18, 1864.
William Dye	20	Private	Aug. 14, '62	
William M. Fulton	17	Private	Aug. 19, '62	
Frederick Hedinger	19	Private	Aug. 14, '62	
Denning O. C. Henthorn	18	Private	Aug. 14, '62	
Joseph A. Hall	22	Private	Aug. 20, '62	Was prisoner of war from October 15, 1864, till February 15, 1865.

ONE HUNDRED AND SIXTEENTH O. V. I.   341

Name	Age	Rank	Enlisted	Remarks
William Q. Hall	18	Private	Aug. 20, '62	
Anthony Howell	20	Private	Aug. 18, '62	
Isaac Howell	18	Private	Aug. 18, '62	
Levi Howell	28	Private	Aug. 20, '62	Transferred from Company I, July 25, 1863; wounded at Fort Gregg, Va., April 2, 1865.
David Howard	35	Private	Aug. 22, '62	Appointed Corporal, September 18, 1862; returned to ranks July 1, 1864.
John Laniger	37	Private	Aug. 16, '62	
John Moore	27	Private	Aug. 19, '62	In hospital, July, August, September and October, of 1864.
John Morrow	18	Private	Aug. 20, '62	Taken prisoner at Winchester, Va., June 15, 1863; returned to regiment, July 22, 1863.
Milton Mozena	20	Private	Aug. 12, '62	Wounded at Opequan, Va., September 19, 1864.
John Nasperly	24	Private	Aug. 18, '62	
Adam H. Ollom	31	Private	Aug. 18, '62	Taken prisoner at Moorefield, Va., January 3, 1863; returned to regiment, January 11, 1863.
Benjamin Ridgway	22	Private	Aug. 14, '62	Taken prisoner at Winchester, Va., June 15, 1863; returned to regiment, August 7, 1863.
Adam Rolde	21	Private	Aug. 21, '62	
Frederick Shafroth	20	Private	Aug. 14, '62	
John L. Snively	18	Private	Aug. 14, '62	
David Spring	32	Private	Aug. 14, '62	
Henry Stevens	34	Private	Aug. 14, '62	
Leander Thompson	22	Private	Aug. 22, '62	
Jacob Fisher	37	Private	Aug. 19, '62	Taken prisoner at Hancock, Md., June 17, 1863.
William Fisher	18	Private	Aug. 12, '62	
John White	18	Private	Aug. 18, '62	
Ephraim Williams	23	Private	Aug. 19, '62	
Jacob Wolnuhaus	21	Private	Aug. 19, '62	Transferred from Company H, October 15, 1862, by order Colonel Washburn.
Stephen Ward	26	Private	Aug. 12, '62	Transferred from Company I, July 25, 1864, by order Colonel Washburn.

ABSENT TO BE MUSTERED OUT.

Name	Age	Rank	Enlisted	Remarks
Joseph Skiles	24	Sergeant	Aug. 20, '62	Appointed Corporal, September 18, 1862; promoted to Sergeant, May 1, 1865; in hospital at Philadelphia.
John J. Atkinson	21	Corporal	Aug. 19, '62	Appointed Corporal, September 1, 1863; detached in Q. M. Department at Stevenson's Depot, Va.
Harrison Cochran	23	Corporal	Aug. 14, '62	At Camp Chase, O.; appointed Corporal July 1, 1863; wounded at Piedmont, Va., June 5, 1864; was taken prisoner and confined at Andersonville, Ga.; escaped June 27, 1865; reached Union lines at Cedar Keys, Fla., April 27, 1865; no white man saw him during all this time, he was taken care of by colored people.
John M. Bougimer	28	Private	Aug. 19, '62	In hospital at Fortress Monroe; wounded at Fort Gregg, Va., April 2, 1865; served as Corporal from September 18, 1862, till September 1, 1863; returned to the ranks at his own request.
John Clegg	18	Private	Aug. 22, '62	In hospital at Annapolis, Md.
Samuel Hartlein	20	Private	Aug. 20, '62	In hospital at Philadelphia, Pa.
Conrad Hartlein	33	Private	Aug. 21, '62	In hospital at Baltimore, Md.
Ephraim Heathorn	22	Private	Aug. 18, '62	In hospital at Baltimore, Md.
Jacob S. Hurd	21	Private	Aug. 19, '62	Taken prisoner at Winchester, Va., June 14, 1863; wounded at Fort Gregg, Va., April 2, 1865; in hospital at Fortress Monroe since that time.
Isaac Littleton	34	Private	Aug. 16, '62	Wounded at Fort Gregg, April 2, 1865; in hospital at Fortress Monroe.
Samuel McConnell	41	Private	Aug. 19, '62	Wounded at River's Station, Va., April 6, 1865; in hospital at Baltimore, Md.

Record of Company E, 116th Regiment O. V. I., in the Service of the United States.—(CONTINUED.)

NAME.	AGE	RANK.	DATE OF ENLISTMENT	GENERAL HISTORY AND FINAL RECORD.
William B. McFarland	21	Private	Aug. 19, '62	Wounded at Rice's Station, Va., April 6, 1865; in hospital at Fortress Monroe.
John Rothaker	26	Private	Aug. 19, '62	In hospital at Wheeling, W. Va.
John K. Rush	22	Private	Aug. 22, '62	In hospital at Cumberland, Md.
John Schappat	30	Private	Aug. 22, '62	Wounded at Fort Gregg, Va., April 2, 1865; in hospital at Fortress Monroe since then.
Frederick Stevens	24	Private	Aug. 22, '62	Wounded at Fort Gregg, Va., April 2, 1865; in hospital at Fortress Monroe since then.
Charles Sappers	31	Private	Aug. 22, '62	In hospital at Columbus, O.
Jacob Walter	25	Private	Aug. 21, '62	Taken prisoner at Winchester, Va., June 15, 1863; in hospital at Annapolis, Md.
George W. Wiley	25	Private	Aug. 20, '62	In hospital at Baltimore, Md.
John J. Walter	21	Private	Aug. 22, '62	Taken prisoner at Moorefield, Va., January 3, 1863; also at Winchester, Va., June 15, 1863; appointed Corporal, Sept. 18, 1862; reduced July 1, 1864; in hospital at Columbus, Ohio.

DISCHARGED.

Joshua Ady	41	Private	Aug. 20, '62	Discharged for disability, March 22, 1865, at York, Pa.
Thomas J. Clegg	21	Private	Aug. 22, '62	Discharged for disability, May 9, 1863, at Gallipolis, O., by order General Ewing.
Andrew J. Curliss	32	Private	Aug. 21, '62	Discharged May 27, 1865, on account of wounds received at Fort Gregg, Va., April 2, 1865.
Andrew J. Henthorn	28	Private	Aug. 22, '62	Discharged for disability at Grafton, Va., date not known.

TRANSFERRED.

Charles A. Cline	21	1st. Sergeant	Aug. 14, '62	Enrolled as Sergeant; promoted to First Sergeant, September 6, 1863; to Second Lieutenant, April 2, 1865, and assigned to Company B of this regiment.
Christian Miller	27	Private	Aug. 15, '62	Transferred to Veteran Reserve Corps.

DIED.

John G. Reithmiller	32	Sergeant	Aug. 18, '62	Killed in action at Fort Gregg, Va., April 2, 1865.
Wilson S. Buskirk	21	Corporal	Aug. 22, '62	Died of disease at Halltown, Va., August 25, 1864.
Lewis W. Moxena	22	Corporal	Aug. 13, '62	Killed in action at Fort Gregg, Va., April 2, 1865.
Dickerson Archer	22	Corporal	Aug. 16, '62	Killed in action at Cedar Creek, Va., October 13, 1864; appointed Corporal, September 1, 1863.
Moses Clegg	31	Corporal	Aug. 22, '62	Died in hospital at Frederick, Md., October 13, 1864; appointed Corporal, Sept. 1, 1863.
Nathaniel Ady	16	Private	M'ch 7, '64	Accidentally killed near Berryville, Va., August 11, 1864.
George Blair	20	Private	Aug. 19, '62	Killed in action at Lynchburg, Va., June 18, 1864.
David Bruny	18	Private	Aug. 15, '62	Killed in action at Cedar Creek, Va., October 19, 1864
Charles Dirkes	36	Private	Aug. 22, '62	Died October 9, 1864, of wounds received in action at Halltown, Va., August 26, 1864.
Leander Eoff	18	Private	Dec. 21, '63	Died at Cumberland, Md., of disease, July —, 1864.
Charles Fulton	19	Private	Aug. 19, '62	Died of disease at Summit Point, Va., September 18, 1864.

Name	Age	Rank	Enlisted	Remarks
Robert J. Hathaway	20	Private	Aug. 29, '62	Died of disease at Annapolis, Md., February 13, 1863; taken prisoner at Moorefield, Va., January 3, 1863.
John Hayward	31	Private	Aug. 15, '62	Died of disease (fever) at Cameron, O., October 18, 1863.
Samuel Henthorn	19	Private	Aug. 20, '62	Died of typhoid fever at Winchester, Va., June 22, 1863.
Robert S. Hutcheson	32	Private	Aug. 19, '62	Died April 12, 1865, of wounds received in action at Ree's Station, April 6, 1865; was taken prisoner at Winchester, Va., June 14, 1863.
Edward C. Loyd	18	Private	Aug. 15, '62	Died of disease at Cumberland, Md., March —, 1864; some records give date of death as April 9, 1864.
Samuel Luthy	23	Private	Aug. 20, '62	Died of wounds received at Winchester, Va., June 15, 1863; date of death not known.
Theodore Mathes	29	Private	Aug. 19, '62	Killed in action at Winchester, Va., June 15, 1863.
Moses M-Collough	23	Private	Aug. 12, '62	Died of wounds received in action at Piedmont, Va., June 5, 1864; date not known.
James McFarland	22	Private	Aug. 19, '62	Died of typhoid fever at Winchester, Va., June 30, 1863.
John McFarland	24	Private	Aug. 19, '62	Died of typhoid fever at Winchester, Va., July 13, 1863.
Gilbert McCoy	25	Private	Aug. 19, '62	Died April 8, 1865, of wounds received at Fort Gregg, Va., April 2, 1865.
Madison G. Miller	42	Private	Aug. 14, '62	Died of wounds received at Piedmont, Va., June 5, 1864, date not known.
Peter Odiom	18	Private	Aug. 12, '62	Died of disease at Winchester, Va., April 25, 1863.
Samuel Rubener	21	Private	Aug. 38, '62	Died, April 8, 1865, of wounds received at Fort Gregg, April 2, 1865.
Charles Schaefer	18	Private	Aug. 18, '62	Died from wounds received in battle of Opequan, Va., September 19, 1864; date not known.
John Smith	19	Private	Aug. 15, '62	Killed in action at Hatcher's Run, Va., March 31, 1865; taken prisoner at Winchester, Va., June 15, 1863.
Francis Swartz	30	Private	Jan. 4, '64	Killed in action at Piedmont, Va., June 5, 1864.

DESERTER.

Name	Age	Rank	Enlisted	Remarks
William Chambers	30	Private	Aug. 15, '62	Deserted from hospital, Bedford, Pa., July 1863
John Lehman	36	Private	Aug. 22, '62	Deserted at Sharpsburg, Md., July 26, 1863.

ONE HUNDRED AND SIXTEENTH O. V. I.

Record of Company F, 116th Regiment O. V. I. in the Service of the United States.

NAME.	AGE	RANK.	DATE OF ENLISTMENT	GENERAL HISTORY AND FINAL RECORD.
Matthew Brown		Captain	Aug. 12, '62	Discharged August 7, 1864.
Wilson S. Martin		Captain	Aug. 12, '62	Enrolled as Second Lieutenant; promoted to First Lieutenant, February 7, 1863; to Captain, February 15, 1864; mustered out with regiment at close of the war.
Henry McElfresh		1st. Lieutenant	Aug. 11, '62	Resigned February 7, 1864.
Milton A. Ellis		2d. Lieutenant	Aug. —, '62	Enrolled as Sergeant Major; promoted to Second Lieutenant, April 1, 1863; mustered out with regiment at close of the war.

TRANSFERRED TO 62D REGIMENT O. V. I.

NAME.	AGE	RANK.	DATE OF ENLISTMENT	GENERAL HISTORY AND FINAL RECORD.
Stephen A. Brown	21	1st. Sergeant	Aug. 15, '62	Appointed Sergeant, October 27, 1862; First Sergeant, June 1, 1863; wounded and taken prisoner at Piedmont, Va., June 5, 1864.
Leander Shahan	28	Sergeant	Aug. 13, '62	Wounded at Halltown, Va., August 26, 1864; commissioned Second Lieutenant, June 29, 1865; not mustered.
Emil L. Kupfer	21	Sergeant	Sept. 27, '62	Sergeant from April 1, 1863; on detached service as clerk at headquarters Second Division 24th Army Corps.
Matthias Rucker		Sergeant	Aug. 15, '62	Captured near Romney, Va., February 16, 1863; paroled February 17; returned for duty March 18, 1863; wounded at Halltown, Va., August 26, 1864.
Joseph Draper	27	Sergeant	Aug. 13, '62	Sergeant since January 1, 1864.
Solomon Railing	25	Sergeant	Aug. 13, '62	Appointed Corporal July 1, 1863; promoted to Sergeant, April 10, 1865.
Edward King	23	Sergeant	Aug. 12, '62	Appointed Corporal, March 30, 1864; promoted to Sergeant, May 10, 1864.
Silas King	26	Corporal	Aug. 21, '62	Appointed Corporal, February 1, 1864; wounded at Piedmont, Va., June 5, 1864; also at Halltown, Va., August 26, 1864.
Lewis Dearth	25	Corporal	Aug. 13, '62	Appointed Corporal, November 1, 1862.
Gardiner Okey		Corporal	Oct. 29, '62	Appointed Corporal, March 1, 1864.
William Allen	29	Private	Aug. 20, '62	Captured near Romney, Va., February 16, 1863; paroled February 17; reported to Camp Chase and placed on detached service; returned to regiment for duty, September 29, 1864; lost an arm at Lynchburg, Va., June 18, 1864.
David Amos	18	Private	Aug. 20, '62	Wounded at Fort Gregg, April 2, 1865.
Lewis Barr	32	Private	Aug. 22, '62	Captured near Romney, Va., February 16, 1863; paroled February 17; returned to duty, March 18, 1863; promoted to Corporal, December 31, 1864.
Shepherd Baruchouse	21	Corporal	Aug. 20, '62	Sick in hospital at Cumberland, Md., since January 11, 1865.
Washington Hartness	35	Private	Aug. —, '62	Captured at Winchester, Va., June 15, 1863; exchanged and returned to duty Nov. 23, 1863.
William H. Bell	19	Private	Aug. 18, '62	Sick in hospital at Annapolis, Md.
Elijah Bunting	42	Private	Aug. —, '62	Captured near Romney, Va., February 16, 1863; paroled February 17; returned to duty March 18, 1863.
Reason Carpenter		Private		
Robert Carpenter	22	Private	Aug. 13, '62	Captured near Romney, Va., February 16, 1863; paroled February 17; returned to duty March 18, 1863; wounded at Cedar Creek, Va., October 19, 1864.
James Carson		Private	Aug. 22, '62	

ONE HUNDRED AND SIXTEENTH O. V. I.

Name	Rank		Date		Remarks
Henry Dillon	Private	19	Aug. 15,	'62	Captured near Romney, Va., February 16, 1863; paroled February 17; returned to duty June 1, 1863; wounded at Fort Gregg, April 2, 1865.
Jacob Dillon	Private	21	Aug. 14,	'62	Captured near Romney, Va., February 16, 1863; paroled February 17; returned to duty June 1, 1863.
John Dillon	Corporal	35	Sept. 30,	'62	Captured near Romney, Va., February 16, 1863; paroled February 17; returned to duty June 1, 1863; appointed Corporal May 19, 1865.
James Early	Private	24	Aug. —,	'62	Captured at Winchester, Va., June 15, 1863; sick in Camp Parole, Annapolis, Md., since September 1, 1863.
Leugenious Efaw	Private	30	Aug. 5,	'62	
Elza Foreshey	Private		Jan. 4,	'64	Deserted at Halltown, Va., August 28, 1864; returned voluntarily March 10, 1865, to make up time, under proclamation of President.
Stephen Hogue	Private	19	Aug. 15,	'62	Appointed Corporal, July 1, 1863; reduced to ranks October 31, 1863.
Henry King	Private	30	Aug. 24,	'62	Captured near Romney, Va., February 16, 1863; paroled February 17; returned to duty March 15, 1863; sick in hospital at Columbus, O., at time of transfer to 62d regiment.
Charles Lutch	Private		Aug. —,	'64	Captured at Winchester, Va., June 15, 1863; returned to duty October 3, 1863.
Peter Lee	Private	20	Oct. 28,	'62	Mustered in with Company K; transferred to Company F, October 29, 1862, order of Colonel Washburn.
Wesley McGee	Private				
Valentine Mahl	Private	36	Aug. 22,	'62	Wounded at Fort Gregg, April 2, 1865.
James Marsh	Private	34	Aug. 20,	'64	Captured at Winchester, Va., June 15, 1863; returned to duty October 15, 1863; on detached service in commissary department at Stevenson's Depot, Va.
Henry Martin	Corporal	27	Aug. 15,	'62	Captured near Romney, Va., February 16, 1863; paroled February 17; returned to duty; promoted to Corporal, April 11, 1865.
Jacob Martin	Private		Aug. 15,	'62	
John Martin	Private		Nov. 8,	'62	Deserted June 15, 1864; returned under President's proclamation of March 10, 1865.
Jacob Matz	Private	25	Aug. 16,	'62	Captured near Romney, Va., February 16, 1863; paroled February 17, and returned to duty June 6, 1863.
John W. Morris	Private		Oct. 18,	'62	
Columbus Nichols	Private		Feb. 21,	'64	
Woodman Okey	Private		Oct. 1,	'63	
Thomas Peterson	Private		Aug. 22,	'62	Captured near Romney, Va., February 16, 1863; paroled February 17; returned to duty June 6, 1863.
Jacob Phelps	Corporal	24	Aug. 15,	'62	Promoted to Corporal, December 31, 1864.
Richard T. Phelps	Private		Feb. 21,	'62	
James T. Piggot	Private		Oct. 18,	'62	Wounded in the head at Piedmont, Va., June 5, 1864.
Jasper Rake	Private	35	Aug. 12,	'62	Captured near Romney, Va., February 16, 1863; paroled February 17; returned for duty June 6, 1863; wounded at Fort Gregg, Va., April 2, 1865.
George Ray	Private				
Abalard Shahan	Private	21	Aug. 15,	'62	Appointed Corporal, July 1, 1863; reduced to ranks February 20, 1864; captured near Romney, Va., February 16, 1863; paroled February 17; reported for duty June 6, 1863.
Christian Rhipes	Private		Aug. 12,	'62	Appointed Corporal, October 17, 1862; reduced July 30, 1864; captured at Winchester, Va., June —.
Thomas Shahan	Private		Feb. 1,	'61	
James L. Smith	Private		Feb. 24,	'64	Sick in U. S. General Hospital at Fortress Monroe at time of transfer.
Robert Smith	Private		Aug. 16,	'62	Captured near Romney, Va., February 16, 1863; paroled February 17; returned for duty September 27, 1863.

Record of Company F, 116th Regiment O. V. I., in the Service of the United States.—(CONTINUED.)

NAME.		RANK.	DATE OF ENLISTMENT	GENERAL HISTORY AND FINAL RECORD.
Miner Starkey		Private	Feb. 16, '64	Wounded at Hatcher's Run; in hospital at Fortress Monroe since April 2, 1865.
Samuel Stephen		Private	Aug. 18, '62	
William Sutton		Private	Aug. 13, '62	Appointed Corporal, October 27, 1862; reduced March 31, 1864; captured near Romney, February 16, 1863; paroled February 17; returned for duty March 18, 1863; wounded at Piedmont, Va., June 5, 1864; leg amputated.
Freeman C. Thompson		Private	Nov. 3, '62	Promoted to Corporal, December 31, 1864; on detached service in Q. M. Department Second Division 24th A. C.; was awarded Medal of Honor by Secretary of War for special bravery at Fort Gregg.
Robert G. Wells		Private	Aug. 12, '62	Transferred from Company G to Company F, September 1, 1863, order Lieutenant Colonel Wildes; sick in hospital at Columbus, O.
James Wilson	20	Private	Aug. 22, '62	Sick in General Hospital at Frederick, Md.; wounded at Cedar Creek, Va., Oct. 19, 1864.
Richard Wilson		Private	Aug. 16, '62	Appointed Corporal, October 17, 1862; reduced June 30, 1863; captured near Romney, Va., February 16, 1863; never returned.
Thomas Simmons	31	Private	Aug. 13, '62	Appointed Corporal, November 1, 1862; reduced December 31, 1864; detailed as blacksmith in U. S. Signal.

DISCHARGED.

Andrew J. Stephen		Sergeant	Aug. —, '62	Discharged at Camp Chase, O., March 30, 1863; captured near Romney, February 16, 1863; paroled and sent to Camp Chase, O.
Benjamin Edwards	18	Private	Aug. —, '62	Discharged from hospital at Cumberland, Md., May 30, 1863.
George Moyer	18	Private	Aug. —, '62	Discharged from hospital at Cumberland, Md., April 11, 1864, by order General Sigel.
George W. Murphy		Private	Aug. 12, '62	Discharged at Camp Chase, O., March 15, 1864; appointed First Sergeant, October 27, 1862; reduced May 31, 1863; captured at Winchester, Va., June 15, 1863; never returned to regiment.
George Piter	25	Private	Aug. —, '62	Discharged from hospital at Cumberland, Md., May 15, 1863.
Jonas A. Steed	24	Private	Aug. —, '62	Discharged December 21, 1863, Camp Chase, O.; captured near Romney, February 16, 1863; returned March 19, 1863.
James Steed	20	Private	Aug. —, '62	Discharged April 1, 1863, Camp Chase, O.; captured near Romney, Va., February 16, 1863; reported to camp and sent to Camp Chase, O.
Samuel Wilson	19	Private	Aug. —, '62	Discharged April 3, 1863, Camp Chase, O.; captured near Romney, Va., February 16, 1863; reported to camp and sent to Camp Chase, O.
George W. Smith	32	Private	Aug. —, '62	Discharged March 31, 1863, General Hospital, Cumberland, Md.; appointed Corporal, October 27, 1862; reduced to ranks January 31 1863.

TRANSFERRED.

Dighton M. Bates	18	Private	Oct. 18, '62	Transferred to Company H, January 1, 1863, order Lieutenant Colonel Wildes.
John R. Brokaw	20	Private	Aug. 22, '62	Transferred to Company H, January 1, 1863; order Lieutenant Colonel Wildes.

ONE HUNDRED AND SIXTEENTH O. V. I.

Name	Rank			Remarks
Jacob Carpenter	Private	22	Aug. 18, '62	Transferred to Company H, January 1, 1863, order Lieutenant Colonel Wildes.
Joel B. Cummings	Private	19	Sept. 2, '62	Transferred to Company G, January 1, 1863, order Lieutenant Colonel Wildes.
Alfred W. Davis	Private	18	Sept. 30, '62	Transferred to Company C, January 1, 1863, order Lieutenant Colonel Wildes.
John S. Egger	Private	18	Sept. 13, '62	Transferred to Company C, January 1, 1863, order Lieutenant Colonel Wildes.
William Flowers	Private	18	Aug. 13, '62	Transferred to Company D, January 1, 1863, order Lieutenant Colonel Wildes.
Johnson Gilbert	Private	33	Aug. 16, '62	Transferred to Company C, January 1, 1863, order Lieutenant Colonel Wildes.
Jehiel Graham	Private	24	Aug. 29, '62	Transferred to Company C, January 1, 1863, order Lieutenant Colonel Wildes.
Jacob Gregg	Private	21	Aug. 29, '62	Transferred to Company H, January 1, 1863, order Lieutenant Colonel Wildes.
Abraham Hall	Private	23	Aug. 16, '62	Transferred to Company G, January 1, 1863, order Lieutenant Colonel Wildes.
James Harrison	Private	22	Aug. 18, '62	Transferred to Company A, January 1, 1863, order Lieutenant Colonel Wildes.
Joseph S. Johnson	Private	22	Aug. 22, '62	Transferred to Company H, January 1, 1863, order Lieutenant Colonel Wildes.
John T. McCoy	Private	29	Oct. 1, '62	Transferred to Company C, January 1, 1863, order Lieutenant Colonel Wildes.
Samuel B. Matthews	Private	18	Oct. 18, '62	Transferred to Company H, January 1, 1863, order Lieutenant Colonel Wildes.
Robert Pethel	Private	35	Oct. 18, '62	Transferred to Company H, January 1, 1863, order Lieutenant Colonel Wildes.
James H. Petty	Private	18	Oct. 18, '62	Transferred to Company C, January 1, 1863, order Lieutenant Colonel Wildes.
John H. Phelps	Private	18	Oct. 18, '62	Transferred to Company C, January 1, 1863, order Lieutenant Colonel Wildes.
Absalom Pittman	Private	27	Sept. 29, '62	Transferred to Company D, November 1, 1862, order Lieutenant Colonel Wildes.
John Rake	Private	24	Aug. 29, '62	Transferred to Company A, January 1, 1862, order Lieutenant Colonel Wildes.
John Rawlings	Private	35	Sept. 15, '62	Transferred to Company G, November 1, 1862, order Lieutenant Colonel Wildes.
Hiram C. Sheldon	Private	18	Oct. 21, '62	Transferred to Company H, November 1, 1862, order Lieutenant Colonel Wildes.
Asa Trux	Private	28	Aug. 21, '62	Transferred to Company D, November 1, 1862, order Lieutenant Colonel Wildes.
Isaac M. Yoho	Private	21	Oct. 1, '62	Transferred to Company H, January 1, 1863, order Lieutenant Colonel Wildes.

DIED.

Name	Rank			Remarks
William Buster	Sergeant	26	Aug. 14, '62	Appointed to Sergeant, July 1, 1863; accidentally shot November 23, 1863.
Robert Bramhall	Corporal	26	Aug. 11, '62	Appointed Corporal, July 1, 1863; died at U. S. Hospital, Martinsburg, Va., August 31, 1863, of dysentery.
Stephen Baker	Private	20	Aug. 14, '62	Died at U. S. Hospital, Cumberland, Md., April 1, 1863, of fever.
Jacob Schusall	Private	21	Aug. 14, '62	Died at U. S. General Hospital, Harrisburg, Pa., August 23, 1863, of typhoid fever.
Robert Martin	Corporal	30	Aug. 16, '62	Captured near Romney, Va., February 16, 1863; returned to duty March 17, 1863; wounded at Piedmont, Va., June 5, 1864; taken prisoner June 8, 1864; died in prison at Andersonville.
William Fisner	Private	43	Aug. 22, '62	Captured near Romney, Va., February 16, 1863; returned to duty June 12, 1863; reduced from Corporal June 30, 1863; captured at Halltown, August 26, 1864; died in Salisbury prison, N. C., date not known.
Asa Foreshey	Private		Jan. 4, '64	Died at Andersonville, Ga., September, 1864.
James F. Hughes	Private		Feb. 13, '64	Killed at Piedmont, Va., June 5, 1864.
George W. Johnson	Private		M'ch 8, '61	Killed at Piedmont, Va., June 5, 1864.
Amos S. Jones	Private		Aug. 13, '62	Captured near Romney, Va., February 16, 1863; returned to duty June 12, 1863; captured at Winchester, Va., June 15, 1863; paroled and returned to duty March 14, October 3, 1863; captured at Halltown, August 26, 1864; died in Salisbury prison, N. C., date not known.
Morris Krouse	Private	19	Jan. 18, '62	Captured near Romney, Va., February 16, 1863; killed at Piedmont, Va., June 5, 1864.
Matthias Light	Private	22	Aug. 13, '62	Died at Frederick, Md., July 8, 1864.
John C. McClain	Private		Feb. 26, '61	Died at Winchester, Va., date not known.

Record of Company F, 116th Regiment O. V. I., in the Service of the United States.—(CONTINUED.)

NAME.	AGE.	RANK.	DATE OF ENLISTMENT.	GENERAL HISTORY AND FINAL RECORD.
Joshua Mercer	29	Private	Aug. 22, '62	Died of wounds received at Piedmont, Va., June 5, 1864
Garrison Mirracle		Private	Aug. 22, '62	Transferred from Company K, October 19, 1862; killed at Piedmont, Va., June 5, 1864
Emanuel Okey	26	Private	Aug. 15, '62	Wounded at Piedmont, Va., June 5, 1864, died in rebel prison at Andersonville, Ga., date not known.
Peter Yoho	33	Private	Aug. 18, '62	Died of wounds received at Opequan, September 19, 1864.

DESERTERS.

Bennett Bryant	23	Private	Aug. 22, '62	Captured near Romney, Va., February 16, 1863; paroled February 17, and went home and never returned.
John Morris	20	Private	Aug. 22, '62	Was captured near Romney, Va., February 16, 1863; went home and never returned.
Samuel King		Private	Jan. 4, '64	Deserted, October 13, 1864, from Cedar Creek.

ONE HUNDRED AND SIXTEENTH O. V. I.   349

Record of Company G, 116th Regiment O. V. I., in the Service of the United States.

NAME.	AGE	RANK.	DATE OF ENLISTMENT	GENERAL HISTORY AND FINAL RECORD.
John C. Golden		Captain	Aug. 12, '62	Resigned January 31, 1863, on account of disability.
Hamilton L. Karr		Captain	Aug. 12, '62	Enrolled as First Lieutenant; promoted to Captain, January 31, 1863; mustered out with regiment at close of the war.
J. C. H. Cobb		1st Lieutenant	Aug. 12, '62	Enrolled as Second Lieutenant; promoted to First Lieutenant, January 31, 1863; promoted to Captain, December 27, 1864, and transferred to Company H; wounded at Cedar Creek, October 19, 1864
Ransom Griffin		1st Lieutenant	Aug. 14, '62	Enrolled as First Sergeant; promoted to Second Lieutenant, January 31, 1864; to First Lieutenant, January 2, 1865; mustered out with regiment at close of the war.

PRESENT TO BE MUSTERED OUT AT CLOSE OF WAR.

NAME.	AGE	RANK.	DATE OF ENLISTMENT	GENERAL HISTORY AND FINAL RECORD.
Francis A. Bartley	23	1st Sergeant	Aug. 13, '62	Promoted from Sergeant, August 26, 1864; commissioned Second Lieutenant, June 26, 1865; not mustered
Joseph C. Stewart	27	Sergeant	Aug. 18, '62	
William H. H. Dye	22	Sergeant	Aug. 15, '62	Promoted from Corporal, April 1, 1864
Joseph F. Christy	26	Sergeant	Sept. 1, '62	Promoted from Corporal, January 1, 1863
Leander R. Sayler	38	Sergeant	Aug. 13, '62	Promoted from Corporal, August 26, 1864
William C. Miller	21	Corporal	Aug. 14, '62	
John A. Crosby	22	Corporal	Aug. 16, '62	
Benoma C. Evans	31	Corporal	Aug. 13, '62	Promoted from private, April 1, 1863
William J. Chase	18	Corporal	Aug. 13, '62	Promoted from private, August 1, 1864; taken prisoner at Winchester, Va., June 15, 1863
Daniel H. Howe	22	Corporal	Aug. 14, '62	Promoted from private, August 26, 1864
Ira Wood	36	Wagoner	Aug. 11, '62	Taken prisoner at Winchester, Va., June 15, 1863
Charles J. Adkins	26	Private	Aug. 11, '62	
Wesley Bowers	22	Private	Aug. 15, '62	
Matthias Bratton		Private	Sept. 7, '62	
Fernando G. Canney	23	Private	Aug. 33, '62	
George J. Davis		Private	Aug. 14, '62	
James Davis	34	Private	Aug. 14, '62	Was taken prisoner at Winchester, Va., June 15, 1863; was the last man wounded in the regiment; was knocked down by the last shell fired by the rebels at Appomattox, Va., April 9, 1865.
William M. Davis	18	Private	Aug. 14, '62	
Archibald Denny	31	Private	Aug. 18, '62	Was prisoner of war; taken at Winchester, Va., June 15, 1863
Elias Dickson	18	Private	Aug. 16, '62	
John Fisher		Private	Aug. 14, '62	Was prisoner of war; taken at Winchester, Va., June 15, 1863
George W. Fisher	26	Private	Aug. 14, '62	
James W. Fitzpatrick	23	Private	Aug. 11, '62	
Stephen Gilmore		Private	Aug. 13, '62	
Isaac N. Hendry	18	Private	Aug. 14, '62	

Record of Company G, 116th Regiment O. V. I., in the Service of the United States.—(CONTINUED.)

NAME.	AGE.	RANK.	DATE OF ENLISTMENT	GENERAL HISTORY AND FINAL RECORD.
John Hewett	30	Private	Aug. 19, '62	Taken prisoner at Winchester, Va., June 15, 1863.
George W. Hysell	21	Private	Aug. 16, '62	Was prisoner of war; taken at Winchester, Va., June 15, 1863.
Ebenezer Hysell	21	Private	Aug. 15, '62	
John Lindsey	26	Private	Aug. 14, '62	
Alexander McFarland	23	Private	Aug. 14, '62	Wounded at Piedmont, Va., June 5, 1864.
William Mooney	25	Private	Aug. 18, '62	
Andrew Perry	27	Private	Aug. 15, '62	
Freeland Perry		Private	Aug. 16, '62	
Royal Phelps	18	Private	Aug. 16, '62	Wounded at Cedar Creek, Va., October 14, 1864.
Lemuel W. Powell	18	Private	Aug. 16, '62	Was prisoner of war; taken at Winchester, Va., June 15, 1863.
William M. Sapp	29	Private	Aug. 15, '62	Was taken prisoner of war at Winchester, Va., June 15, 1863.
James Saxton	35	Private	Aug. 15, '62	Wounded at Snicker's Ferry, Va., July 18, 1864.
Samuel Smith	44	Private	Aug. 13, '62	Was taken prisoner at Winchester, Va., June 15, 1863.
Horace W. Stoddard	18	Private	Aug. 13, '62	
Michael Strausbaugh	41	Private	Aug. 16, '62	
Isaac C. Sweet	34	Private	Aug. 15, '62	Was taken prisoner at Winchester, Va., June 15, 1863.
Henry Sweatengarn	32	Private	Aug. 19, '62	Granted thirty days' furlough and awarded Medal of Honor for special bravery at Fort Gregg, Va., April 2, 1865.
Joseph Vanmater	37	Private	Aug. 16, '63	
John Waterhouse	25	Private	Sept. 15, '62	
James Whiteman	26	Private	Aug. 19, '62	Taken prisoner at Cedar Creek Va., October 19, 1864.
David C. Wood	18	Private	Aug. 14, '62	

ABSENT TO BE MUSTERED OUT.

NAME.	AGE.	RANK.	DATE OF ENLISTMENT	GENERAL HISTORY AND FINAL RECORD.
James B. Miller	25	Corporal	Aug. 19, '62	Wounded and taken prisoner at Lynchburg, Va., June 18, 1864.
David Longstreth	23	Corporal	Aug. 20, '62	In hospital on account of wound received at Fort Gregg, Va., April 2, 1865; lost an eye at Winchester, Va., 1863.
Edward Lowrey	31	Corporal	Aug. 16, '62	In hospital on account of wound received at Fort Gregg, Va., April 2, 1865; wounded at Fisher's Hill, Va., September 22, 1864.
Samuel Barrett	37	Private	Aug. 15, '62	In hospital on account of wounds received at Fort Gregg, Va., April 2, 1865.
Joel B. Cummins		Private		In hospital on account of wound received at Snicker's Ferry, Va., July 18, 1864.
Samuel G. Christy	22	Private	Aug. 18, '62	In confinement at Harper's Ferry for desertion.
Jesse Frasier	18	Private	Aug. 15, '62	In hospital on account of wounds received at Cedar Creek, Va., October 13, 1864; (arm shot off.)
Arthur Gibson	23	Private	Aug. 15, '62	Prisoner of war since July 25, 1864.
John J. Martin	22	Private	Aug. 14, '62	Sick in hospital April 21, 1865.
Erastus Stowe	43	Private	Aug. 16, '62	Sick in hospital since December 31, 1864.

Name	Rank		Enlisted		Remarks
Jonathan VanInbber	38	Private	Aug. 16, '62	Detailed in reserve ambulance corps, February 15, 1865; was prisoner of war.
William B. Yeanger	18	Private	Aug. 15, '62	Taken prisoner at Cedar Creek, Va., October 19, 1864.

DISCHARGED.

Name		Rank	Enlisted		Remarks
John Rawlings	38	Private	Oct. 2, '62	Discharged for disability, May 19, 1865, order of War Department; was taken prisoner at Cedar Creek, Va., October 19, 1864; was wounded at Piedmont, Va., June 5, 1864.
Columbus Ralph	18	Private	Aug. 16, '62	Discharged Feb. 23, 1863, at Cumberland, Md., for disability, by order Surgeon Olliver.
Erastus Young	21	Private	Aug. 15, '62	Discharged May 20, 1863, at Cumberland, Md., for disability, by order Surgeon Lewis.
Thomas J. Moore	23	Private	Aug. 16, '62	Discharged May 12, 1865, at Philadelphia, Pa., for disability, by order War Department May 3, 1865.
James F. Bullock	29	Corporal	Aug. 14, '62	Discharged May 16, 1865, at Camp Lee, Va., for disability, order War Department, May 3, 1865; was captured at Cedar Creek, Va., October 13, 1864.
John W. Harrison	27	Corporal	Dec. 26, '63	Discharged by order War Department, May 3, 1865, at McClellan Hospital, Philadelphia, Pa., on account of wounds.

TRANSFERRED.

Name		Rank	Enlisted		Remarks
Milton A. Ellis	21		Aug. 14, '62	Transferred by promotion to Sergeant Major of regiment.
George Hutchinson	34	Corporal	Aug. 19, '62	Transferred to Veteran Reserve Corps, November 27, 1864.
Joel B. Lauther	21	Musician	Aug. 14, '62	Transferred by promotion to principal musician, August 18, 1862; order Col. Washburn.
Robert G. Wells	22	Private	Aug. 13, '62	Transferred to Company F, August 12, 1863, order Major Morris; reduced from Sergeant June 1, 1863
Ezra L. Walker	23	Private	Sept. 4, '62	Transferred by promotion to Commissary Sergeant of regiment September 4, 1862, order of Colonel Washburn.
William J. Lee	21	Private	Sept. 4, '62	Transferred by promotion to Q. M. Sergeant of regiment, September 4, 1862, order Col. Washburn.

DESERTED.

Name		Rank	Enlisted		Remarks
Dillon J. Haning	18	Private	Aug. 13, '62	Deserted August 13, 1863, from hospital.
Cornelius A. Johnson	27	Private	Aug. 16, '62	Deserted June 27, 1863 from hospital at Cumberland, Md.
George L. Story	18	Private	Aug. 19, '62	Deserted March 10, 1863, from hospital.
Charles N. Webster	34	Private	Aug. 15, '62	Deserted May 9, 1863, at Winchester, Va

NAMES OMITTED.

Edward H. Bradley	
DeWitt J. Canny	
William D. Christy	
Jehiel Graham	
Isaac P. Hanning	
Samuel R. Halladay	Wounded at Cedar Creek, Va., October 19, 1864; also at Opequan, September 19, 1864.
William Hovey	
William Kidwell	
Benjamin E. McLane	

Record of Company G, 116th Regiment O. V. I. in the Service of the United States.—(CONTINUED.)

NAME.	AGE.	RANK.	DATE OF ENLISTMENT	GENERAL HISTORY AND FINAL RECORD.
Hiram C. Sheldon.				Court martialed for cowardice at Fort Gregg and sentenced to two years' imprisonment at Rip Raps; parloned by the President.
John R. Steel.				
James Stowe.				
James A. Strong.				Wounded at Hatcher's Run; discharged from hospital.
Jesse Vanlahher.		Drummer		
Henry D. Weynud.				
Benjamin Yeager.				Discharged from hospital.

DIED.

Jacob Butts.	21	Private	Aug. 14, '62	Died June 4, 1863, at Winchester, Va., of lung fever.
Elza A. Bowers.	28	Private	Aug. 14, '62	Died August 4, 1863, at Woodyard, O.; (at home on sick furlough when he died.)
Josephus Comstock.	18	Musician	Aug. 16, '62	Died December 16, 1862, at Cumberland, Md.
Joshua Farley.	24	Private	Aug. 15, '62	Killed in action at Snicker's Ferry, Va., July 18, 1864.
Martin Hysell.	27	Private	Aug. 14, '62	Killed in action at Fort Gregg, Va., April 2, 1865.
James T. McKenzie.	34	1st Sergeant	Aug. 12, '62	Died August 30, 1864, at Sandy Hook. Md.; promoted from Sergeant April 1, 1863.
David A. Moore.	27	Private	Aug. 13, '62	Taken prisoner at Lynchburg, Va. June 18, 1864; died in Andersonville, Ga., prison, August 15, 1864.
John G. Russell.	42	Private	Dec. 31, '63	Died August 14, 1864, at Andersonville, Ga.; taken prisoner June 10, 1864, near Staunton, Va.

Record of Company H, 116th Regiment, O. V. I., in the Service of the United States.

NAME.	AGE	RANK.	DATE OF ENLISTMENT	GENERAL HISTORY AND FINAL RECORD.
Wilbert B. Teters		Captain	Aug. 17, '62	Promoted to Major December 27, 1864; wounded at Piedmont, Va., June 5, 1864; also at Cedar Creek, Va., October 19, 1864.
John C. H. Cobb	29	Captain	Aug. 13, '62	Original Second Lieutenant of Company G; promoted to First Lieutenant January 3, 1863, and to Captain January 2, 1864.
William L. Moseley	32	2d Lieutenant	Aug. 18, '62	Promoted to First Lieutenant September 8, 1864; to Captain March 18, 1865; honorably discharged March 30, 1865, on account of wounds received in action at Opequan, Va., September 19, 1864.
Joseph Parkey	25	1st Lieutenant	Aug. 22, '62	Wounded and taken prisoner at the battle of Piedmont, Va., June 5, 1864; was at Andersonville, Ga., from June 10, to November 19, 1864; was First Sergeant from enlistment; promoted to Second Lieutenant January 19, 1865.
William S. Spriggs	24	1st Lieutenant	Aug. 29, '62	Dishonorably dismissed for disloyalty and drunkenness, per general court martial at Martinsburg, Va., November 1863.

PRESENT TO BE MUSTERED OUT.

Benjamin F. Sammons	29	1st Sergeant	Aug. 22, '62	Promoted from Sergeant March 31, 1865; wounded at Fort Gregg, Va., April 2, 1865; commissioned Second Lieutenant June 29, 1865; not mustered.
William A. Arnold	29	Sergeant	Aug. 22, '62	Was Corporal to July 25, 1864; wounded in left knee at Halltown, Va., August 26, 1864.
Jesse Joseph	35	Sergeant	Aug. 19, '62	Promoted from Corporal January 15, 1865.
Joseph Sevress	28	Sergeant	Aug. 22, '62	Promoted from Corporal March 23, 1865.
Benjamin B. Tifton	30	Corporal	Aug. 22, '62	Wounded in right leg at Piedmont, Va., June 5, 1864; wounded.
Jeremiah Smith	18	Corporal	Aug. 22, '62	Wounded at Fort Gregg, April 2, 1865.
Samuel Carpenter		Corporal	Aug. 22, '62	
John W. Rackley	20	Corporal	Aug. 22, '62	Wounded at Piedmont, Va., June 5, 1864.
William H. Williams	18	Corporal	Aug. 22, '62	
Mark E. Ward	21	Corporal	Aug. 22, '62	
William H. Hesson	23	Wagoner	Aug. 22, '62	
Pyan Bartlett	27	Private	Aug. 22, '62	
Lloyd Bock	35	Private	Aug. 22, '62	Taken prisoner at Winchester, Va., June 15, 1863.
Nathaniel Butler	30	Private	Aug. 22, '62	Taken prisoner at Moorefield, Va., December 29, 1862; wounded at Fort Gregg, Va., April 2, 1865.
William V. Cann	18	Private	Aug. 22, '62	
John Cutliff	28	Private	Aug. 22, '62	
Henry C. Gary	14	Private	Aug. 22, '62	
Henderson G. Crooks	21	Private	Aug. 22, '62	
Jacob L. Ingram	21	Private	Aug. 22, '62	
William J. Emmons		Private	Aug. 22, '62	
Joseph Gerlds	25	Private	Aug. 22, '62	Was prisoner of war.

Record of Company H, 116th Regiment O. V. I., in the Service of the United States.—(CONTINUED.)

NAME.	AGE.	RANK.	DATE OF ENLISTMENT	GENERAL HISTORY AND FINAL RECORD.
Mathew Grandon	29	Private	Aug. 22, '62	Taken prisoner at Winchester, Va., June 15, 1863.
Charles A. Golly	19	Private	Aug. 22, '62	
John J. Keyser	20	Private	Aug. 22, '62	Wounded in right leg at Piedmont, Va., June 5, 1864, and taken prisoner.
James R. P. Keyser	18	Private	Sept. 3, '64	Wounded at Fort Gregg, Va., April 2, 1865.
Eli T. Kirklride	18	Private	Aug. 22, '62	
Elijah J. Mathews	33	Private	Aug. 22, '62	Taken prisoner at Winchester, Va., June 15, 1863.
Lafayette Moore	20	Private	Aug. 22, '62	Taken prisoner at W inchester, Va., June 15, 1863.
Michael J. Moore	31	Private	Aug. 22, '62	Taken prisoner at Winchester, Va., June 15, 1863.
William Moran	18	Private	Aug. 22, '62	
Aaron Morris	21	Private	Aug. 22, '62	
John W. Mott	18	Private	Aug. 22, '62	Wounded at Piedmont, Va., June 5, 1864
Andrew Powell	22	Private	Aug. 22, '62	
William C. Roland	22	Private	Aug. 22, '62	
Isaac Russel	19	Private	Aug. 22, '62	Wounded at Lynchburg, Va., June 18, 1864.
Simon Secrest	20	Private	Aug. 22, '62	
Hugh Shafer	30	Private	Aug. 22, '62	Taken prisoner at Winchester, Va., June 15, 1863.
John Watson	40	Private	Aug. 22, '62	
Wesley J. Westbrooks	44	Private	Aug. 22, '62	
George Whaff	21	Private	Aug. 22, '62	
Pardon J. Wiley	19	Private	Aug. 22, '62	Wounded at Opequan, Va., September 19, 1864.
John W. Williams	20	Private	Aug. 22, '62	
James I. Shafer	22	Private	Aug. 22, '62	

ABSENT TO BE MUSTERED OUT.

NAME.	AGE.	RANK.	DATE OF ENLISTMENT	GENERAL HISTORY AND FINAL RECORD.
Joseph C. Wilson	21	Corporal	Aug. 22, '62	Wounded in left leg at Piedmont, Va., June 5, 1864, and taken prisoner at Staunton, Va., June 10, 1864.
Armstrong Johnson	19	Corporal	Aug. 22, '62	Wounded in left arm at Fort Gregg, Va., April 2, 1865; sent to hospital at Point of Rocks.
Reason Baker	21	Private	Aug. 22, '62	Wounded in right hand at Piedmont, Va., June 5, 1864.
Leonard Craig	18	Private	Aug. 22, '62	Wounded in right foot at Berryville, Va., September 3, 1864.
James M. Unizel	22	Private	Aug. 22, '62	
Jacob Dudley	21	Private	Aug. 22, '62	Taken prisoner at High Bridge, Va., April 6, 1865.
Joseph Dudley	26	Private	Aug. 22, '62	Taken prisoner at Winchester, Va., June 15, 1863, and also at Piedmont, Va., June 5, 1864.
John A. Groves	35	Private	Aug. 22, '62	Wounded in left knee and taken prisoner at Piedmont, Va., June 5, 1864.
Isaac Groves	18	Private	Aug. 22, '62	In hospital at Washington, D. C., August 25, 1864; transferred to invalid corps.
Alrah D. Hopper	18	Private	Aug. 22, '62	On detached duty at Draft Rendezvous, Columbus, O.
Wesley John James	18	Private	Aug. 22, '62	Wounded in right shoulder and taken prisoner at Piedmont, Va., June 5, 1864.

Name	Rank	Date	Remarks
Henry C. Mathews	18 Private	Aug. 22, '62	Wounded in right foot in assault on Fort Gregg, Va., April 2, 1865.
David Shepherd	20 Private	Aug. 22, '62	In hospital at Martinsburg, Va., September 19, 1864; discharged at Cumberland, Md., May 30, 1865.
Joseph Smith	31 Private	Aug. 22, '62	Taken prisoner at Winchester, Va., June 15, 1863; wounded in neck at Fort Gregg, Va., April 2, 1865.
Thomas Spear	21 Private	Aug. 22, '62	Wounded in arm and taken prisoner at Piedmont, Va., June 5, 1864.
Andrew Trimmer	21 Private	Aug. 22, '62	In hospital at Cumberland, March 13, 1863; returned to the ranks from Sergeant, August 1, 1864, on account of disability.
Duncan A. Wharton	22 Private	Aug. 22, '62	At convalescent camp, Harper's Ferry, August 10, 1864; returned to the ranks from Corporal, April 1, 1863, on account of disability.

DISCHARGED.

Name	Rank	Date	Remarks
Benjamin C. Drake	22 Sergeant	Aug. 22, '62	Wounded in left thigh and ankle at Piedmont, Va., June 5, 1864; discharged on account of wounds, May 24, 1865.
Reese Williams	18 Sergeant	Aug. 22, '62	Wounded in right side at Piedmont, Va., June 5, 1864; discharged November 2, 1864.
Uriah J. Chessear	26 Private	Aug. 22, '62	Discharged at Cumberland, Md., April 3, 1865, on surgeon's certificate of disability.
William McBride	21 Private	Aug. 22, '62	Wounded at Piedmont, Va., June 5, 1864; discharged, on account of wounds, at Annapolis, Md., January 19, 1865.
Zachariah Raney	21 Private	Aug. 22, '62	Discharged at Martinsburg, Va., October 15, 1863, on account of rupture.
Jeremiah R. Rhodes	18 Private	Aug. 22, '62	Discharged at Cumberland, Md., April 7, 1865, on account of disability; reduced to ranks from Sergeant August 1, 1863.
Dexter W. Sullivan	32 Private	Oct. 1, '62	Discharged at Winchester, Va., June 12, 1865, on account of disability, by order general Milroy.
George Walters	44 Private	Aug. 22, '62	Discharged at Columbus, O., 1863, on account of disability.
Oliver K. Wharff	44 Private	Aug. 22, '62	Discharged at Harper's Ferry, Va., May 10, 1864, by order general court martial, on account of mental and physical disability.

TRANSFERRED.

Name	Rank	Date	Remarks
Henry T. Johnson	20 Corporal	Aug. 22, '62	Wounded in right arm at Opequan, Va., September 19, 1864; transferred to V. R. C. April 11, 1865.
George Morrison	21 Private	Aug. 22, '62	Taken prisoner at Winchester, Va., June 15, 1863; transferred to V. R. C. on account of rupture.
Jacob Wonhas	30 Private	Aug. 22, '62	Transferred to Company E, 116th O. V. I. by order of Colonel James Washburn.

DIED.

Name	Rank	Date	Remarks
Jacob Gregg	35 Corporal	Aug. 22, '62	Died at Annapolis, Md., April 23, 1865, on account of wound received at Piedmont, Va., June 5, 1864, and disease.
Charles W. Engle	21 Private	Aug. 22, '62	Died at Hookensville, O., September 2, 1863, of disease contracted in the service.
Daniel Gorley	22 Private	Aug. 22, '62	Died at Shepardstown, Va., August 29, 1864, of typhoid fever.
James Harrison	27 Private	Aug. 22, '62	Died at Piedmont, Va., June 6, 1864, on account of wounds received at battle of Piedmont, Va., June 5, 1864.
Samuel Hull	18 Private	Dec. 26, '63	Died at Sandy Hook, Md., August 4, 1864, of chronic diarrhoea.

Record of Company H, 116th Regiment O. V. I., in the Service of the United States.—(CONTINUED.)

NAME.	AGE	RANK.	DATE OF ENLISTMENT	GENERAL HISTORY AND FINAL RECORD.
John Larrick	30	Private	Aug. 22, '62	Died at Savannah, Ga., September 12, 1864, on account of wounds received at Piedmont, Va., June 5, 1864.
Benjamin Larrick	18	Private	Aug. 22, '62	Died at Frederick, Md., October 2, 1864, on account of wounds received at Berryville, Va., September 3, 1864.
George Lamp	18	Musician	Aug. 22, '62	Killed in action at Snicker's Ferry, Va., July 18, 1864.
Stephen C. McCoy	21	Private	Aug. 22, '62	Taken prisoner at Winchester, Va., June 15, 1863; killed in action at Piedmont, Va., June 5, 1864.
John T. McCoy	27	Private	Oct. 1, '62	Died at Chambersburg, Pa., August 2, 1863, of disease.
John A. McIlvee	18	Private	Mch. 31, '64	Killed in action at Opequan, Va., September 19, 1864.
Apollo Morris	23	Private	Aug. 22, '62	Died at Salisbury, N. C., January 1, 1863, on account of disease.
Robert Pethel	22	Private	Oct. 1, '62	Died at Winchester, Va., May 23, 1863, on account of disease.
George C. Pickenpaugh	22	Private	Aug. 22, '62	Died at Shepardstown, Va., October 4, 1862, of typhoid fever.
Solomon Rich	20	Private	Aug. 22, '62	Died at Port Republic, July 1, 1864, on account of wounds received at Piedmont, Va., June 5, 1864.
James I. Rodgers	18	Private	Aug. 22, '62	Killed in action at Fort Gregg, Va., April 2, 1865.
James A. Stoneking	22	Private	Aug. 22, '62	Died at Cumberland, Md., November 30, 1862, of typhoid fever.
Reuben Yoho	18	Private	Feb. 27, '64	Died at Martinsburg, Va., April 1, 1864, of measles.
Isaiah Tribby		Private		Died of wounds received at battle of Opequan, Va., September 19, 1864.

DESERTED.

NAME	AGE	RANK	DATE OF ENLISTMENT	GENERAL HISTORY AND FINAL RECORD
James H. Petty	22	Private	Oct. 17, '62	Deserted at Springfield, Va., March 13, 1863.
Michael Swaney	25	Private	Aug. 22, '62	Deserted at Parkersburg, Va., July 6, 1864.
William Voorhees	24	Private	Aug. 22, '62	Deserted at Orleans Station, B. & O. R. R., June 17, 1863.

RECRUITS TRANSFERRED TO 62D REGIMENT O. V. I.

NAME	AGE	RANK	DATE OF ENLISTMENT	GENERAL HISTORY AND FINAL RECORD
Samuel B. Mathews	28	Sergeant	Oct. 1, '62	Taken prisoner at Winchester, Va., June 15, 1863; was transferred from Company F to Company H 116th O. V. I.
Nathan Archer	18	Private	Aug. 21, '63	Was transferred from Company F to Company H 116th O. V. I.
Lighton M. Bates	18	Private	Oct. 1, '62	Was transferred from Company F to Company H 116th O. V. I.
John R. Brokaw	21	Private	Aug. 22, '62	
Leroy Brown	19	Private	Feb. 3, '64	Wounded October 13, 1864.
Jacob Carpenter	22	Private	Oct. 14, '62	Taken prisoner at Cedar Creek, Va., October 19, 1864; was transferred from Company F to Company H 116th O. V. I.
Jacob L. Gregg	28	Private	Aug. 21, '62	Was transferred from Company F to Company H 116th O. V. I.

ONE HUNDRED AND SIXTEENTH O. V. I. 357

Alexander D. Kockley	18	Private	Jan. 11, '64	Sick in hospital at Annapolis, Md., since May, 1864.
Noah Larock	18	Private	Mar. 31, '64	
Barney Moore	19	Private	Jan. 13, '64	
Greenberry Murdock	20	Private	Dec. 24, '63	
John H. Phelps	28	Private	Oct. 1, '62	In hospital at Cumberland, Md., April 1, 1863; was transferred from Company F to Company H 116th O. V. I.
Irwin T. Smith	22	Private	Jan. 2, '64	
Asbury Stephens	21	Private	Jan. 5, '64	Wounded and taken prisoner at Staunton, Va., June 10, 1864.
Elisha D. Williams	18	Private	Jan. 11, '64	
Isaac W. Toho	28	Private	Oct. 1, '62	Wounded at Fort Gregg, Va., April 2, 1865; transferred from Company F to Company H 116th O. V. I.

358   ONE HUNDRED AND SIXTEENTH O. V. I.

Record of Company I, 116th Regiment O. V. I., in the Service of the United States.

NAME.	NO.	RANK.	DATE OF ENLISTMENT	GENERAL HISTORY AND FINAL RECORD.
Edward Fuller	32	Captain	Aug. 18, '62	Resigned at Romney, Va., January 31, 1863.
*Alexander Cochran	40	Captain	Aug. 16, '62	Promoted from First Lieutenant January 31, 1863.
Adolphus B. Frame	23	Captain	Aug. 16, '62	Promoted from Second Lieutenant to First Lieutenant January 31, 1863, and to Captain December 25, 1864; honorably discharged by order of Secretary of War and transferred to 186th regiment O. V. I.
Richmond O. Knowles	40	Captain	Aug. 15, '62	Promoted from First Sergeant to Second Lieutenant, January 31, 1863; to First Lieutenant November 3, 1864, and to Captain March 29, 1865.

PRESENT TO BE MUSTERED OUT AT CLOSE OF WAR.

John C. Chuck	29	1st Sergeant	Aug. 19, '62	Was Sergeant from date of muster to August 31, 1864; commissioned Second Lieutenant June 20, 1865; not mustered.
Luther C. Wedge	24	Sergeant	Aug. 18, '62	
Edgar Humphrey	24	Sergeant	Aug. 22, '62	Wounded in neck at Snicker's Ferry, July 18, 1864.
Wesley Mickle	21	Sergeant	Aug. 19, '62	Taken prisoner at Winchester, Va., June 15, 1863.
Joseph P. Parrish	26	Corporal	Aug. 18, '62	Taken prisoner at Winchester, Va., June 15, 1863.
William Scott	23	Corporal	Aug. 17, '62	First man in the regiment wounded; wounded at Lynchburg, Va., June 18, 1864.
Harvey V. Cooley	23	Corporal	Aug. 22, '62	
Ebenezer Finley	27	Corporal	Aug. 22, '62	
Edwin G. Fuller	26	Corporal	Aug. 18, '62	Wounded through hips and taken prisoner at Piedmont, Va., June 5, 1864.
Fayette Paugh	20	Corporal	Aug. 22, '62	Wounded in arm and taken prisoner at Piedmont, Va., June 5, 1864.
Bradley P. Barrows	44	Corporal	Aug. 22, '62	Taken prisoner at Bunker Hill, Va., June 13, 1863; wounded in arm at Piedmont, Va., June 5, 1864.
Jacob E. Athey	29	Corporal	Aug. 19, '62	Taken prisoner at Bunker Hill, Va., June 14, 1863.
Jasper Secoy	23	Wagoner	Aug. 19, '62	
Elias Baker	24	Private	Aug. 19, '62	Taken prisoner at Bunker Hill, Va., June 13, 1863.
Hiram L. Baker	25	Private	Aug. 18, '62	Regimental wagonmaster.
William M. Bancroft	40	Private	Aug. 18, '62	Regimental blacksmith.
Henry M. Blagg	24	Private	Aug. 22, '62	
Jesse Borton	30	Private	Aug. 19, '62	Taken prisoner at Bunker Hill, Va., June 13, 1863.
George W. Burch	36	Private	Aug. 19, '62	Wounded in left thigh and taken prisoner at Bunker Hill, Va., June 13, 1863.
Asher Buckley	20	Private	Aug. 19, '62	Taken prisoner at Winchester, Va., June 15, 1863.
Francis M. Byers	25	Private	Aug. 19, '62	Wounded in thigh at Snicker's Ferry, Va., July 18, 1864.
William Cabeen	21	Private	Aug. 19, '62	
Joseph A. Campbell	25	Private	Aug. 20, '62	Taken prisoner at Romney, Va., Feb. 16, 1863, and at Bunker Hill, Va., June 13, 1863.
Alvah D. Carlton	22	Private	Aug. 20, '62	Taken prisoner at Winchester, Va., June 15, 1863.

*Capt. Cochran was wounded in the right elbow at Bunker Hill, Va., June 14, 1863, and was never after able to do duty with the Regiment.

Name	Age	Rank	Date	Year	Remarks
Luther H. Cayton	31	Private	Aug. 20,	'62	Taken prisoner at Winchester, Va., June 15, 1863.
Hiram G. Connett	25	Private	Aug. 22,	'62	Assistant commissary of the regiment.
Samuel H. Crumblet	22	Private	Aug. 20,	'62	Taken prisoner at Bunker Hill, Va., June 13, 1863, and wounded at Fisher's Hill, Va., September 22, 1864.
Milton Ewers	31	Private	Aug. 19,	'62	
James R. Finley	21	Private	Aug. 19,	'62	Wounded in leg at Halltown, Va., August 26, 1864.
Samuel P. Fleak	21	Private	Aug. 19,	'62	Taken prisoner at Bunker Hill, Va., June 13, 1863, and escaped; wounded at Piedmont, Va., June 5, 1864.
William L. Frost	21	Private	Aug. 22,	'62	Taken prisoner at Bunker Hill, Va., June 13, 1863.
James H. Gilchrist	22	Private	Aug. 22,	'62	Taken prisoner at Bunker Hill, Va., June 13, 1863; wounded in leg at Piedmont, Va., June 5, 1864.
James W. Glazier	21	Private	Aug. 21,	'62	Taken prisoner at Bunker Hill, Va., June 13, 1863.
Jesse Green	28	Private	Aug. 18,	'62	
Frank Hannon	35	Private	Aug. 19,	'62	
Michael T. Manning	34	Private	Aug. 22,	'62	
Samuel McColloch	31	Private	Aug. 22,	'62	Taken prisoner at Bunker Hill, Va., June 13, 1863; wounded in thigh at Piedmont, Va., June 5, 1864.
William McMullen	32	Private	Aug. 19,	'62	Taken prisoner at Bunker Hill, Va., June 13, 1863.
Leonard S. Mickle	23	Private	Aug. 20,	'62	Taken prisoner at Bunker Hill, Va., June 13, 1863.
Sheldon Parker	23	Private	Aug. 22,	'62	Taken prisoner at Bunker Hill, Va., June 13, 1864.
William S. Parrott	25	Private	Aug. 21,	'62	Taken prisoner at Bunker Hill, Va., June 13, 1863; wounded and taken prisoner at Cedar Creek, Va., October 19, 1864.
Amanuel Russell	27	Private	Aug. 22,	'62	Wounded in left knee and taken prisoner at Piedmont, Va., June 5, 1864.
Joshua Safreed	22	Private	Aug. 22,	'62	
Rufus B. Stanley	25	Private	Aug. 22,	'62	Taken prisoner at Winchester, Va., June 15, 1863; wounded in thigh at Piedmont, Va., June 5, 1864.
George W. Tacker	25	Private	Aug. 22,	'62	Taken prisoner at Bunker Hill, Va., June 13, 1863; wounded in abdomen at Piedmont, Va., June 5, 1864.
Enoch Taylor	46	Private	Aug. 22,	'62	Taken prisoner at Winchester, Va., June 15, 1863.
George W. Wallace	25	Private	Aug. 22,	'62	Ward master in hospital at Harper's Ferry, Va.
Charles W. Waterman	44	Private	Aug. 19,	'62	Taken prisoner at Winchester, Va., June 15, 1863; private secretary and orderly to Colonel Washburn.
Albert Woodruff	29	Private	Aug. 19,	'62	

ABSENT TO BE MUSTERED OUT.

Name	Age	Rank	Date	Year	Remarks
George H. Bean	21	Sergeant	Aug. 19,	'62	Wounded at Fort Gregg, Va., April 2, 1865; taken prisoner at Bunker Hill, Va., June 13, 1863.
John C. Bailey	22	Private	Aug. 22,	'62	Taken prisoner at Bunker Hill, Va., June 13, 1863, and also at High Bridge, Va., April 6, 1865.
John E. Ewers	21	Private	Aug. 19,	'62	Regimental pioneer; taken prisoner at High Bridge, Va., April 6, 1865.
Morris Humphrey	30	Private	Aug. 19,	'62	Taken prisoner at Winchester, Va., June 15, 1863.
John B. Humphrey	25	Private	Aug. 22,	'62	Taken prisoner at Winchester, Va., June 15, 1863.
Joseph Morrison	19	Private	Aug. 20,	'62	Taken prisoner at Bunker Hill, Va., June 13, 1863; wounded in both legs and taken prisoner at Piedmont, Va., June 5, 1864.

Record of Company I, 116th Regiment O. V. I. in the Service of the United States.—(CONTINUED.)

NAME.	ARMY	RANK.	DATE OF ENLISTMENT	GENERAL HISTORY AND FINAL RECORD.
John J. Norris	44	Private	Aug. 19, '62	Taken prisoner at Bunker Hill, Va., June 13, 1863; wounded in foot at Opequan, Va., September 19, 1864.
Hopson L. Sherman	25	Private	Aug. 20, '62	Taken prisoner at Bunker Hill, Va., June 13, 1863; also captured at High Bridge, Va., April 6, 1865.

TRANSFERRED.

Caleb I. Baker	45	Private	Aug. 19, '62	Wounded in thigh and taken prisoner at Bunker Hill, Va., June 13, 1863; transferred to V. R. C.
George Bates	24	Private	Aug. 22, '62	Taken prisoner at Winchester, Va., June 15, 1863; wounded in hand at Berryville, Va., September 3, 1864; transferred to V. R. C.
Lemuel Griffen	24	Private	Aug. 20, '62	Transferred to Company E, 116th O. V. I., July 25, 1863.
Levi Howell	22	Private	Aug. 16, '62	Transferred to Company E, 116th O. V. I., July 25, 1863.
William T. Patterson	25	Private	Aug. 22, '62	Promoted to Commissary Sergeant and transferred to field and staff.
Frank O. Pickering	28	Private	Aug. 22, '62	Transferred to field and staff by promotion to Commissary Sergeant.
Stephen Ward	35	Private	Aug. 12, '62	Transferred to Company E, 116th O. V. I., July 25, 1863.

DISCHARGED.

John Mitchell	21	Corporal	Aug. 19, '62	Discharged for promotion in 116th O. V. I. per order Secretary of War, March 14, 1865.
John G. Athey	36	Musician	Aug. 19, '62	Discharged on surgeon's certificate of disability, at Annapolis, Md., September, 1863.
Edward Bridge	25	Private	Aug. 22, '62	Discharged on surgeon's certificate of disability, at Romney, Va., March, 1863.
John Brown	30	Private	Aug. 22, '62	Discharged on surgeon's certificate of disability, at Winchester Va., March, 1863.
Daniel Connor	36	Private	Aug. 22, '62	Discharged by reason of accidental gun shot wound, at Cumberland, Md., March, 1863.
Henry T. Finley	18	Private	Oct. 27, '62	Discharged on surgeon's certificate of disability, at Cumberland, Md., February 28, 1863.
Marion Frost	36	Private	Aug. 22, '62	Taken prisoner at Winchester, Va., June 15, 1863; discharged for disability at Parkersburg, Va., March 4, 1864.
Elijah Patton	38	Private	Dec. 31, '63	Wounded in arm at Piedmont, Va., June 5, 1864; discharged February 27, 1865.

DIED.

Samuel Baker	21	Private	Aug. 19, '62	Died at Martinsburg, Va., October 17, 1862, of congestive chills.
John A. Dennis	22	Private	Aug. 22, '62	Taken prisoner at Winchester, Va., June 15, 1863; killed at Chapin's Farm, Va., February 10, 1865, by falling of a tree.
Consider Frost	33	Private	Jan. 1, '64	Wounded in both legs at Piedmont, Va., June 5, 1864, and died at Staunton, Va., June 26, 1864, of wounds.
Ephraim W. Frost	23	Private	Aug. 22, '62	Taken prisoner at Bunker Hill, Va., June 13, 1863; wounded and taken prisoner at Piedmont, Va., June 5, 1864; died at Annapolis, Md., January 13, 1865.

ONE HUNDRED AND SIXTEENTH O. V. I.

Name	Rank	Age	Date	Remarks
Jonathan C. S. Gilbert	Private	32	Aug. 21, '62	Taken prisoner at Winchester, Va., June 15, 1863; wounded and taken prisoner at Piedmont, Va., June 5, 1864; died at Savannah, Ga., October 9, 1864.
Wesley Griffin	Private	21	Aug. 22, '62	Died at Cumberland, Md., December 15, 1862.
Richard B. Miller	Private	25	Aug. 22, '62	Killed in action at Piedmont, Va., June 5, 1864.
William Stoneman	Private	21	Aug. 20, '62	Killed in action at Snicker's Ferry, Va., July 18, 1864.
Jacob C. Sichlers	Corporal	23	Aug. 22, '62	Wounded at Halltown, Va., August 26, 1864; died of wounds at Sandy Hook, Md., September 19, 1864.
Gilbert Vanhorn	Private	11	Dec. 25, '63	Killed in action at Lynchburg, Va., June 18, 1864.
Frederick Warren	Private	25	Aug. 18, '62	Wounded at Piedmont, Va., June 5, 1864, and died of wounds June 30, 1864.
Joseph H. Watson	Private	23	Dec. 25, '63	Died at Coolville, O., January 16, 1865, of consumption.

DESERTED.

Name	Rank	Age	Date	Remarks
Frederick Huson	Private	26	Aug. 22, '62	At Winchester, Va., May, 1863.
Edward Furgerson	Private	45	Dec. 24, '63	At Berryville, Va., September 3, 1864.
Mark W. McAtee	Private	22	Aug. 22, '62	In action at Cedar Creek, Va., October 19, 1864.
John H. Pamphrey	Private	18	Aug. 22, '62	At Gallipolis, O., October 6, 1862.
John A. White	Private	21	Jan. 3, '64	At Berryville, Va., September 3, 1864.

RECRUITS TRANSFERRED TO 62D REGIMENT O. V. I.

Name	Rank	Age	Date	Remarks
Jesse Anson	Private	34	Dec. 25, '63	
James R. Brown	Private	18	Jan. 1, '64	
Nathan Hatch	Private	20, '63	Dec. 29, '63	Wounded in shoulder and taken prisoner at Piedmont, Va., June 5, 1864.
Silas Hall	Private	20	Dec. 25, '63	
Alfred L. Shell	Private	19	Dec. 25, '63	
Charles C. Watson	Private	18	Dec. 21, '63	Wounded at Halltown, Va., August 26, 1864.

Record of Company K, 116th Regiment O. V. I., in the Service of the United States.

NAME.	AGE.	RANK.	DATE OF ENLISTMENT	GENERAL HISTORY AND FINAL RECORD.
John Hall		Captain	Aug. 18, '62	Resigned March 11, 1863.
William Sears		1st Lieutenant	Sept. 18, '62	Resigned January 21, 1861.
John F. Welch		1st Lieutenant	Aug. 18, '62	Enrolled as Second Lieutenant; promoted to First Lieutenant, January 31, 1863; promoted to Captain November 3, 1864, and assigned to Company B.
Gotlieb Shotley		2d. Lieutenant	Aug. 18, '62	Enrolled as First Sergeant; promoted to Second Lieutenant, April 1, 1863; resigned September 17, 1861

TRANSFERRED TO 62D REGIMENT O. V. I.

Benjamin Sheffield		Sergeant	Aug. 18, '62	Taken prisoner at Moorefield, Va., January 3, 1863; returned January 17, 1863; commissioned Second Lieutenant January 29, 1865; not mustered.
Charles P. Allison		Sergeant	Aug. 18, '62	Taken prisoner at Moorefield, Va., January 10, 1861.
William Drinkwater		Sergeant	Aug. 18, '62	
Michael J. Bole		Sergeant	Aug. 18, '62	Promoted from Corporal April 1, 1861; in hospital at Petersburg, Va., at time of transfer.
John Young		Corporal	Aug. 18, '62	Wounded at Lynchburg, Va., June 18, 1861.
Christopher Dawson		Sergeant	Aug. 18, '62	Promoted from Corporal May 6, 1865.
Hiram Andrews		Corporal	Aug. 18, '62	Wounded near New Market, Va., June 1, 1861; discharged February, 1865.
Perry Gardner		Corporal	Aug. 18, '62	Taken prisoner at ——— April 7, 1865; paroled April 9, 1865, at Camp Parole, Annapolis, Md.
Alexander F. Swain		Sergeant	Aug. 28, '62	Promoted to Sergeant from Corporal, March 28, 1865.
Jesse Allen		Corporal	Aug. 21, '62	Reduced to ranks March 8, 1865; order Captain Peters.
Thomas Berry		Corporal	Aug. 22, '62	Captured at Winchester, Va., June 15, 1863; prisoner of war at time of transfer.
Carmon M. Allison		Private	Aug. 18, '62	Wounded April 7, 1865; in hospital at Fortress Monroe, Va., January 10, 1861; at Winchester, Va., June 15, 1863; taken prisoner at Moorefield, Va., January 10, 1861; at Winchester, Va., June 15, 1861; at parole camp at time of transfer.
Charles Anders		Private	Aug. 18, '62	Wounded at Ft. Gregg, Va., April 2, 1865; in hospital at Fortress Monroe at time of transfer.
Rawly Anslaerry		Private	Nov. 12, '62	In hospital at Annapolis, Md.
Craven Ayers		Private	Aug. 11, '62	
William H. Brown			Aug. 22, '62	Captured at Moorefield, Va., January 3, 1863; released January 10, 1863.
Rufus P. Brooks			Aug. 21, '62	
Joseph D. Butts			Aug. 18, '62	
Abraham Butterworth		Private	Nov. 12, '62	Captured at Moorefield, Va., January 3, 1863; also at Winchester, Va., June 15, 1863; released July 1, 1863.
Nelson B. Clements			Aug. 21, '62	Wounded at Piedmont, Va., June 5, 1861; died in hospital at Grafton, Va.
William Clark			Feb. 21, '61	Prisoner since July 21, 1861
Elihu Cox		Corporal	Aug. 21, '62	Appointed Corporal February 27, 1865.
Albert Cook		Private	Nov. 12, '62	Missing at Little Orleans, Md., June 18, 1861.

*A Sergeant Charles F. Alford was commissioned 2d Lieut. Nov. 12, 1864, and 1st Lieut. March 18, 1865, and must have been mustered as 2d Lieut, though probably never mustered as 1st Lieut.

Name	Rank	Date	Remarks
Samuel Dye	Private	Oct. 25, '62	
Orlando Griffith	Corporal	Aug. 18, '62	Appointed Corporal March 28, 1865; wounded at Cedar Creek, Va., October 19, 1864
Marion V. Gabriel	Private	Feb. 27, '64	
William Gabriel	Private	Feb. 27, '64	
John Hartley	Private	Aug. 18, '62	Taken prisoner at Winchester, Va., June 15, 1863; returned July 1, 1863
Pardon C. Hewitt	Private	Aug. 18, '62	Wounded at Cedar Creek, Va., October 19, 1864; in hospital at Philadelphia since that time
William Hunter	Private	Aug. 18, '62	
James Jones		Feb. , '64	
John Kislow	Private	Aug. 18, '62	Taken prisoner at Winchester, Va., June 15, 1863; exchanged July 1, 1863
John Keep	Private	Aug. 18, '62	Taken prisoner at Winchester, Va., June 15, 1863; exchanged July 1, 1863
Ami Ladd	Private	Aug. 18, '62	Taken prisoner at Moorefield, Va., January 3, 1863; returned July 14, 1863
John Lewellen	Private	Aug. 18, '62	
Thomas Lewellen	Private	Aug. 18, '62	
Robert Love	Corporal	Aug. 18, '62	Date of appointment not given
Joseph Love	Private	Aug. 18, '62	
Isaiah Mattheny	Private	Oct. 27, '62	Taken prisoner at Moorefield, Va., January 3, 1863; returned June 11, 1863
George McDonald	Private	Aug. 18, '62	Taken prisoner at Winchester, Va., June 15, 1863; returned July 1, 1863
John McGonigale	Private	Aug. 18, '62	
Joseph McNeal	Private	Aug. 22, '62	
Josiah McNeal	Private	Feb. 1, '64	
William McNeal	Private	Feb. , '64	
Emory Newton	Private	Aug. 22, '62	Taken prisoner June 15, 1864, at Winchester, Va.; returned July 1, 1863; accidentally shot in the hand, June 15, 1864
Hiram Peacock		Aug. 22, '62	Taken prisoner at Winchester, Va., June 15, 1863; returned July 2, 1863
Reason Risley		Aug. 18, '62	Captured at Winchester, Va., June 15, 1863; prisoner till July 1, 1863
William Roberts		Aug. 18, '62	Captured at Moorefield, Va., January 3, 1863; prisoner till June 1, 1864
William Rutter		Aug. 22, '62	Absent without leave since October 1, 1863
Lewis Six	Corporal	Aug. 20, '63	Appointed Corporal March 6, 1864
Philip Six	Private	Aug. 20, '63	
Thomas Smith	Private	Aug. 18, '62	Wounded in leg at Piedmont, Va., June 5, 1864
Samuel Spencer	Private	Aug. 18, '62	
Isaac Wagner	Private	Aug. 14, '62	Wounded at Opequan, September 19, 1864
Daniel D. Weddle	Private	Aug. 18, '62	Wounded at Piedmont, Va., June 5, 1864
Thomas Witham	Private	Aug. 18, '62	Taken prisoner at Moorefield, Va., January 3, 1863; returned June 1, 1863
John Wilkinson	Private	Aug. 18, '62	
Aaron Young	Private	Aug. 18, '62	
Alexander Young	Private	Aug. 18, '62	
Hezekiah Razor	Private	M'ch 30, '64	
William Six	Private	M'ch 21, '64	

TRANSFERRED.

Name	Rank	Date	Remarks
Thomas Eaton	Private	Nov. 12, '62	Returned to Company G, 116th regiment O. V. I. where he had been duly enlisted
Byron Button	Private	Nov. 12, '62	Discharged on account of disability, ——— 1863
Joseph Callicum	Private	Aug. 18, '62	Transferred to invalid corps

Record of Company K, 116th Regiment O. V. I., in the Service of the United States.—(CONTINUED.)

NAME.	AGE.	RANK.	DATE OF ENLISTMENT	GENERAL HISTORY AND FINAL RECORD.
Harley Gilbert		Private	Aug. 18, '62	Died at Winchester, Va., June —, 1863.
Morgan Lady		Private	" " "	Died in hospital at Martinsburg, Va., March —, 1864; (a new recruit.)
Nathaniel Smith		Private	Aug. 20, '62	Died in hospital at Winchester, Va., March —, 1864.
Jacob Wyckoff		1st Sergeant	Aug. 18, '62	Promoted to Second Lieutenant, January 18, 1864, and assigned to Company B.

DIED.

Andrew G. Cagg			Aug. 18, '62	Prisoner of war since June 10, 1864; died at Andersonville, Ga., date not known.
Nelson B. Clements			Aug. 21, '62	Wounded at Piedmont, Va., June 5, 1864; died in hospital at Grafton, Va.
David L. Grove			Aug. 18, '62	Killed at Fort Gregg, Va., April 2, 1865.
Edward Hanishaw			Feb. 1, '64	Prisoner of war since June 10, 1864; died at Andersonville, Ga., date not known.
James Landsey			Oct. 15, '62	Killed at Fort Gregg, Va., April 2, 1865.
George Lyons			Aug. 18, '62	Killed at Lynchburg, Va., June 18, 1864.
George Sigler			Aug. 20, '62	Killed at Opequan, Va., September 19, 1864.

www.ingramcontent.com/pod-product-compliance
Lightning Source LLC
Chambersburg PA
CBHW032028220426
43664CB00006B/405